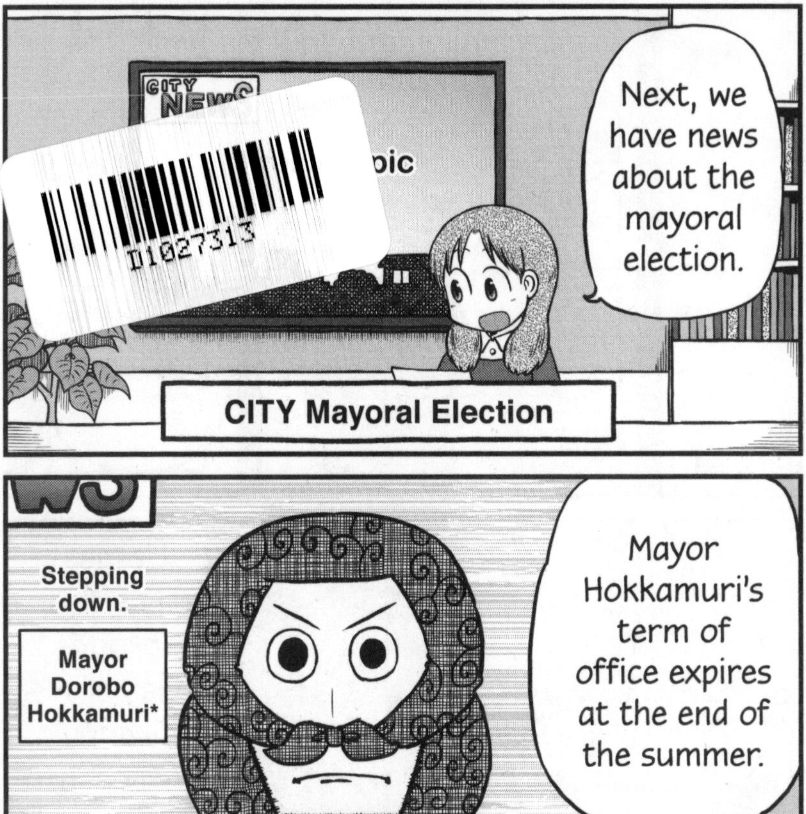
Next, we have news about the mayoral election.
CITY Mayoral Election
Mayor Hokkamuri's term of office expires at the end of the summer.
Stepping down.
Mayor Dorobo Hokkamuri*

* "Dorobo" is a pun on the word "thief," and "Hokkamuri" is a pun on "*hookaburi*," the head covering he wears, which is an old-fashioned disguise for a thief.

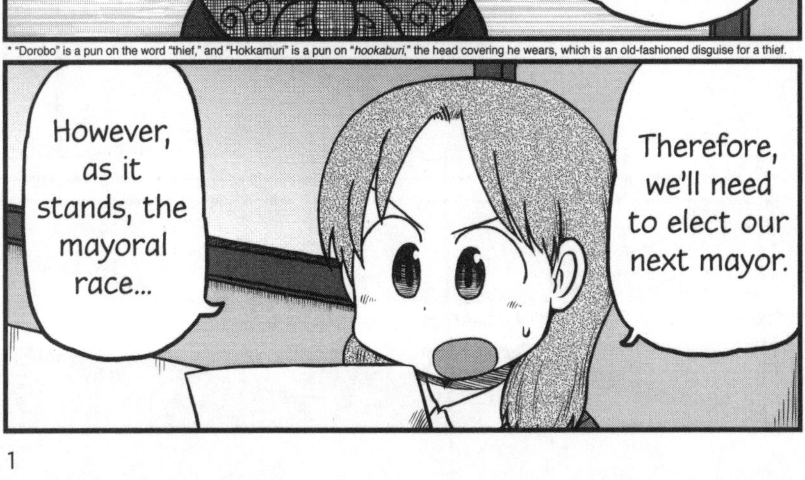
Therefore, we'll need to elect our next mayor.
However, as it stands, the mayoral race...

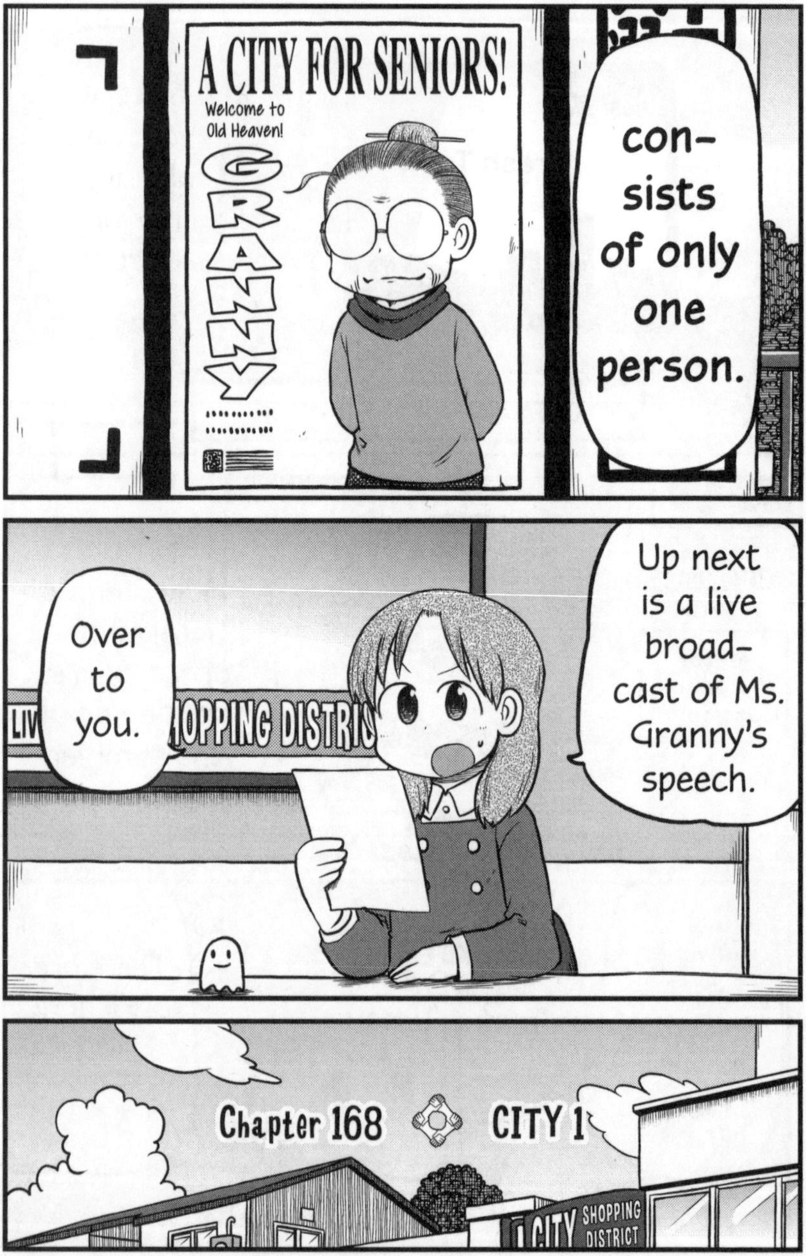
con-sists of only one person.
A CITY FOR SENIORS!
Welcome to Old Heaven!
GRANNY
Up next is a live broadcast of Ms. Granny's speech.
Over to you.
Chapter 168 CITY 1
CITY SHOPPING DISTRICT

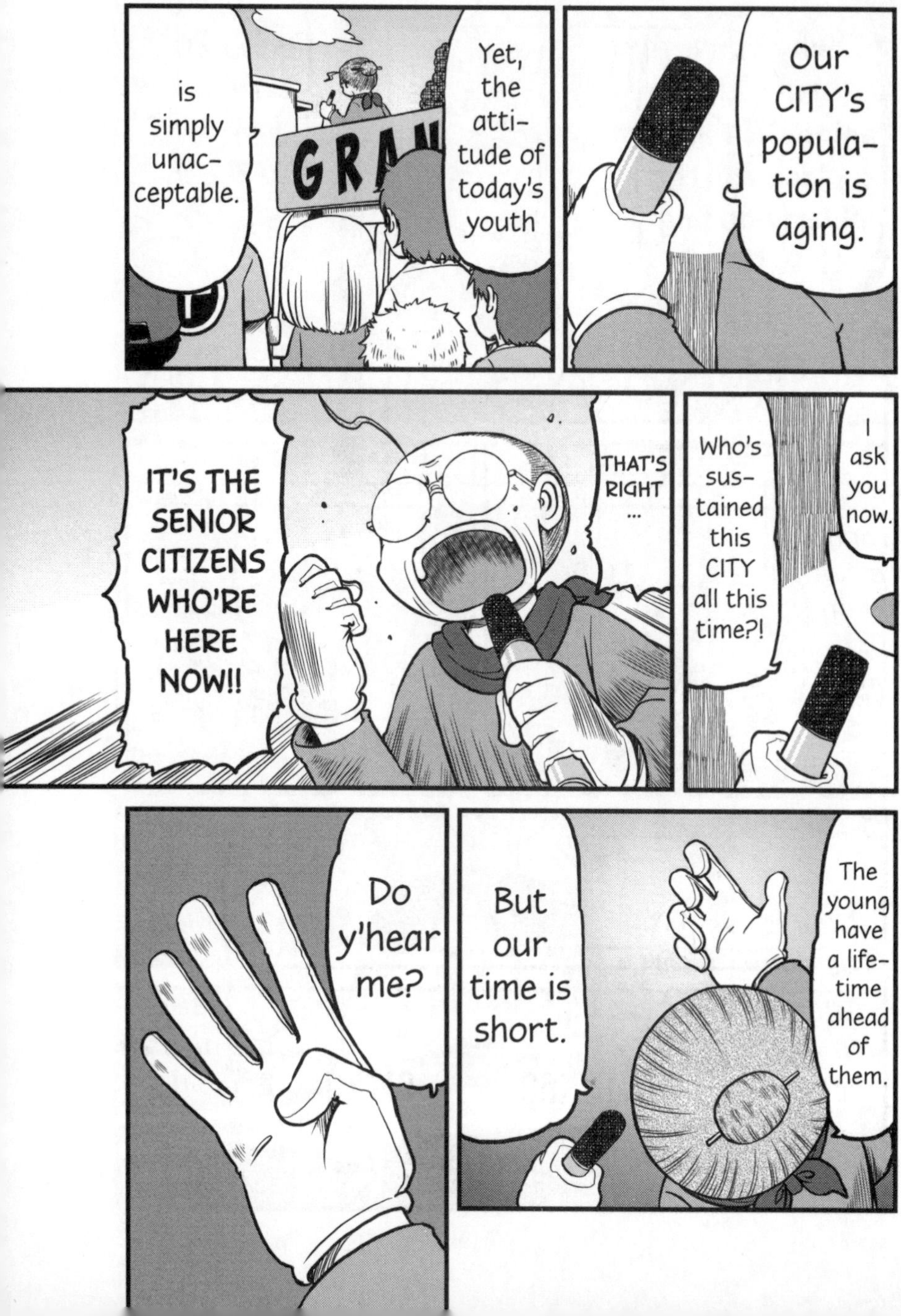
Our CITY's population is aging.
Yet, the attitude of today's youth
is simply unacceptable.
I ask you now.
Who's sustained this CITY all this time?!
THAT'S RIGHT...
IT'S THE SENIOR CITIZENS WHO'RE HERE NOW!!
The young have a lifetime ahead of them.
But our time is short.
Do y'hear me?

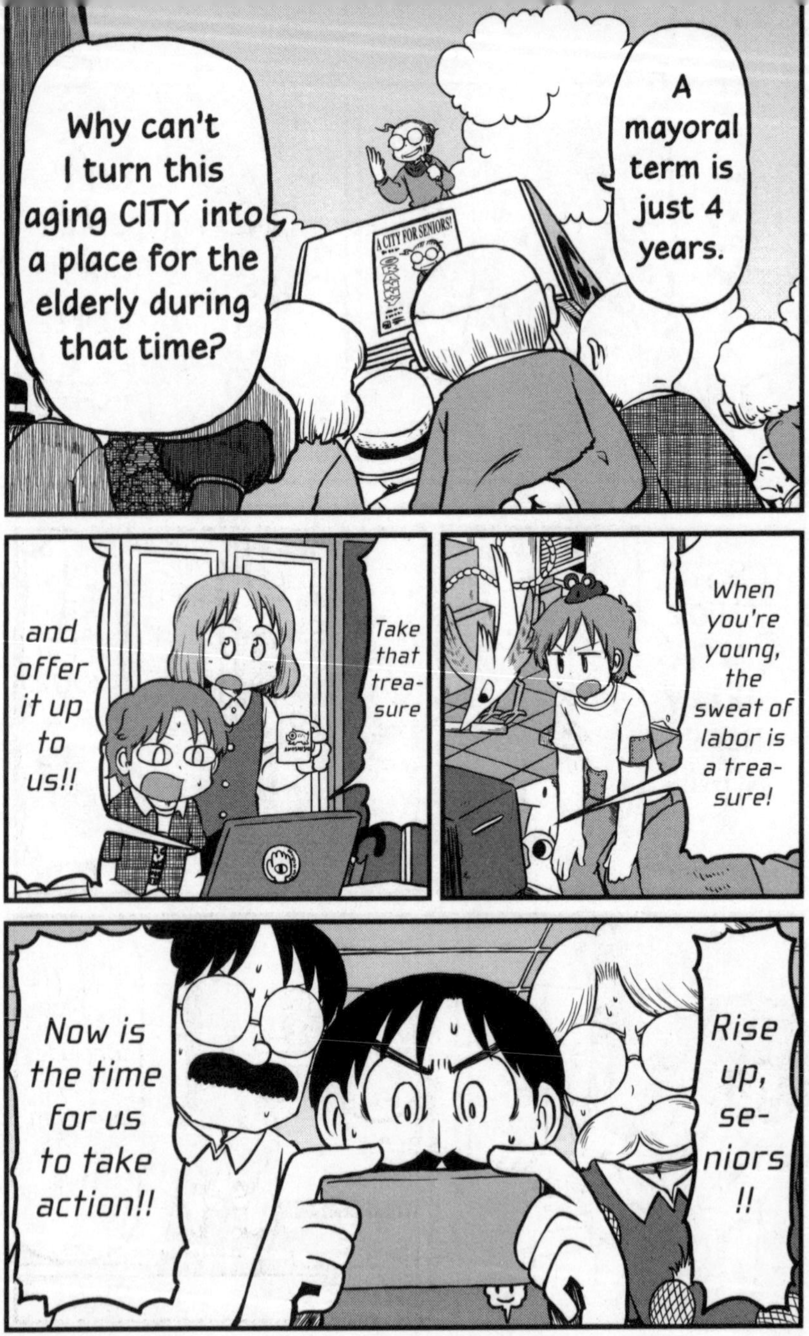
A mayoral term is just 4 years.
A CITY FOR SENIORS!
Why can't I turn this aging CITY into a place for the elderly during that time?
When you're young, the sweat of labor is a treasure!
Take that treasure
and offer it up to us!!
Rise up, seniors!!
Now is the time for us to take action!!

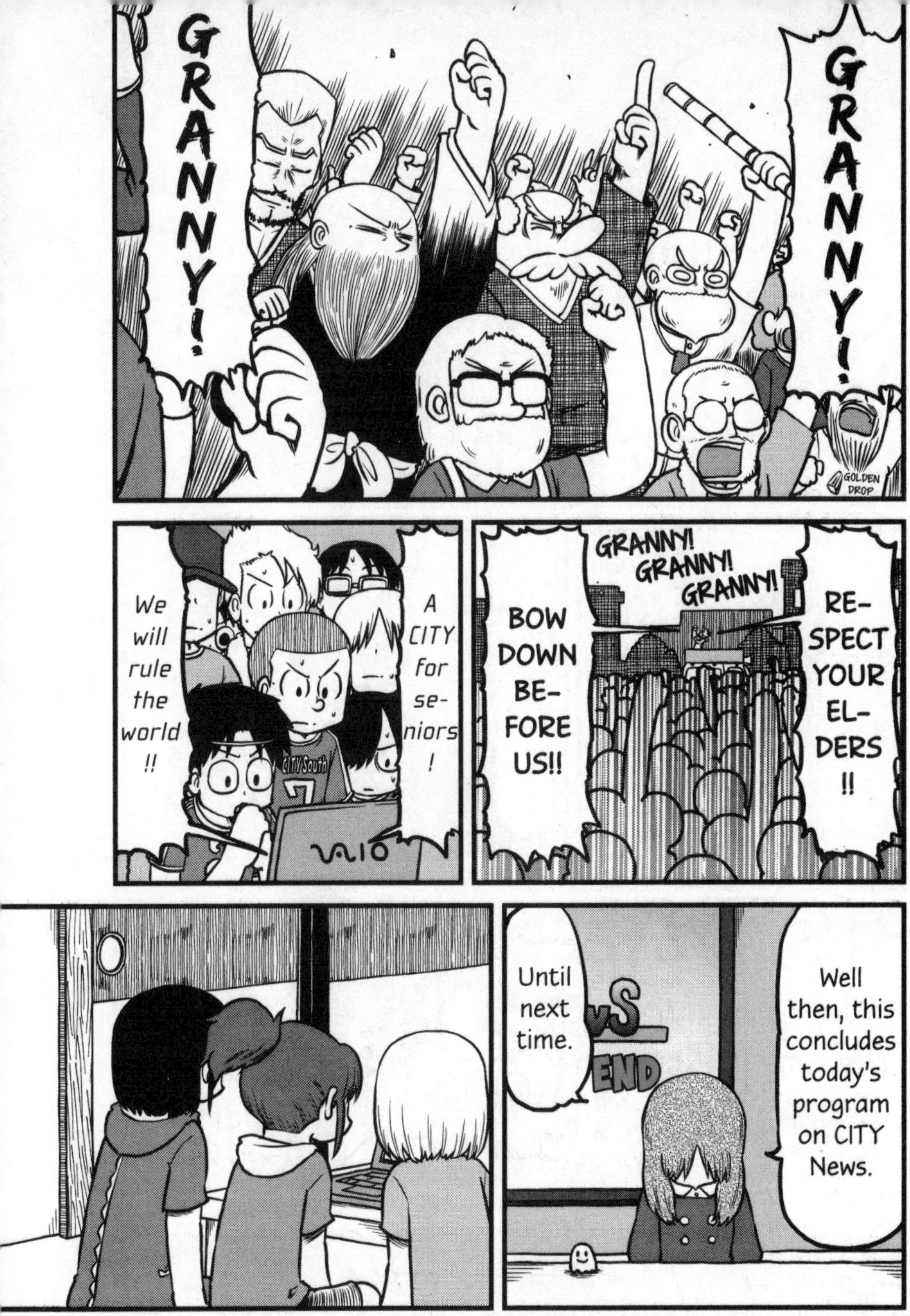
GRANNY!
GRANNY!
GOLDEN DROP
RE-SPECT YOUR EL-DERS!!
GRANNY! GRANNY! GRANNY!
BOW DOWN BE-FORE US!!
A CITY for se-niors!
CITY South
We will rule the world!!
VAIO
Well then, this concludes today's program on CITY News.
Until next time.
END

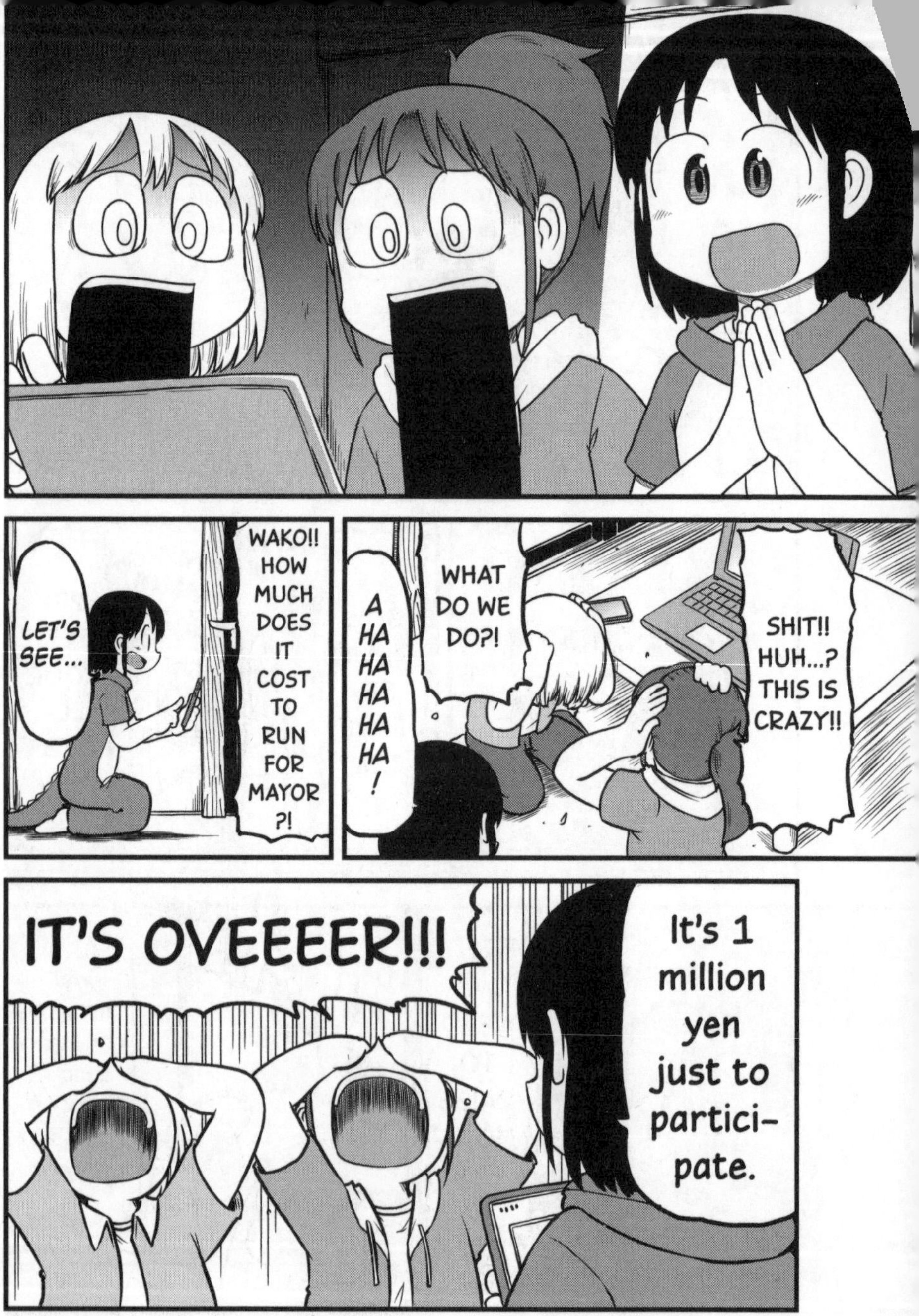
SHIT!! HUH...? THIS IS CRAZY!!
WHAT DO WE DO?!
A HA HA HA HA HA!
WAKO!! HOW MUCH DOES IT COST TO RUN FOR MAYOR?!
LET'S SEE...
It's 1 million yen just to partici-pate.
IT'S OVEEEER!!!

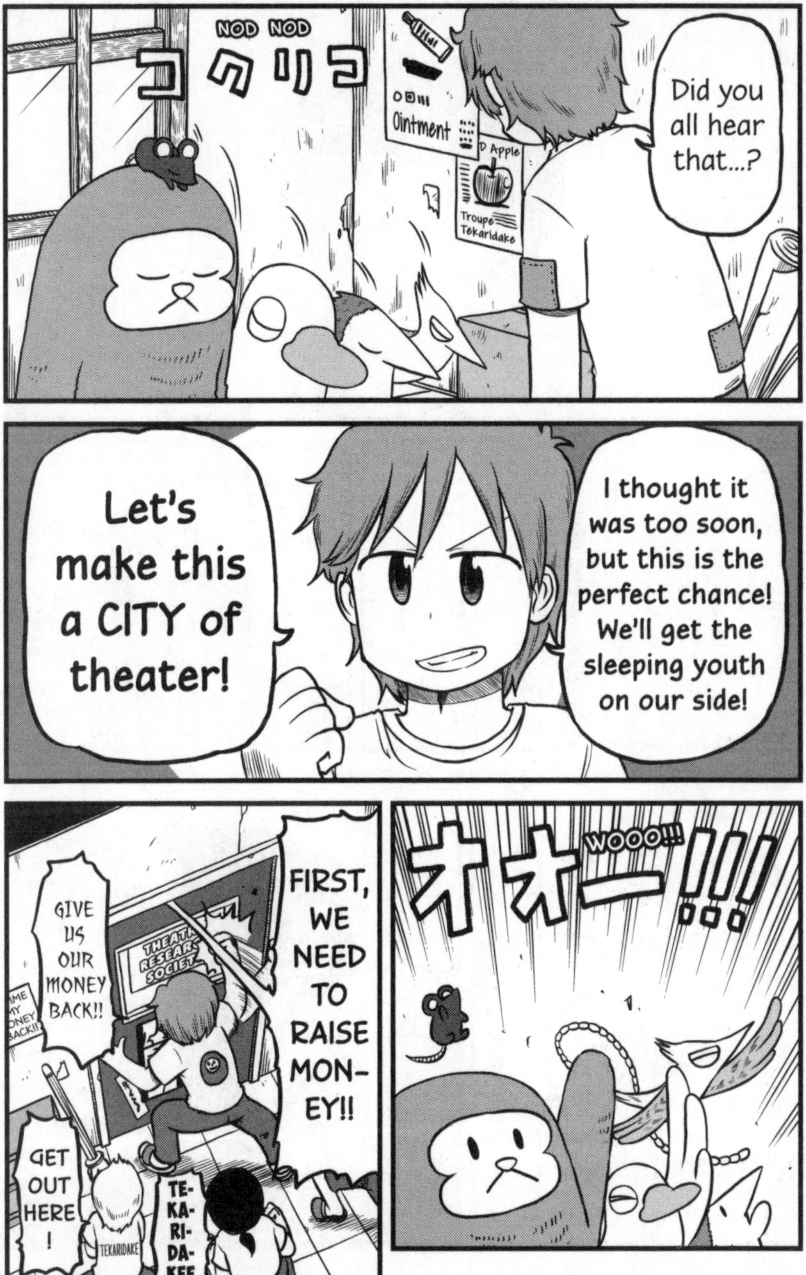
NOD NOD
コクリコ
Ointment
D Apple
Troupe Tekaridake
Did you all hear that...?
I thought it was too soon, but this is the perfect chance! We'll get the sleeping youth on our side!
Let's make this a CITY of theater!
オオー!!!
WOOO!!!
FIRST, WE NEED TO RAISE MON-EY!!
GIVE US OUR MONEY BACK!!
GET OUT HERE!
TE-KA-RI-DA-KEE!!
TEKARIDAKE

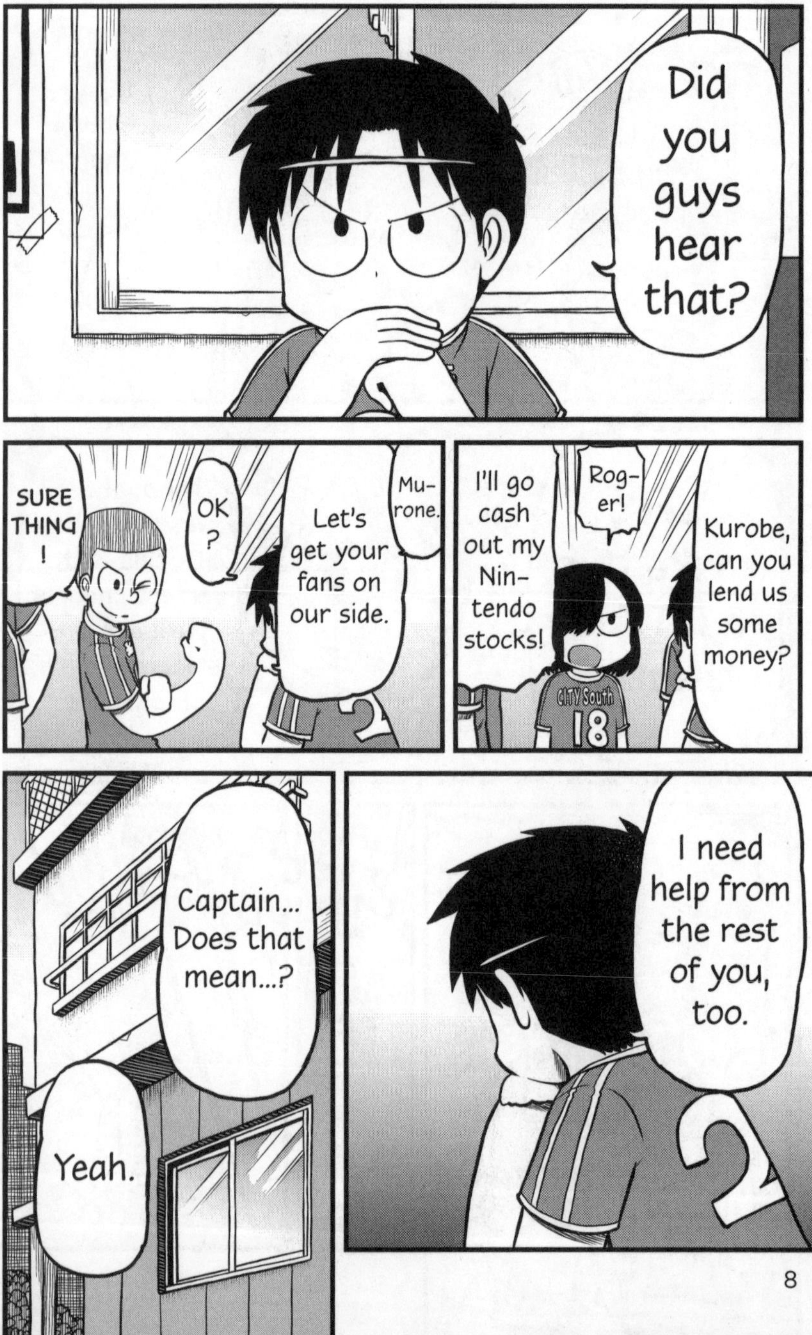

Did you guys hear that?
Kurobe, can you lend us some money?
Roger!
I'll go cash out my Nintendo stocks!
Murone.
Let's get your fans on our side.
OK?
SURE THING!
I need help from the rest of you, too.
Captain... Does that mean...?
Yeah.

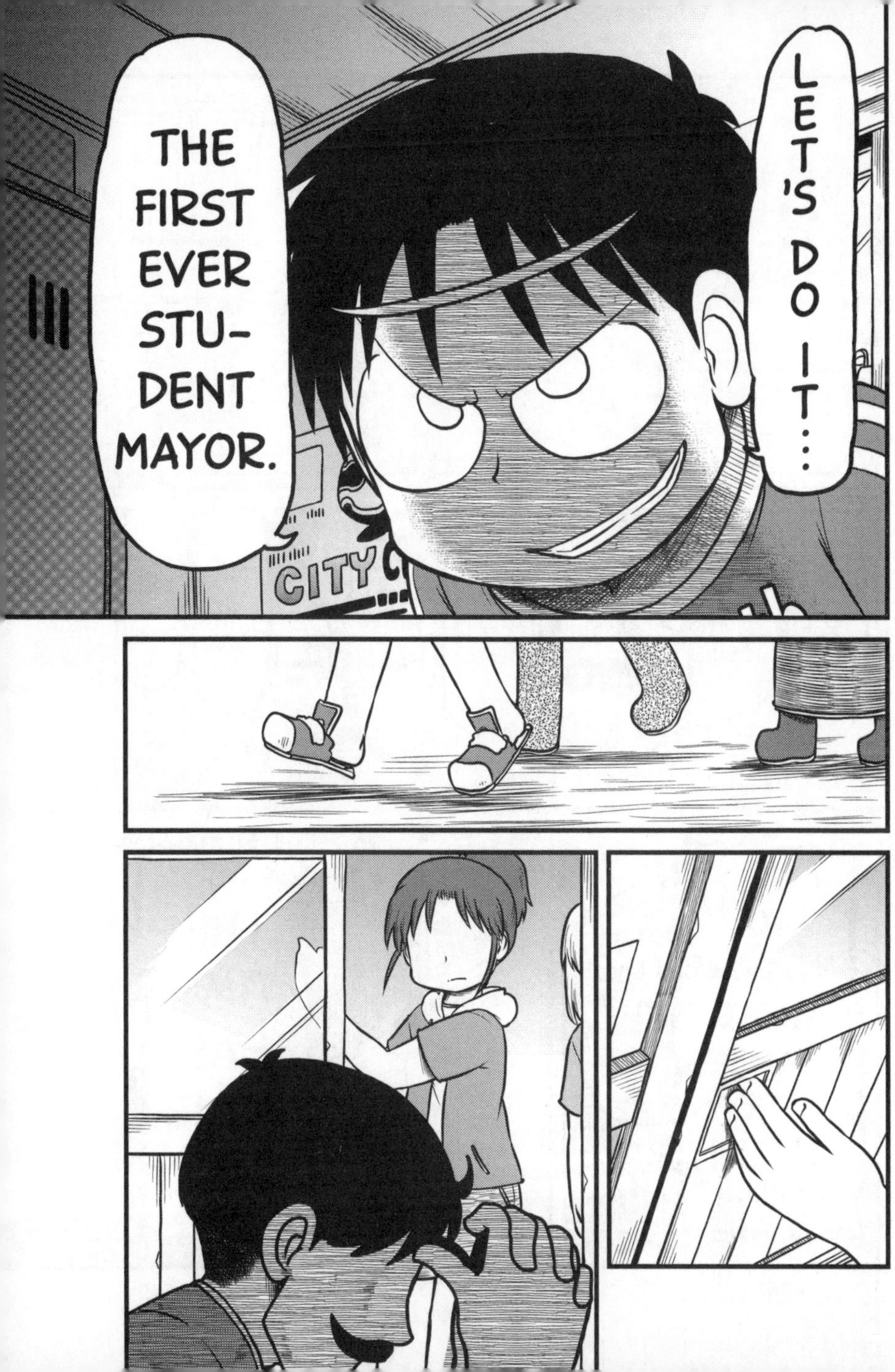
LET'S DO IT...
THE FIRST EVER STU-DENT MAYOR.
CITY

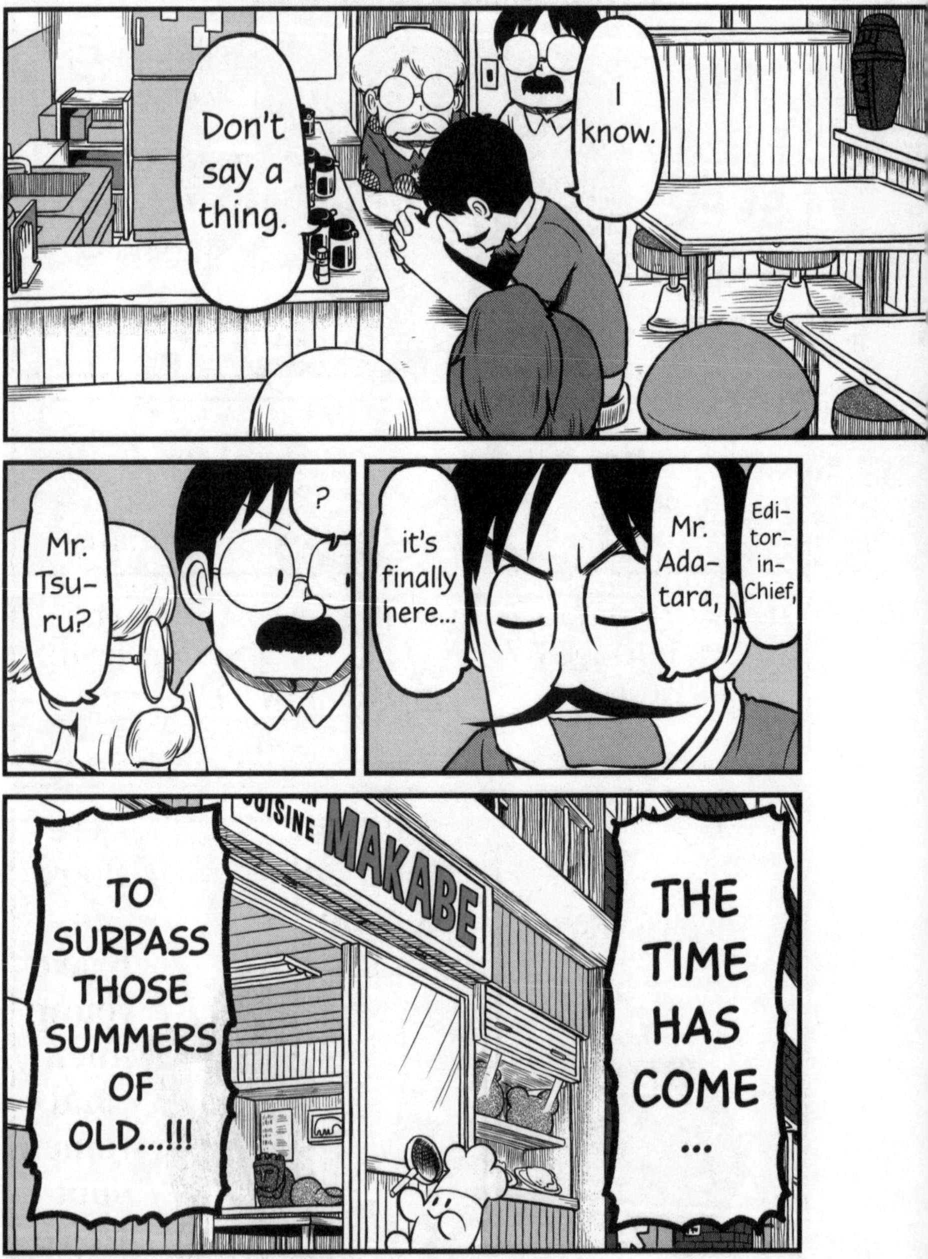
I know.
Don't say a thing.
Editor-in-Chief,
Mr. Adatara,
it's finally here...
?
Mr. Tsuru?
MAKABE
THE TIME HAS COME...
TO SURPASS THOSE SUMMERS OF OLD...!!!

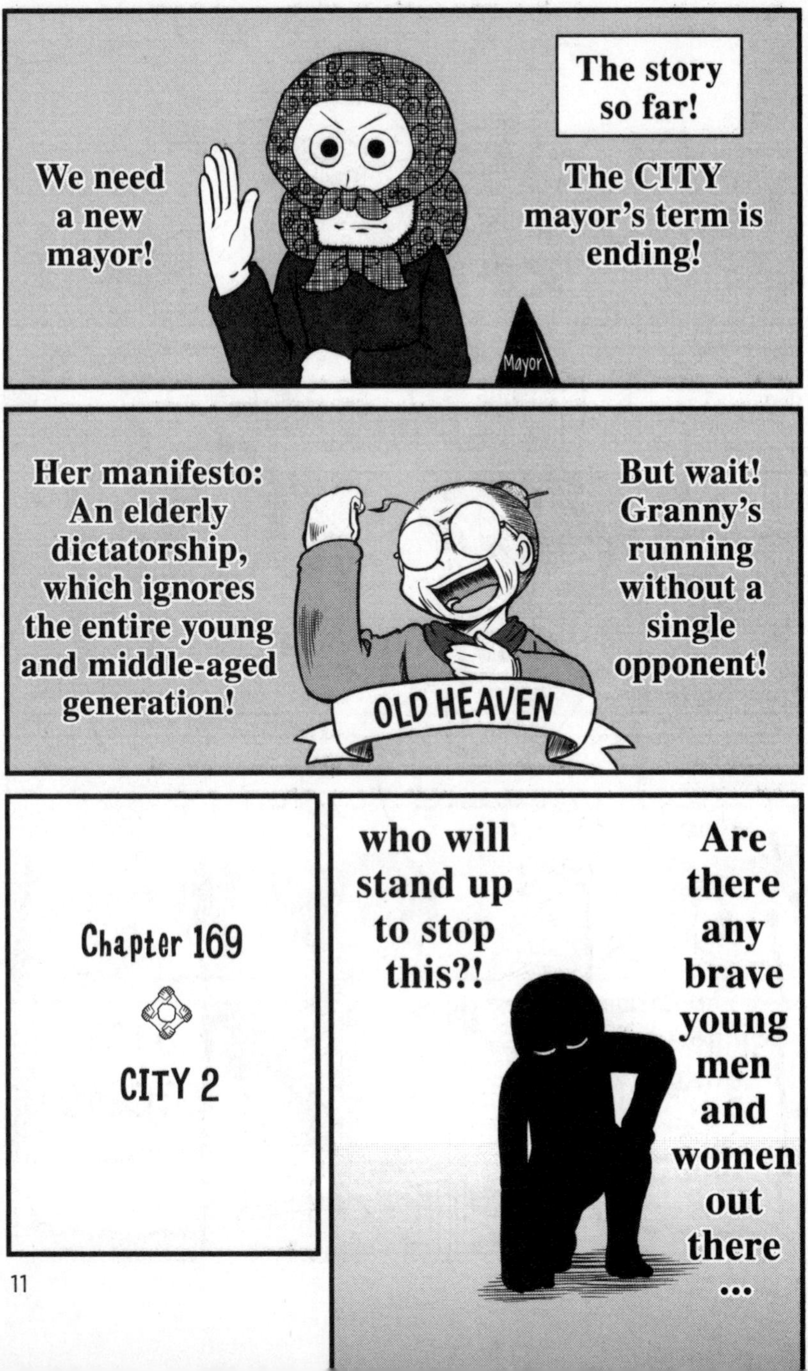
The story so far!
The CITY mayor's term is ending!
We need a new mayor!
Mayor
But wait! Granny's running without a single opponent!
Her manifesto: An elderly dictatorship, which ignores the entire young and middle-aged generation!
OLD HEAVEN
Are there any brave young men and women out there…
who will stand up to stop this?!
Chapter 169
CITY 2

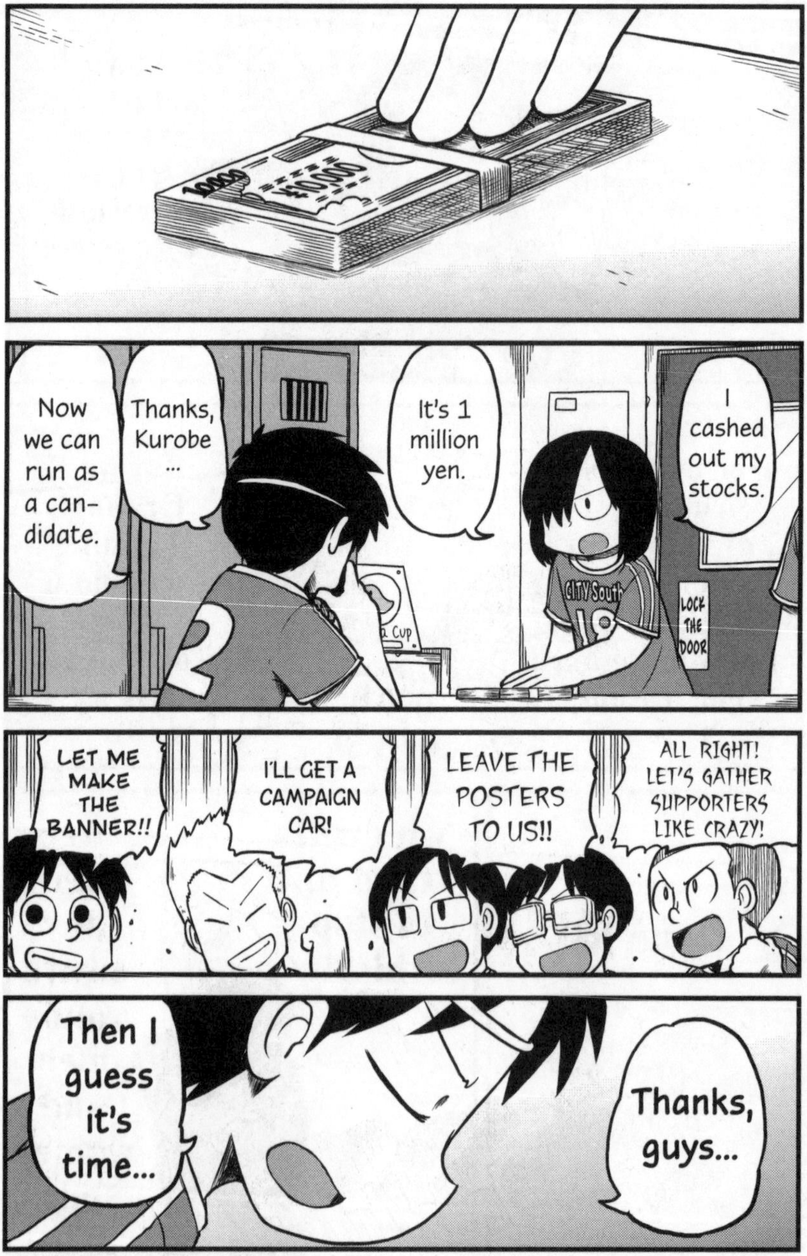
¥10000
I cashed out my stocks.
It's 1 million yen.
Thanks, Kurobe ...
Now we can run as a candidate.
CITY South
LOCK THE DOOR
ALL RIGHT! LET'S GATHER SUPPORTERS LIKE CRAZY!
LEAVE THE POSTERS TO US!!
I'LL GET A CAMPAIGN CAR!
LET ME MAKE THE BANNER!!
Thanks, guys...
Then I guess it's time...

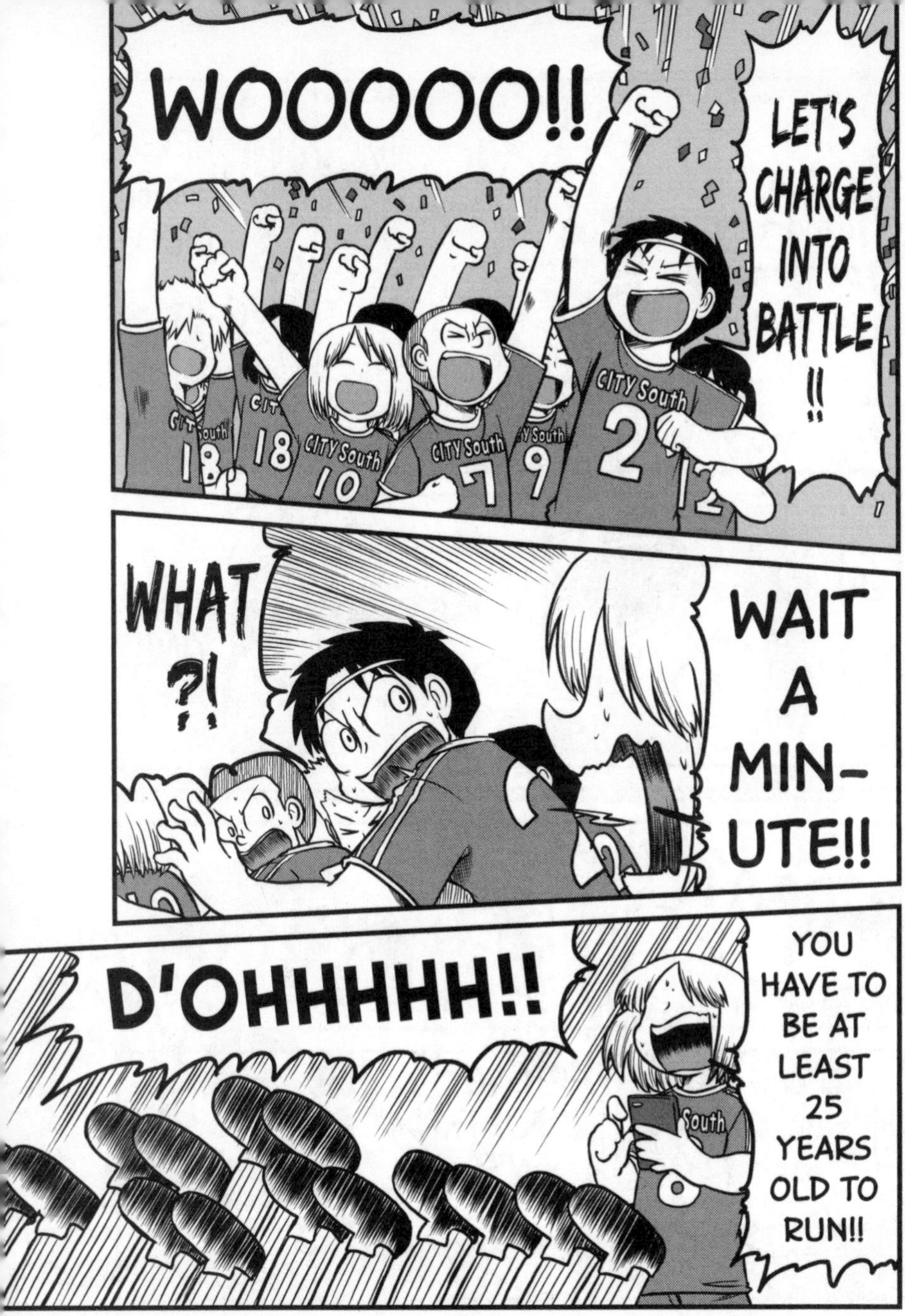
LET'S CHARGE INTO BATTLE!!
WOOOOO!!
WAIT A MIN-UTE!!
WHAT?!
YOU HAVE TO BE AT LEAST 25 YEARS OLD TO RUN!!
D'OHHHHH!!

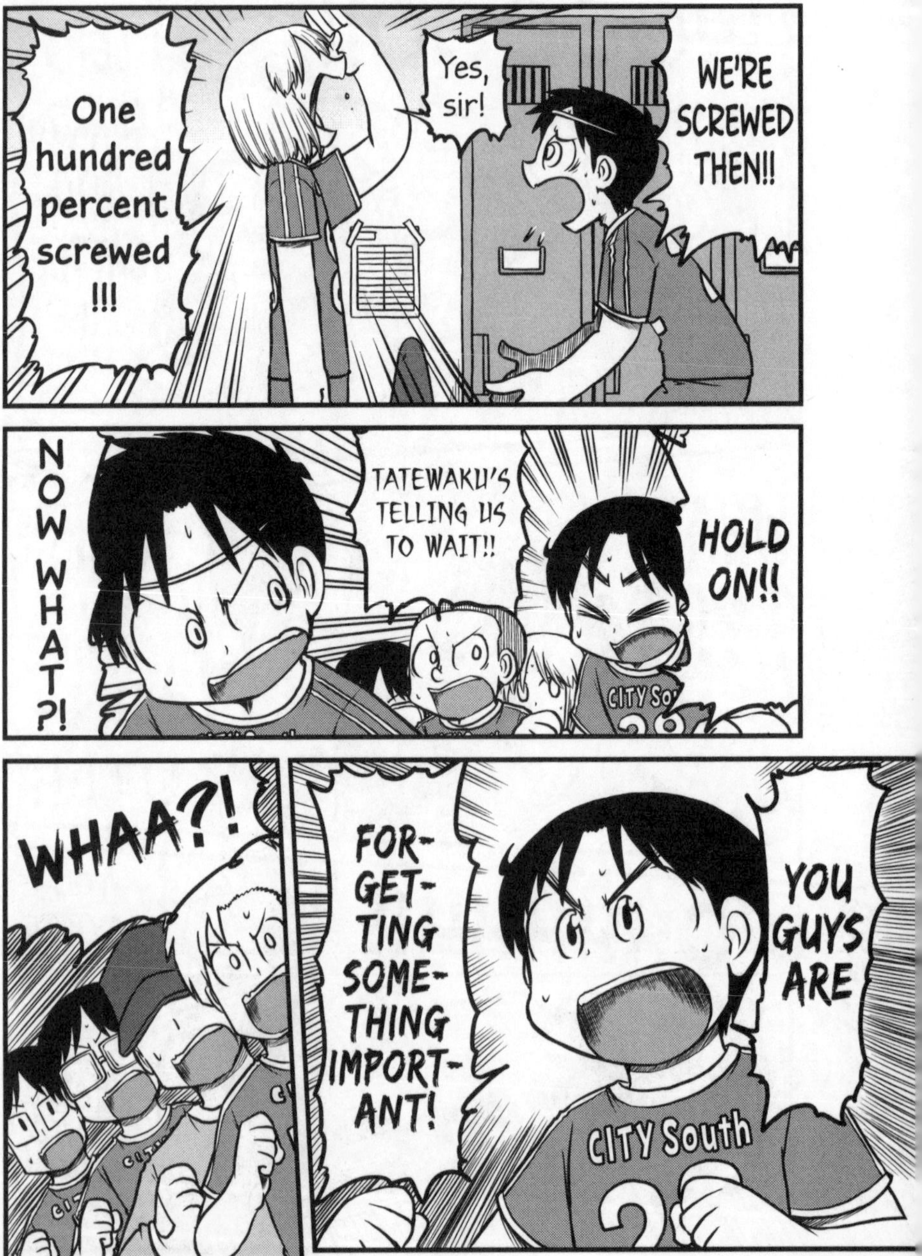
WE'RE SCREWED THEN!!
Yes, sir!
One hundred percent screwed !!!
HOLD ON!!
TATEWAKU'S TELLING US TO WAIT!!
NOW WHAT?!
YOU GUYS ARE
FOR-GET-TING SOME-THING IMPORT-ANT!
CITY South
WHAA?!

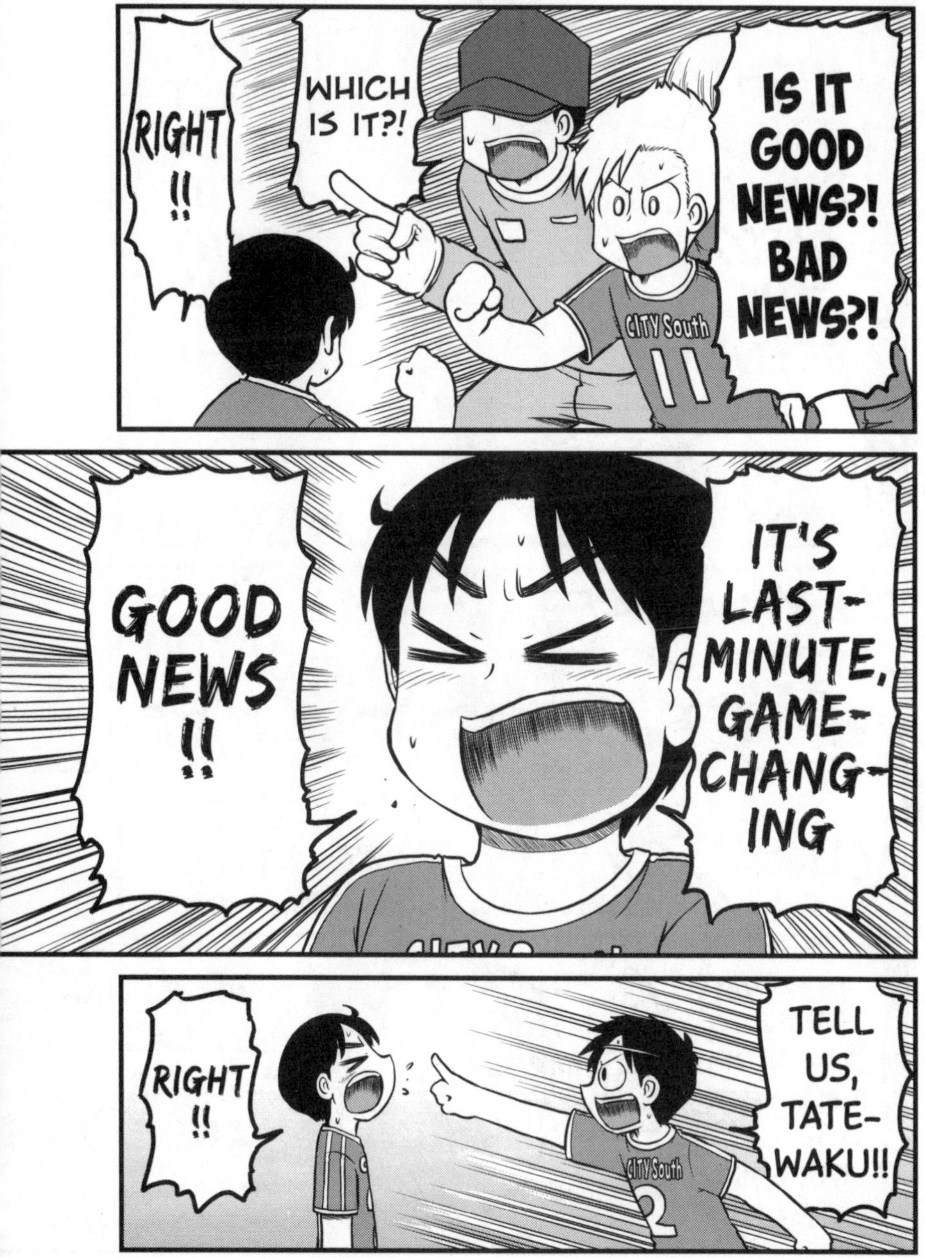
IS IT GOOD NEWS?! BAD NEWS?!
WHICH IS IT?!
CITY South
11
RIGHT!!
IT'S LAST-MINUTE, GAME-CHANGING
GOOD NEWS!!
TELL US, TATEWAKU!!
CITY South
2
RIGHT!!

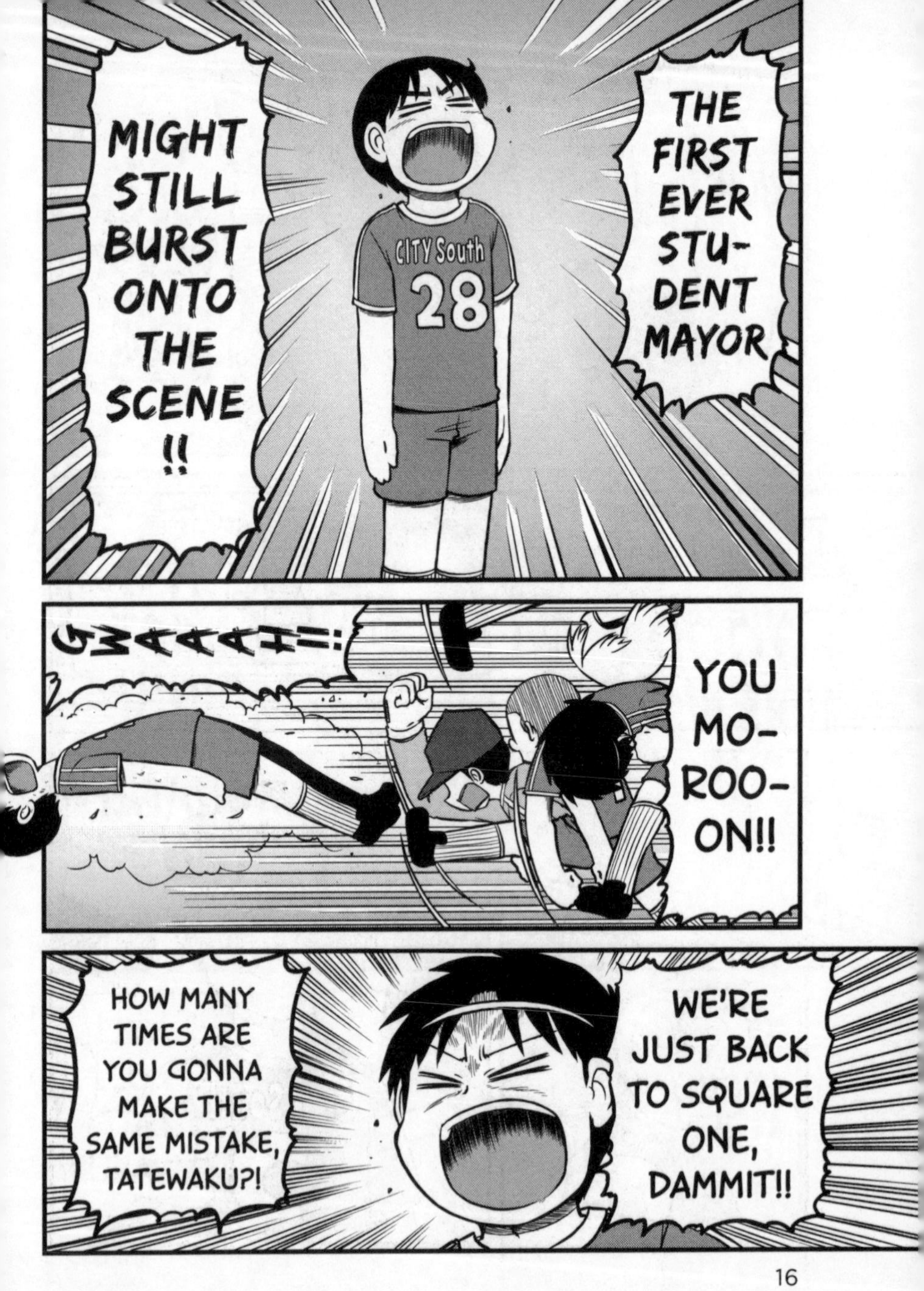

THE FIRST EVER STU-DENT MAYOR
MIGHT STILL BURST ONTO THE SCENE !!
YOU MO-ROO-ON!!
GWAAAH!!
WE'RE JUST BACK TO SQUARE ONE, DAMMIT!!
HOW MANY TIMES ARE YOU GONNA MAKE THE SAME MISTAKE, TATEWAKU?!

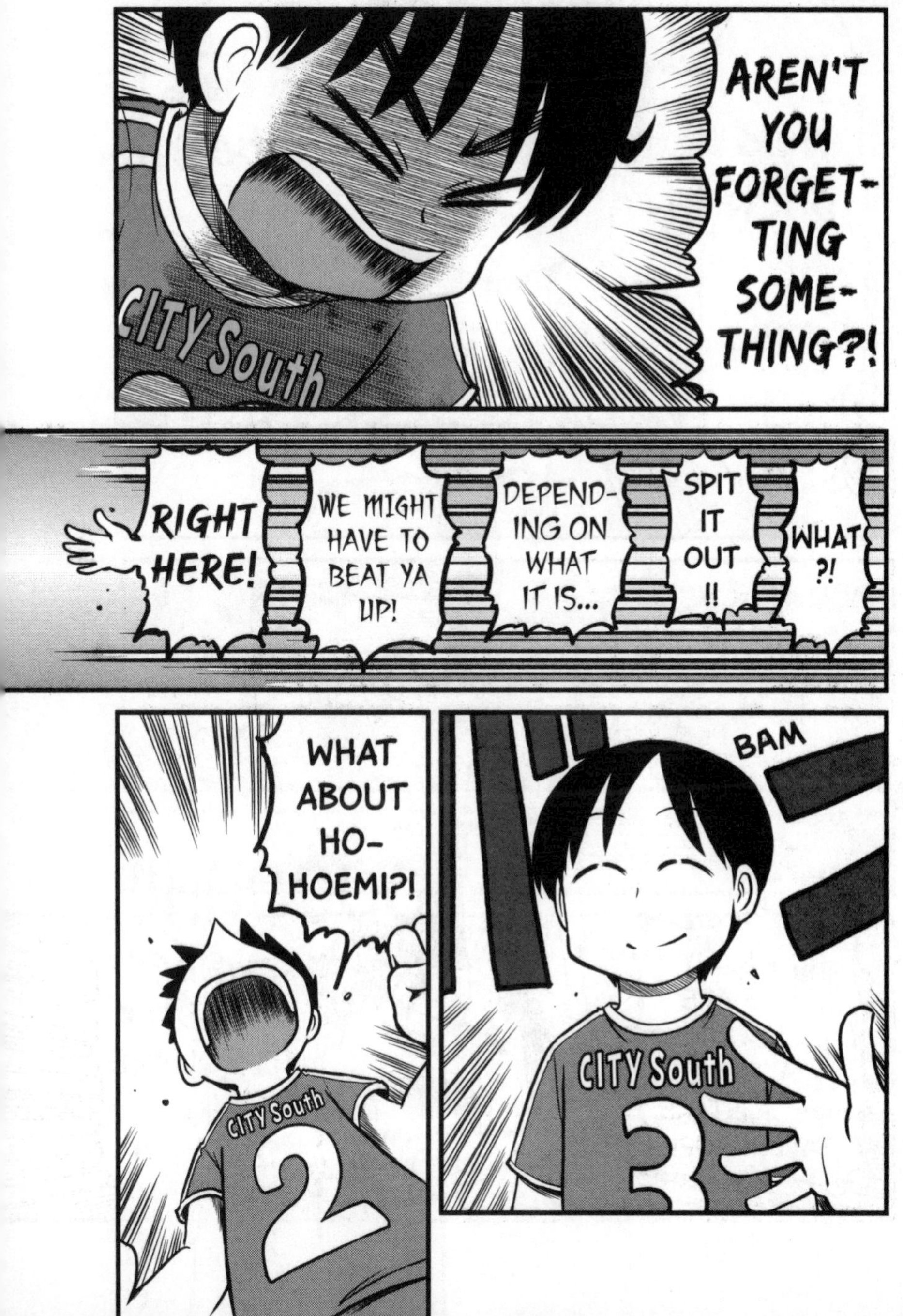
AREN'T YOU FORGETTING SOMETHING?!
CITY South
WHAT?!
SPIT IT OUT!!
DEPENDING ON WHAT IT IS...
WE MIGHT HAVE TO BEAT YA UP!
RIGHT HERE!
BAM
CITY South
3
WHAT ABOUT HO-HOEMI?!
CITY South
2

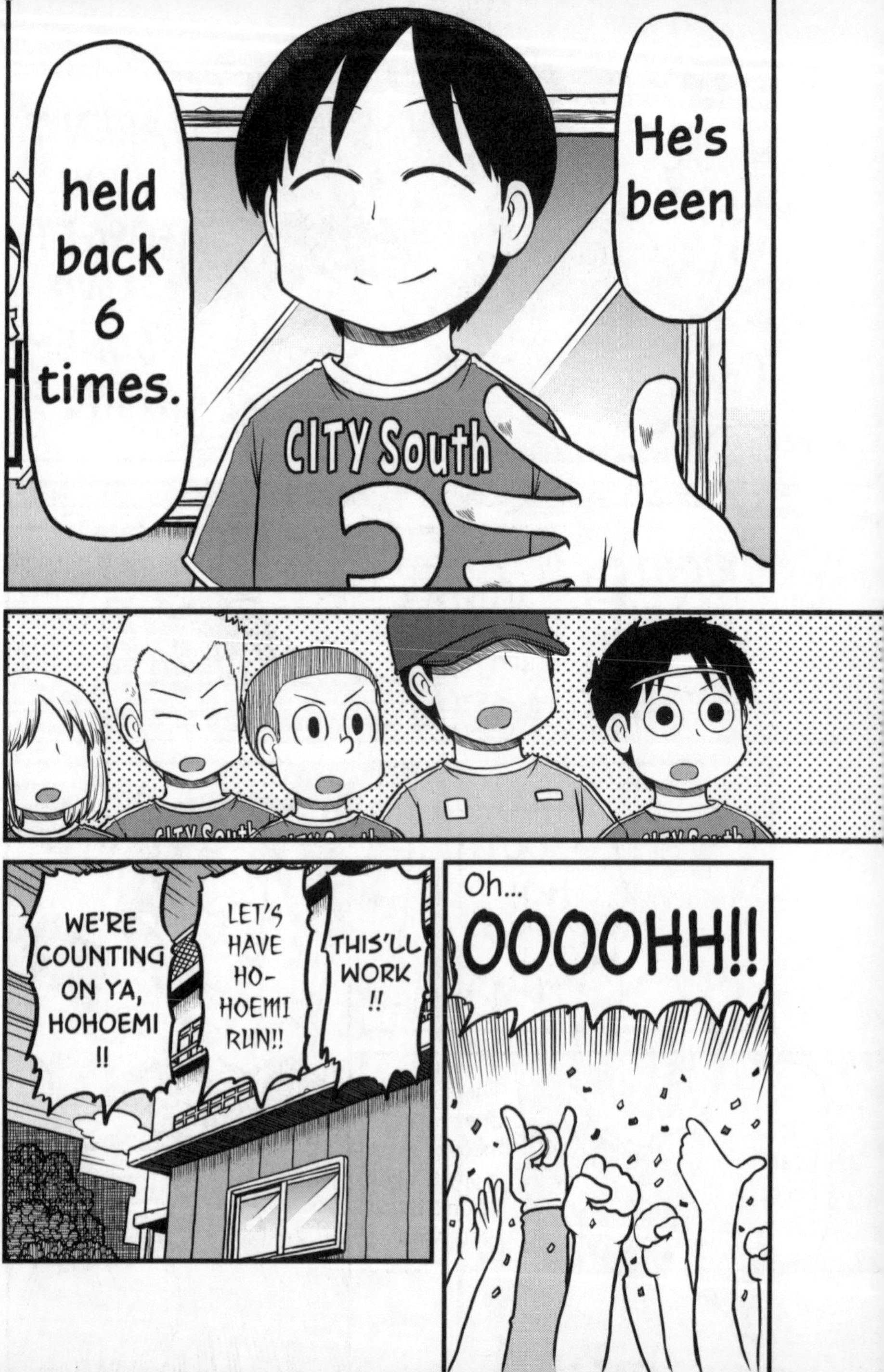
He's been
held back 6 times.
CITY South
Oh...
OOOOHH!!
THIS'LL WORK!!
LET'S HAVE HO-HOEMI RUN!!
WE'RE COUNTING ON YA, HOHOEMI!!

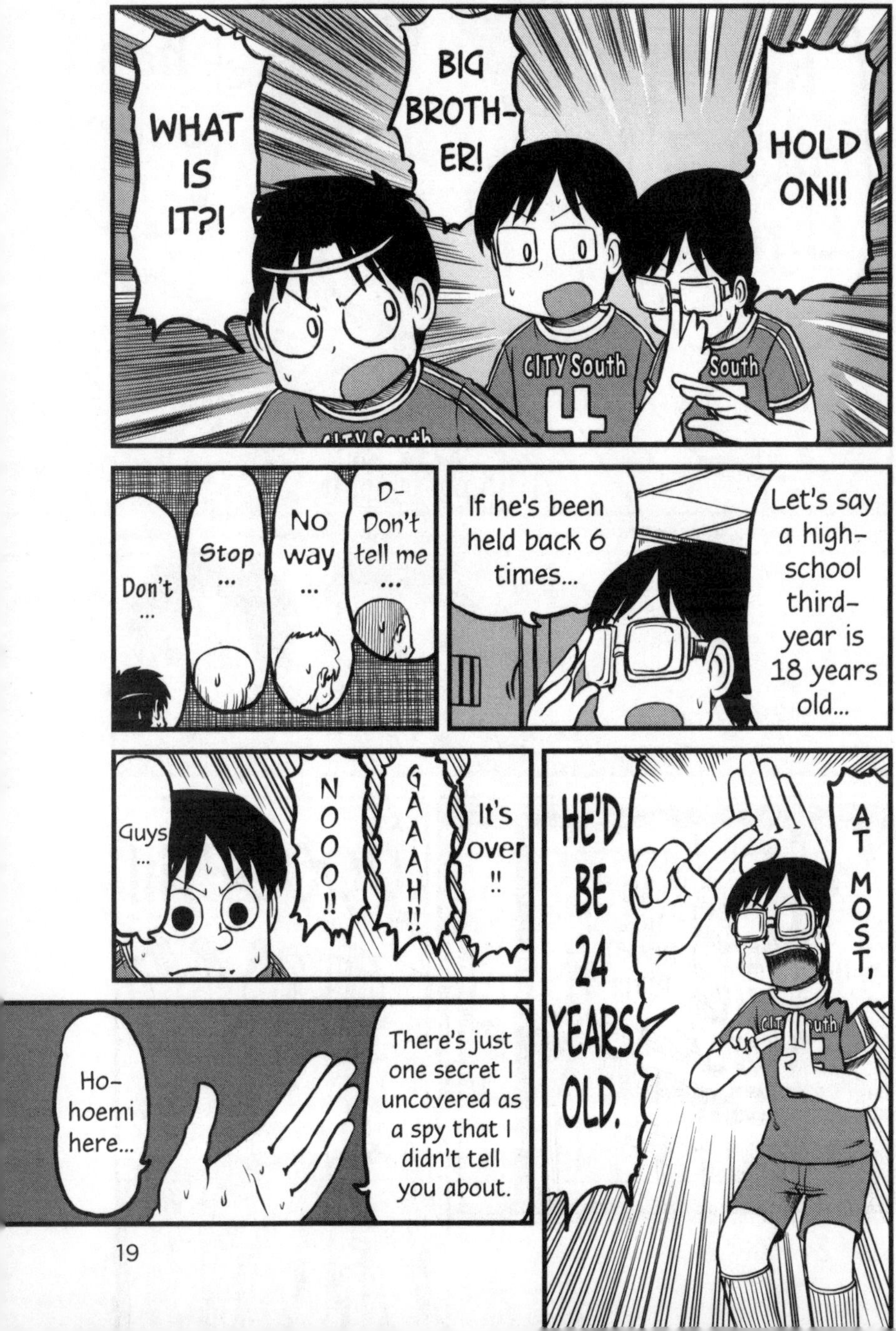
HOLD ON!!
BIG BROTH-ER!
WHAT IS IT?!
CITY South
Let's say a high-school third-year is 18 years old...
If he's been held back 6 times...
D- Don't tell me ...
No way ...
Stop ...
Don't ...
AT MOST,
HE'D BE 24 YEARS OLD.
It's over !!
GAAAAH!!
NOOOO!!
Guys ...
There's just one secret I uncovered as a spy that I didn't tell you about.
Ho-hoemi here...

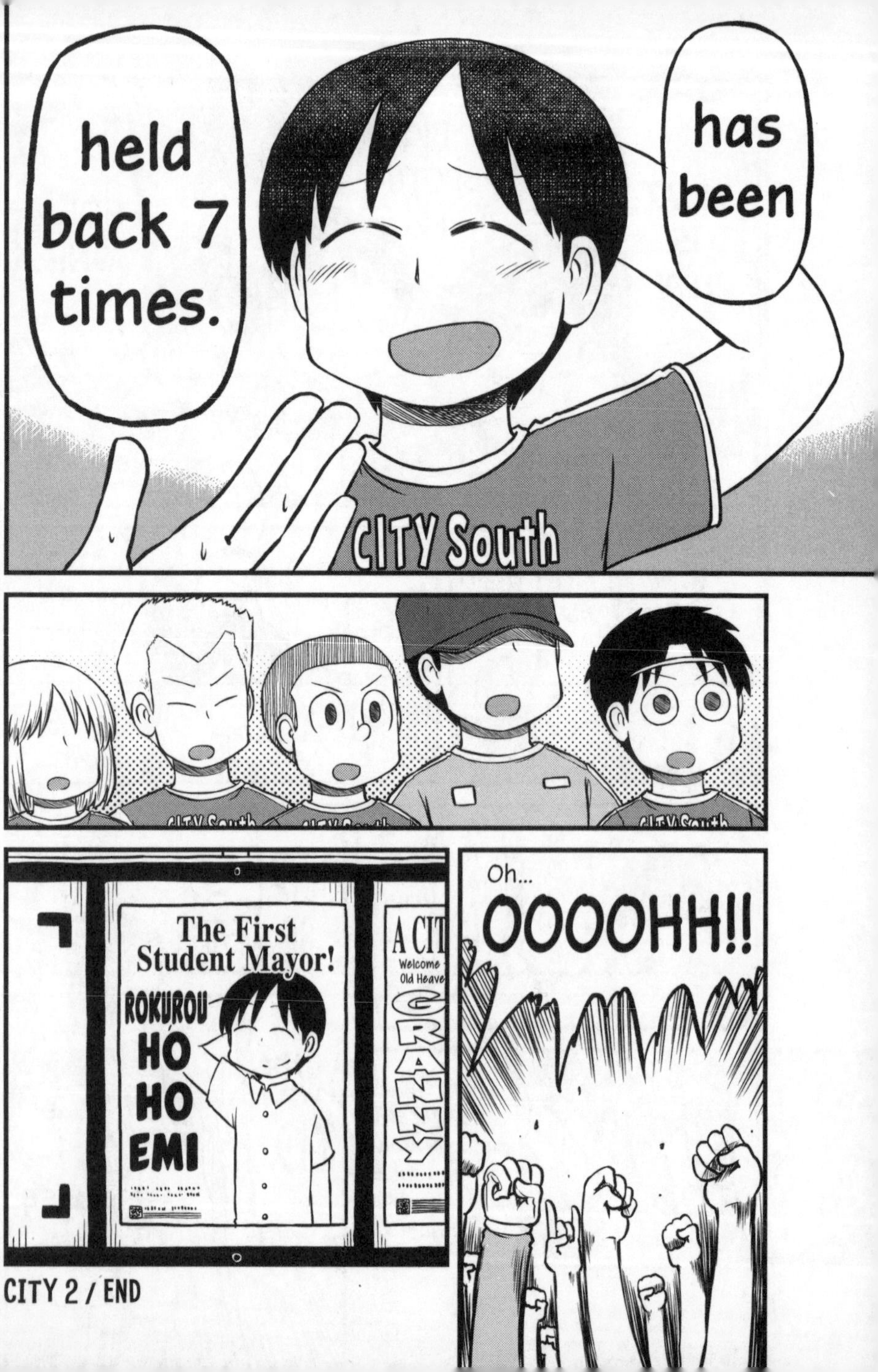

has been
held back 7 times.
CITY South
CITY South
CITY South
Oh...
OOOOHH!!
The First Student Mayor!
ROKUROU
HO
HO
EMI
A CIT
Welcome
Old Heave
GRANNY

CITY 2 / END

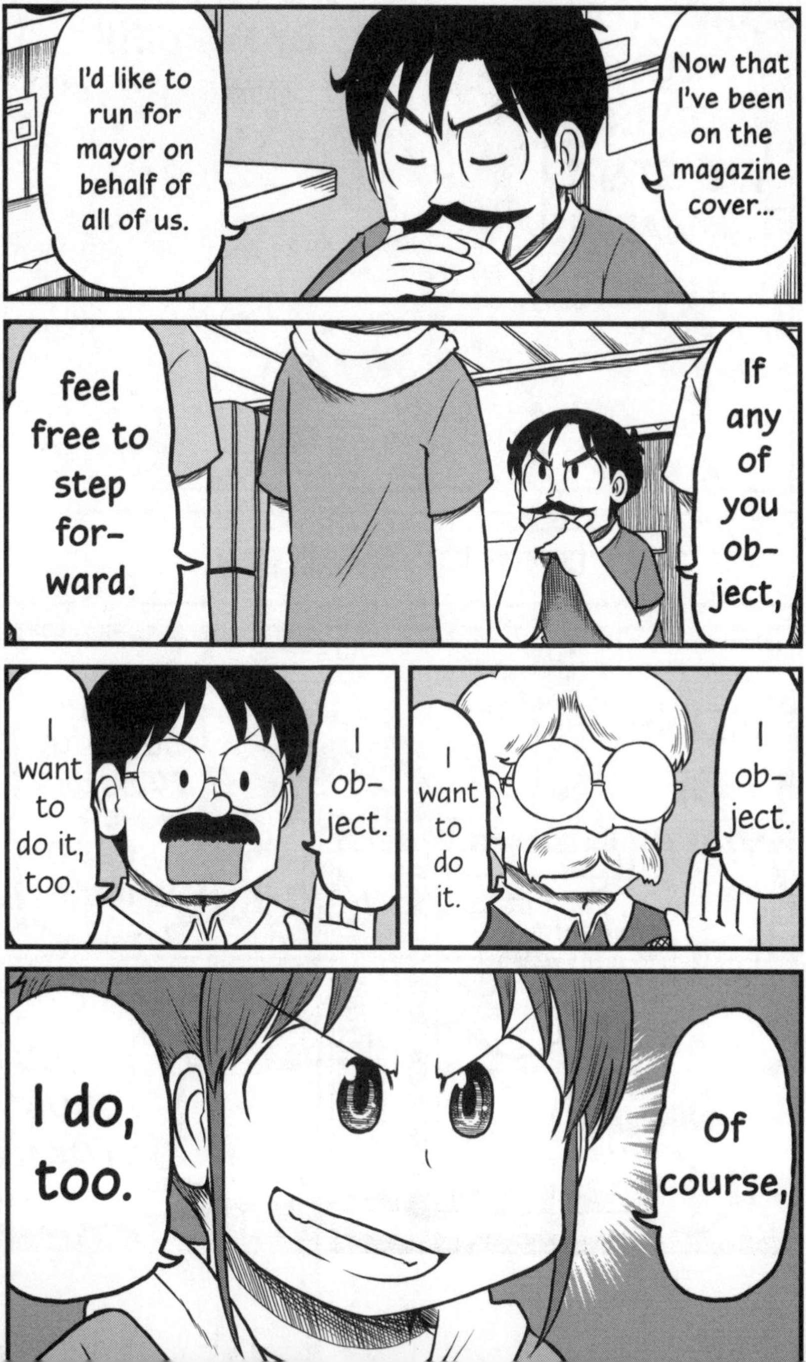
Now that I've been on the magazine cover...
I'd like to run for mayor on behalf of all of us.
If any of you ob-ject,
feel free to step for-ward.
I ob-ject.
I want to do it.
I ob-ject.
I want to do it, too.
Of course,
I do, too.

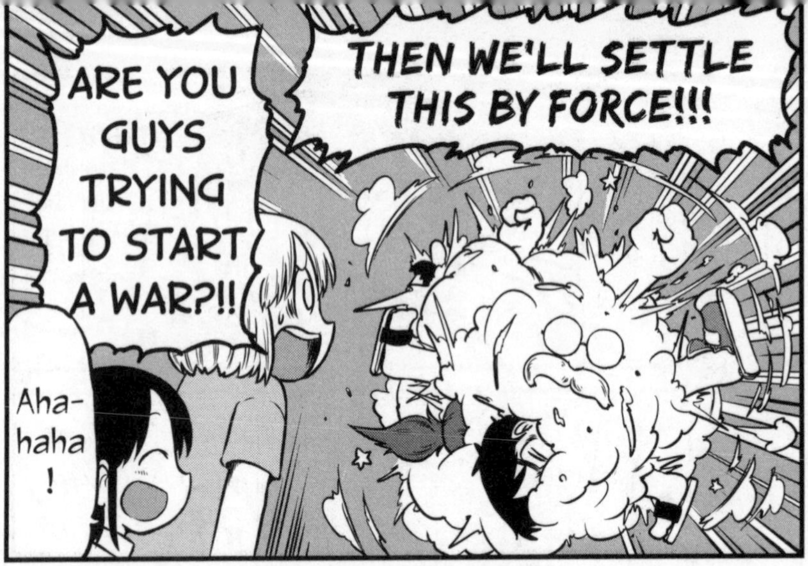
THEN WE'LL SETTLE THIS BY FORCE!!!
ARE YOU GUYS TRYING TO START A WAR?!!
Aha-haha!

Chapter 170 CITY 3

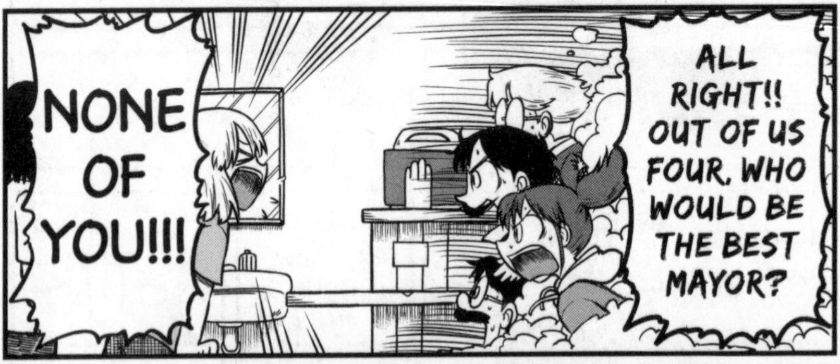
ALL RIGHT!! OUT OF US FOUR, WHO WOULD BE THE BEST MAYOR?
NONE OF YOU!!!

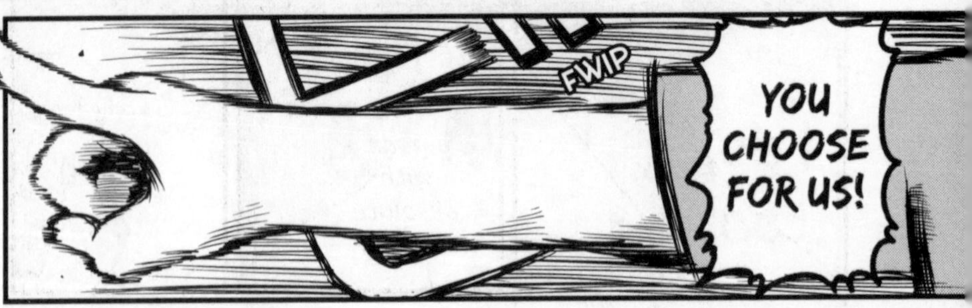
YOU CHOOSE FOR US!
FWIP

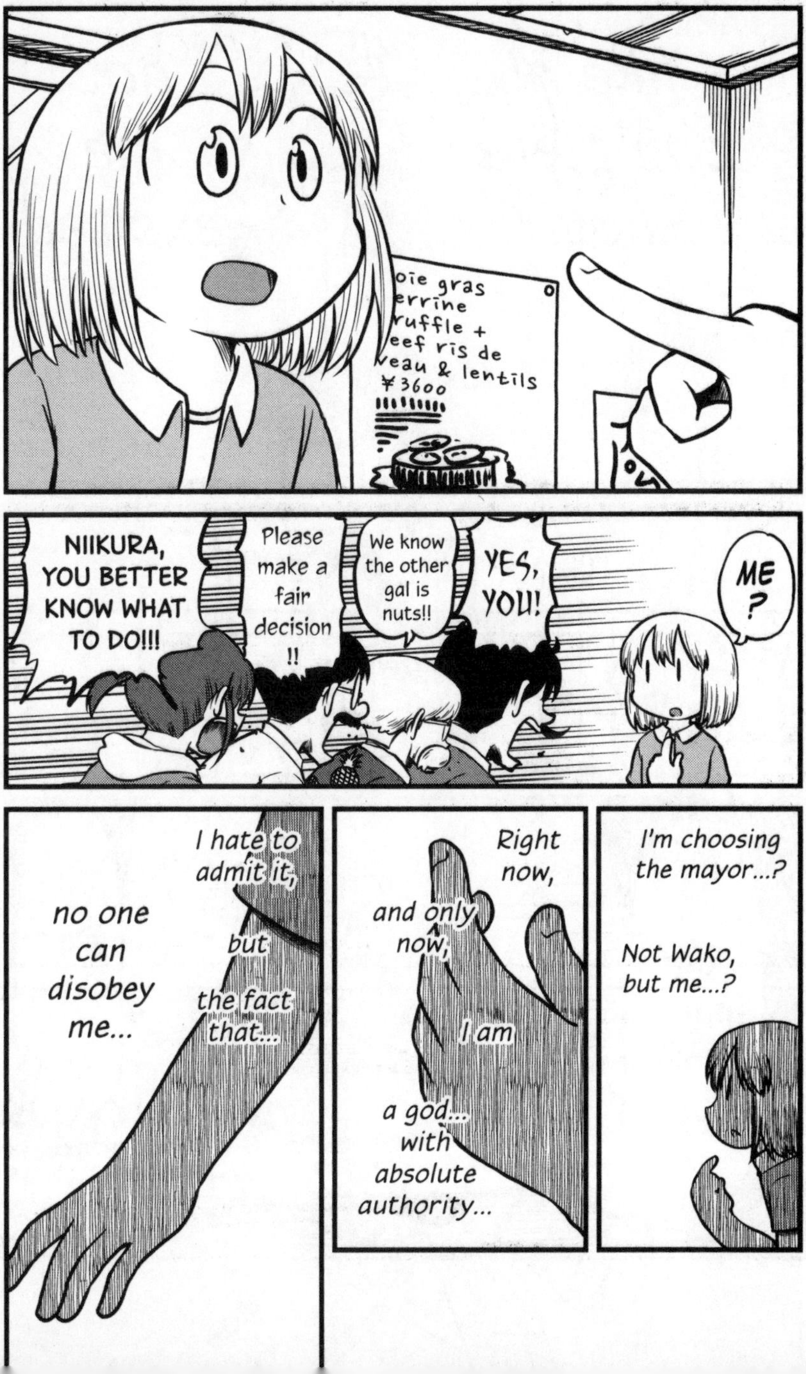
oie gras
errine
ruffle +
eef ris de
veau & lentils
¥3600
ME?
YES, YOU!
We know the other gal is nuts!!
Please make a fair decision!!
NIIKURA, YOU BETTER KNOW WHAT TO DO!!!
I'm choosing the mayor...?
Not Wako, but me...?
Right now,
and only now,
I am
a god... with absolute authority...
I hate to admit it,
but
the fact that...
no one can disobey me...

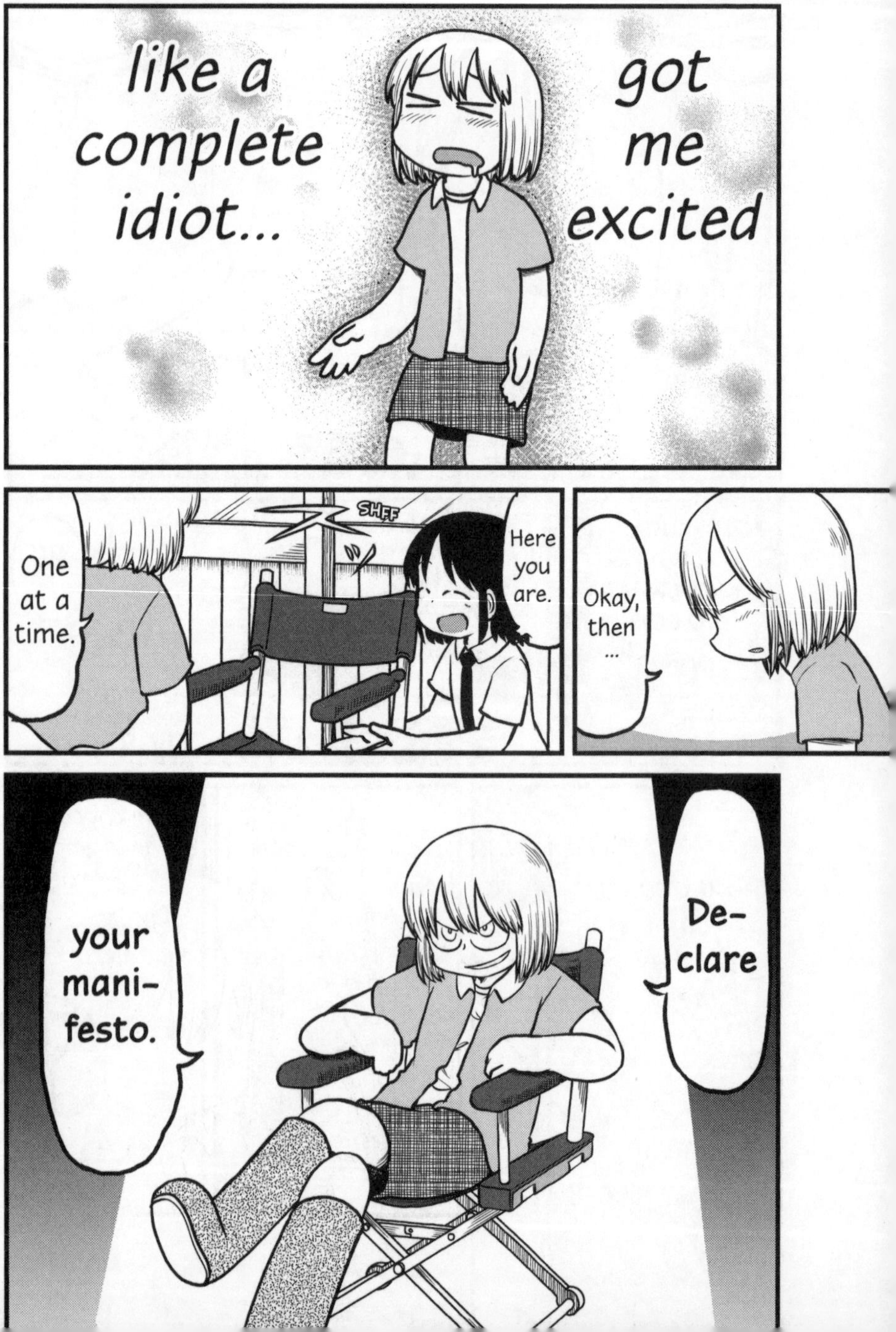
got me excited
like a complete idiot...
Okay, then ...
Here you are.
SHFF
One at a time.
De-clare
your mani-festo.

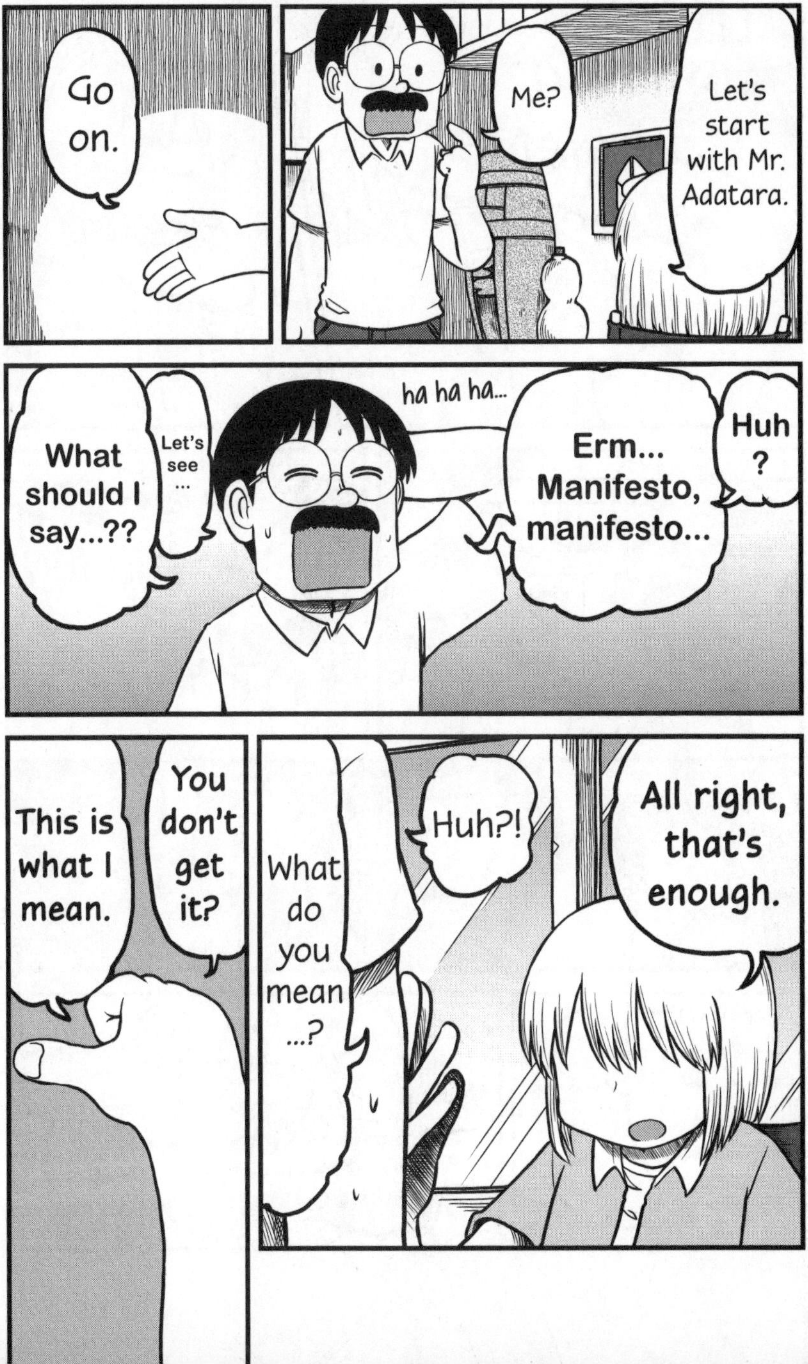
Let's start with Mr. Adatara.
Me?
Go on.
Huh?
Erm... Manifesto, manifesto...
ha ha ha...
Let's see ...
What should I say...??
All right, that's enough.
Huh?!
What do you mean ...?
You don't get it?
This is what I mean.

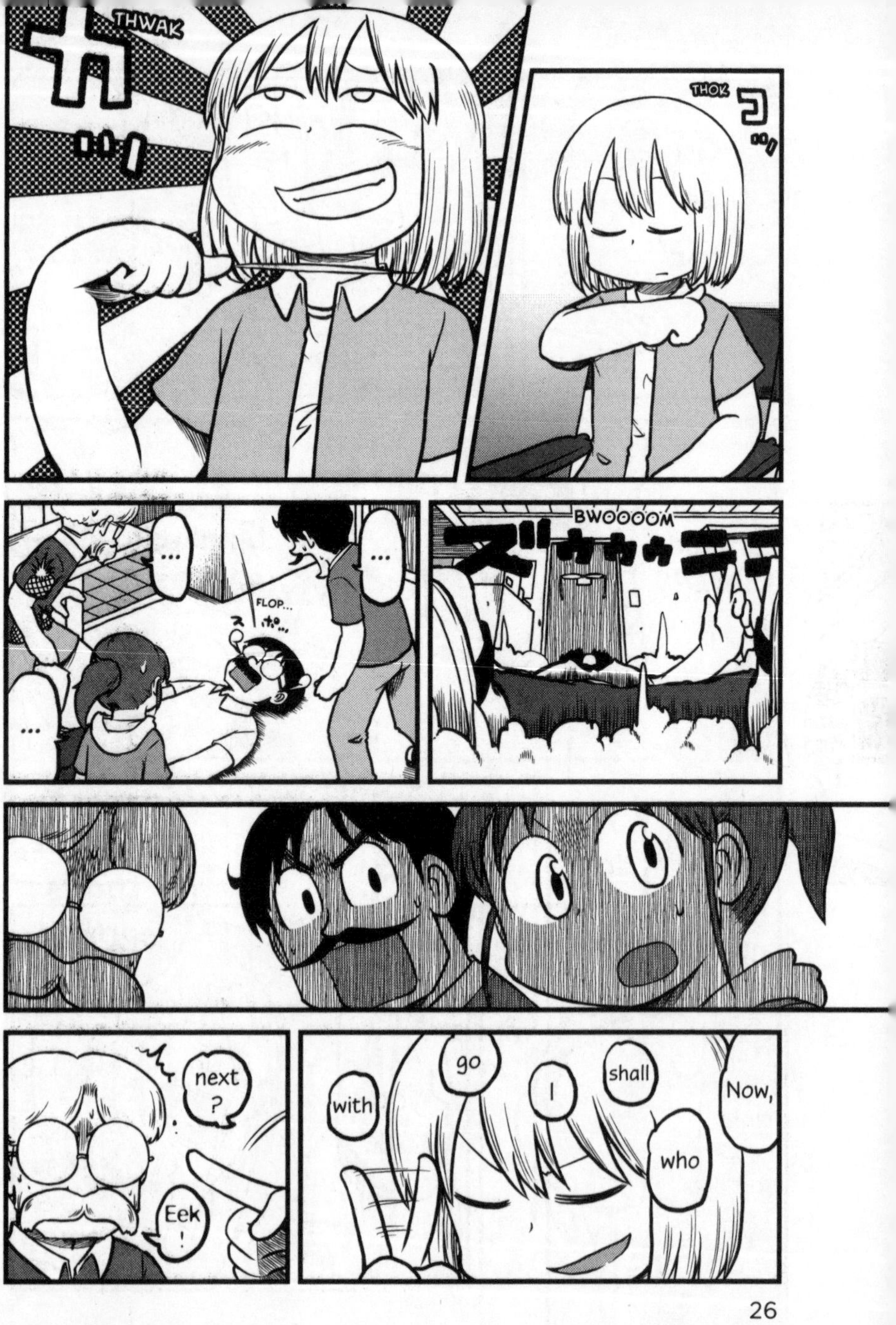

THOK
THWAK
BWOOOOM
...
...
FLOP...
...
Now,
who
shall
I
go
with
next?
Eek!

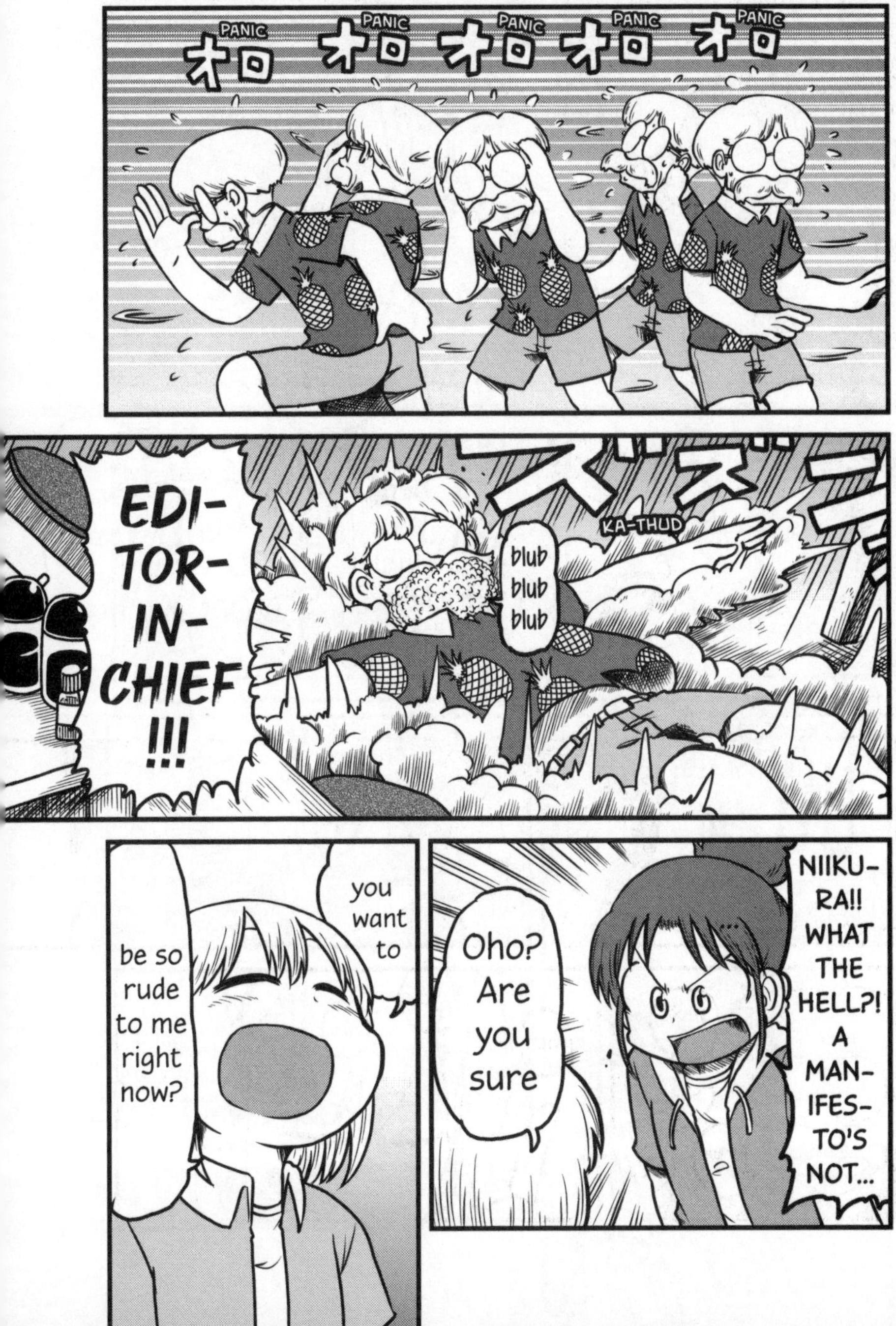
PANIC オロ PANIC オロ PANIC オロ PANIC オロ PANIC オロ
KA-THUD
blub blub blub
EDI-TOR-IN-CHIEF !!!
NIIKU-RA!! WHAT THE HELL?! A MAN-IFES-TO'S NOT...
Oho? Are you sure
you want to
be so rude to me right now?

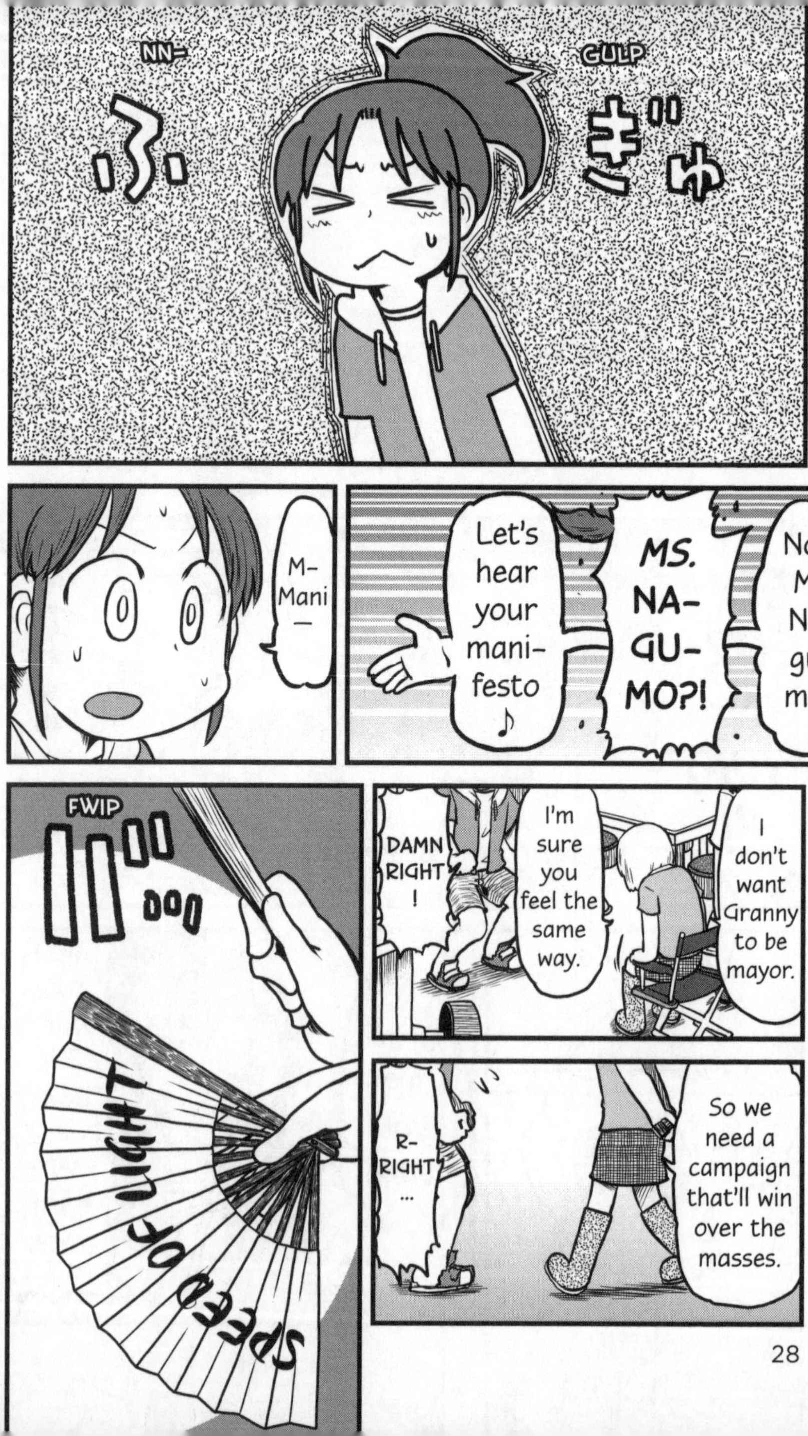
GULP
NN-
Now, Ms. Nagumo...
MS. NAGUMO?!
Let's hear your manifesto ♪
M-Mani—
I don't want Granny to be mayor.
I'm sure you feel the same way.
DAMN RIGHT!
So we need a campaign that'll win over the masses.
R-RIGHT...
FWIP
SPEED OF LIGHT

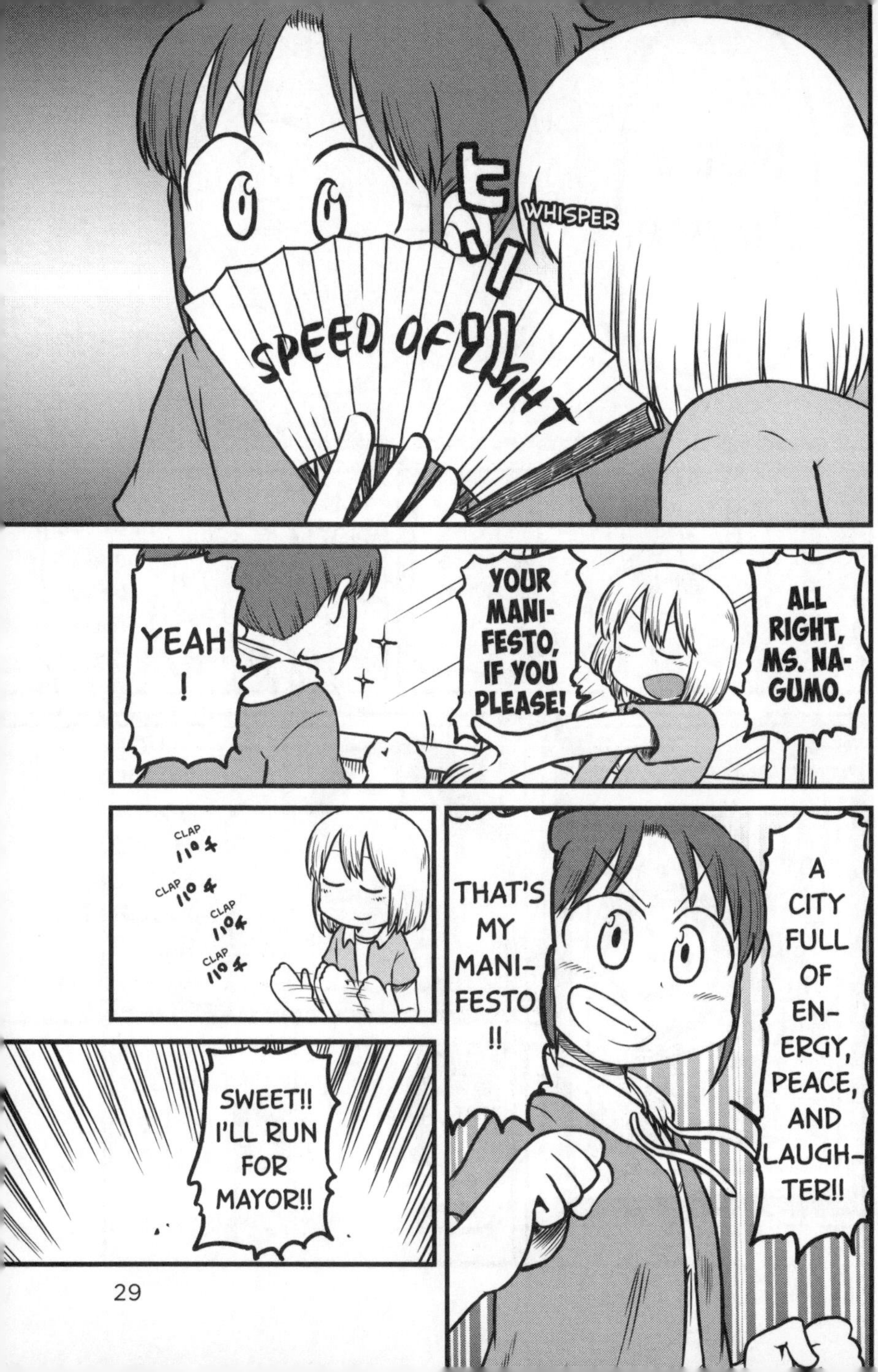
WHISPER
SPEED OF LIGHT
ALL RIGHT, MS. NAGUMO.
YOUR MANIFESTO, IF YOU PLEASE!
YEAH!
A CITY FULL OF ENERGY, PEACE, AND LAUGHTER!!
THAT'S MY MANIFESTO!!
CLAP
CLAP
CLAP
CLAP
SWEET!! I'LL RUN FOR MAYOR!!

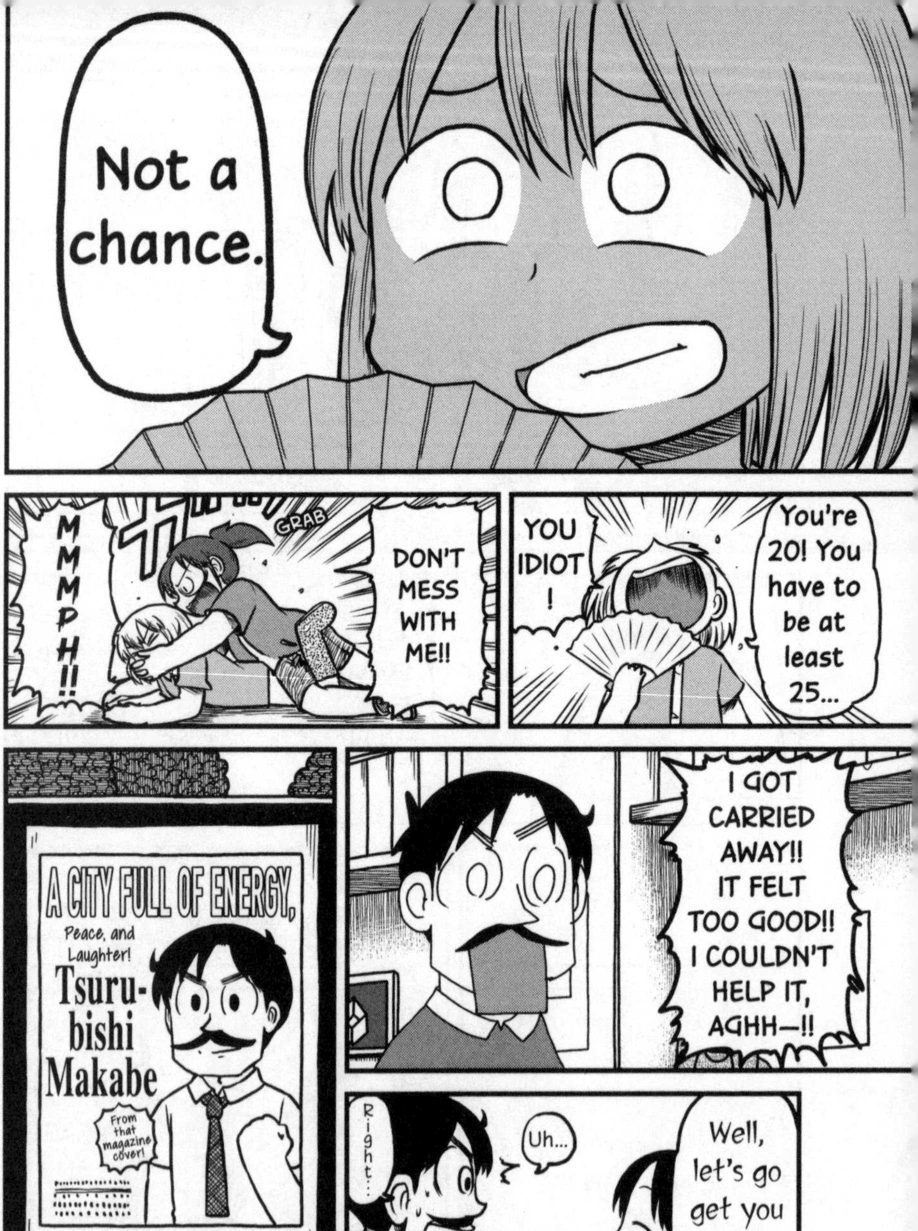
Not a chance.
You're 20! You have to be at least 25...
YOU IDIOT!
DON'T MESS WITH ME!!
GRAB
MMMPH!!
I GOT CARRIED AWAY!! IT FELT TOO GOOD!! I COULDN'T HELP IT, AGHH—!!
Well, let's go get you regis-tered.
Uh...
Right...
A CITY FULL OF ENERGY,
Peace, and Laughter!
Tsuru-bishi Makabe
From that magazine cover!

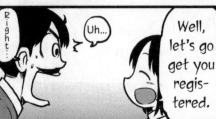

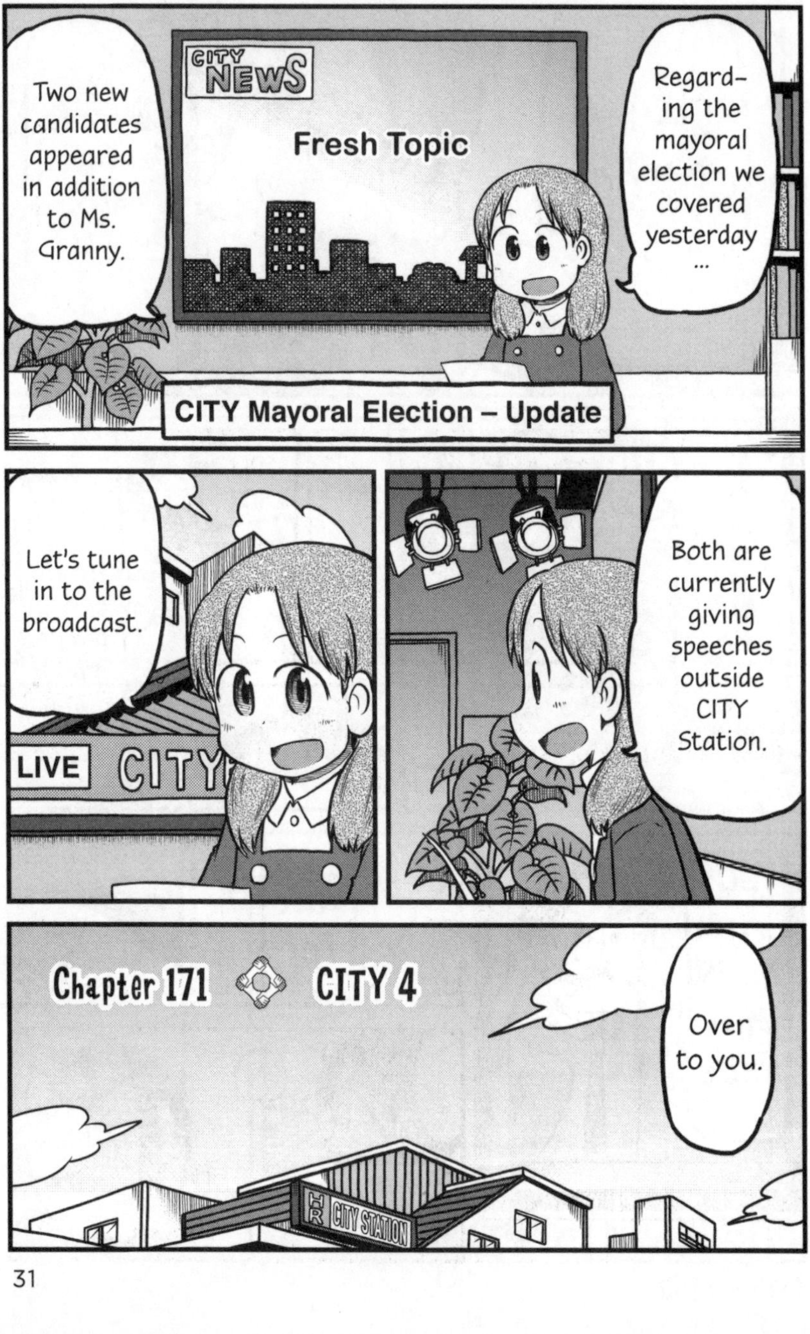

Regard-ing the mayoral election we covered yesterday ...
CITY NEWS
Fresh Topic
Two new candidates appeared in addition to Ms. Granny.
CITY Mayoral Election – Update
Both are currently giving speeches outside CITY Station.
Let's tune in to the broadcast.
LIVE
CITY
Chapter 171 CITY 4
Over to you.
HR CITY STATION

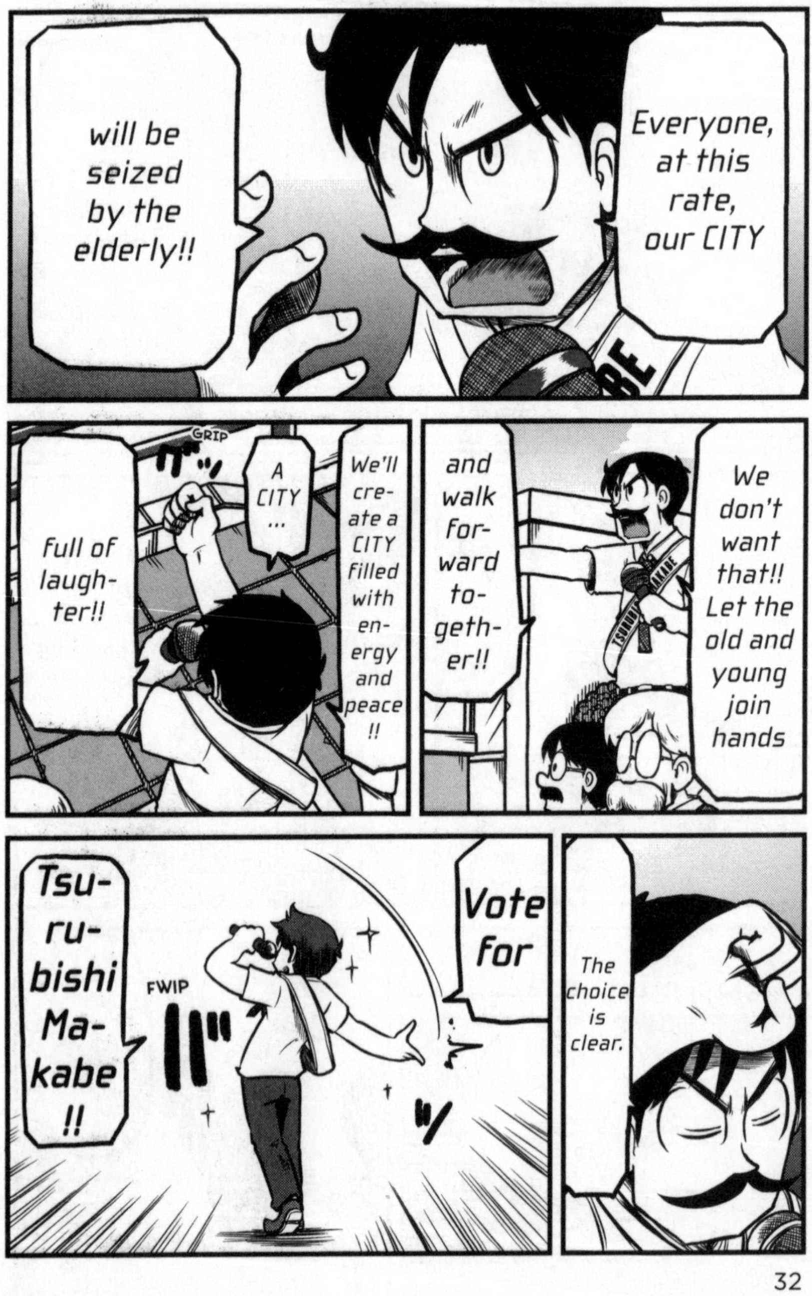
Everyone, at this rate, our CITY
will be seized by the elderly!!
We don't want that!! Let the old and young join hands
and walk for-ward to-geth-er!!
We'll cre-ate a CITY filled with en-ergy and peace!!
A CITY...
GRIP
full of laugh-ter!!
The choice is clear.
Vote for
FWIP
Tsu-ru-bishi Ma-kabe!!

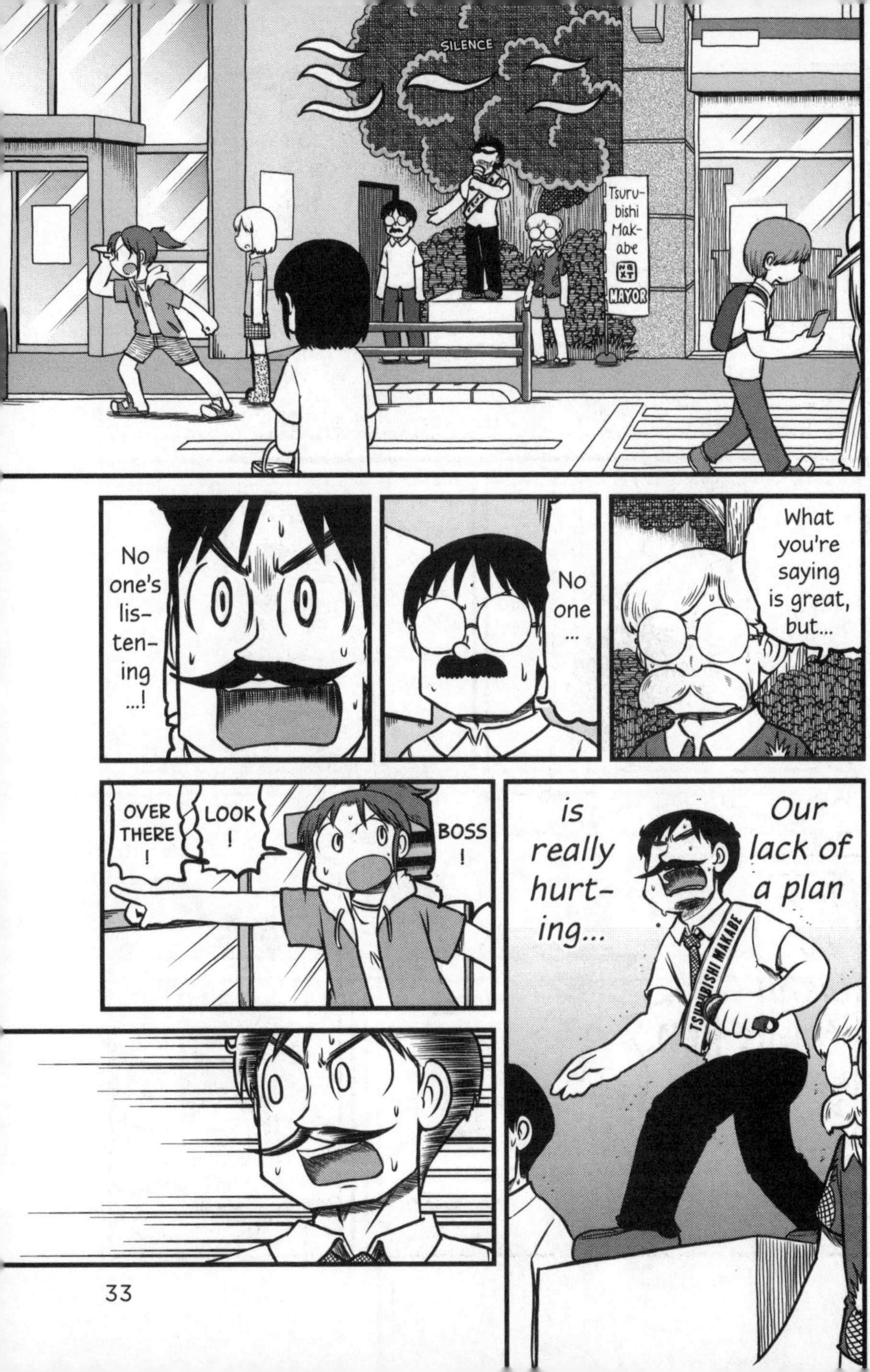
SILENCE
Tsuru-bishi Mak-abe NEXT MAYOR
What you're saying is great, but...
No one ...
No one's lis-ten-ing ...!
Our lack of a plan
is really hurt-ing...
TSURUBISHI MAKABE
BOSS!
LOOK!
OVER THERE!

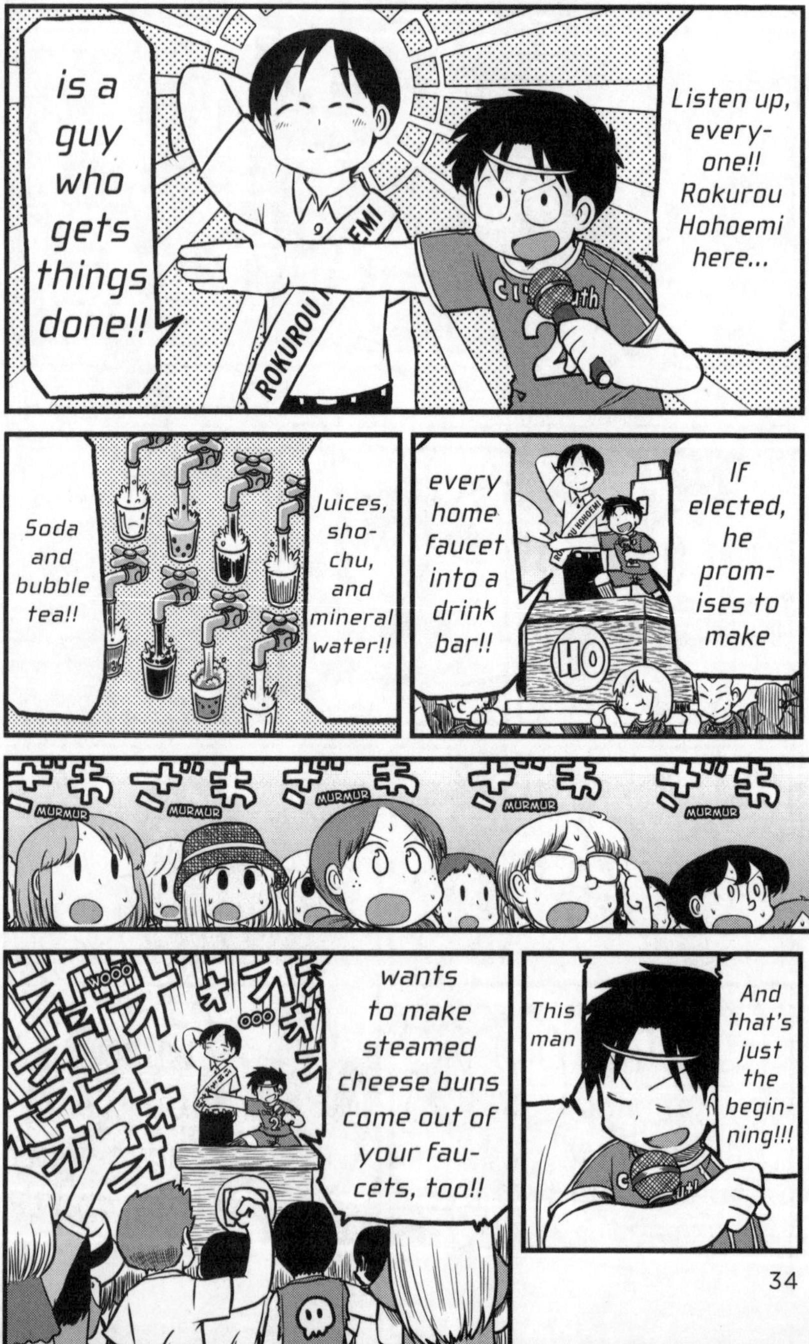
Listen up, every-one!! Rokurou Hohoemi here...
is a guy who gets things done!!
If elected, he prom-ises to make
every home faucet into a drink bar!!
ROKUROU HOHOEMI
HO
Juices, sho-chu, and mineral water!!
Soda and bubble tea!!
MURMUR
MURMUR
MURMUR
MURMUR
MURMUR
And that's just the begin-ning!!!
This man
wants to make steamed cheese buns come out of your fau-cets, too!!
WOOO
OOO

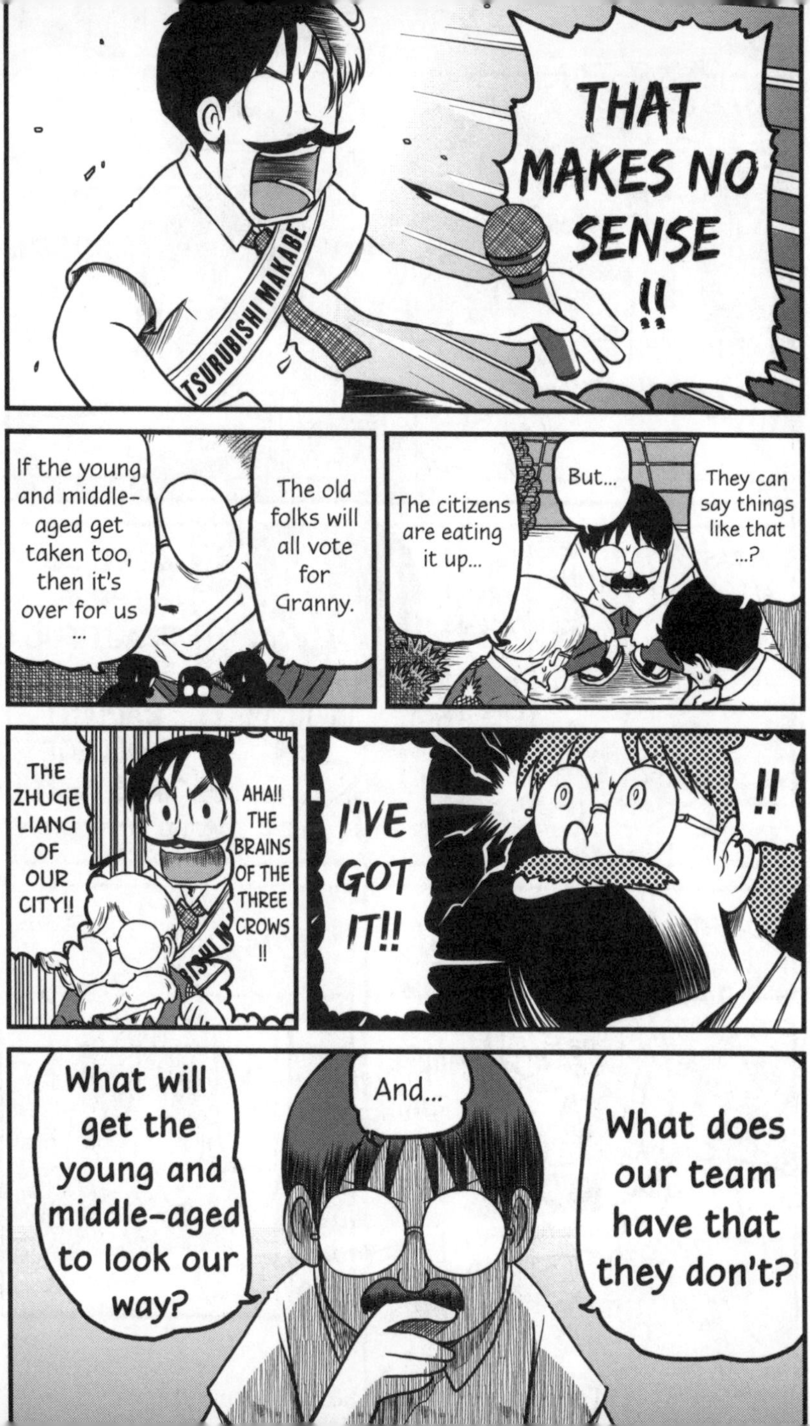
TSURUBISHI MAKABE
THAT MAKES NO SENSE !!
They can say things like that ...?
But...
The citizens are eating it up...
The old folks will all vote for Granny.
If the young and middle-aged get taken too, then it's over for us ...
!!
I'VE GOT IT!!
AHA!! THE BRAINS OF THE THREE CROWS !!
THE ZHUGE LIANG OF OUR CITY!!
What does our team have that they don't?
And...
What will get the young and middle-aged to look our way?

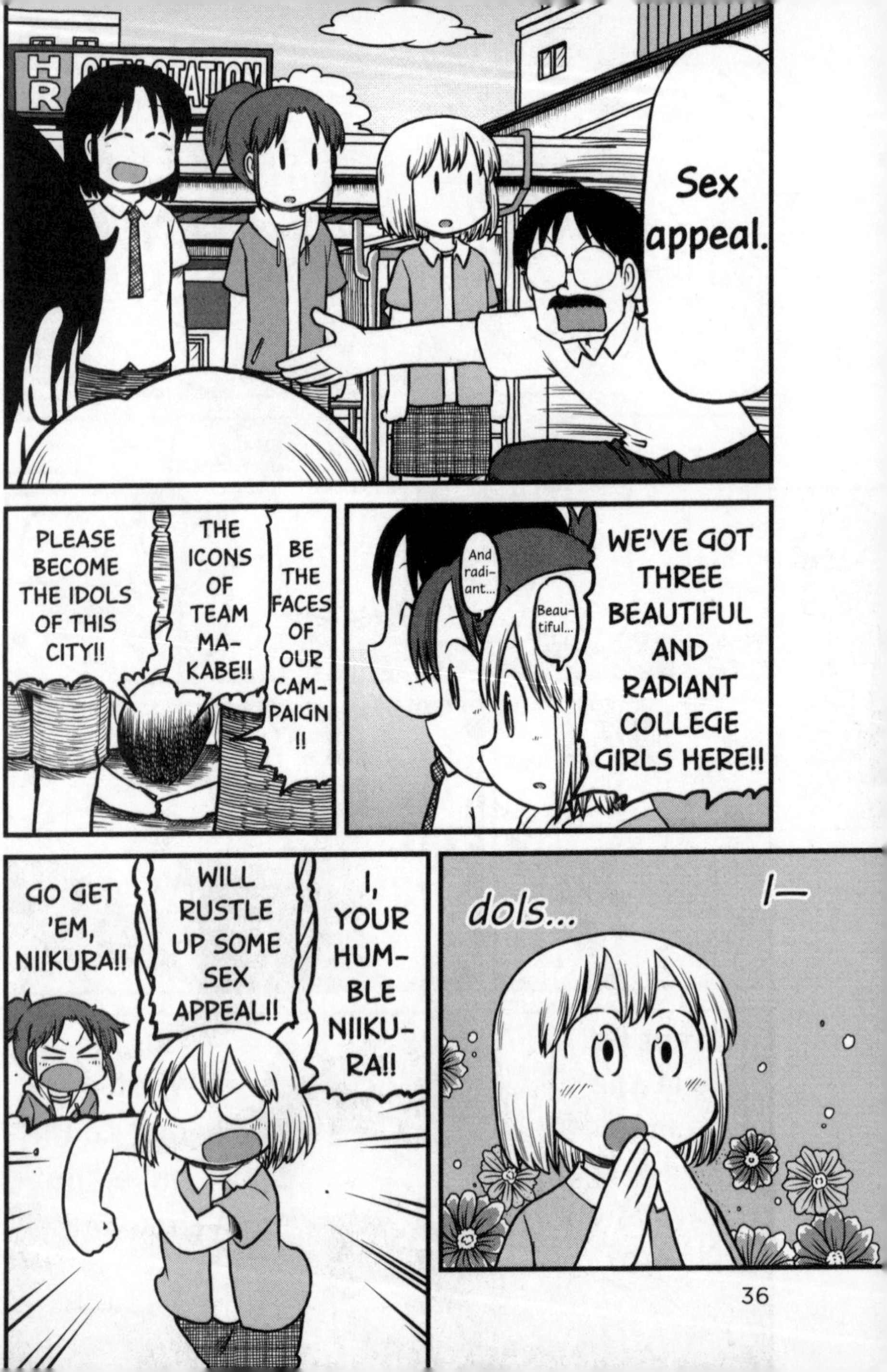
Sex appeal.
WE'VE GOT THREE BEAUTIFUL AND RADIANT COLLEGE GIRLS HERE!!
Beautiful...
And radiant...
BE THE FACES OF OUR CAMPAIGN!!
THE ICONS OF TEAM MAKABE!!
PLEASE BECOME THE IDOLS OF THIS CITY!!
I—
dols...
I, YOUR HUMBLE NIIKURA!!
WILL RUSTLE UP SOME SEX APPEAL!!
GO GET 'EM, NIIKURA!!

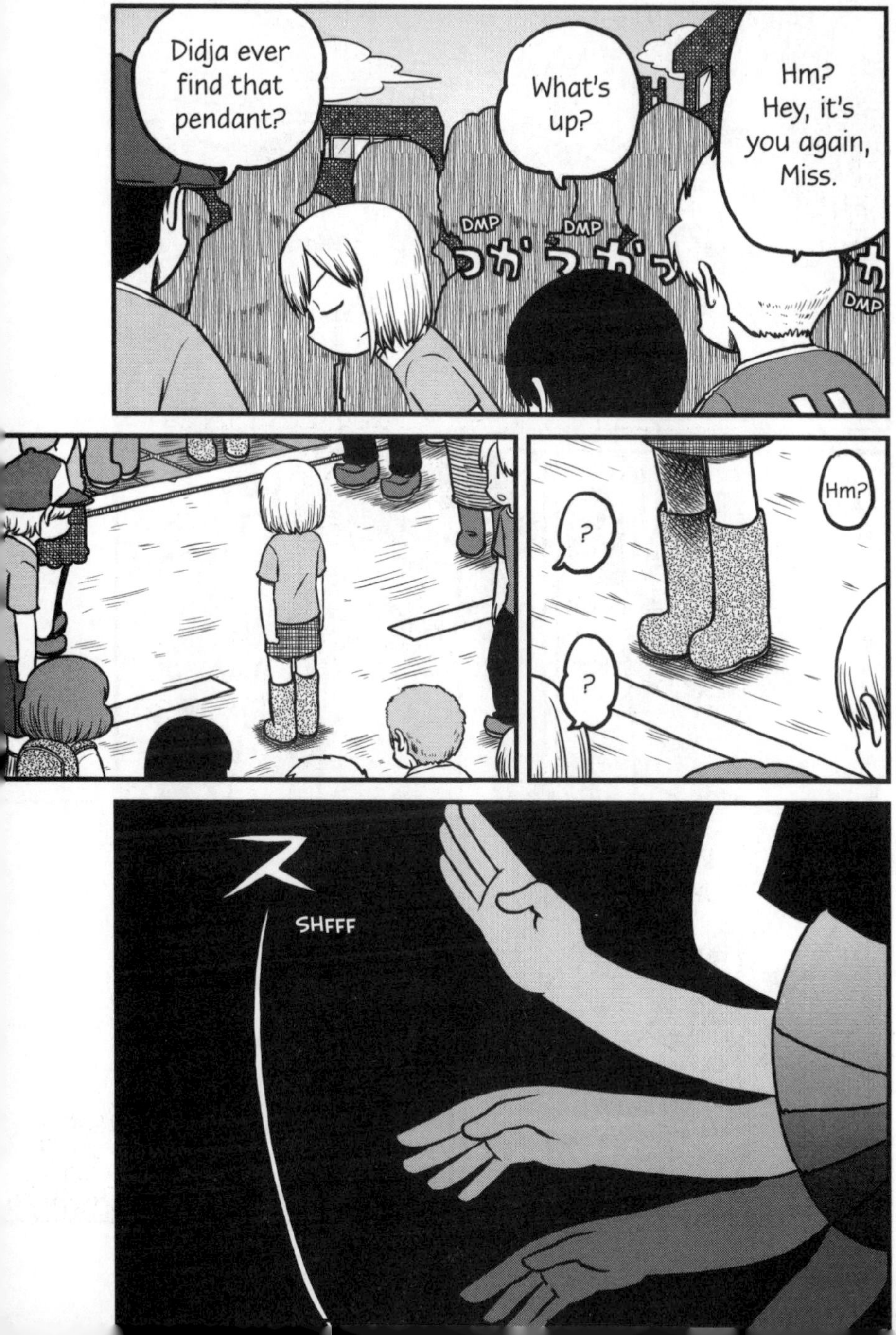
Hm? Hey, it's you again, Miss.
DMP
What's up?
DMP
Didja ever find that pendant?
DMP
Hm?
?
?
ス
SHFFF

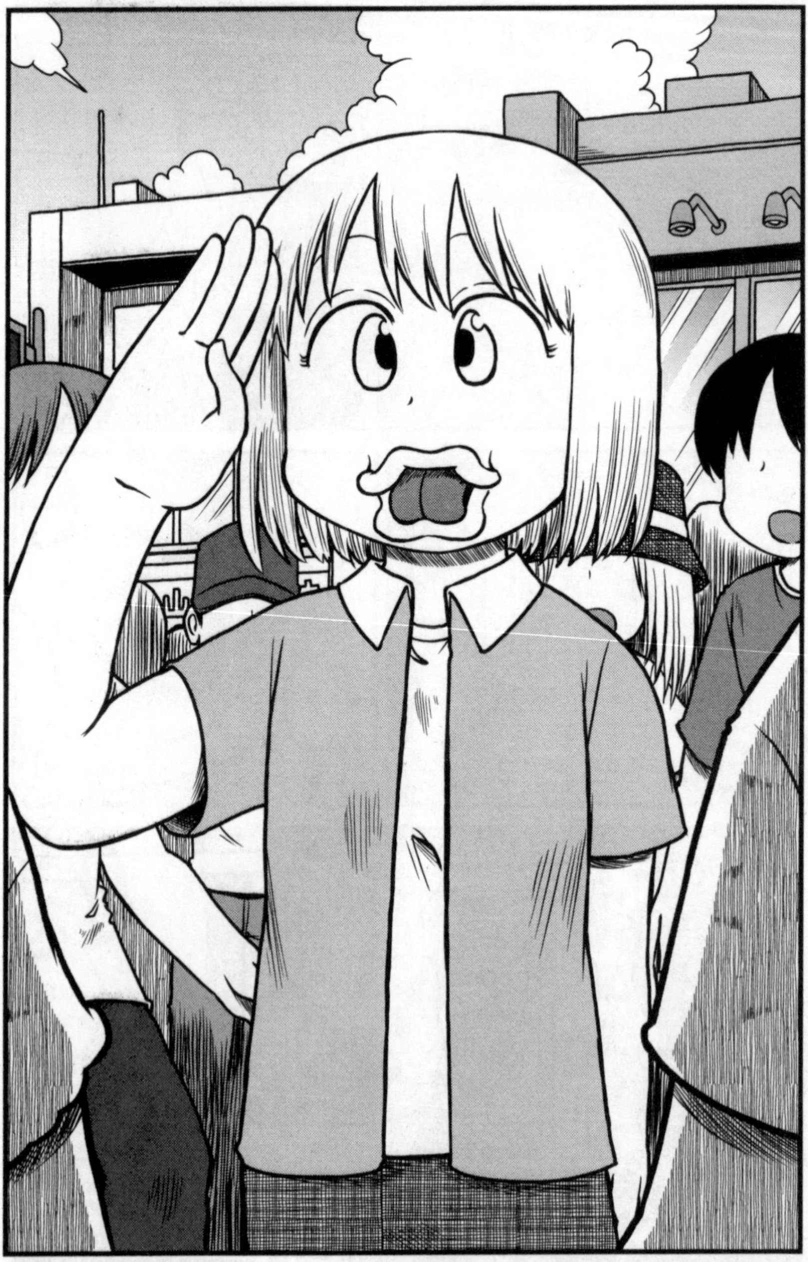

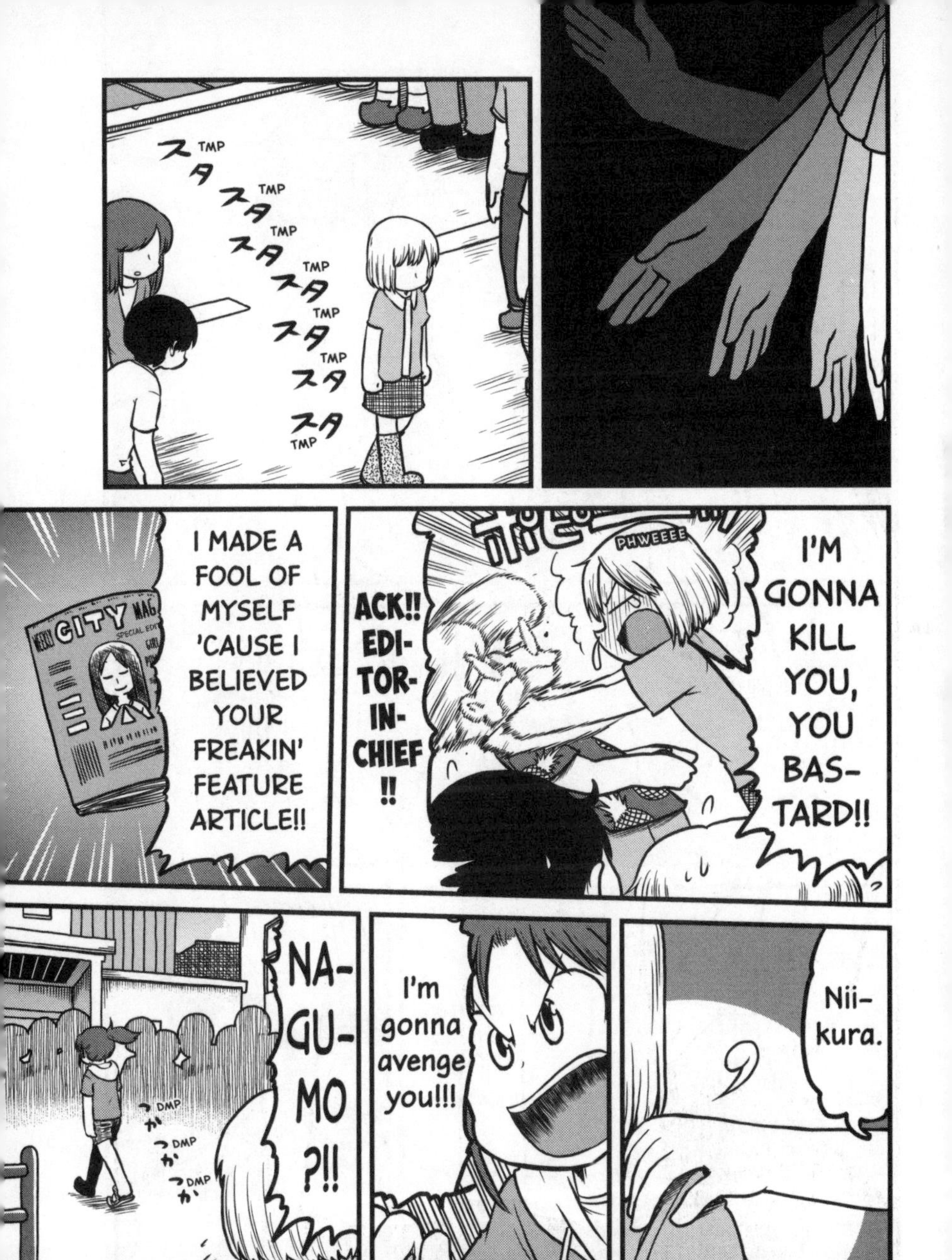
スタ TMP
スタ TMP
スタ TMP
スタ TMP
スタ TMP
スタ TMP
スタ TMP
PHWEEEE
I'M GONNA KILL YOU, YOU BAS-TARD!!
ACK!! EDI-TOR-IN-CHIEF!!
I MADE A FOOL OF MYSELF 'CAUSE I BELIEVED YOUR FREAKIN' FEATURE ARTICLE!!
CITY MAG
Nii-kura.
I'm gonna avenge you!!!
NA-GU-MO?!!
DMP
DMP
DMP

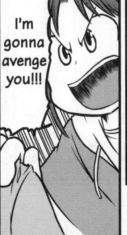

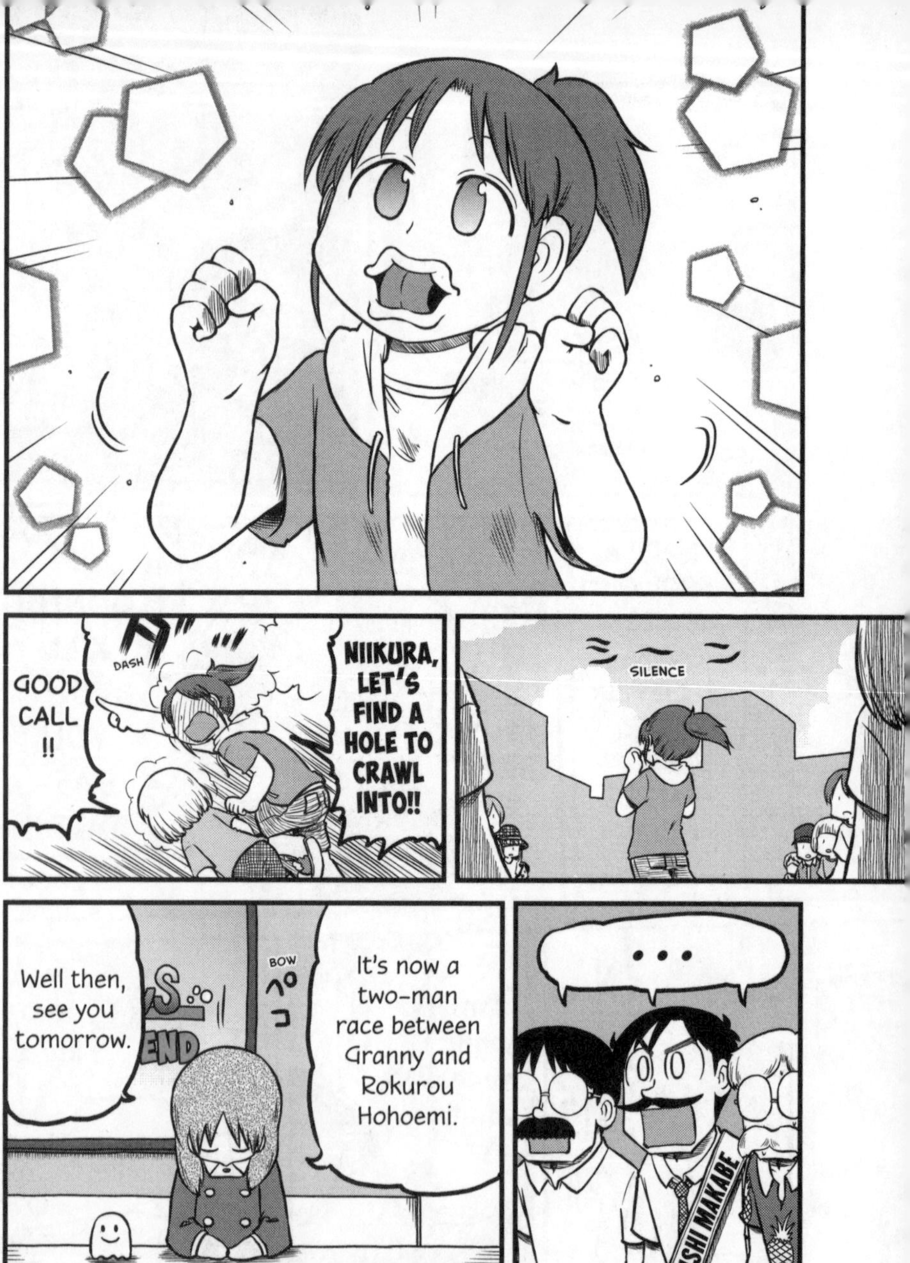
SILENCE
NIIKURA, LET'S FIND A HOLE TO CRAWL INTO!!
DASH
GOOD CALL !!
...
SURUBISHI MAKABE
It's now a two-man race between Granny and Rokurou Hohoemi.
BOW
Well then, see you tomorrow.

CITY 4 / END

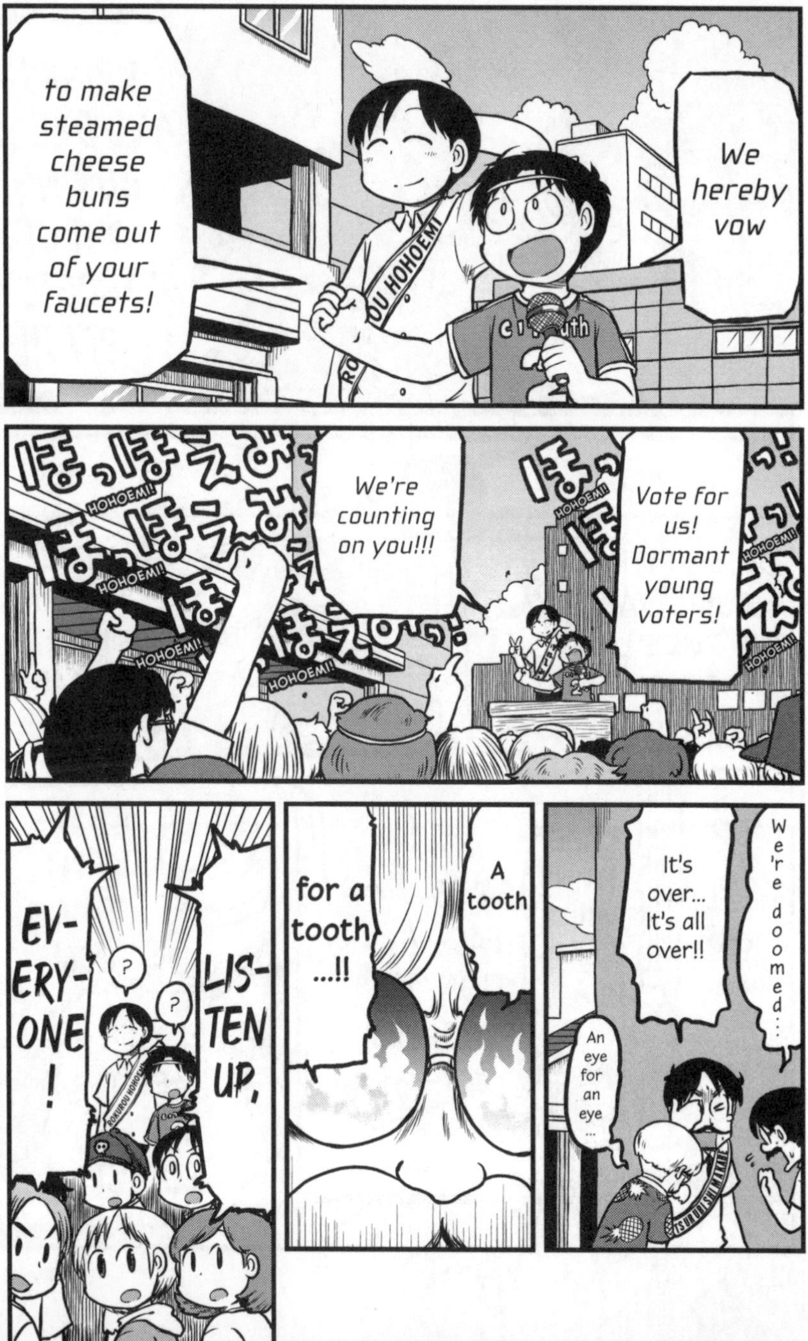
We hereby vow
to make steamed cheese buns come out of your faucets!
Vote for us! Dormant young voters!
We're counting on you!!!
ほっほえみっ
HOHOEMI!
HOHOEMI!
HOHOEMI!
We're doomed...
It's over... It's all over!!
An eye for an eye...
A tooth
for a tooth ...!!
LIS-TEN UP,
EV-ERY-ONE!
?
?

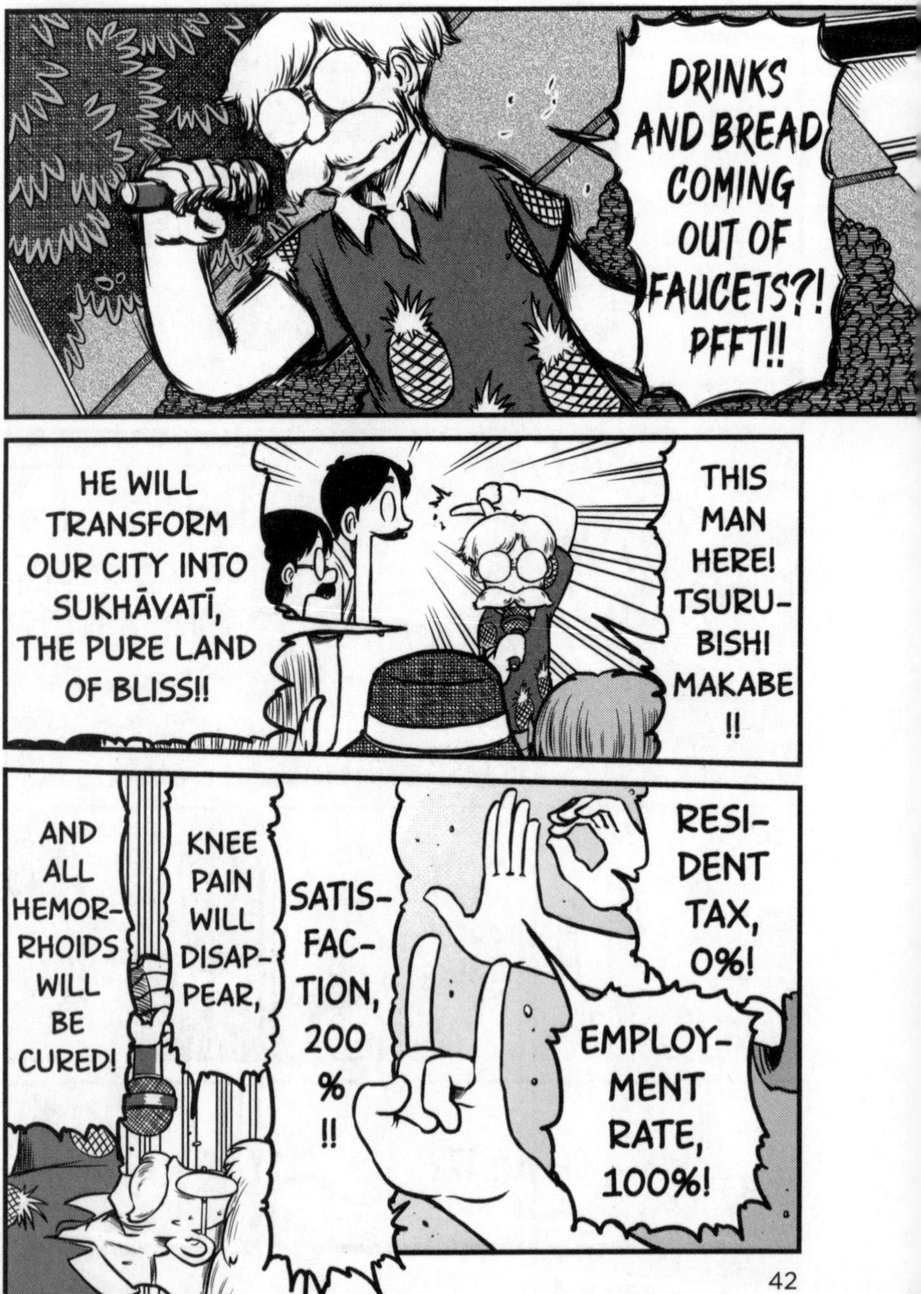
DRINKS AND BREAD COMING OUT OF FAUCETS?! PFFT!!
THIS MAN HERE! TSURUBISHI MAKABE!!
HE WILL TRANSFORM OUR CITY INTO SUKHĀVATĪ, THE PURE LAND OF BLISS!!
RESIDENT TAX, 0%!
EMPLOYMENT RATE, 100%!
SATISFACTION, 200%!!
KNEE PAIN WILL DISAPPEAR,
AND ALL HEMORRHOIDS WILL BE CURED!

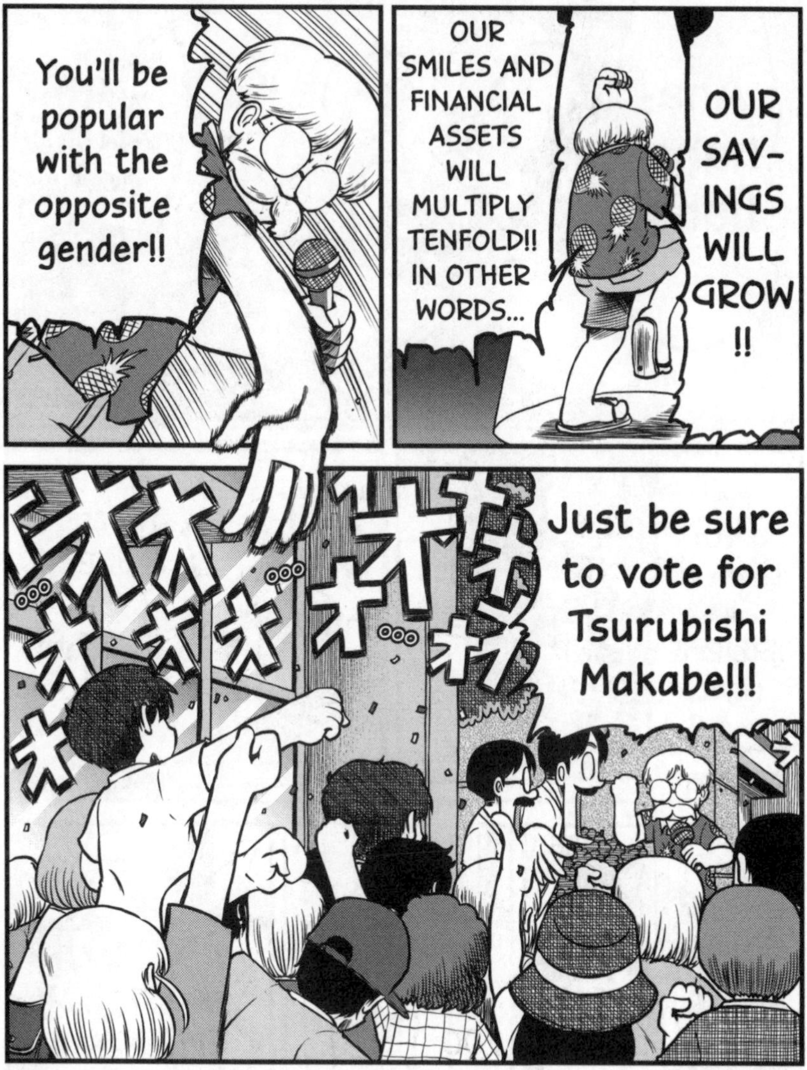
OUR SMILES AND FINANCIAL ASSETS WILL MULTIPLY TENFOLD!! IN OTHER WORDS...
OUR SAVINGS WILL GROW!!
You'll be popular with the opposite gender!!
Just be sure to vote for Tsurubishi Makabe!!!

Chapter 172 CITY 5

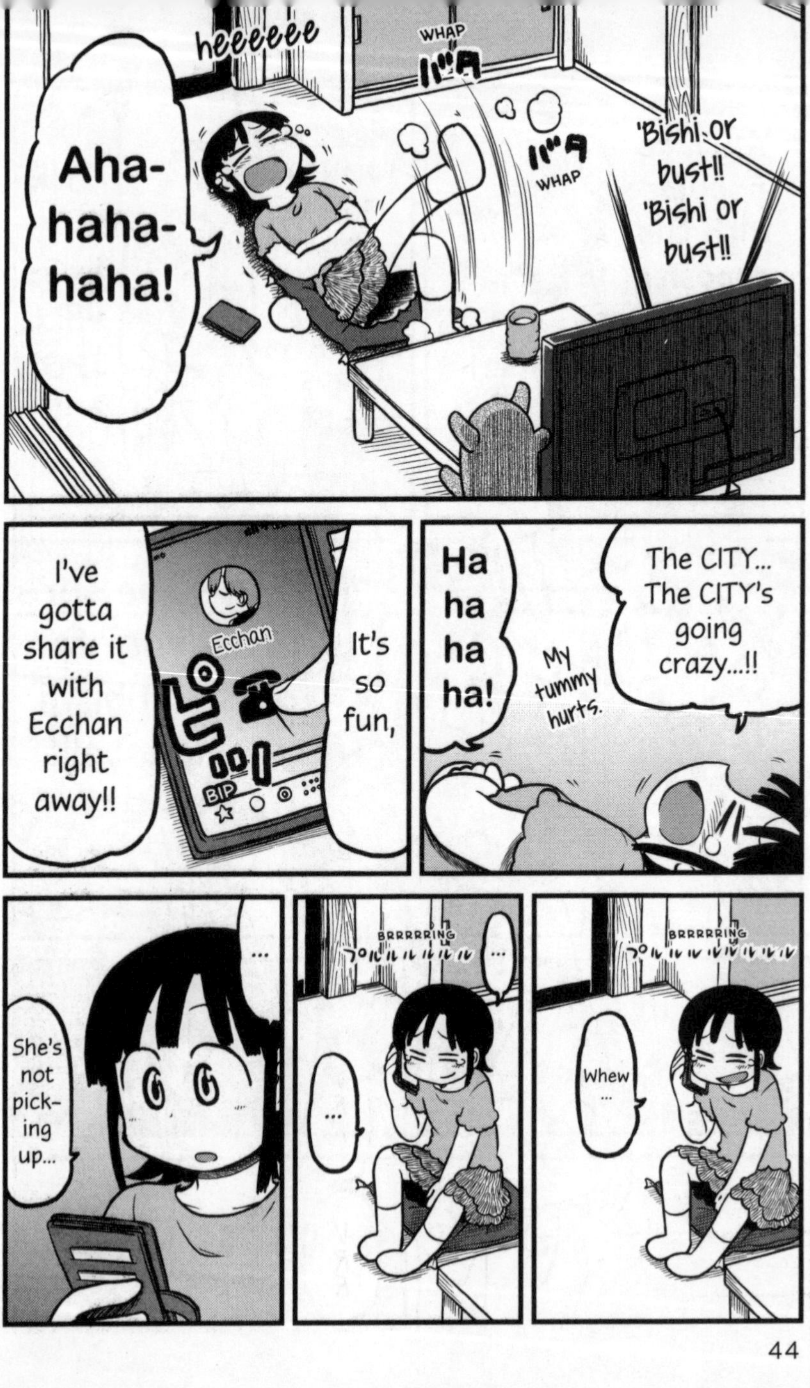
'Bishi or bust!! 'Bishi or bust!!
WHAP
バタ
バタ
WHAP
heeeeee
Aha-haha-haha!
The CITY... The CITY's going crazy...!!
My tummy hurts.
Ha ha ha ha!
It's so fun,
Ecchan
BIP
I've gotta share it with Ecchan right away!!
BRRRRRING
プルルルルルルルル
Whew ...
BRRRRRING
プルルルルルル
...
...
...
She's not pick-ing up...

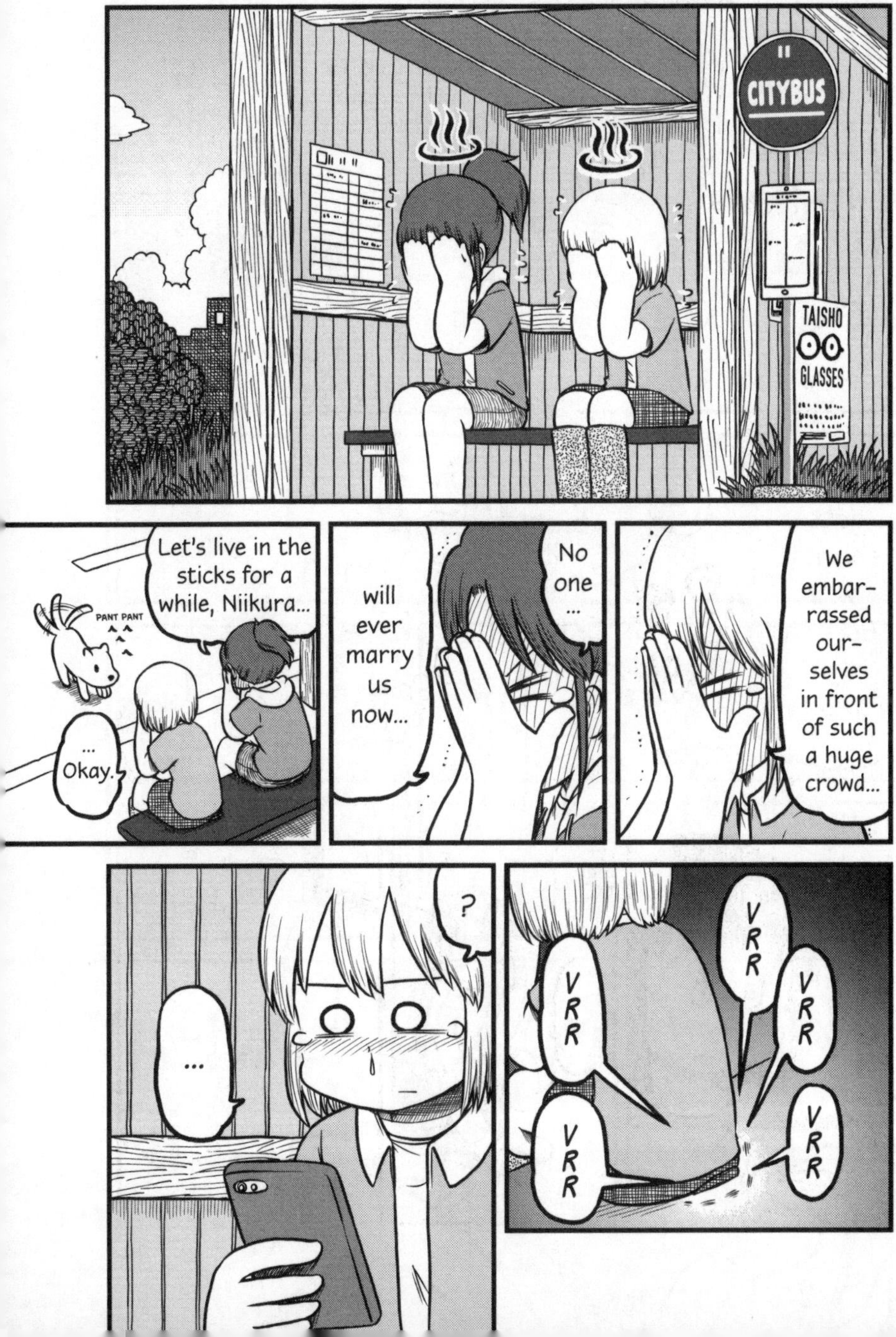
CITYBUS
TAISHO
GLASSES
We embarrassed ourselves in front of such a huge crowd...
No one ...
will ever marry us now...
Let's live in the sticks for a while, Niikura...
PANT PANT
... Okay.
VRR
VRR
VRR
VRR
?
...

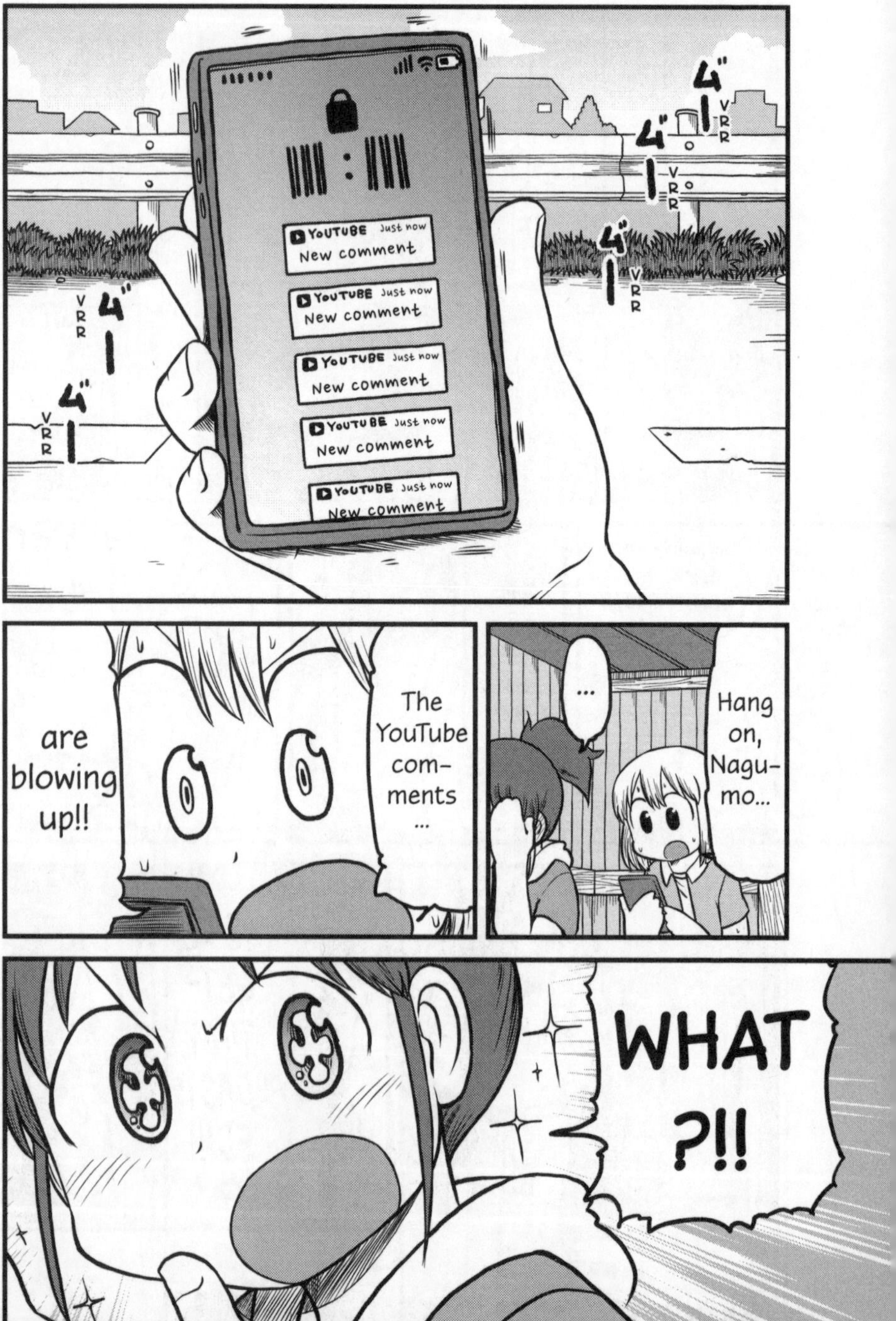

VRR
VRR
VRR
YOUTUBE Just now
New comment
YOUTUBE Just now
New comment
YOUTUBE Just now
New comment
YOUTUBE Just now
New comment
YOUTUBE Just now
New comment
VRR
VRR
Hang on, Nagumo...
...
The YouTube comments...
are blowing up!!
WHAT?!!

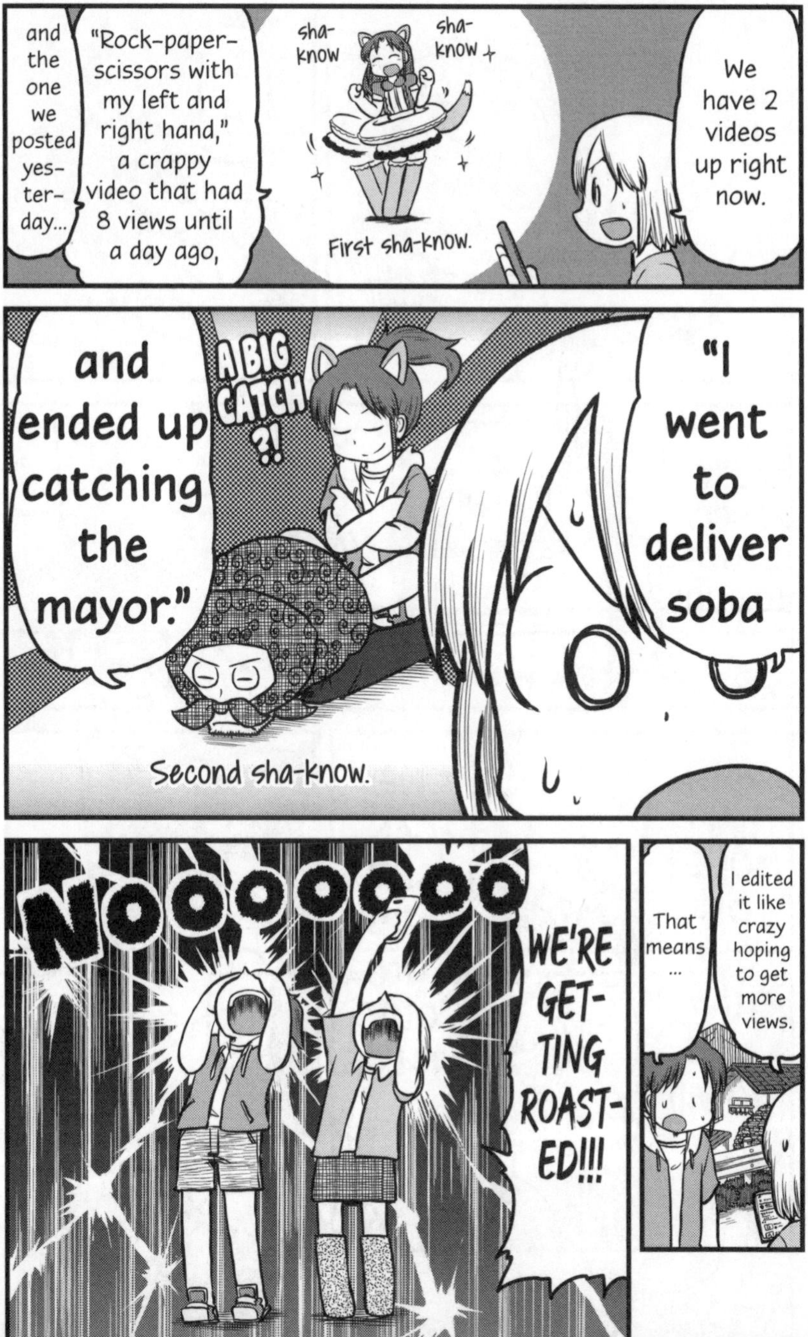
We have 2 videos up right now.
sha-know
sha-know
First sha-know.
"Rock-paper-scissors with my left and right hand," a crappy video that had 8 views until a day ago,
and the one we posted yes-ter-day...
"I went to deliver soba
A BIG CATCH?!
and ended up catching the mayor."
Second sha-know.
I edited it like crazy hoping to get more views.
That means...
WE'RE GET-TING ROAST-ED!!!
NOOOOOOO

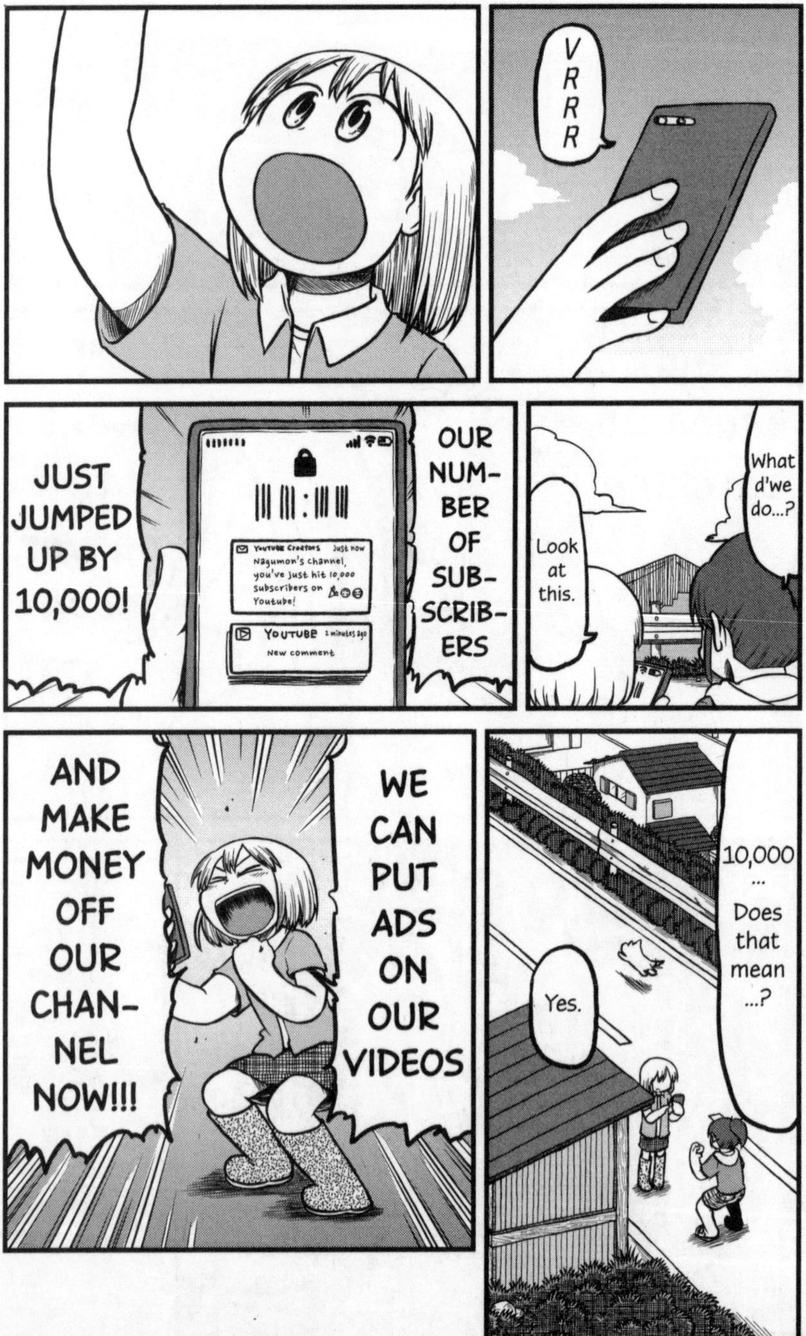
VRRR
What d'we do...?
Look at this.
OUR NUMBER OF SUBSCRIBERS
YouTube Creators Just now
Nagumon's channel, you've just hit 10,000 subscribers on Youtube!
YOUTUBE 2 minutes ago
New comment
JUST JUMPED UP BY 10,000!
10,000 ... Does that mean ...?
Yes.
WE CAN PUT ADS ON OUR VIDEOS
AND MAKE MONEY OFF OUR CHANNEL NOW!!!

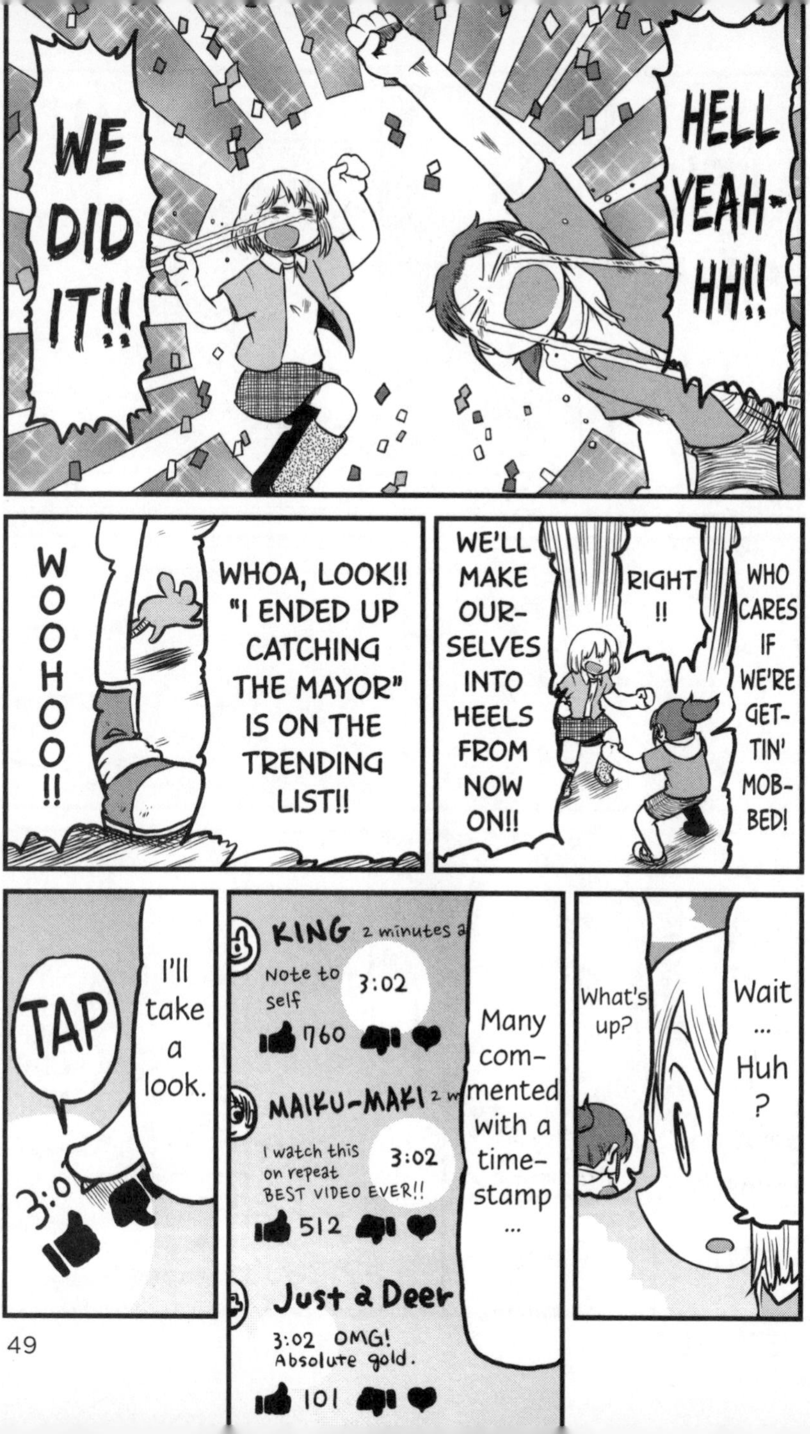
HELL YEAH-HH!!
WE DID IT!!
WHO CARES IF WE'RE GET-TIN' MOB-BED!
RIGHT!!
WE'LL MAKE OUR-SELVES INTO HEELS FROM NOW ON!!
WHOA, LOOK!! "I ENDED UP CATCHING THE MAYOR" IS ON THE TRENDING LIST!!
WOOHOOO!!
Wait... Huh?
What's up?
Many com-mented with a time-stamp...
KING 2 minutes a
Note to self
3:02
760
MAIKU-MAKI 2 m
I watch this on repeat BEST VIDEO EVER!!
3:02
512
Just a Deer
3:02 OMG! Absolute gold.
101
I'll take a look.
TAP

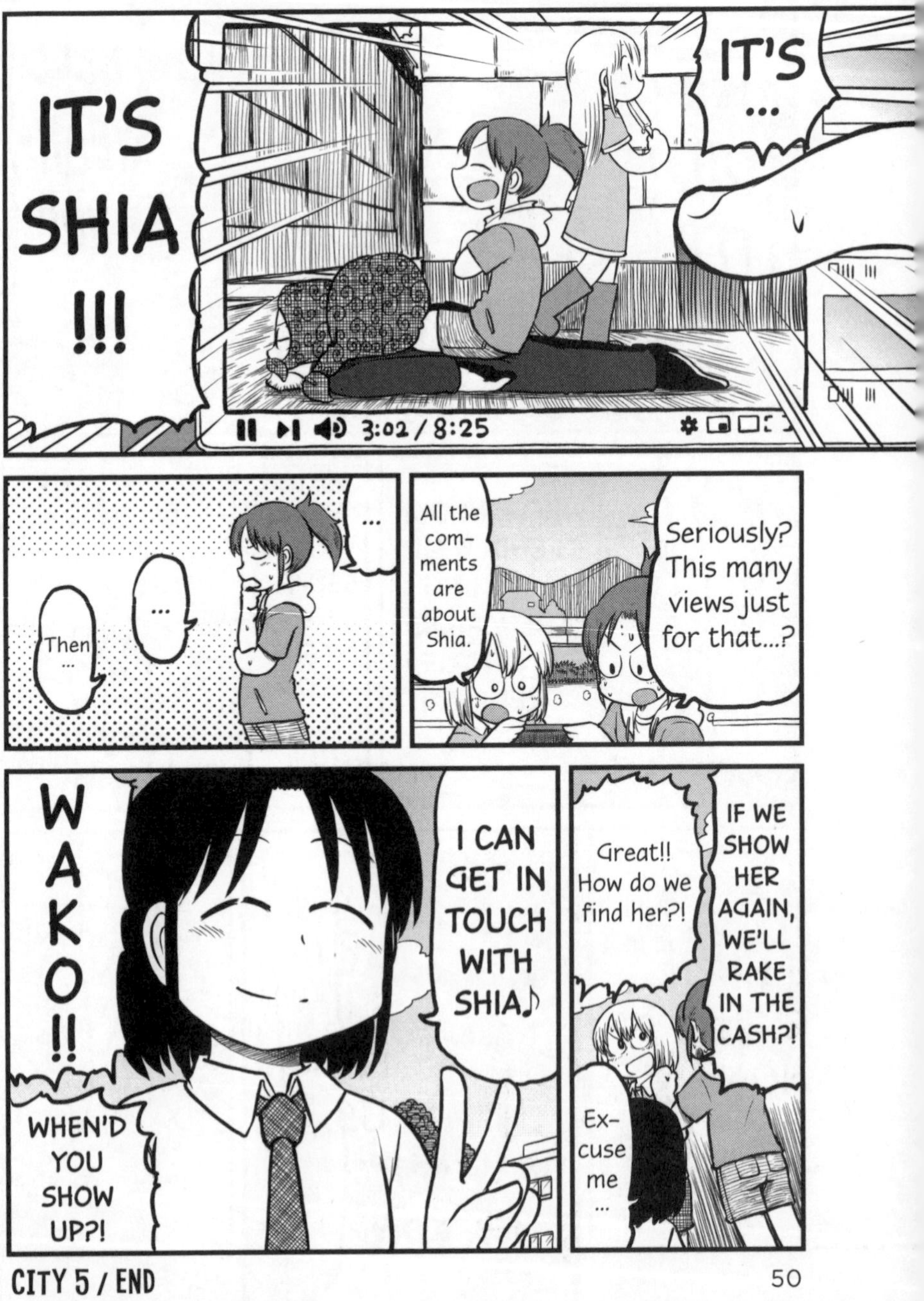
IT'S ...
IT'S SHIA !!!
3:02 / 8:25
Seriously? This many views just for that...?
All the comments are about Shia.
...
...
Then ...
IF WE SHOW HER AGAIN, WE'LL RAKE IN THE CASH?!
Great!! How do we find her?!
Excuse me ...
I CAN GET IN TOUCH WITH SHIA♪
WAKO!!
WHEN'D YOU SHOW UP?!

CITY 5 / END

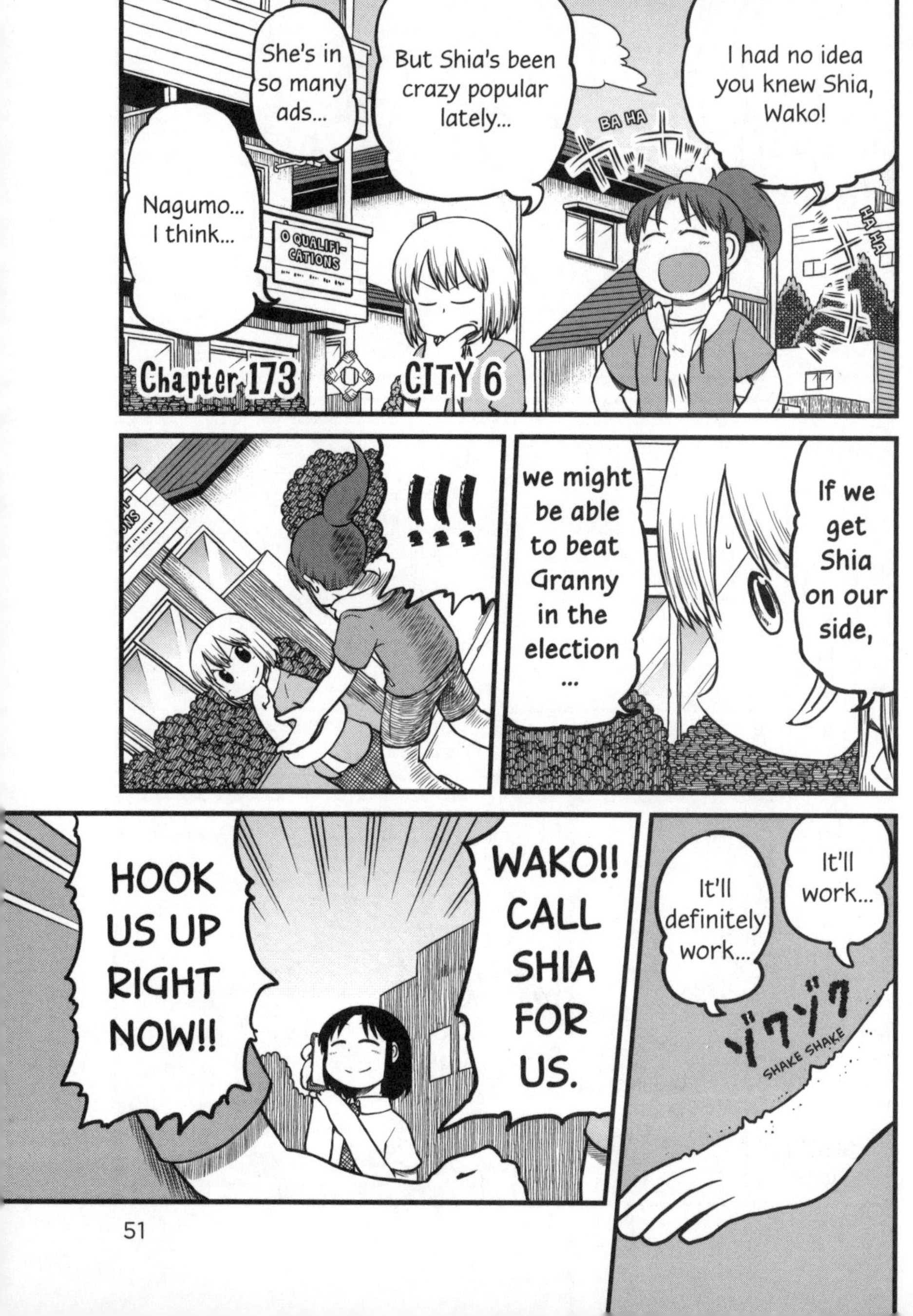

I had no idea you knew Shia, Wako!
BA HA
HA HA
But Shia's been crazy popular lately...
She's in so many ads...
Nagumo... I think...
QUALIFI-CATIONS
Chapter 173 CITY 6
If we get Shia on our side,
we might be able to beat Granny in the election ...
!!!
It'll work...
It'll definitely work...
SHAKE SHAKE
WAKO!! CALL SHIA FOR US.
HOOK US UP RIGHT NOW!!

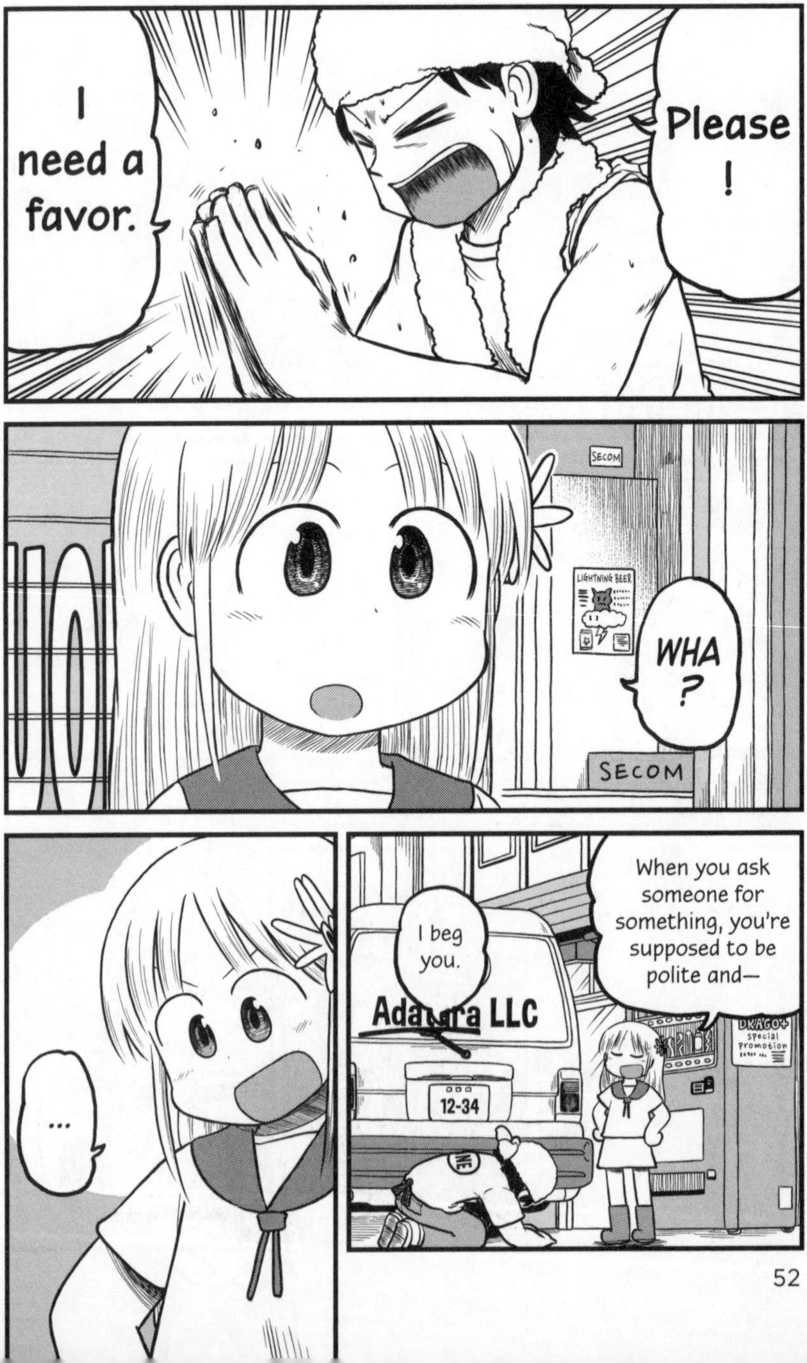
Please !
I need a favor.
SECOM
LIGHTNING BEER
WHA ?
SECOM
When you ask someone for something, you're supposed to be polite and—
I beg you.
Adatara LLC
special promotion
12-34
...

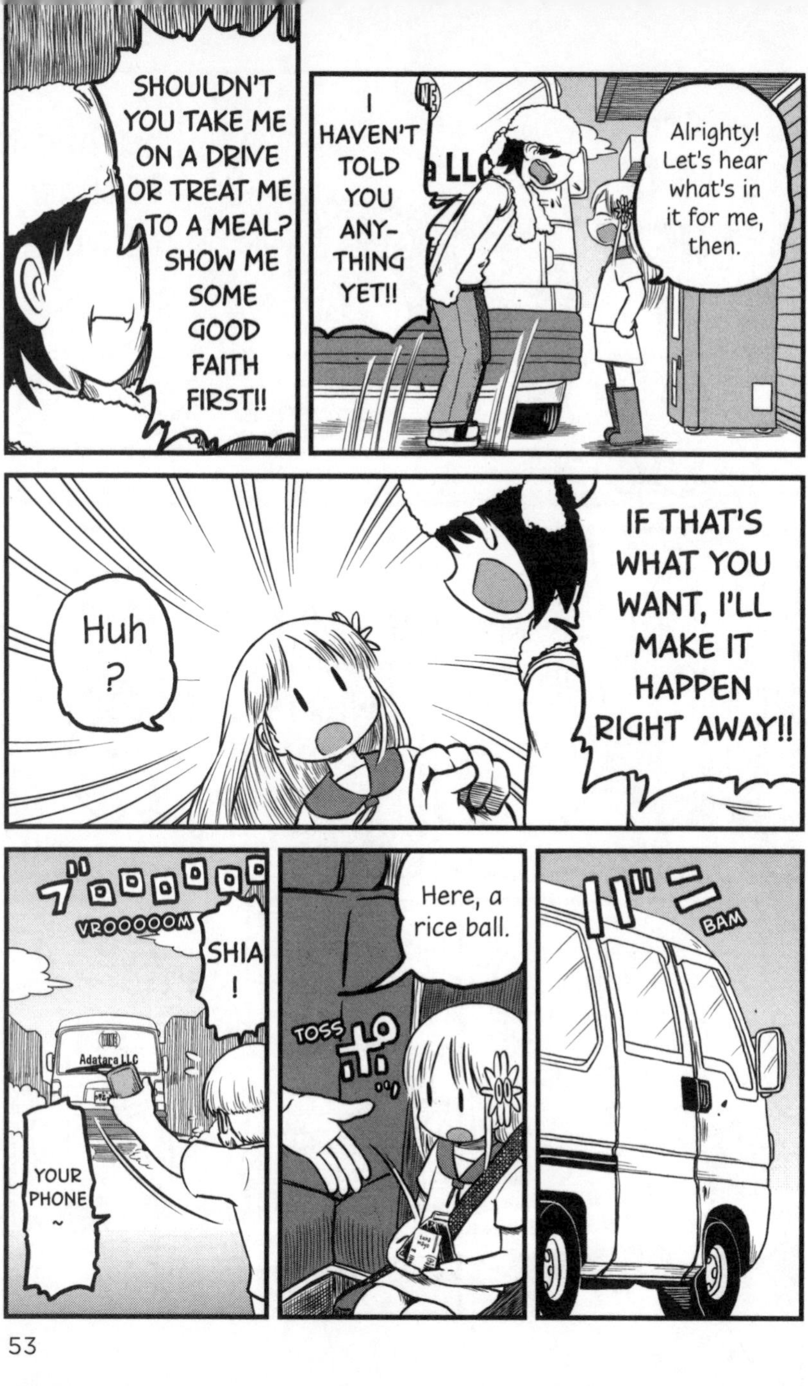
Alrighty! Let's hear what's in it for me, then.
I HAVEN'T TOLD YOU ANYTHING YET!!
SHOULDN'T YOU TAKE ME ON A DRIVE OR TREAT ME TO A MEAL? SHOW ME SOME GOOD FAITH FIRST!!
IF THAT'S WHAT YOU WANT, I'LL MAKE IT HAPPEN RIGHT AWAY!!
Huh?
BAM
Here, a rice ball.
TOSS
VROOOOOM
SHIA!
Adatara LLC
YOUR PHONE ~

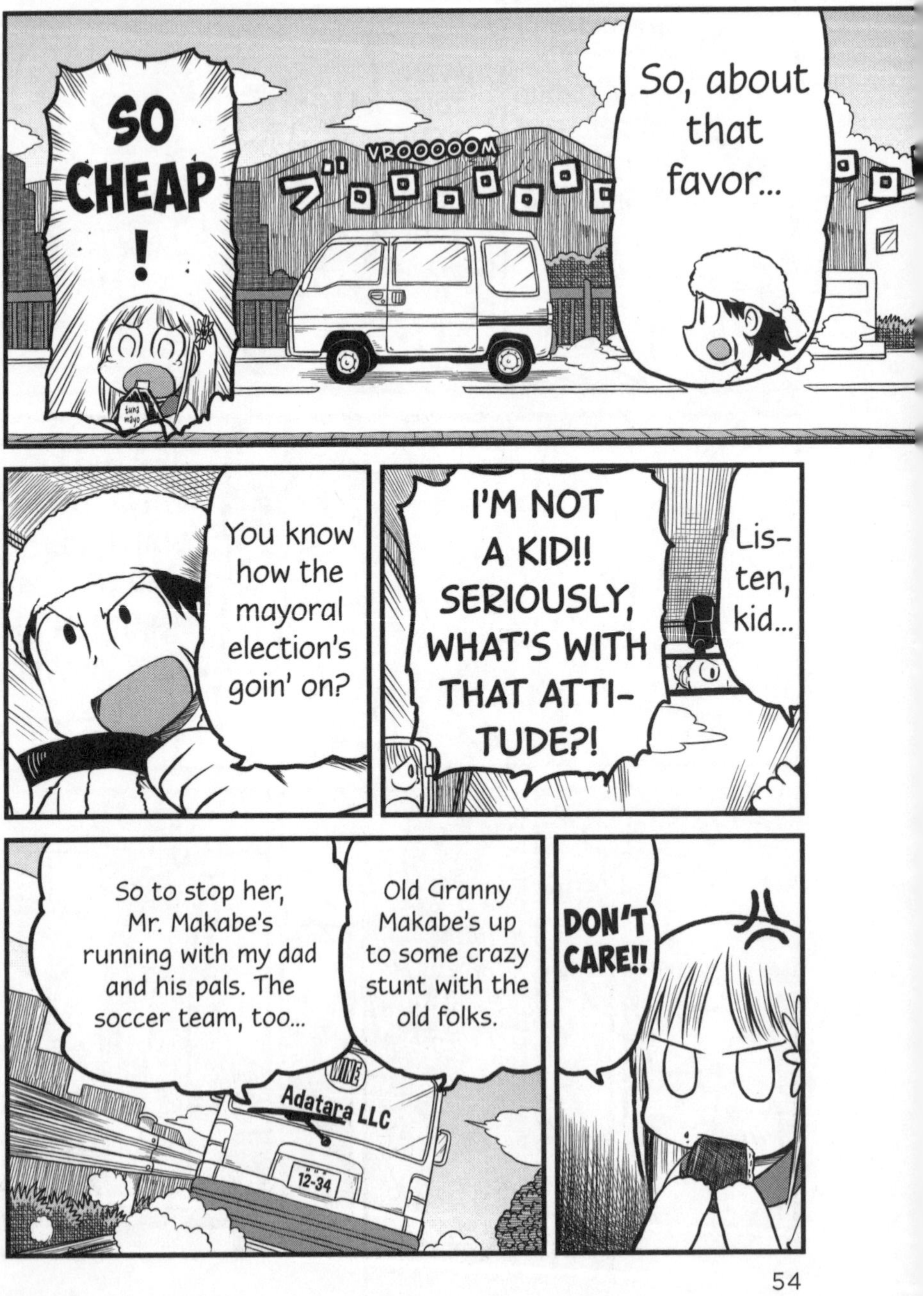
So, about that favor...
VROOOOOM
SO CHEAP!
tuna mayo
Lis- ten, kid...
I'M NOT A KID!! SERIOUSLY, WHAT'S WITH THAT ATTI- TUDE?!
You know how the mayoral election's goin' on?
DON'T CARE!!
Old Granny Makabe's up to some crazy stunt with the old folks.
So to stop her, Mr. Makabe's running with my dad and his pals. The soccer team, too...
Adatara LLC
12-34

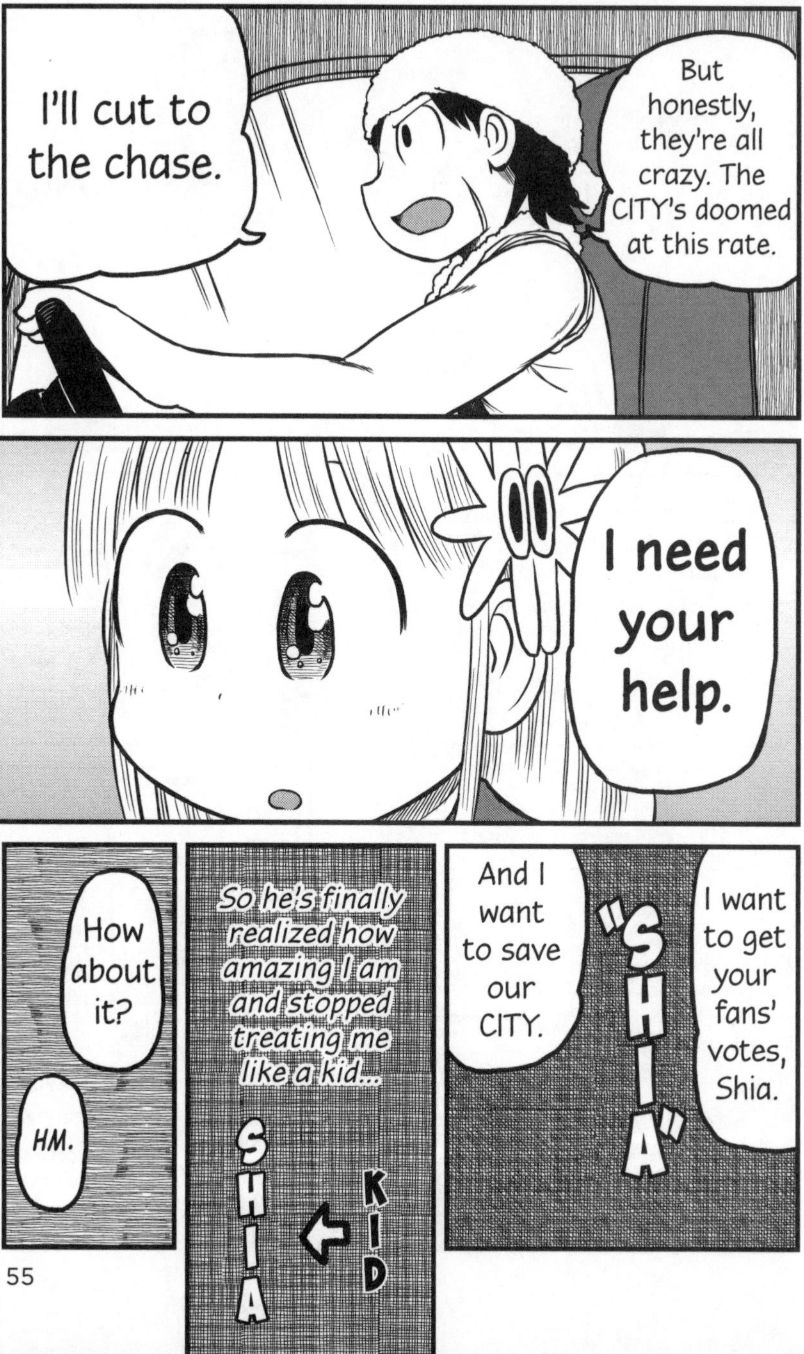
But honestly, they're all crazy. The CITY's doomed at this rate.
I'll cut to the chase.
I need your help.
I want to get your fans' votes, Shia.
"SHIA"
And I want to save our CITY.
So he's finally realized how amazing I am and stopped treating me like a kid...
KID
SHIA
How about it?
HM.

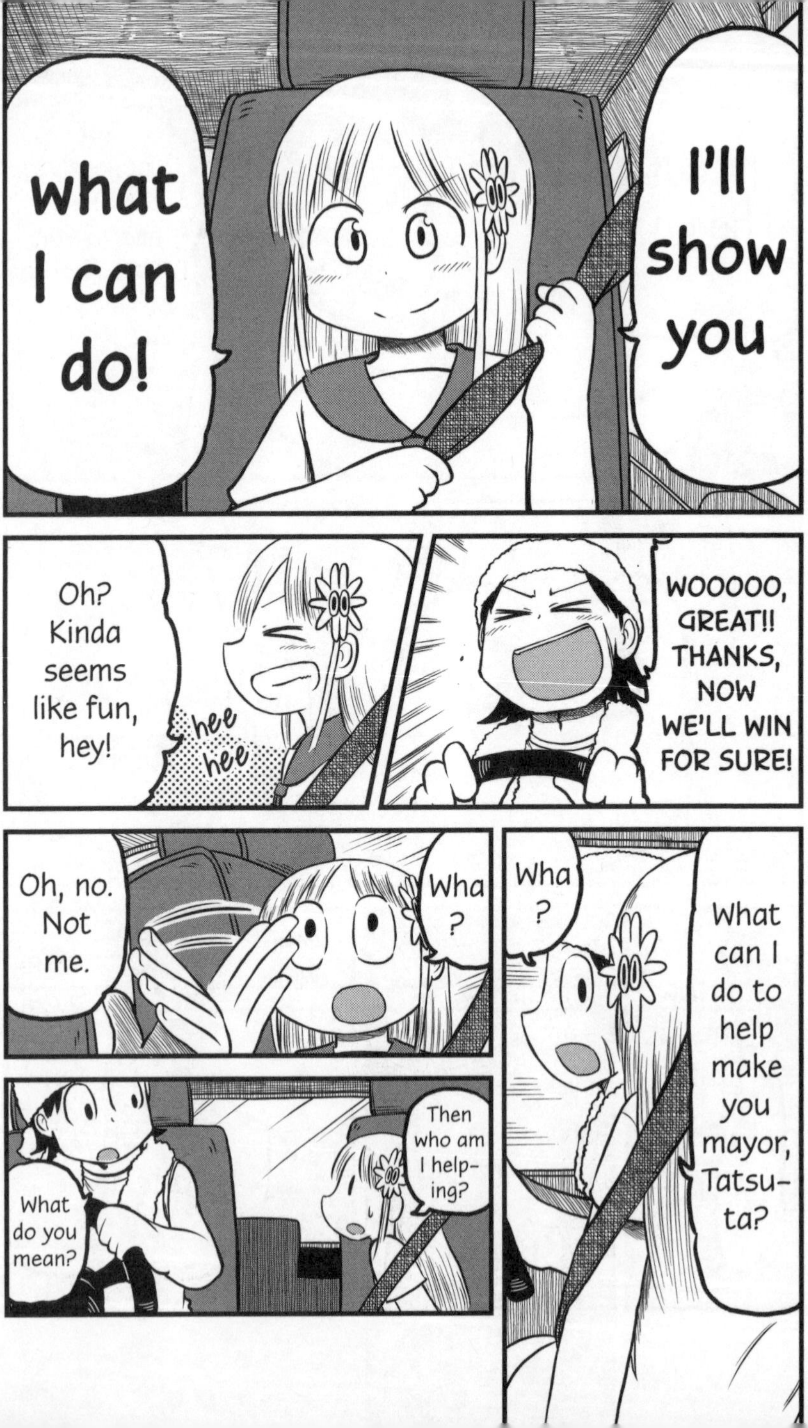
I'll show you
what I can do!
WOOOOO, GREAT!! THANKS, NOW WE'LL WIN FOR SURE!
Oh? Kinda seems like fun, hey!
hee hee
What can I do to help make you mayor, Tatsuta?
Wha ?
Wha ?
Oh, no. Not me.
Then who am I helping?
What do you mean?

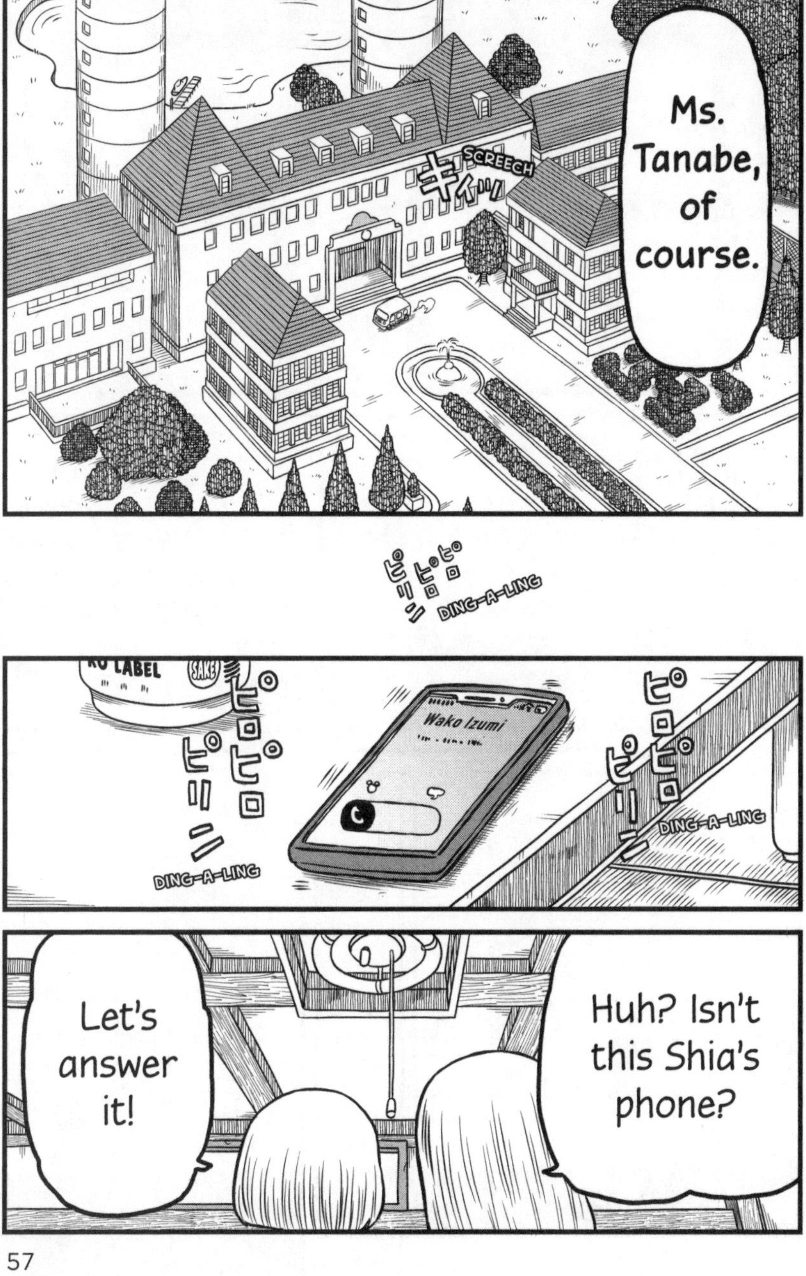
SCREECH
Ms. Tanabe, of course.
DING-A-LING
DING-A-LING
Wako Izumi
SAKE
DING-A-LING
Huh? Isn't this Shia's phone?
Let's answer it!

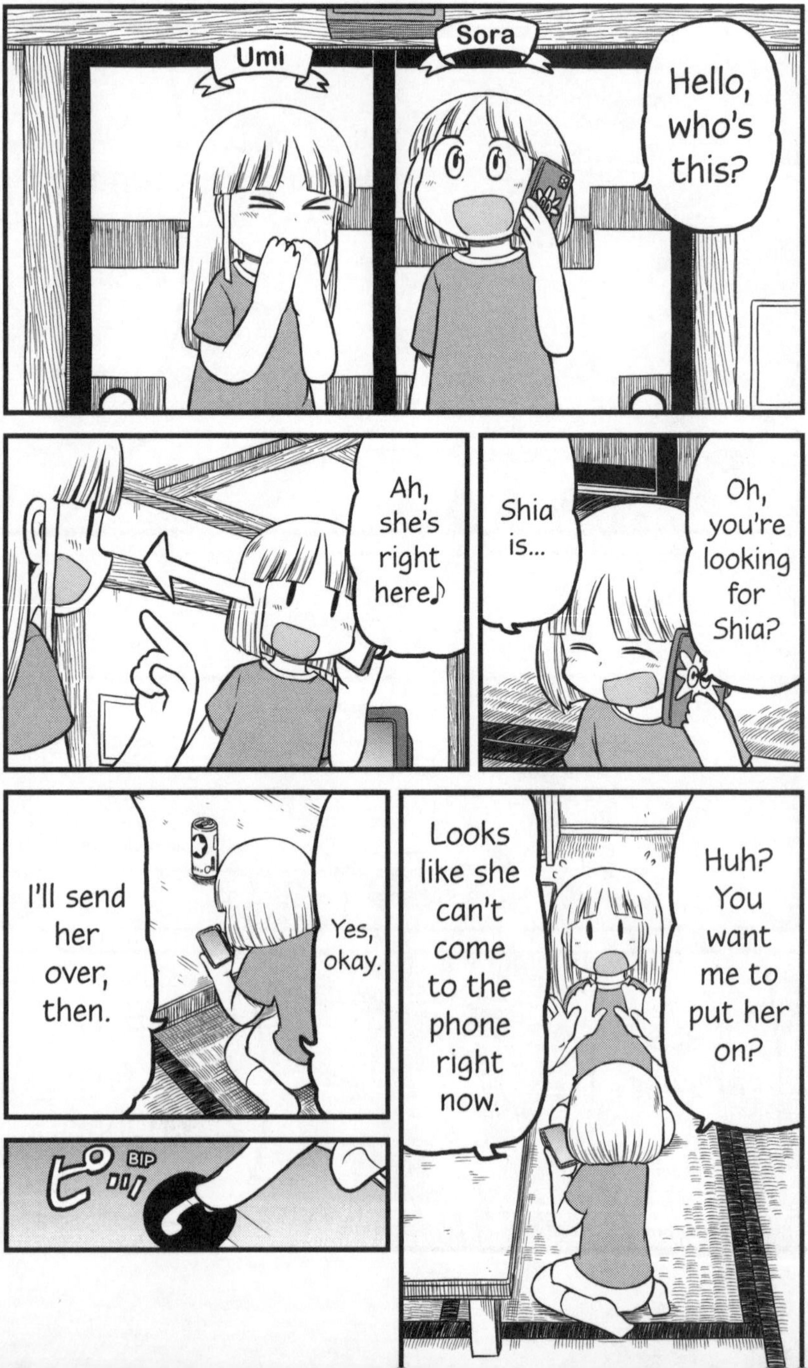
Hello, who's this?
Sora
Umi
Oh, you're looking for Shia?
Shia is...
Ah, she's right here♪
Huh? You want me to put her on?
Looks like she can't come to the phone right now.
Yes, okay.
I'll send her over, then.
BIP

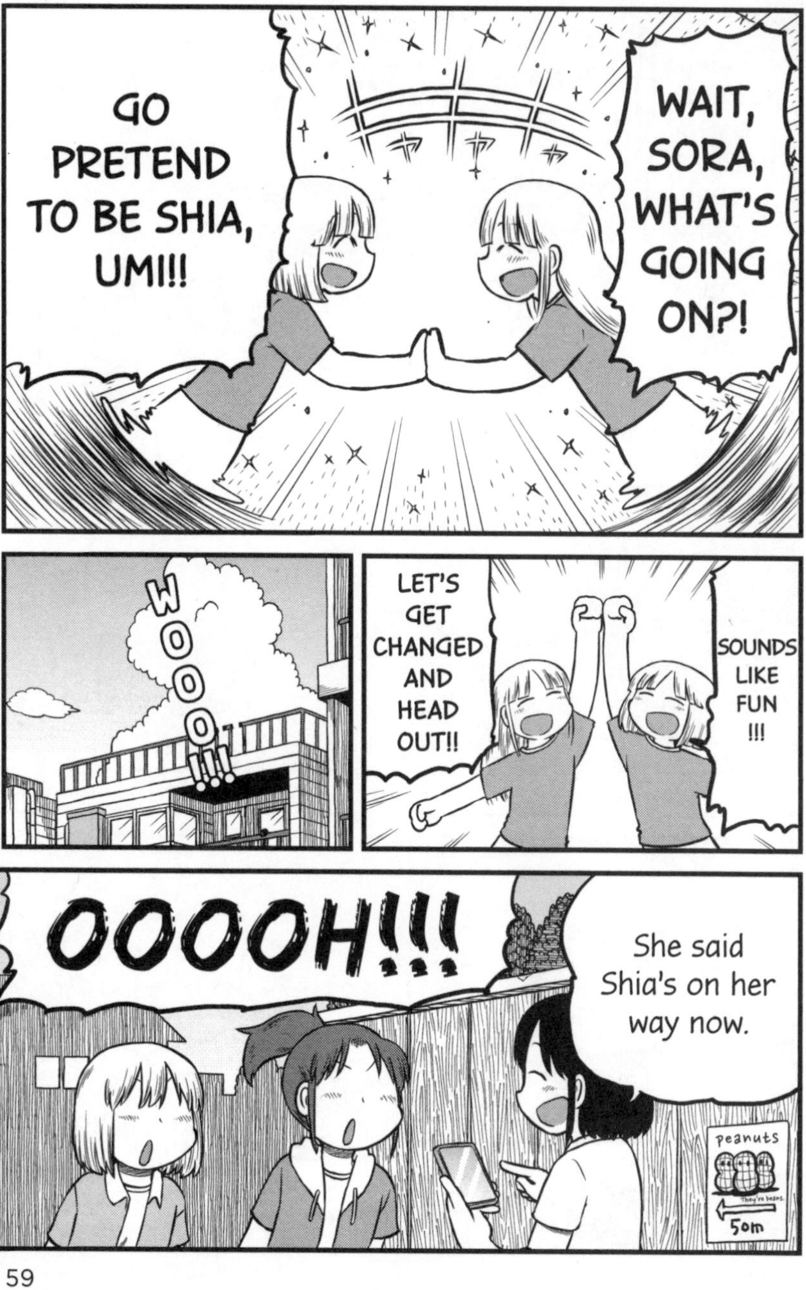
WAIT, SORA, WHAT'S GOING ON?!
GO PRETEND TO BE SHIA, UMI!!
LET'S GET CHANGED AND HEAD OUT!!
SOUNDS LIKE FUN!!!
WOOOO!!!
She said Shia's on her way now.
peanuts
They're beans.
50m
OOOOH!!!

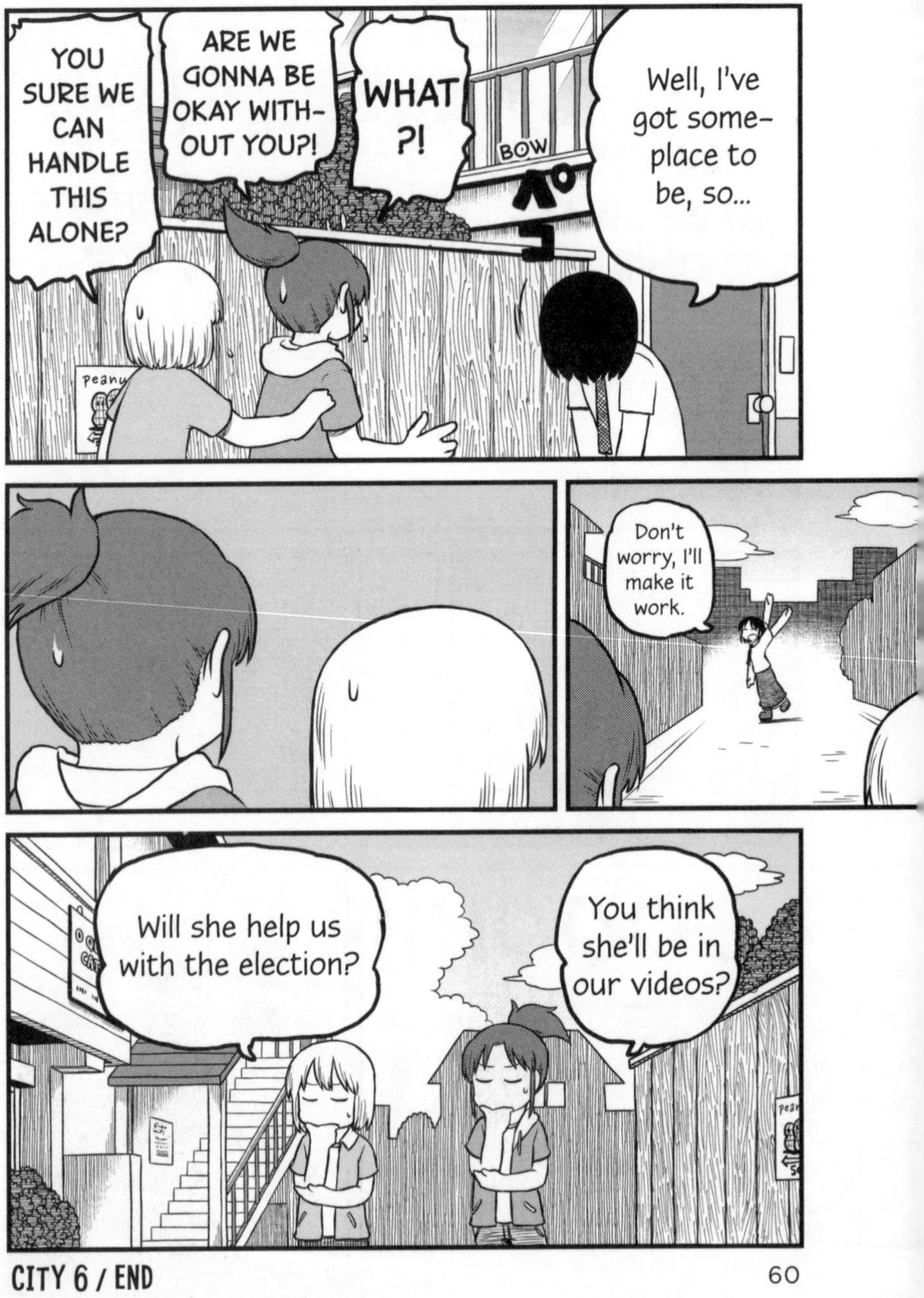
Well, I've got some-place to be, so...
BOW
WHAT?!
ARE WE GONNA BE OKAY WITH-OUT YOU?!
YOU SURE WE CAN HANDLE THIS ALONE?
Don't worry, I'll make it work.
You think she'll be in our videos?
Will she help us with the election?

CITY 6 / END

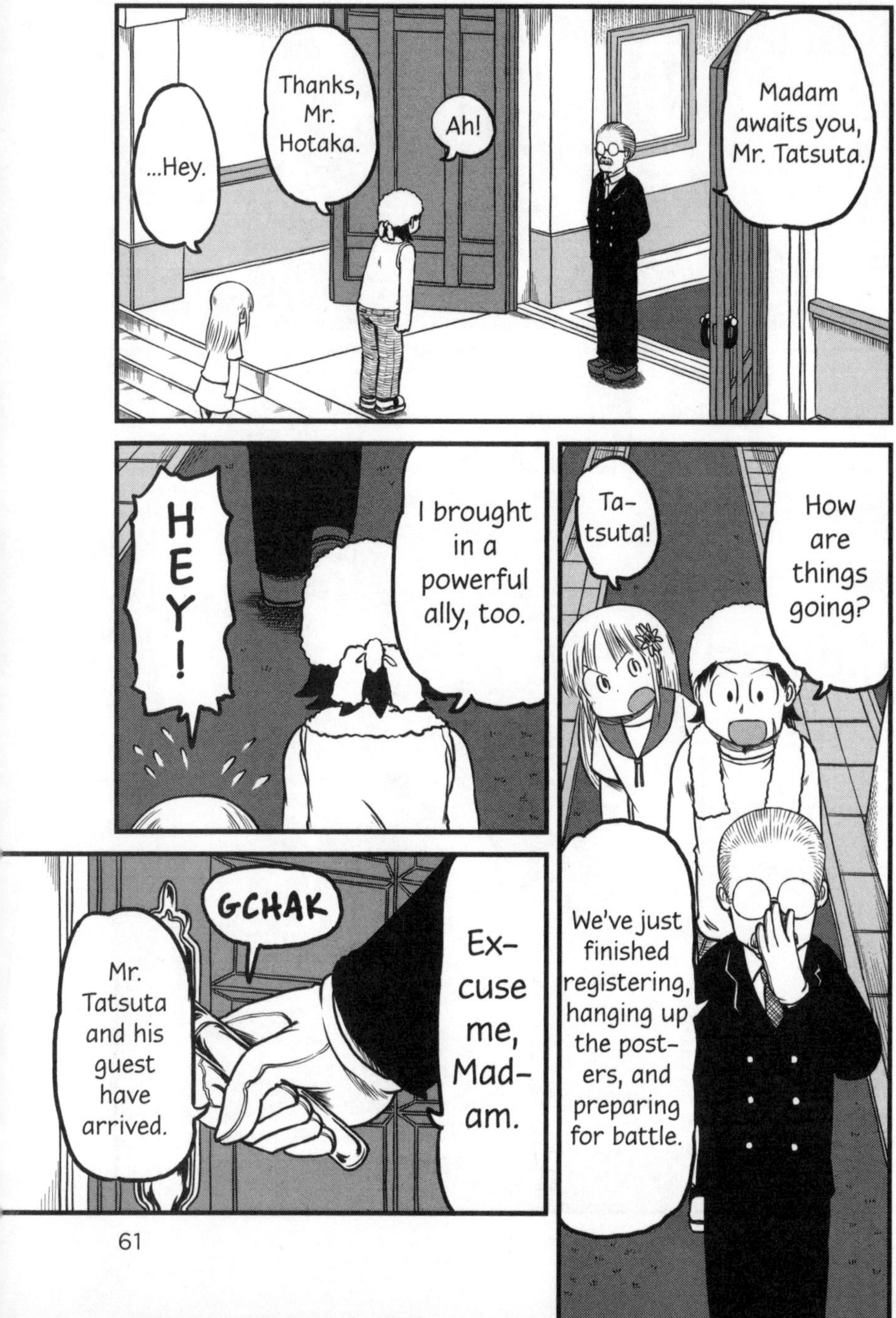
Madam awaits you, Mr. Tatsuta.
Ah!
Thanks, Mr. Hotaka.
...Hey.
How are things going?
Ta-tsuta!
We've just finished registering, hanging up the post-ers, and preparing for battle.
I brought in a powerful ally, too.
HEY!
Ex-cuse me, Mad-am.
GCHAK
Mr. Tatsuta and his guest have arrived.

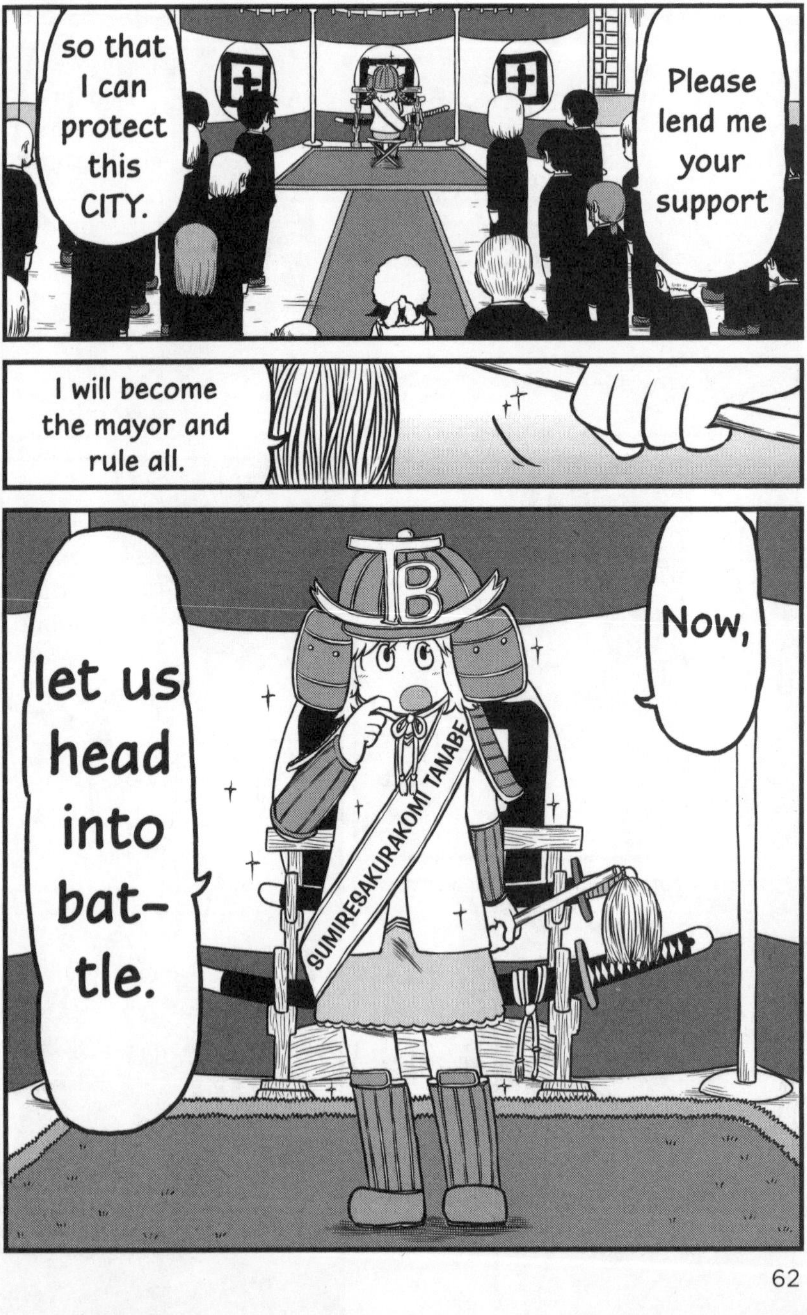
Please lend me your support
so that I can protect this CITY.
I will become the mayor and rule all.
Now,
let us head into bat- tle.
SUMIRESAKURAKOMI TANABE

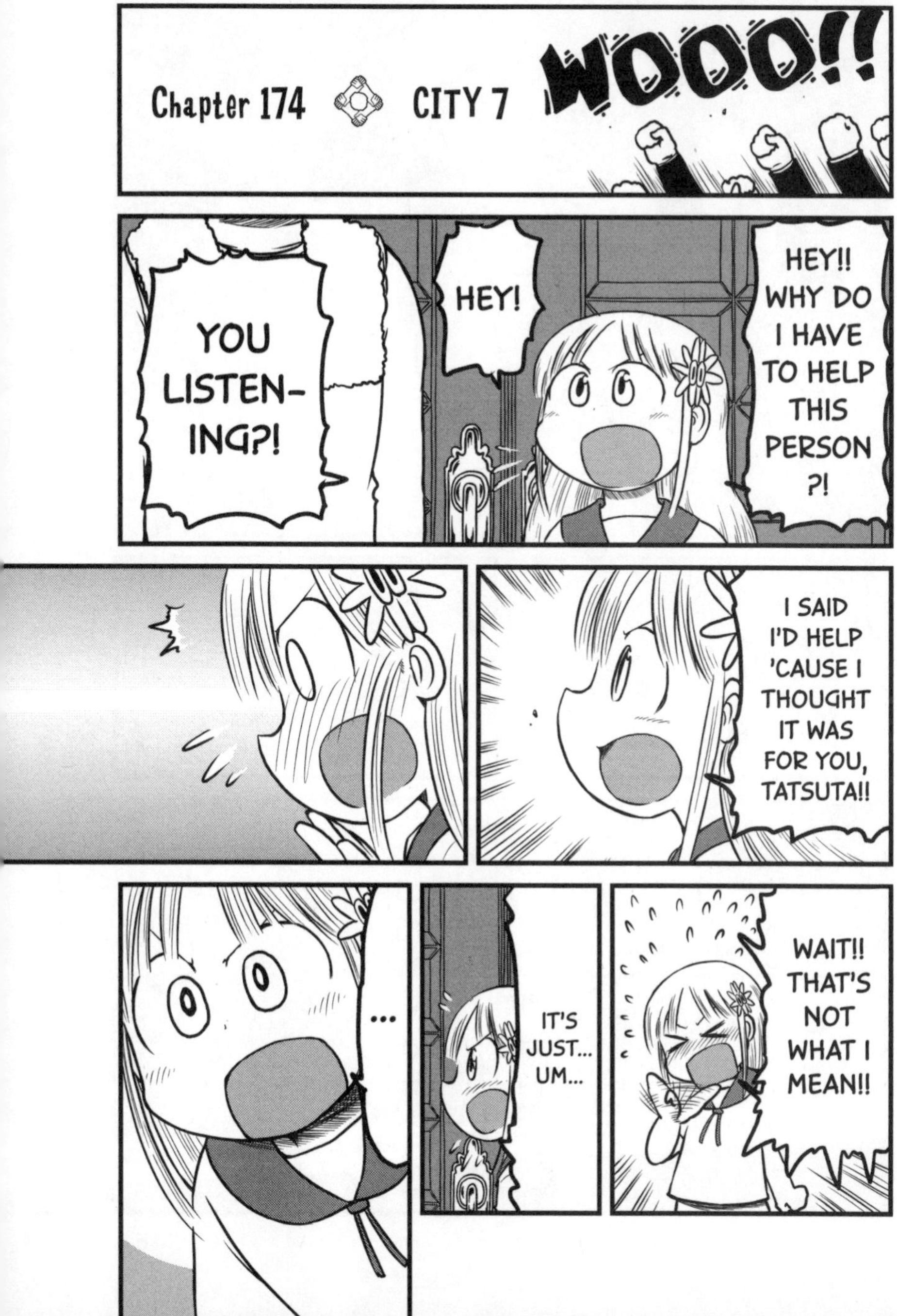
Chapter 174 CITY 7
WOOO!!
HEY!! WHY DO I HAVE TO HELP THIS PERSON ?!
HEY!
YOU LISTEN-ING?!
I SAID I'D HELP 'CAUSE I THOUGHT IT WAS FOR YOU, TATSUTA!!
WAIT!! THAT'S NOT WHAT I MEAN!!
IT'S JUST... UM...
...

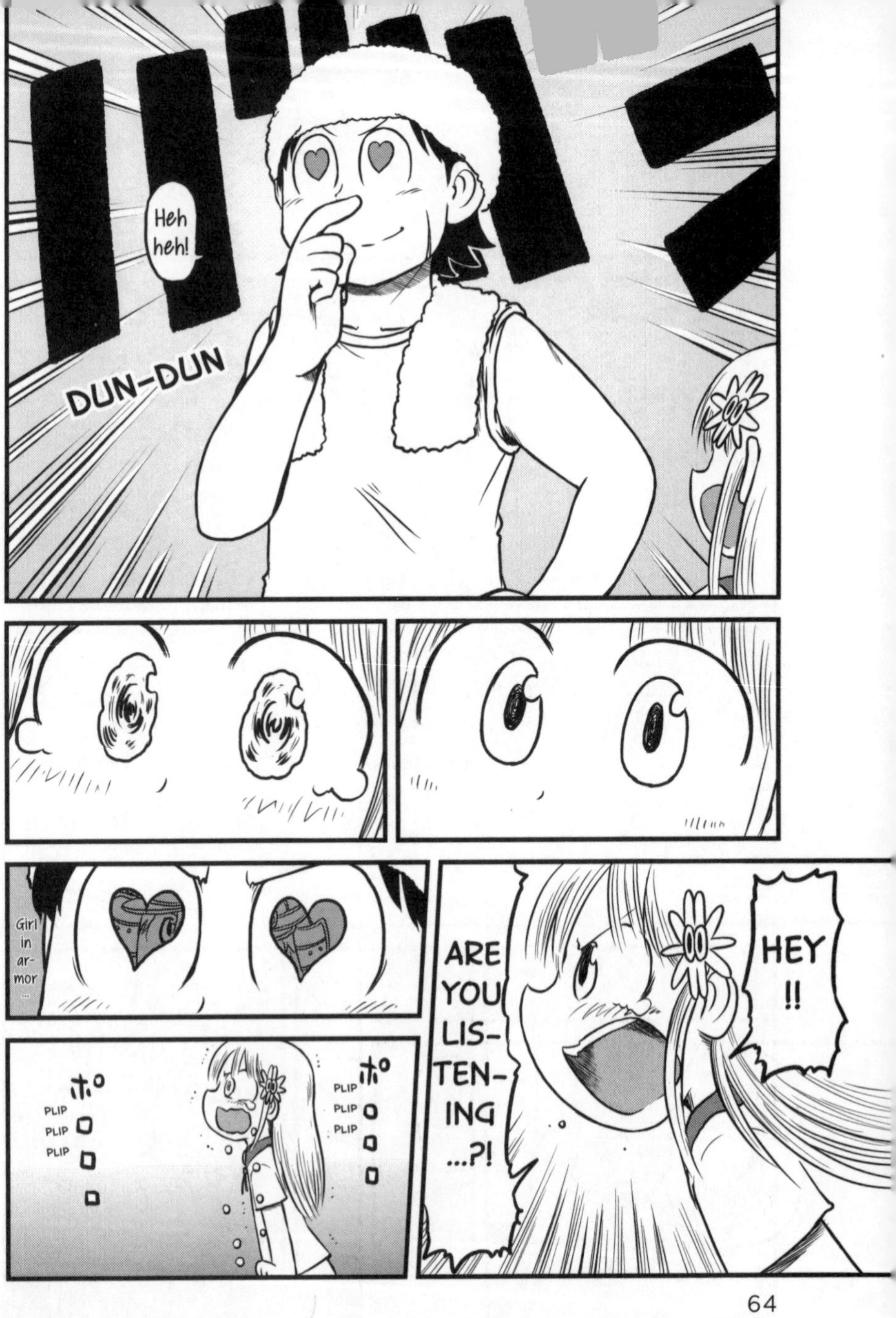
Heh heh!
DUN-DUN
HEY !!
ARE YOU LIS-TEN-ING ...?!
Girl in ar-mor ...
ポロロロ
PLIP PLIP PLIP
ポロロロ
PLIP PLIP PLIP

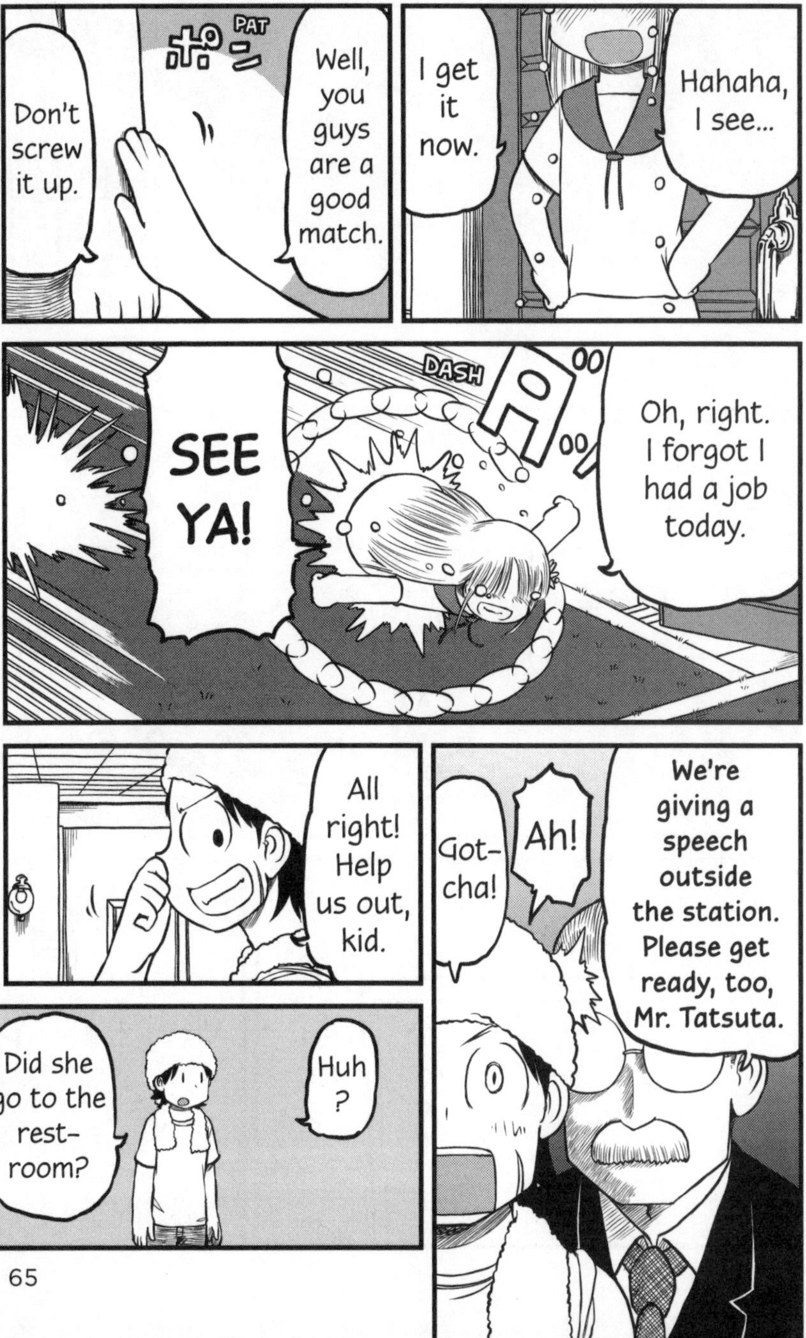
Hahaha, I see...
I get it now.
PAT
Well, you guys are a good match.
Don't screw it up.
Oh, right. I forgot I had a job today.
DASH
SEE YA!
We're giving a speech outside the station. Please get ready, too, Mr. Tatsuta.
Ah!
Got-cha!
All right! Help us out, kid.
Huh?
Did she go to the rest-room?

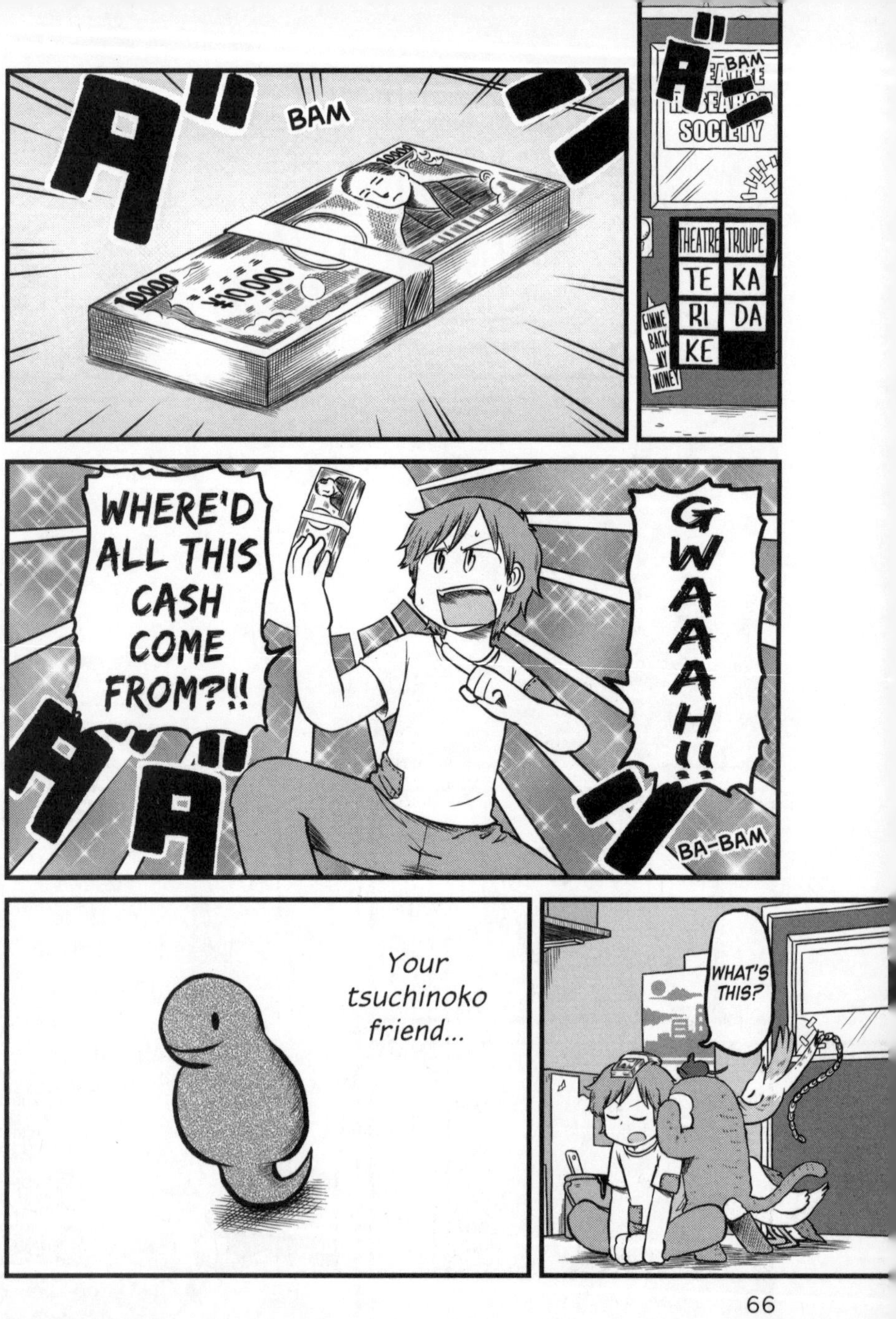
BAM
SOCIETY
THEATRE TROUPE
TE KA
RI DA
KE
GIMME BACK MY MONEY
BAM
GWAAAAH!!
WHERE'D ALL THIS CASH COME FROM?!!
BA-BAM
WHAT'S THIS?
Your tsuchinoko friend...

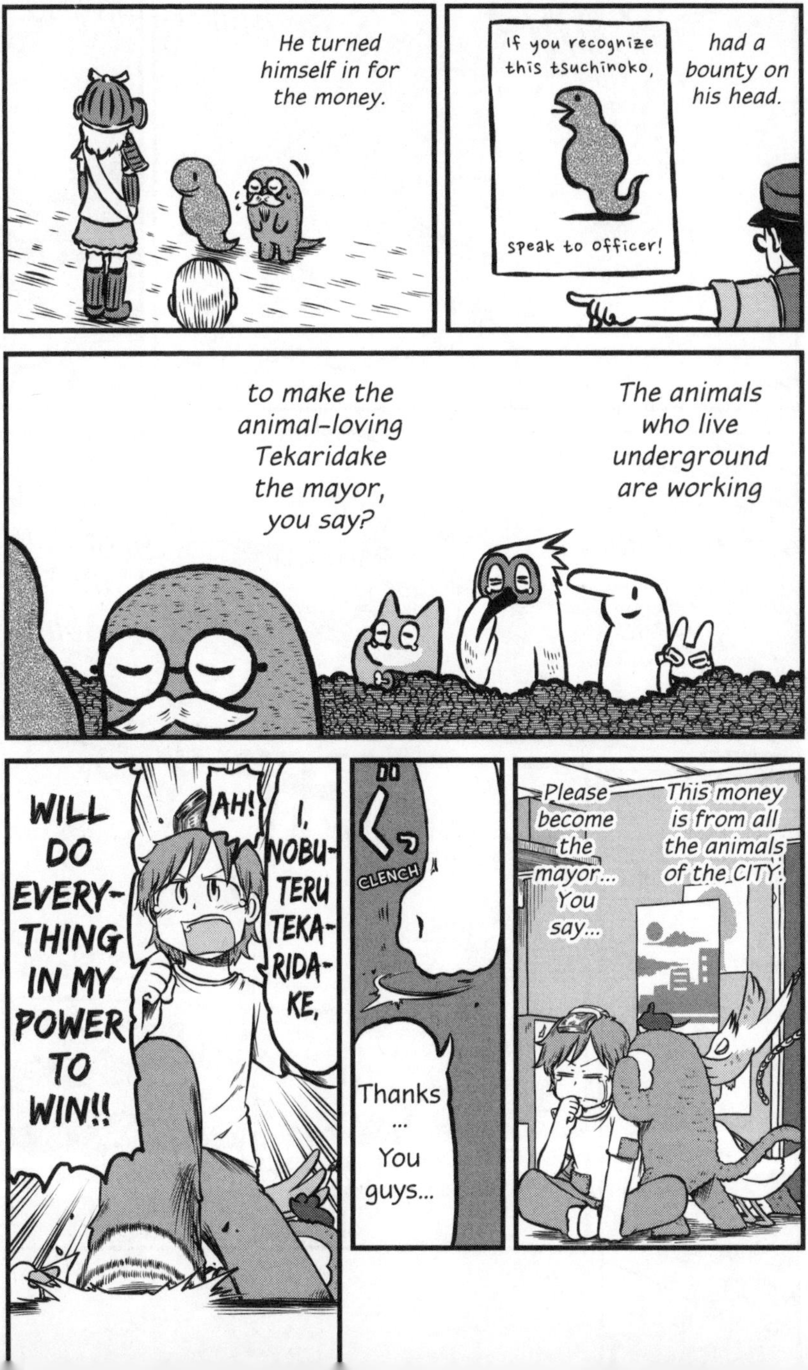
had a bounty on his head.
If you recognize this tsuchinoko,
Speak to Officer!
He turned himself in for the money.
The animals who live underground are working
to make the animal-loving Tekaridake the mayor, you say?
This money is from all the animals of the CITY.
Please become the mayor... You say...
CLENCH
Thanks... You guys...
AH!
I, NOBUTERU TEKARIDAKE,
WILL DO EVERYTHING IN MY POWER TO WIN!!

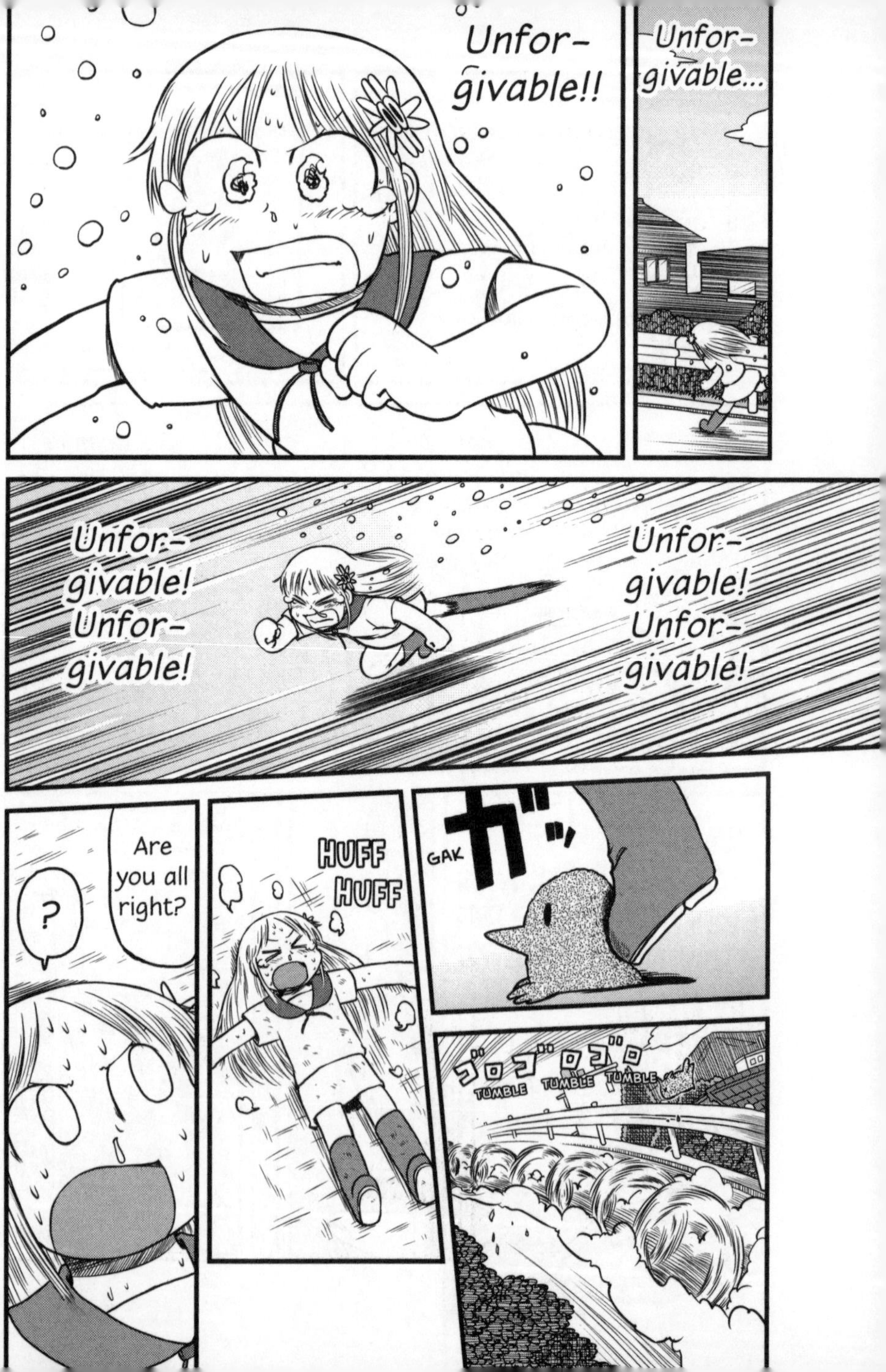
Unfor-
givable...
Unfor-
givable!!
Unfor-
givable!
Unfor-
givable!
Unfor-
givable!
Unfor-
givable!
ガッ
GAK
ゴロゴロゴロ
TUMBLE TUMBLE TUMBLE
HUFF HUFF
Are you all right?
?

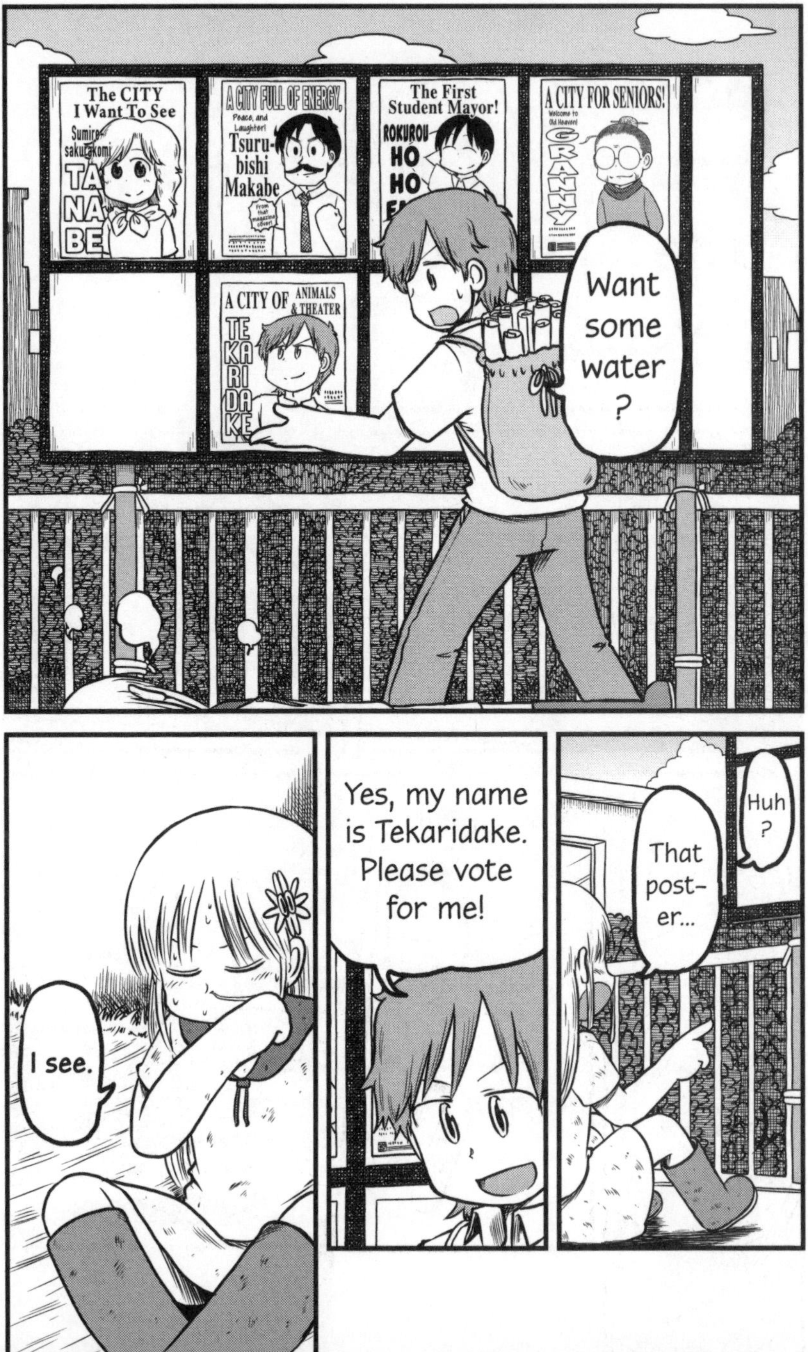
A CITY FOR SENIORS!
Welcome to Old Heaven!
GRANNY
The First Student Mayor!
ROKUROU
HO
HO
A CITY FULL OF ENERGY,
Peace, and Laughter!
Tsuru-bishi Makabe
From that magazine cover!
The CITY I Want To See
Sumire-sakurakomi
TA NA BE
Want some water?
A CITY OF ANIMALS & THEATER
TE KA RI DA KE
Huh?
That post-er...
Yes, my name is Tekaridake. Please vote for me!
I see.

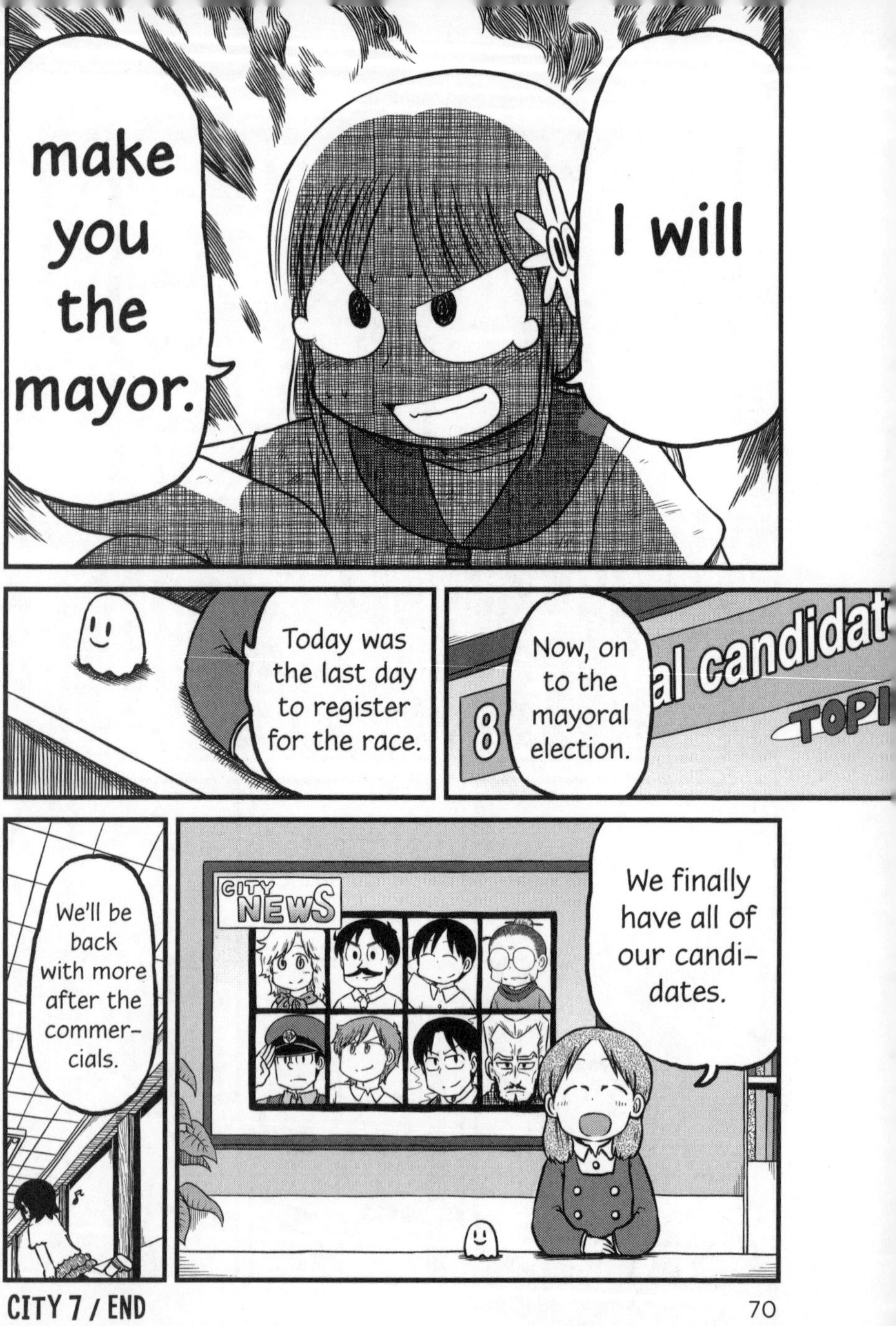
I will
make you the mayor.
Now, on to the mayoral election.
Today was the last day to register for the race.
CITY NEWS
We finally have all of our candi-dates.
We'll be back with more after the commer-cials.

CITY 7 / END

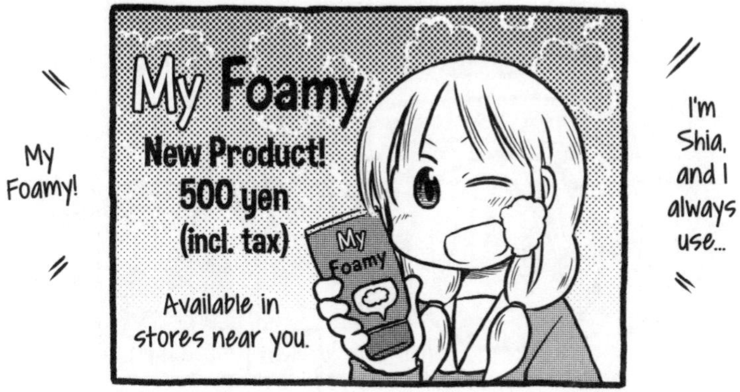
I'm Shia, and I always use...
My Foamy
New Product!
500 yen
(incl. tax)
Available in stores near you.
My Foamy
My Foamy!

CITY

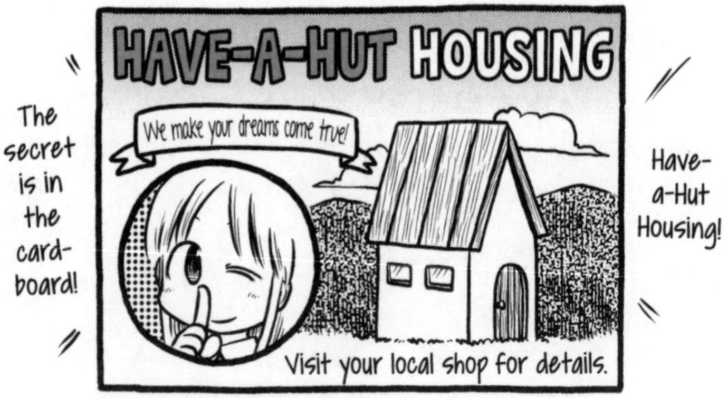
HAVE-A-HUT HOUSING
We make your dreams come true!
Visit your local shop for details.
Have-a-Hut Housing!
The secret is in the cardboard!

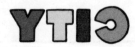

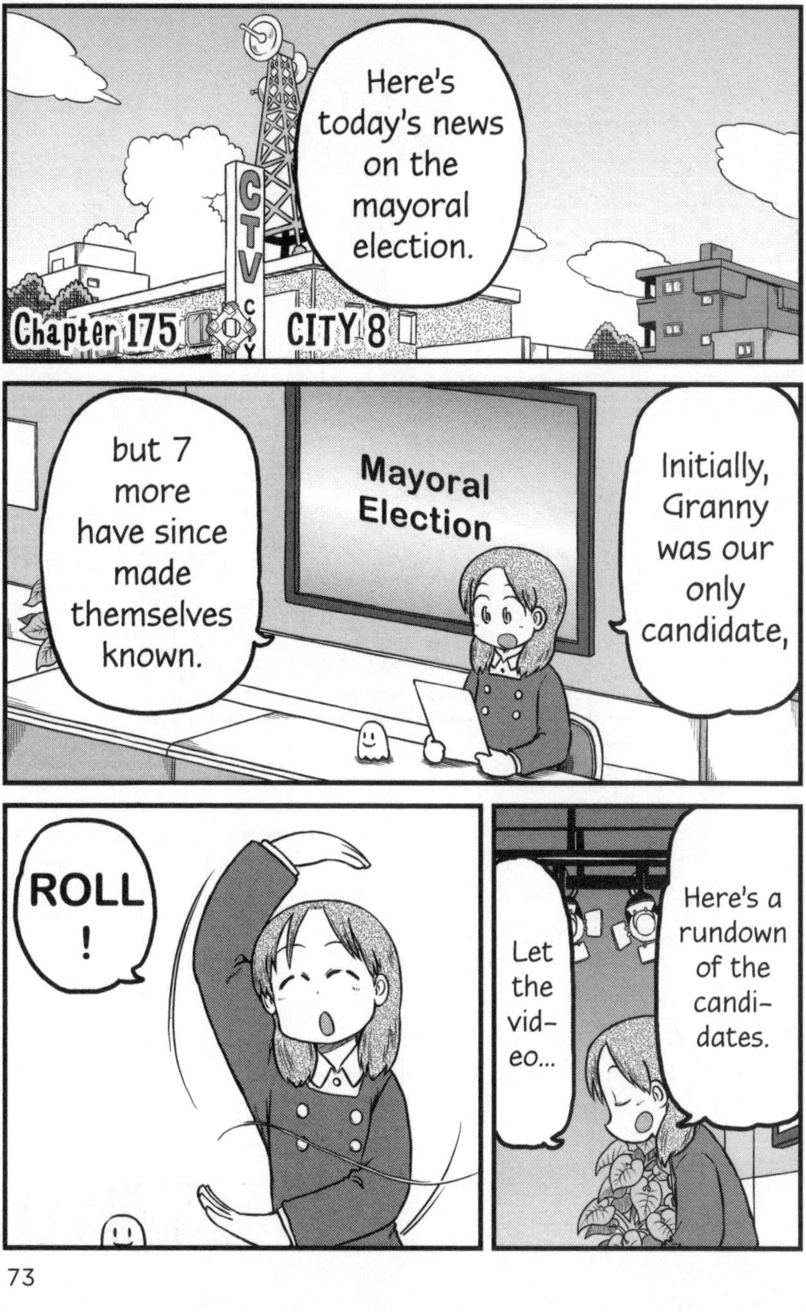
Here's today's news on the mayoral election.
Chapter 175 CITY 8
CTV
CITY
Initially, Granny was our only candidate,
Mayoral Election
but 7 more have since made themselves known.
Here's a rundown of the candi- dates.
Let the vid- eo...
ROLL !

Yes, the CITY mayoral election is upon us.
MAYORAL ELECTION
It's still fresh in our minds that a thief-like fellow won the last election because no one took interest!
Narration: Gorou Kurobe
Well, the candidate to appear this time was Granny!
Her manifesto: "A CITY for seniors!"
She wants to create a community for the old folks!
Her promise for an elderly dictatorship has all the senior citizens charged up!
At first, we thought she'd win uncontested like the last mayor...
ZZHF
ZZFH
But two men stepped forward!

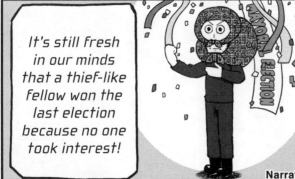

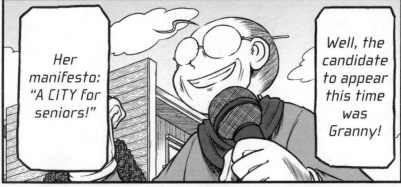

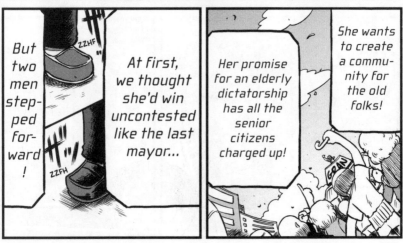

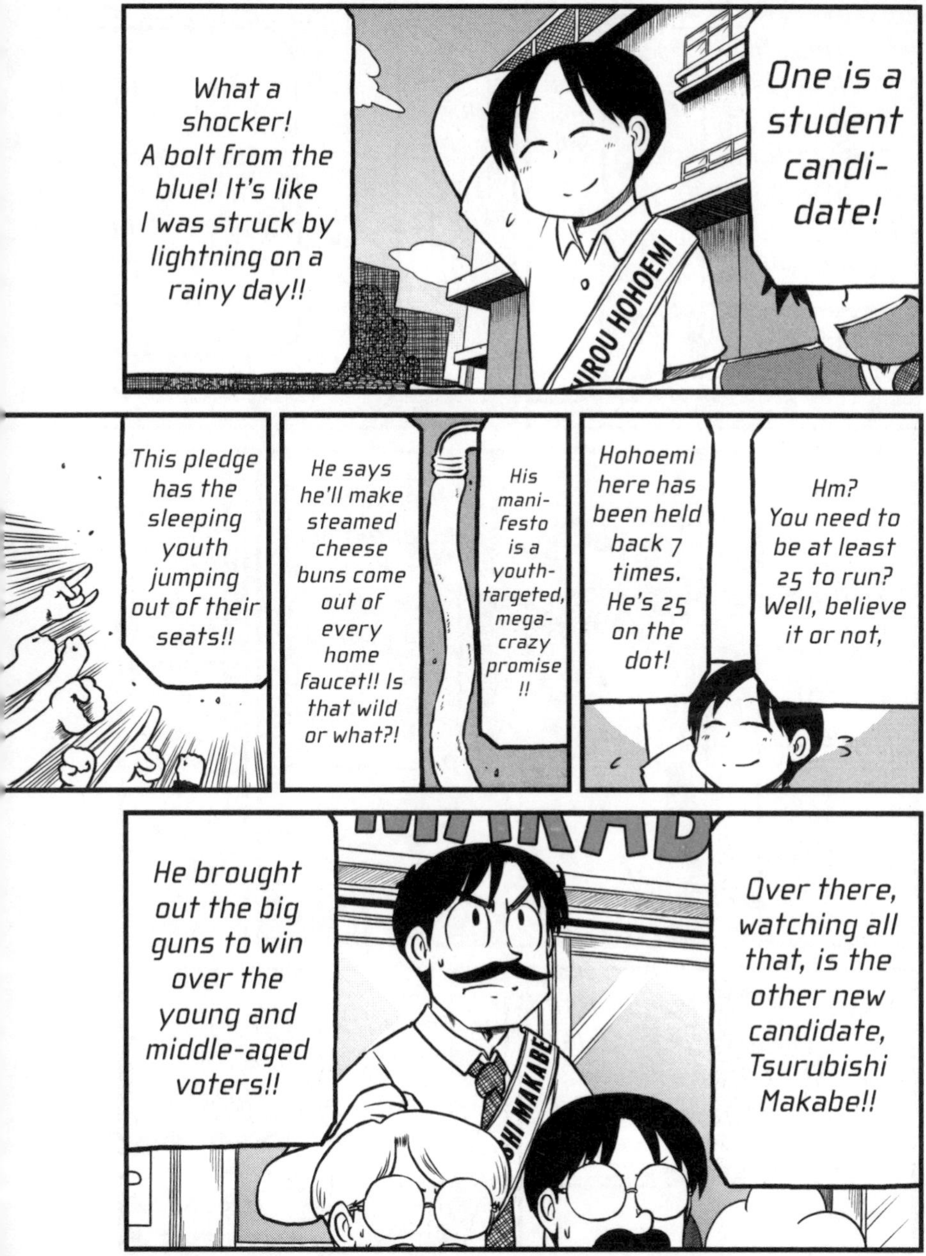
One is a student candi- date!
What a shocker! A bolt from the blue! It's like I was struck by lightning on a rainy day!!
HOHOEMI
Hm? You need to be at least 25 to run? Well, believe it or not,
Hohoemi here has been held back 7 times. He's 25 on the dot!
His mani- festo is a youth- targeted, mega- crazy promise !!
He says he'll make steamed cheese buns come out of every home faucet!! Is that wild or what?!
This pledge has the sleeping youth jumping out of their seats!!
Over there, watching all that, is the other new candidate, Tsurubishi Makabe!!
He brought out the big guns to win over the young and middle-aged voters!!
MAKABE

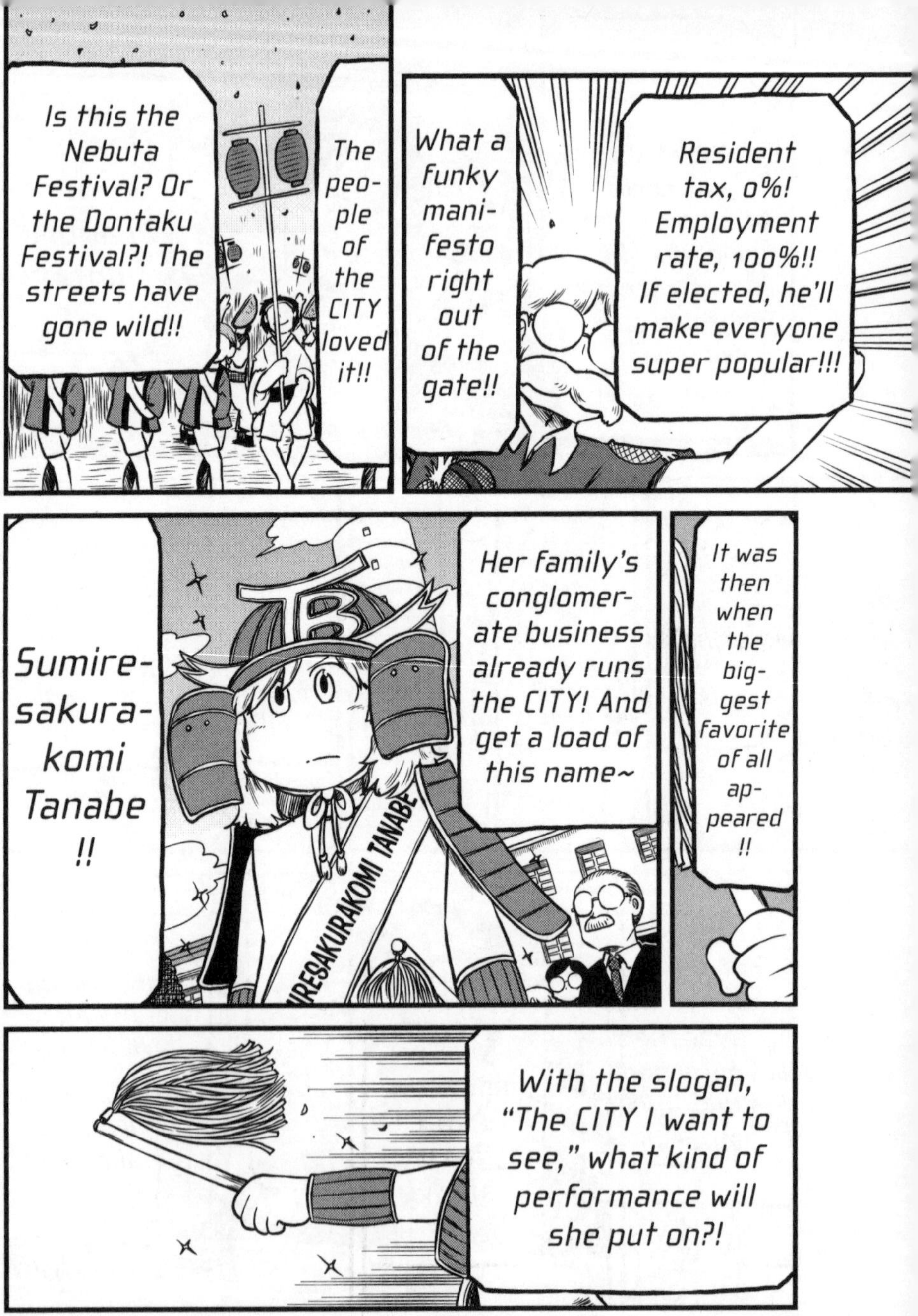
Resident tax, 0%! Employment rate, 100%!! If elected, he'll make everyone super popular!!!
What a funky mani-festo right out of the gate!!
The peo-ple of the CITY loved it!!
Is this the Nebuta Festival? Or the Dontaku Festival?! The streets have gone wild!!
It was then when the big-gest favorite of all ap-peared!!
Her family's conglomer-ate business already runs the CITY! And get a load of this name~
Sumire-sakura-komi Tanabe!!
With the slogan, "The CITY I want to see," what kind of performance will she put on?!

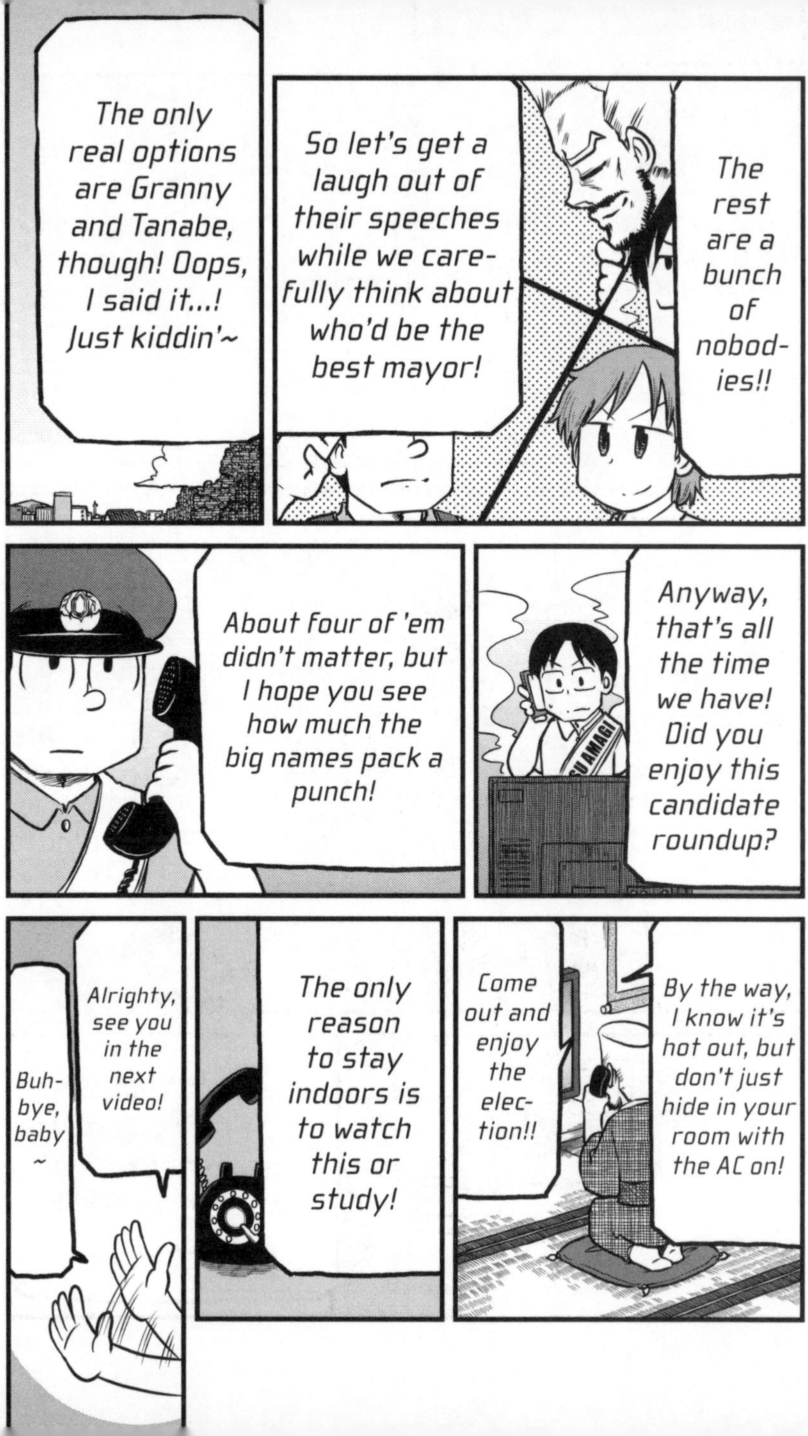

The rest are a bunch of nobodies!!
So let's get a laugh out of their speeches while we carefully think about who'd be the best mayor!
The only real options are Granny and Tanabe, though! Oops, I said it...! Just kiddin'~
Anyway, that's all the time we have! Did you enjoy this candidate roundup?
About four of 'em didn't matter, but I hope you see how much the big names pack a punch!
By the way, I know it's hot out, but don't just hide in your room with the AC on!
Come out and enjoy the election!!
The only reason to stay indoors is to watch this or study!
Alrighty, see you in the next video!
Buh-bye, baby ~

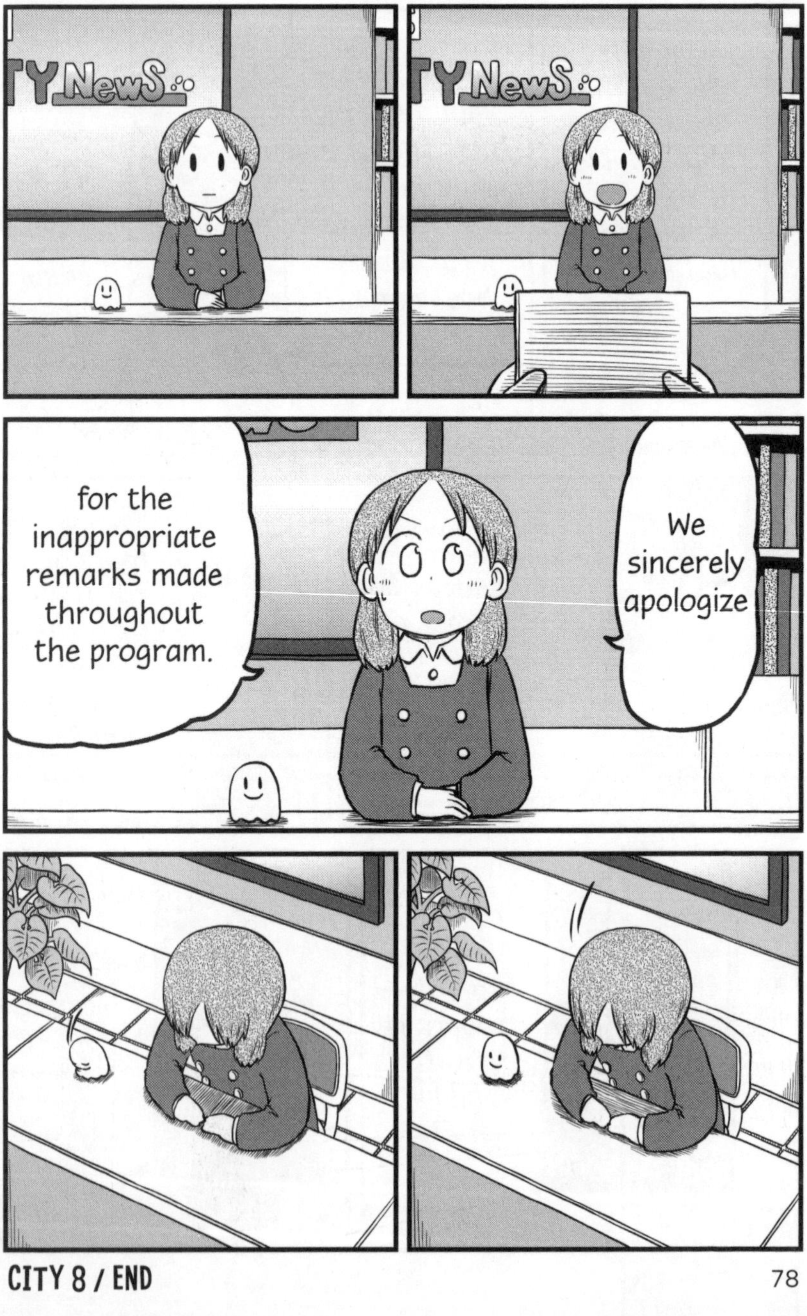
We sincerely apologize
for the inappropriate remarks made throughout the program.

CITY 8 / END

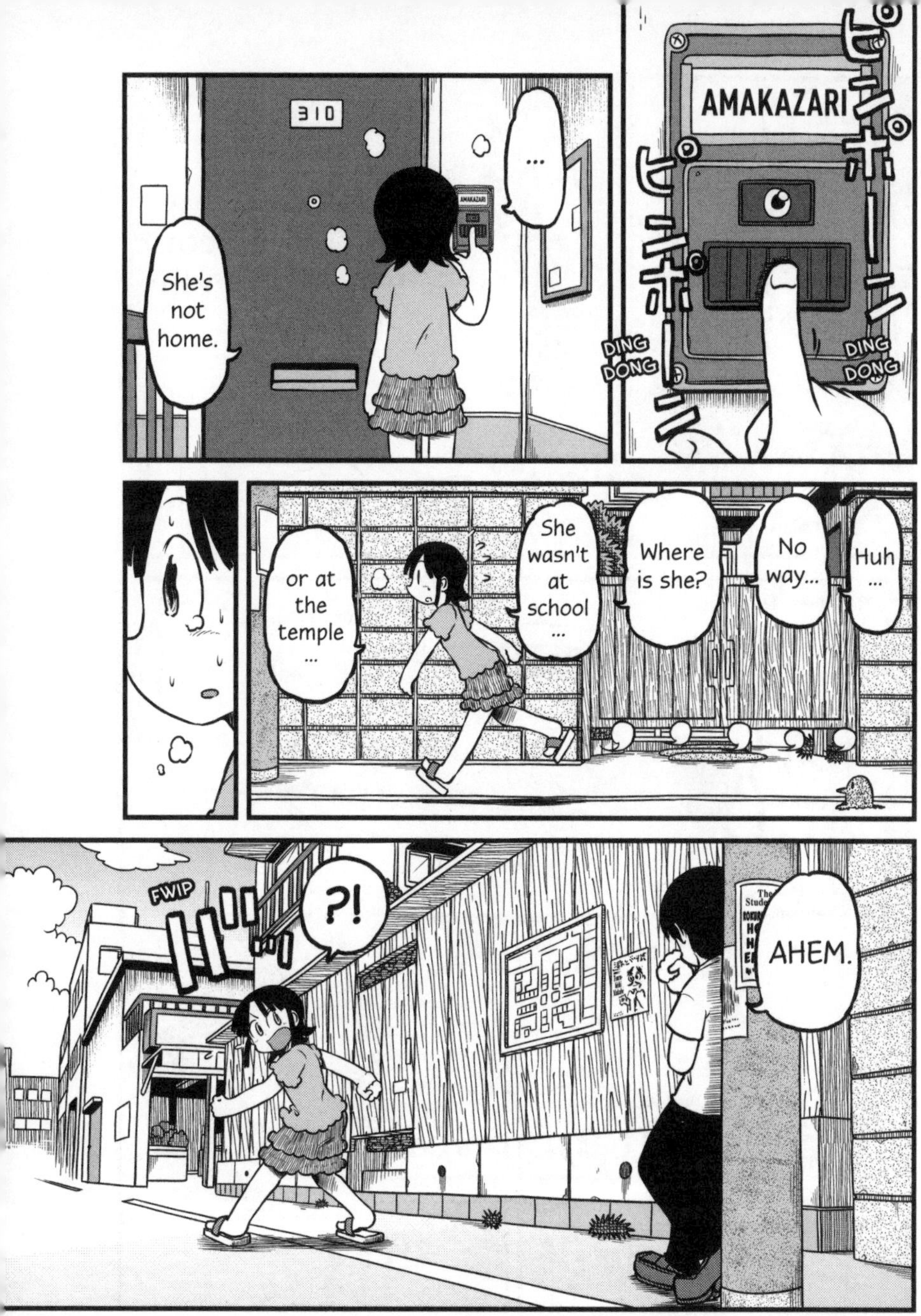
AMAKAZARI
ピンポーン
ピンポーン
DING DONG
DING DONG
...
She's not home.
Huh...
No way...
Where is she?
She wasn't at school...
or at the temple...
AHEM.
?!
FWIP

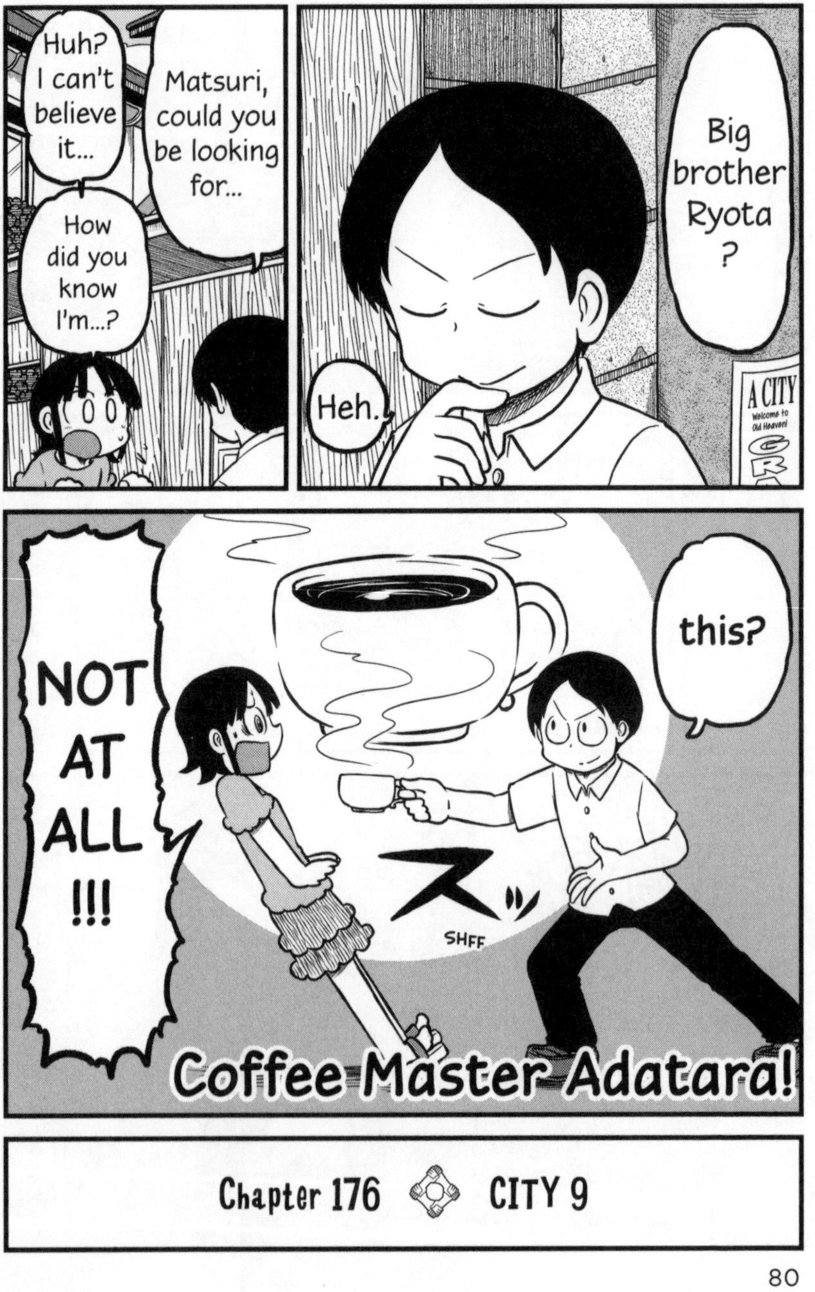
Big brother Ryota?
Heh.
A CITY
Welcome to Old Heaven!
Matsuri, could you be looking for...
Huh? I can't believe it...
How did you know I'm...?
this?
NOT AT ALL!!!
SHFF
Coffee Master Adatara!

Chapter 176 CITY 9

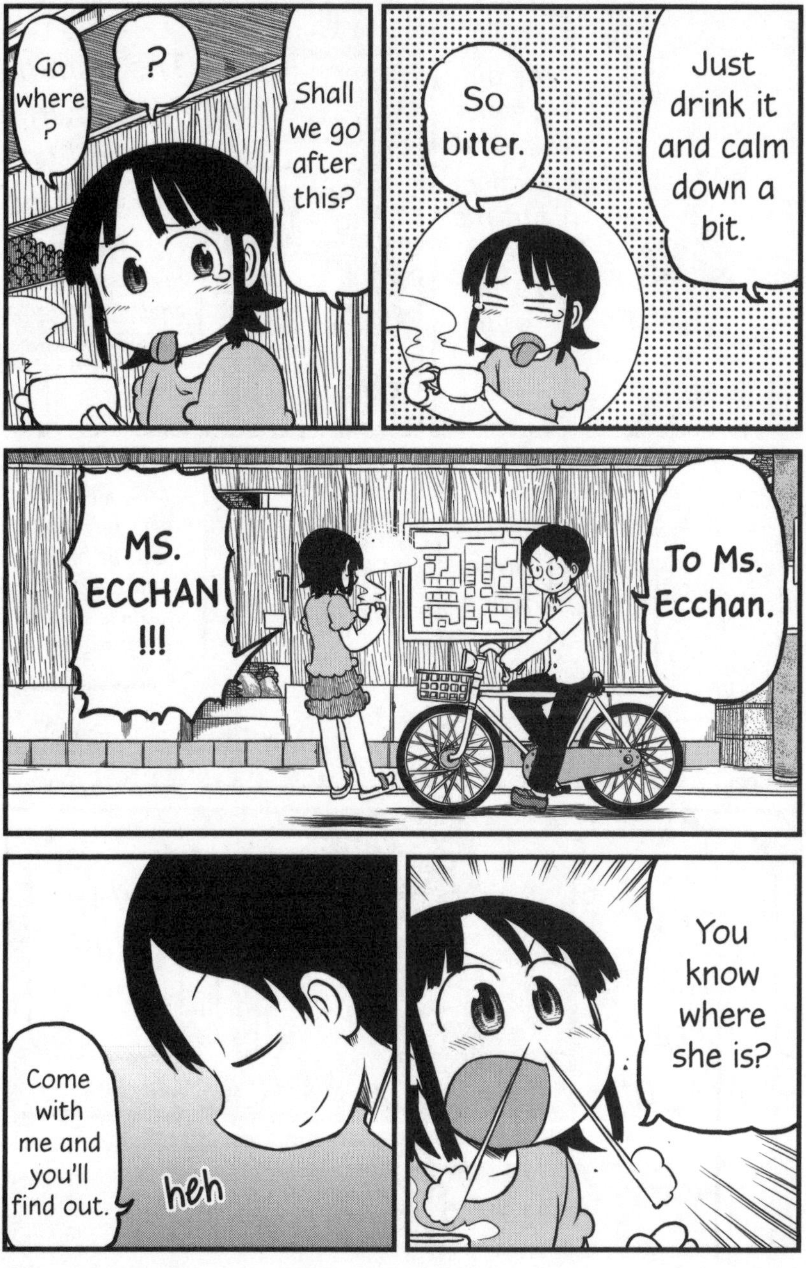
Just drink it and calm down a bit.
So bitter.
Shall we go after this?
?
Go where?
To Ms. Ecchan.
MS. ECCHAN!!!
You know where she is?
Come with me and you'll find out.
heh

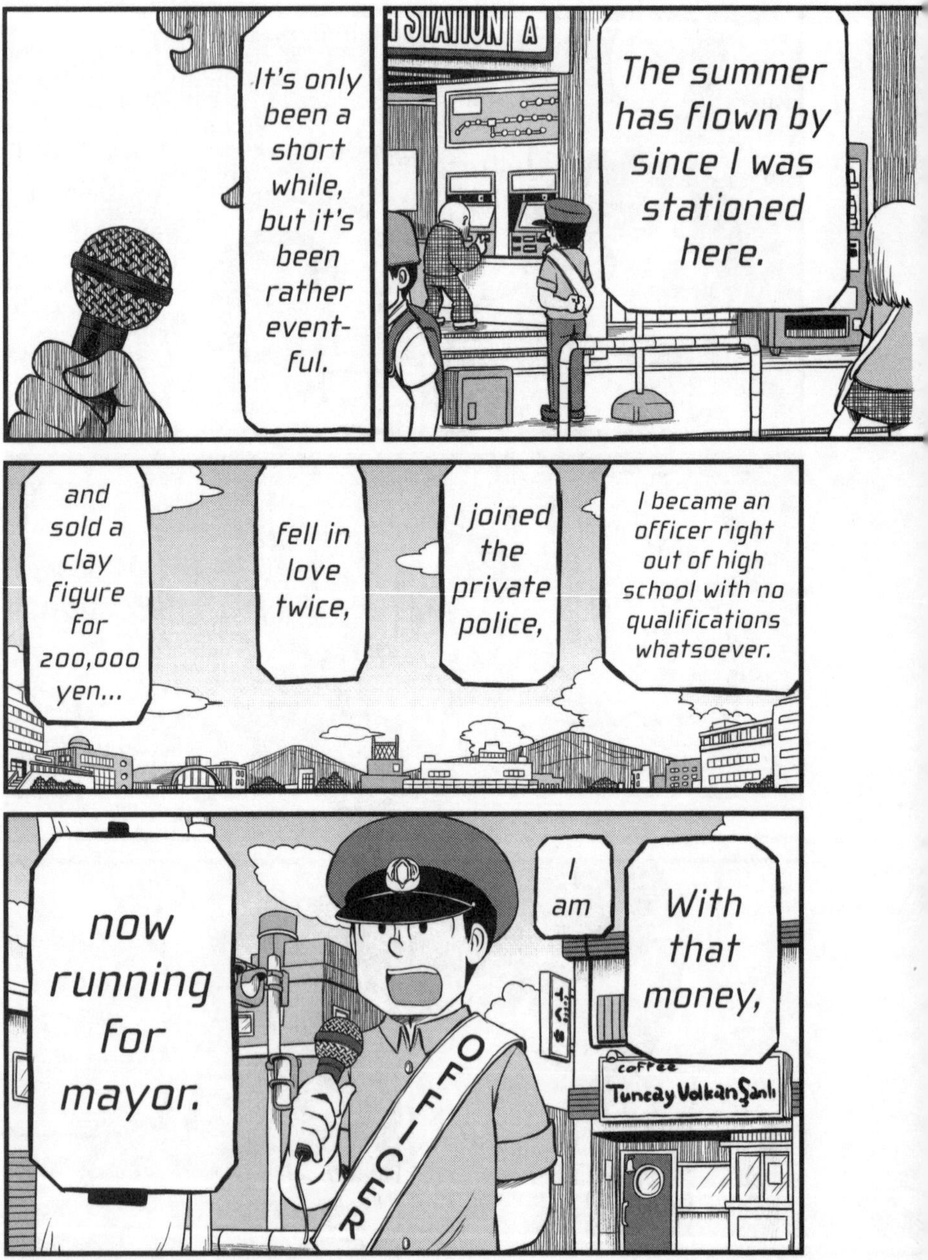
STATION A
The summer has flown by since I was stationed here.
It's only been a short while, but it's been rather eventful.
I became an officer right out of high school with no qualifications whatsoever.
I joined the private police,
fell in love twice,
and sold a clay figure for 200,000 yen...
With that money,
I am
now running for mayor.
OFFICER
coffee
Tuncay Volkan Şanlı

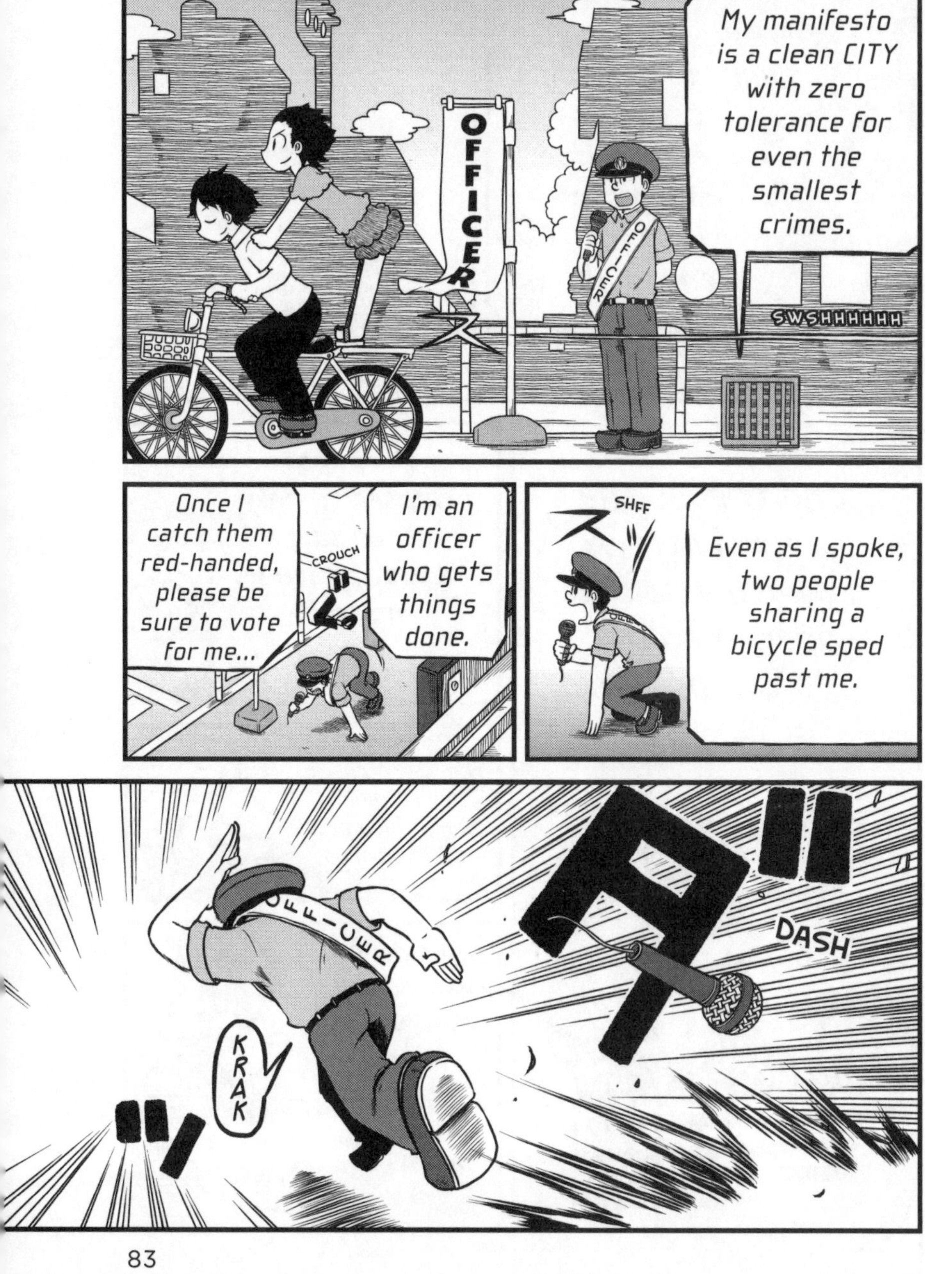

My manifesto is a clean CITY with zero tolerance for even the smallest crimes.
OFFICER
OFFICER
SWSHHHHHH
SHFF
Even as I spoke, two people sharing a bicycle sped past me.
I'm an officer who gets things done.
CROUCH
Once I catch them red-handed, please be sure to vote for me...
DASH
OFFICER
KRAK

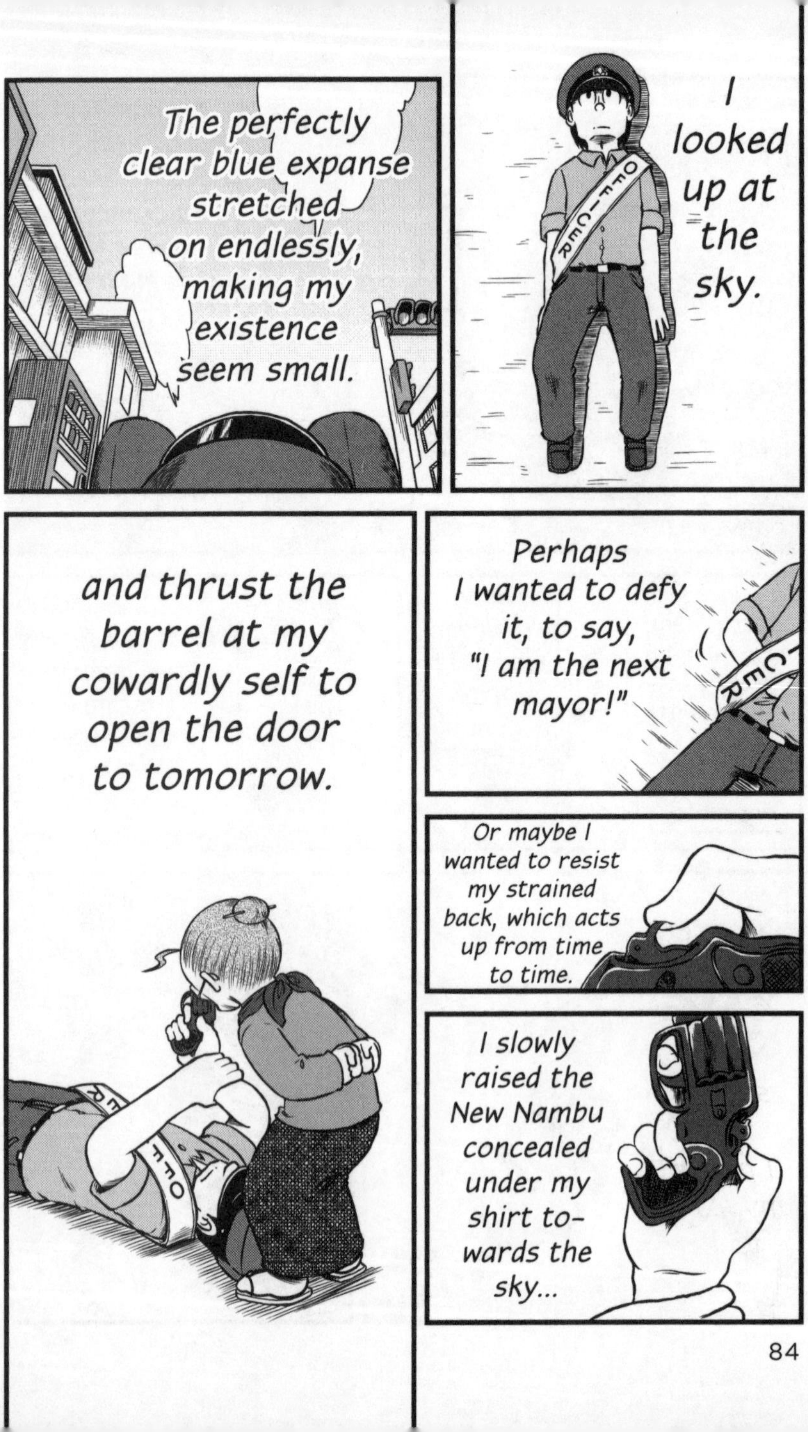
I looked up at the sky.
The perfectly clear blue expanse stretched on endlessly, making my existence seem small.
OFFICER
Perhaps I wanted to defy it, to say, "I am the next mayor!"
Or maybe I wanted to resist my strained back, which acts up from time to time.
I slowly raised the New Nambu concealed under my shirt towards the sky...
and thrust the barrel at my cowardly self to open the door to tomorrow.

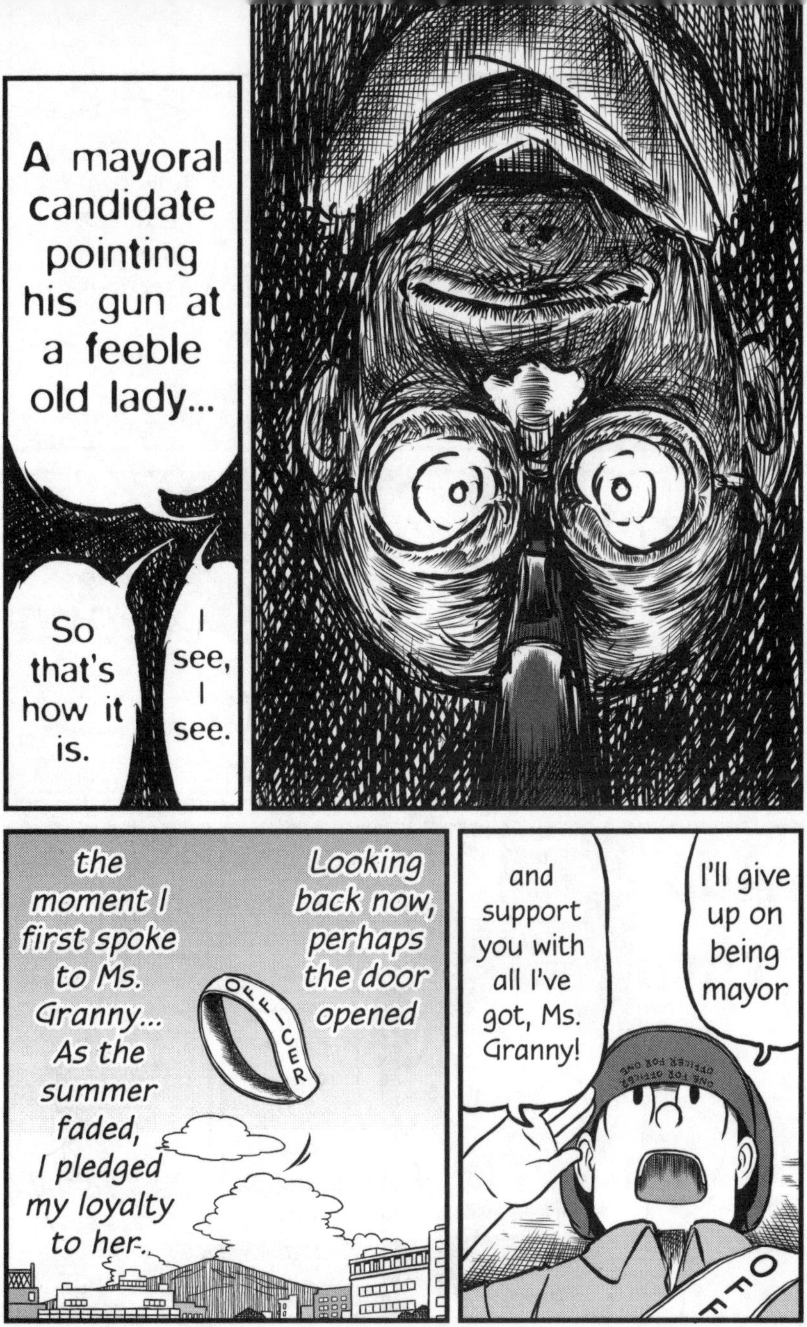
A mayoral candidate pointing his gun at a feeble old lady...
I see, I see.
So that's how it is.
I'll give up on being mayor
and support you with all I've got, Ms. Granny!
Looking back now, perhaps the door opened
the moment I first spoke to Ms. Granny... As the summer faded, I pledged my loyalty to her..
OFFICER

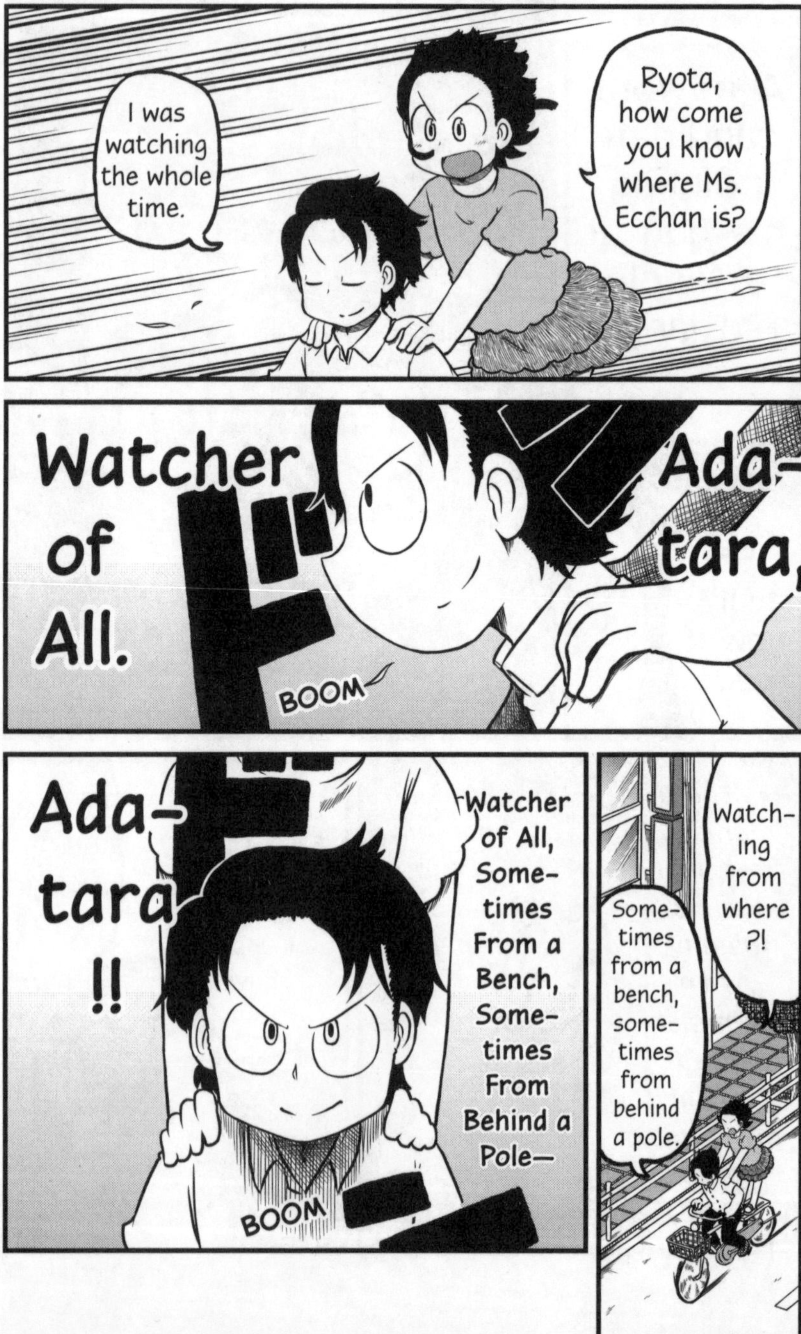
Ryota, how come you know where Ms. Ecchan is?
I was watching the whole time.
Ada-tara,
Watcher of All.
BOOM
Watching from where?!
Sometimes from a bench, sometimes from behind a pole.
Watcher of All, Sometimes From a Bench, Sometimes From Behind a Pole—
Ada-tara!!
BOOM

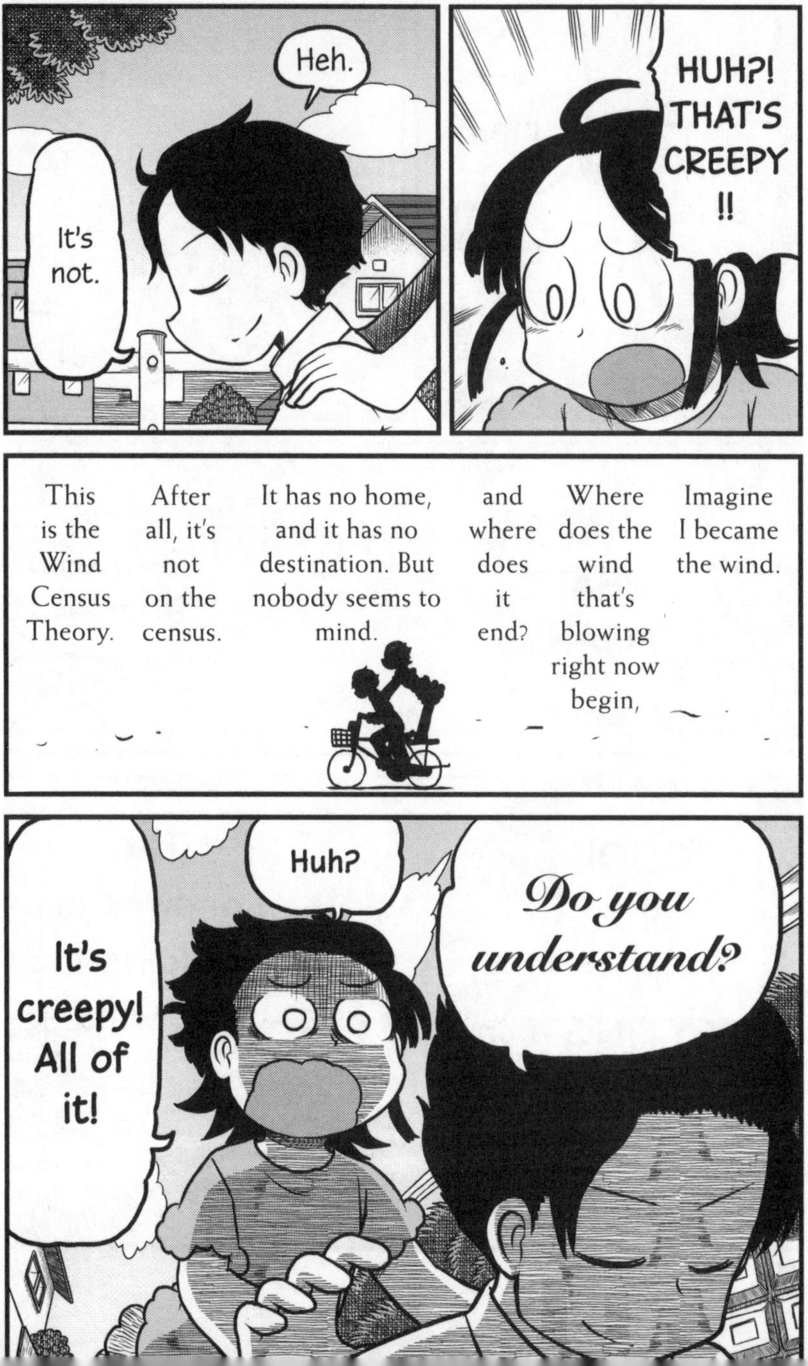
HUH?! THAT'S CREEPY !!
Heh.
It's not.
Imagine I became the wind.
Where does the wind that's blowing right now begin,
and where does it end?
It has no home, and it has no destination. But nobody seems to mind.
After all, it's not on the census.
This is the Wind Census Theory.
Do you understand?
Huh?
It's creepy! All of it!

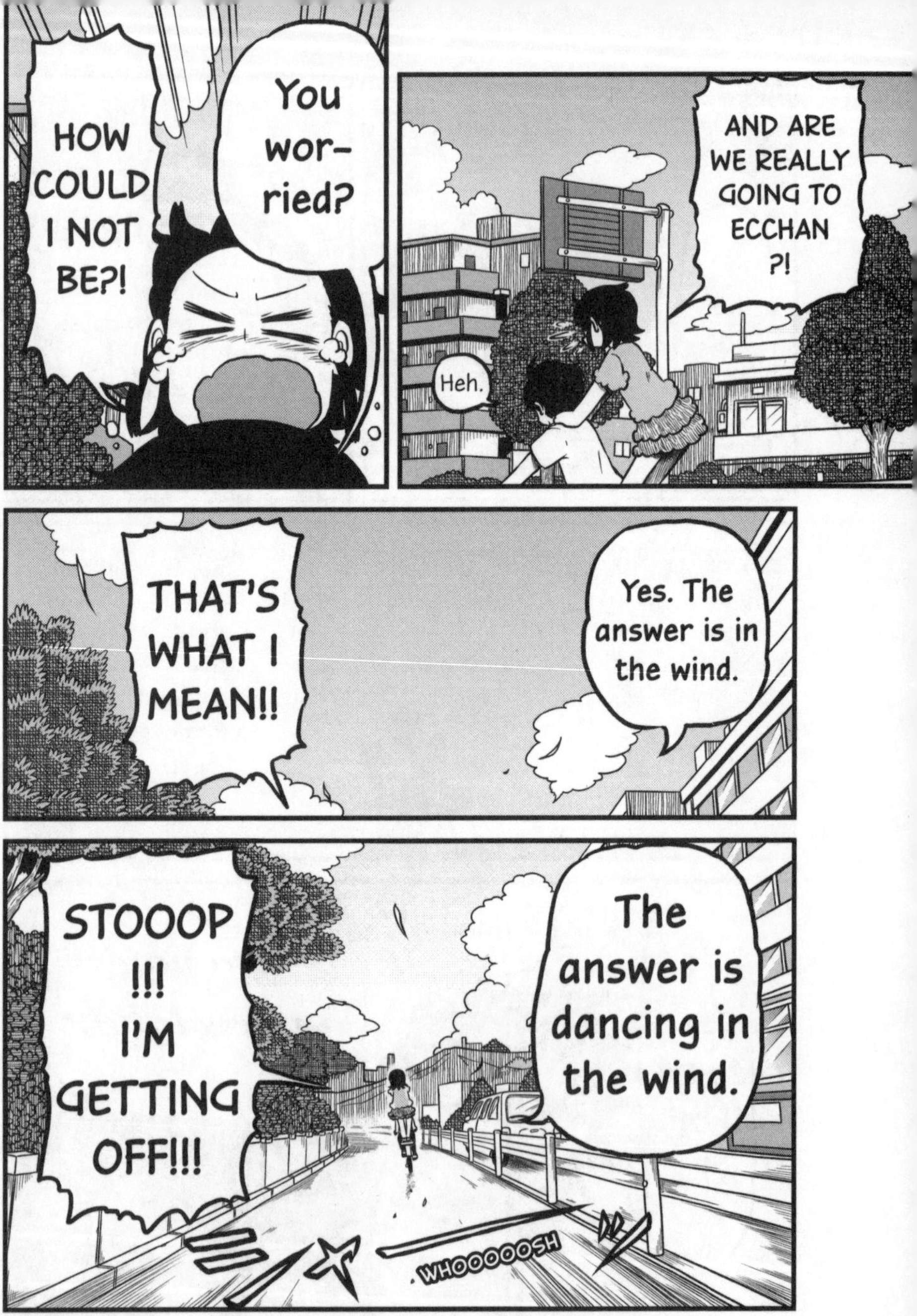
AND ARE WE REALLY GOING TO ECCHAN ?!
Heh.
You wor-ried?
HOW COULD I NOT BE?!
Yes. The answer is in the wind.
THAT'S WHAT I MEAN!!
The answer is dancing in the wind.
STOOOP !!! I'M GETTING OFF!!!
WHOOOOOSH

CITY 9 / END

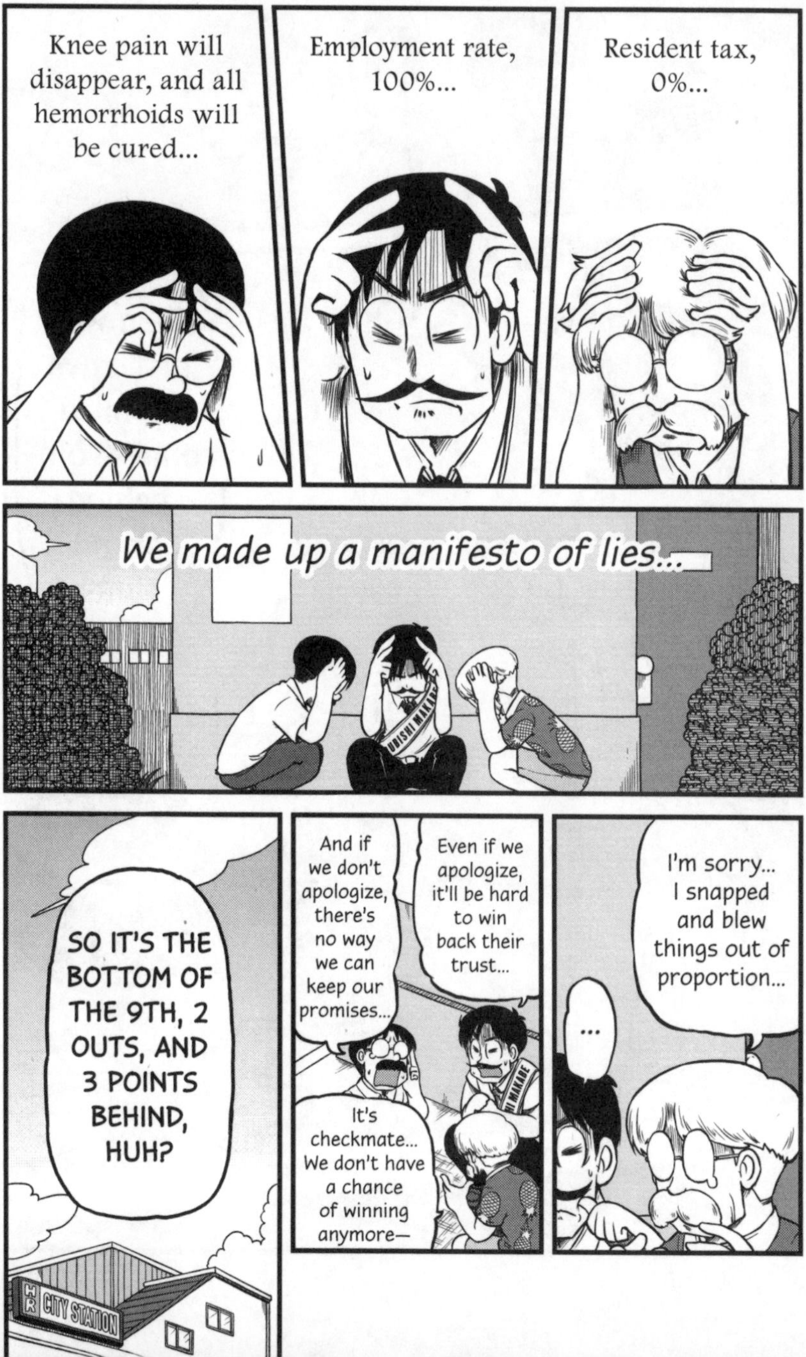
Resident tax, 0%...
Employment rate, 100%...
Knee pain will disappear, and all hemorrhoids will be cured...
We made up a manifesto of lies...
I'm sorry... I snapped and blew things out of proportion...
...
Even if we apologize, it'll be hard to win back their trust...
And if we don't apologize, there's no way we can keep our promises...
It's checkmate... We don't have a chance of winning anymore—
SO IT'S THE BOTTOM OF THE 9TH, 2 OUTS, AND 3 POINTS BEHIND, HUH?
HR
CITY STATION

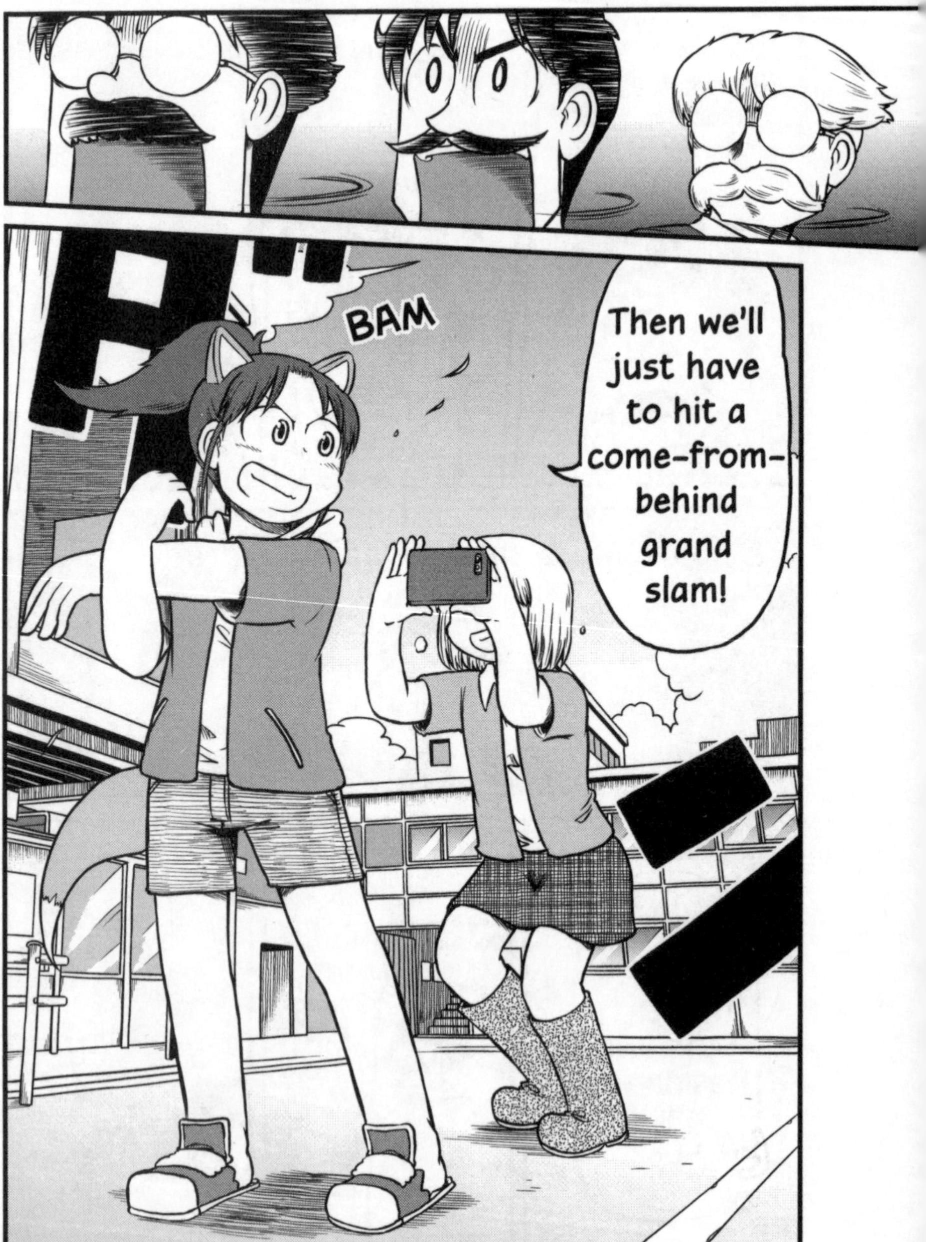
Then we'll just have to hit a come-from-behind grand slam!
BAM

Chapter 177 ◇ CITY 10

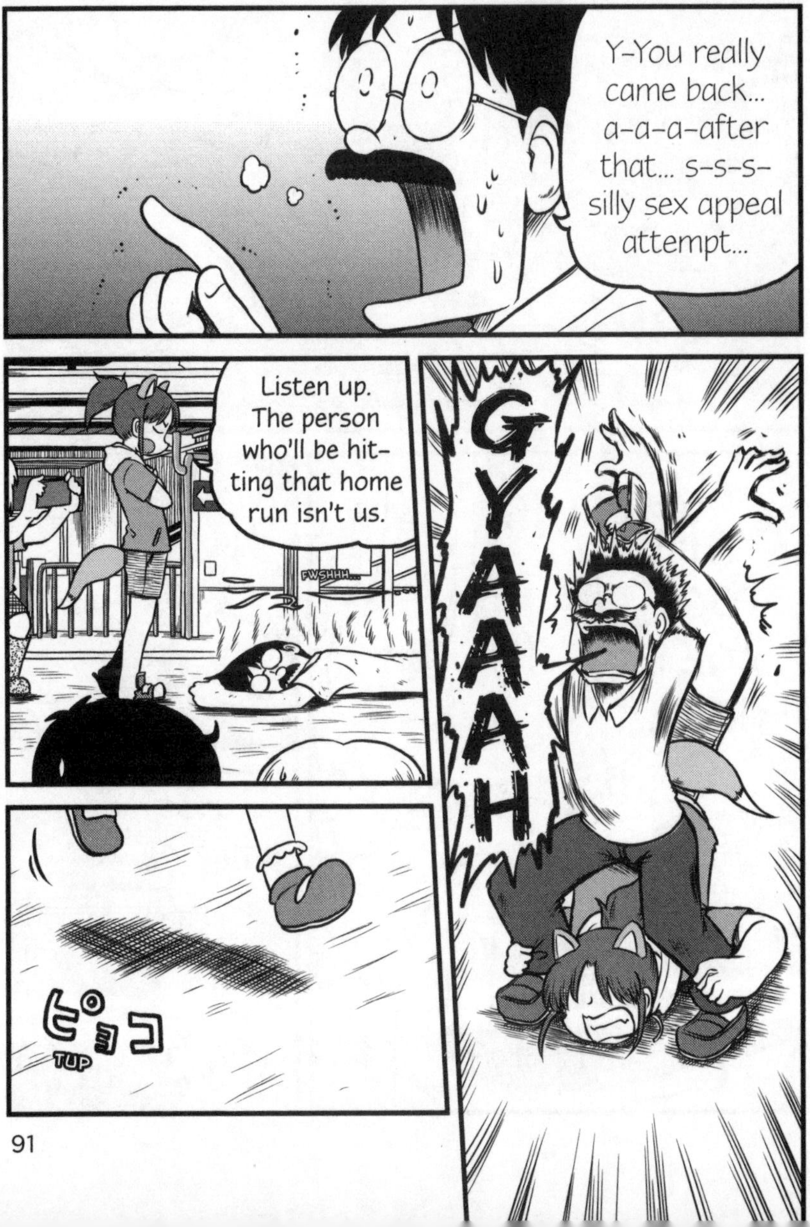

Y-You really came back... a-a-a-after that... s-s-s-silly sex appeal attempt...
GYAAAAH
Listen up. The person who'll be hit-ting that home run isn't us.
FWSHHH...
ピョコ
TUP

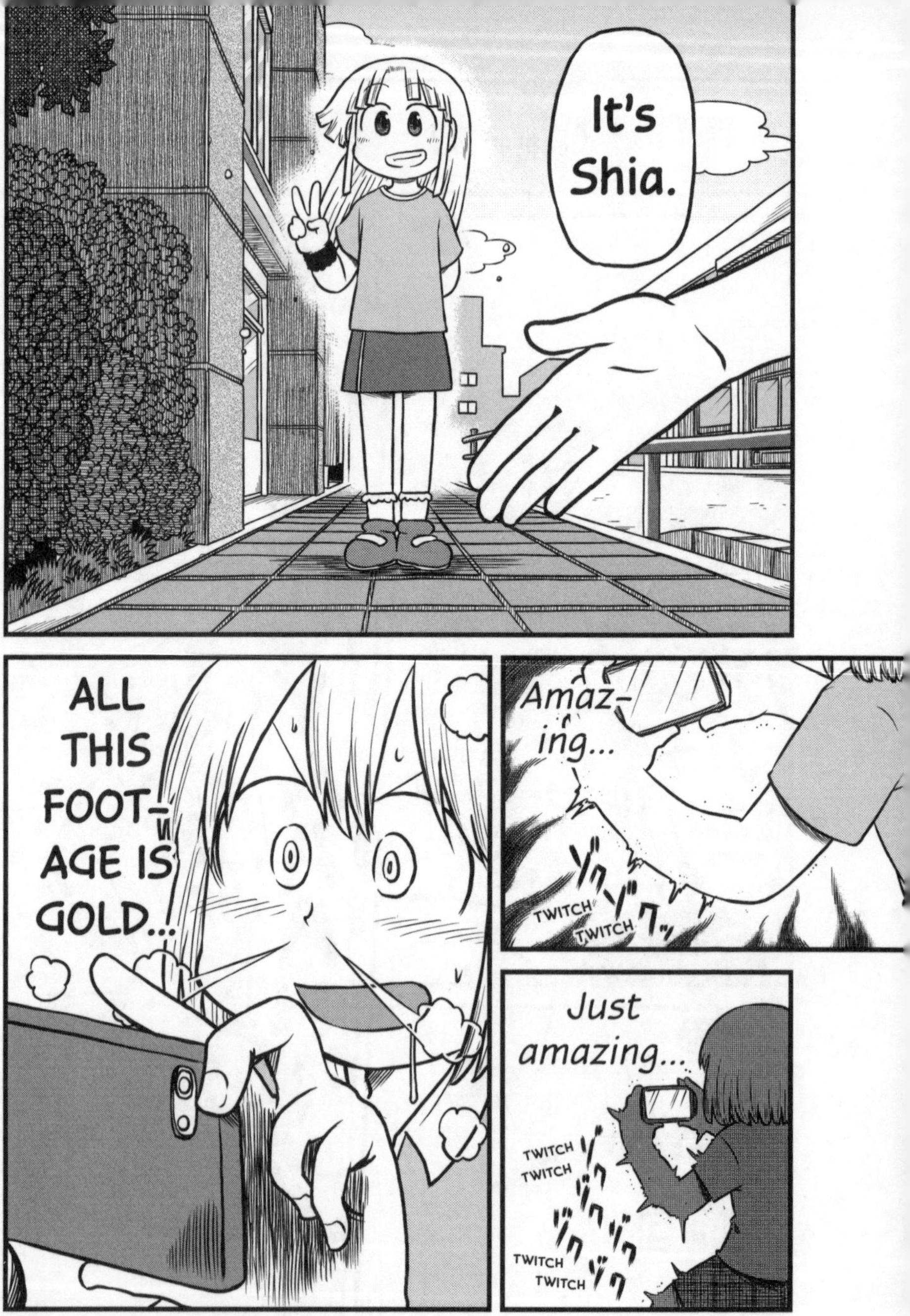
It's Shia.
Amaz-ing...
ゾクゾクッ
TWITCH TWITCH
Just amazing...
TWITCH TWITCH
ゾクゾクゾクゾクゾク
TWITCH TWITCH
ALL THIS FOOT-AGE IS GOLD...

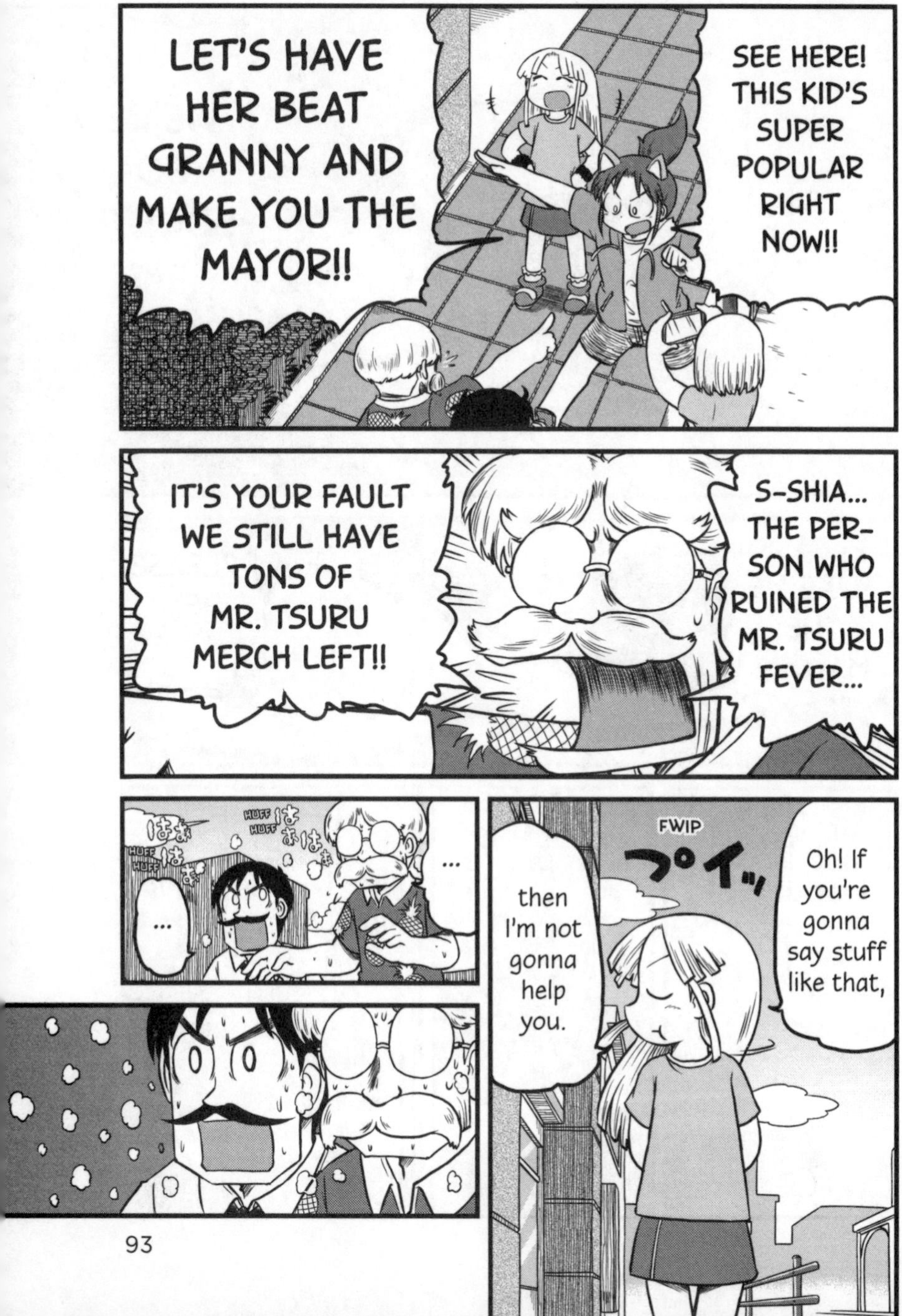
SEE HERE! THIS KID'S SUPER POPULAR RIGHT NOW!!
LET'S HAVE HER BEAT GRANNY AND MAKE YOU THE MAYOR!!
S-SHIA... THE PER-SON WHO RUINED THE MR. TSURU FEVER...
IT'S YOUR FAULT WE STILL HAVE TONS OF MR. TSURU MERCH LEFT!!
Oh! If you're gonna say stuff like that,
FWIP
then I'm not gonna help you.
HUFF HUFF
HUFF HUFF
...
...

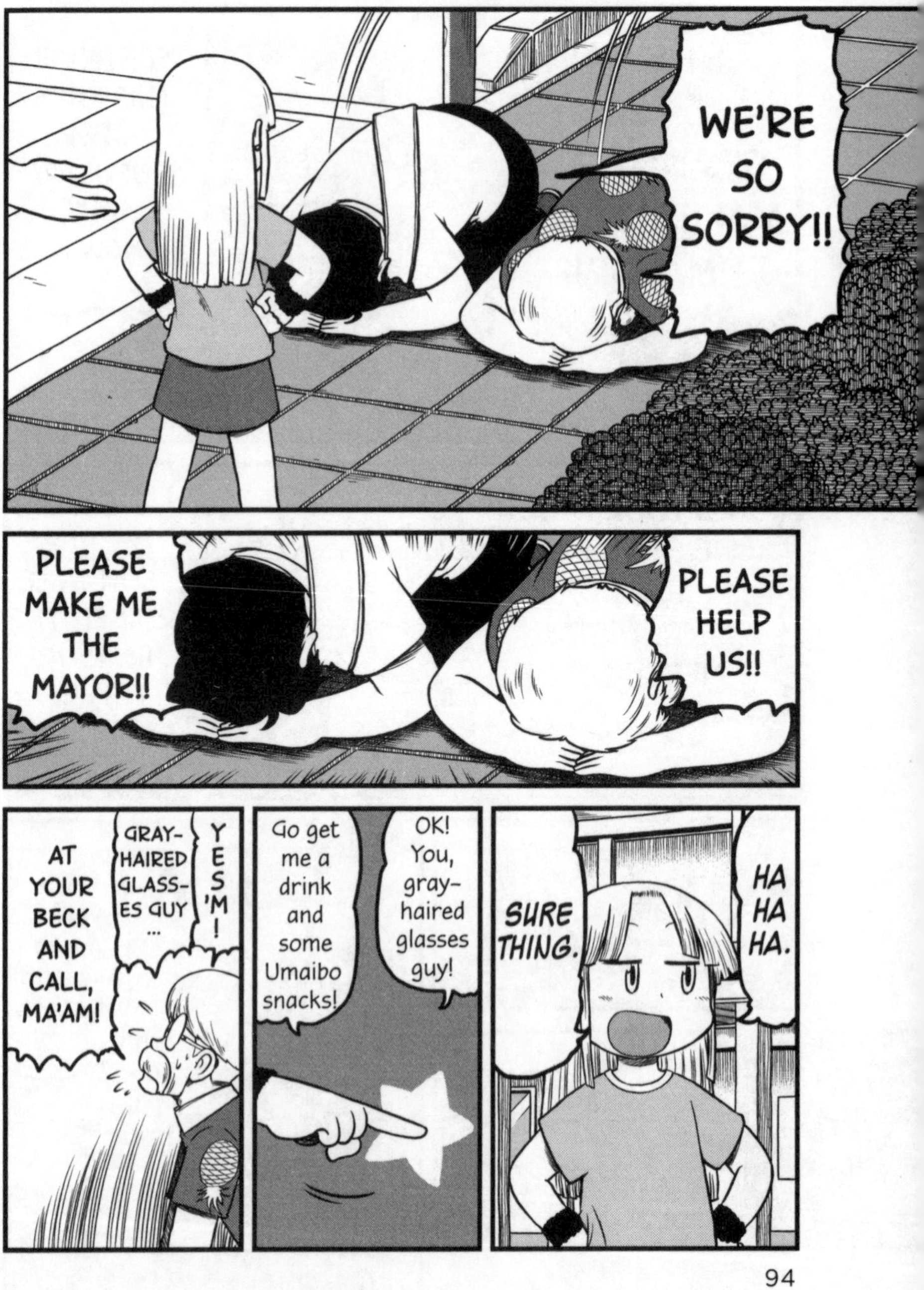
WE'RE SO SORRY!!
PLEASE HELP US!!
PLEASE MAKE ME THE MAYOR!!
HA HA HA.
SURE THING.
OK! You, gray-haired glasses guy!
Go get me a drink and some Umaibo snacks!
YES'M!
GRAY-HAIRED GLASSES GUY ...
AT YOUR BECK AND CALL, MA'AM!

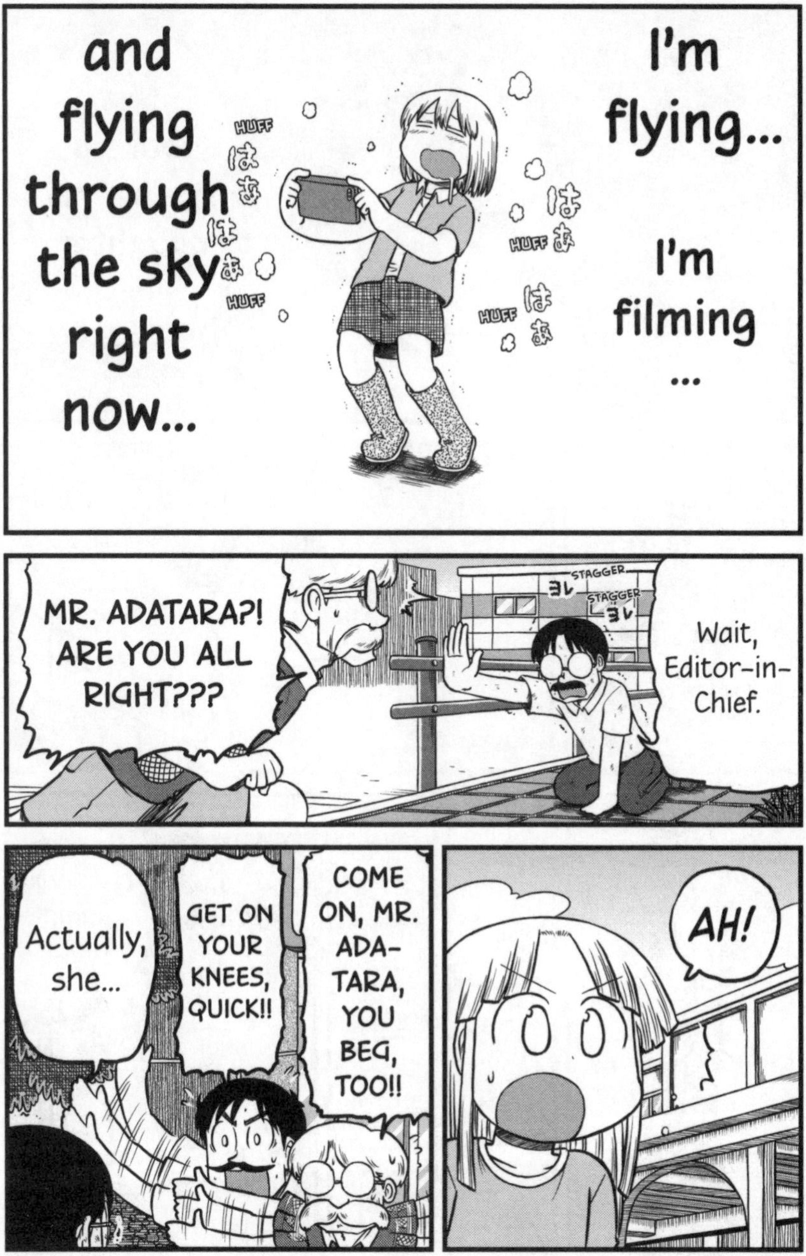
I'm flying...
I'm filming ...
HUFF はあ
HUFF はあ
HUFF はあ
HUFF はあ
and flying through the sky right now...
Wait, Editor-in-Chief.
STAGGER ヨレ
STAGGER ヨレ
MR. ADATARA?! ARE YOU ALL RIGHT???
AH!
COME ON, MR. ADA-TARA, YOU BEG, TOO!!
GET ON YOUR KNEES, QUICK!!
Actually, she...

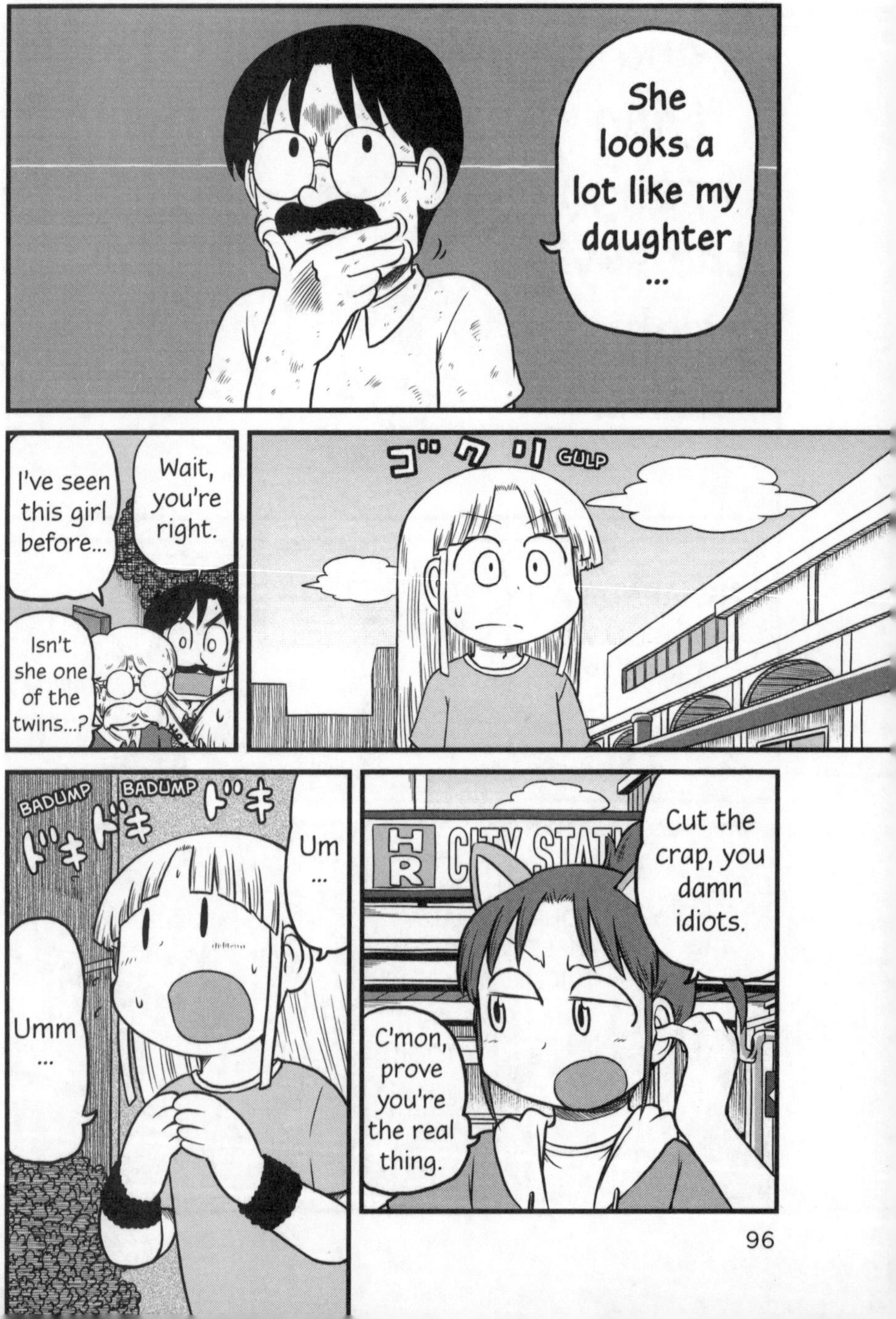
She looks a lot like my daughter ...
ゴクリ GULP
Wait, you're right.
I've seen this girl before...
Isn't she one of the twins...?
Cut the crap, you damn idiots.
C'mon, prove you're the real thing.
ドキドキ
BADUMP BADUMP
Um ...
Umm ...

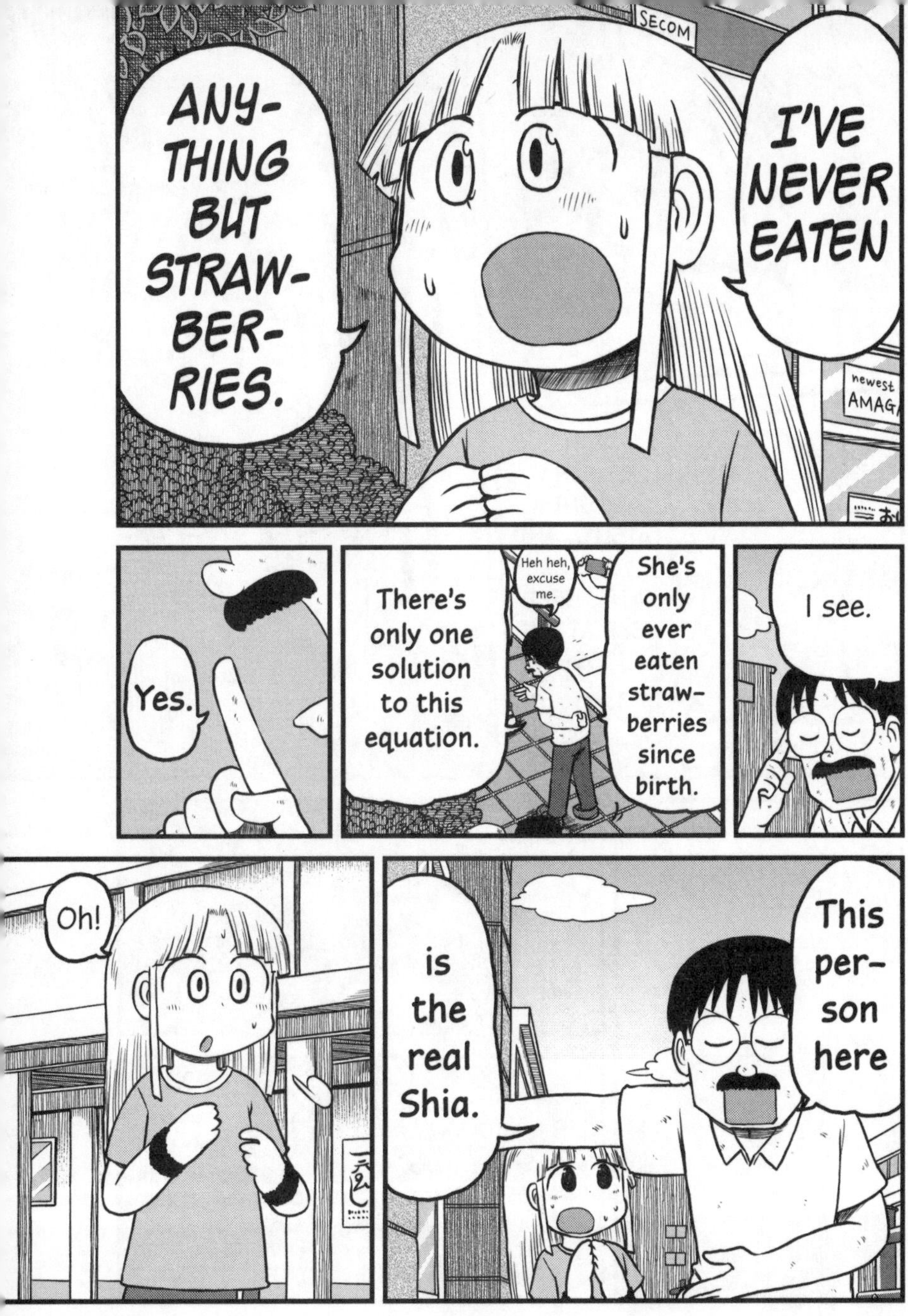
SECOM
newest
I'VE NEVER EATEN
ANY-THING BUT STRAW-BER-RIES.
I see.
She's only ever eaten straw-berries since birth.
Heh heh, excuse me.
There's only one solution to this equation.
Yes.
This per-son here
is the real Shia.
Oh!

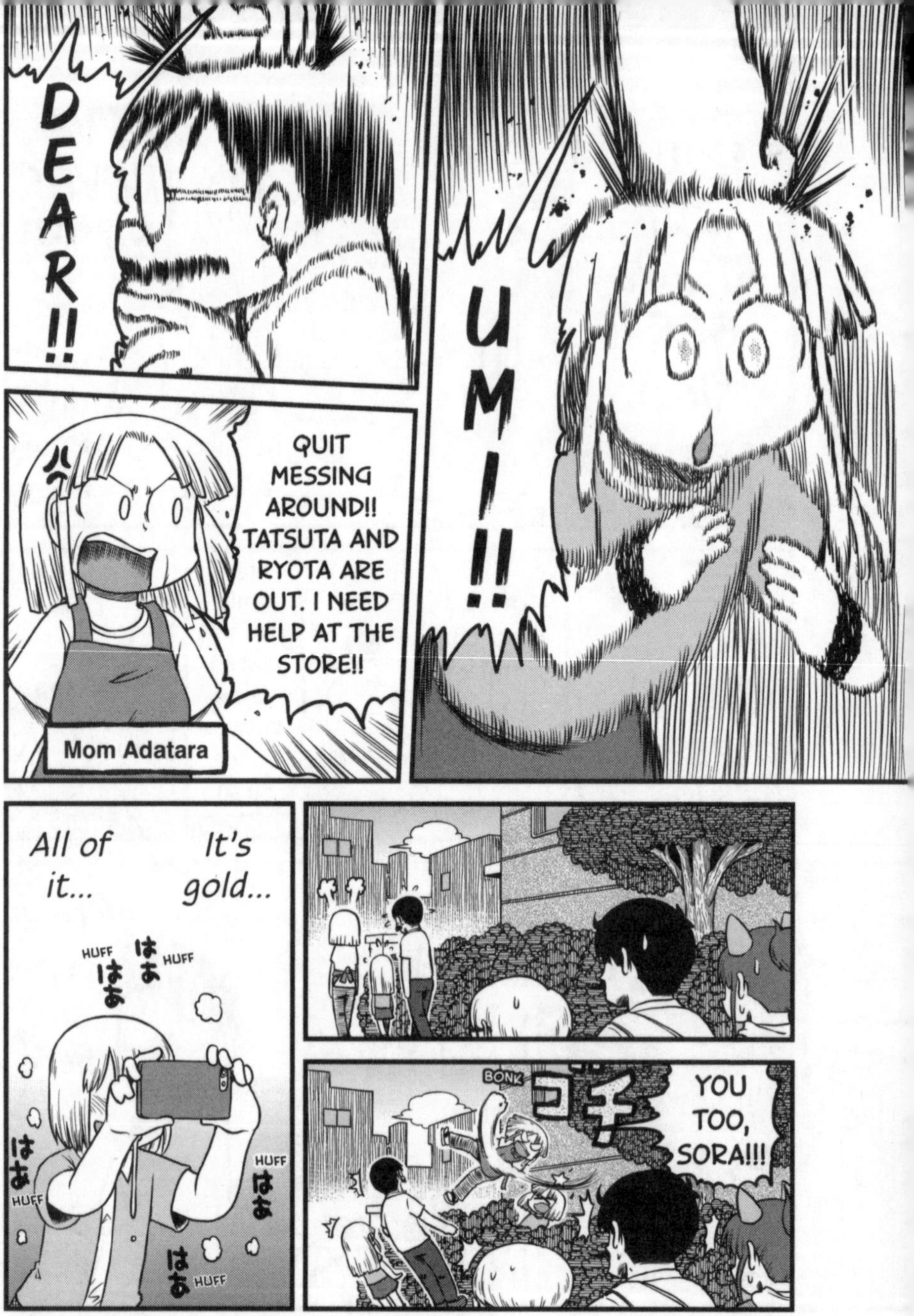
UMI!!
DEAR!!
QUIT MESSING AROUND!! TATSUTA AND RYOTA ARE OUT. I NEED HELP AT THE STORE!!
Mom Adatara
BONK
ゴチ
YOU TOO, SORA!!!
It's gold...
All of it...
はあ HUFF
はあ HUFF
はあ HUFF
はあ HUFF
はあ HUFF

CITY 10 / END

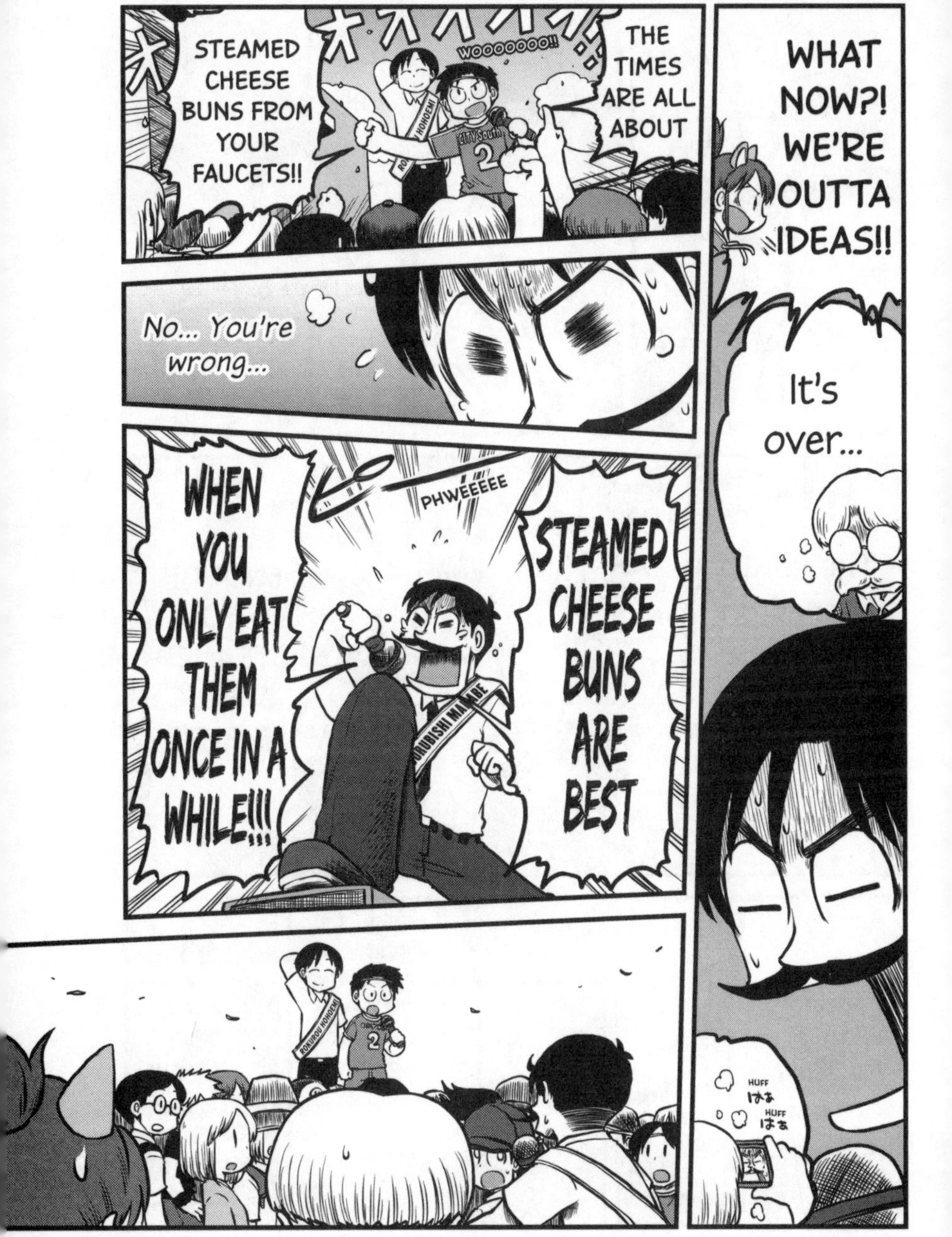
WHAT NOW?! WE'RE OUTTA IDEAS!!
WOOOOOOOO!!
THE TIMES ARE ALL ABOUT
STEAMED CHEESE BUNS FROM YOUR FAUCETS!!
It's over...
No... You're wrong...
PHWEEEEE
STEAMED CHEESE BUNS ARE BEST
WHEN YOU ONLY EAT THEM ONCE IN A WHILE!!!
HUFF はぁ
HUFF はぁ

Chapter 178 CITY 11

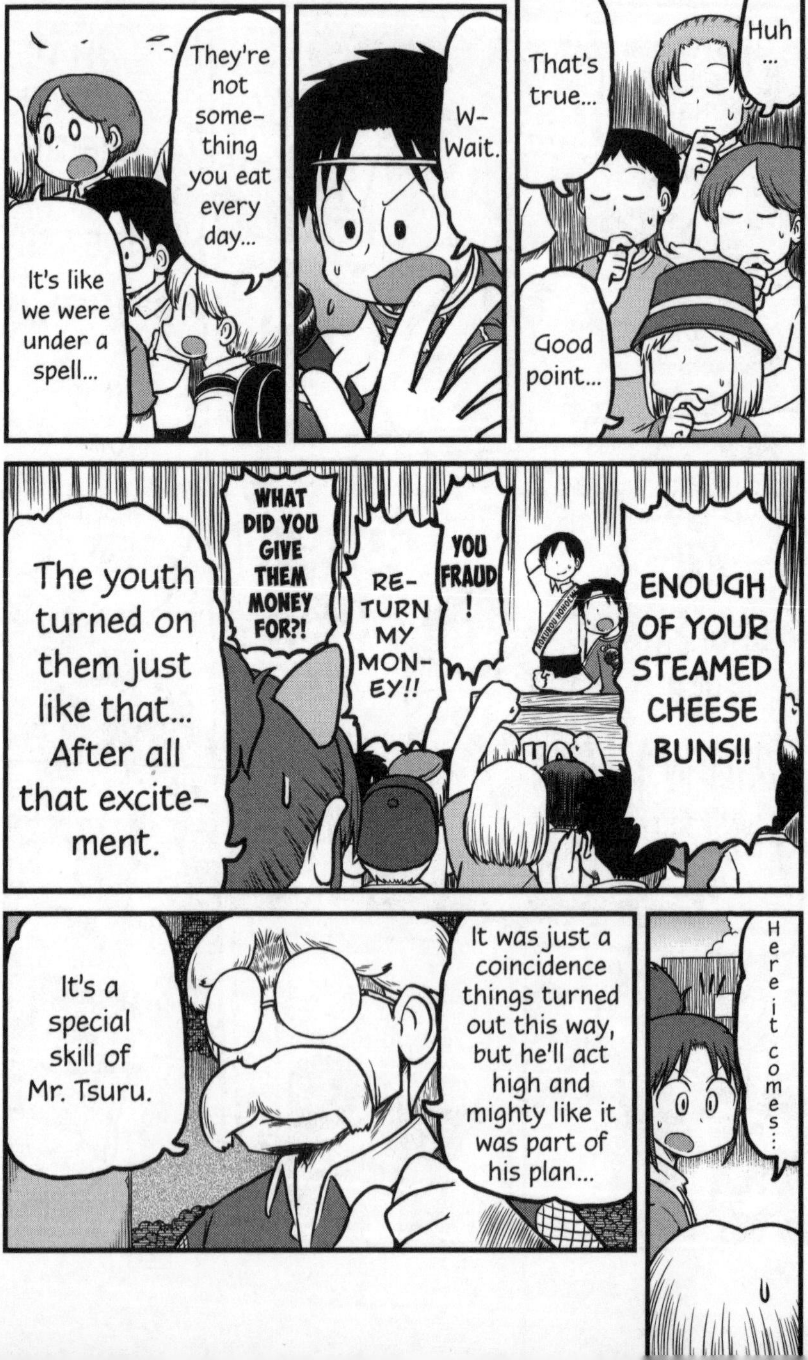
Huh ...
That's true...
Good point...
W- Wait.
They're not some-thing you eat every day...
It's like we were under a spell...
ENOUGH OF YOUR STEAMED CHEESE BUNS!!
YOU FRAUD!
RE-TURN MY MON-EY!!
WHAT DID YOU GIVE THEM MONEY FOR?!
The youth turned on them just like that... After all that excite-ment.
Here it comes...
It was just a coincidence things turned out this way, but he'll act high and mighty like it was part of his plan...
It's a special skill of Mr. Tsuru.

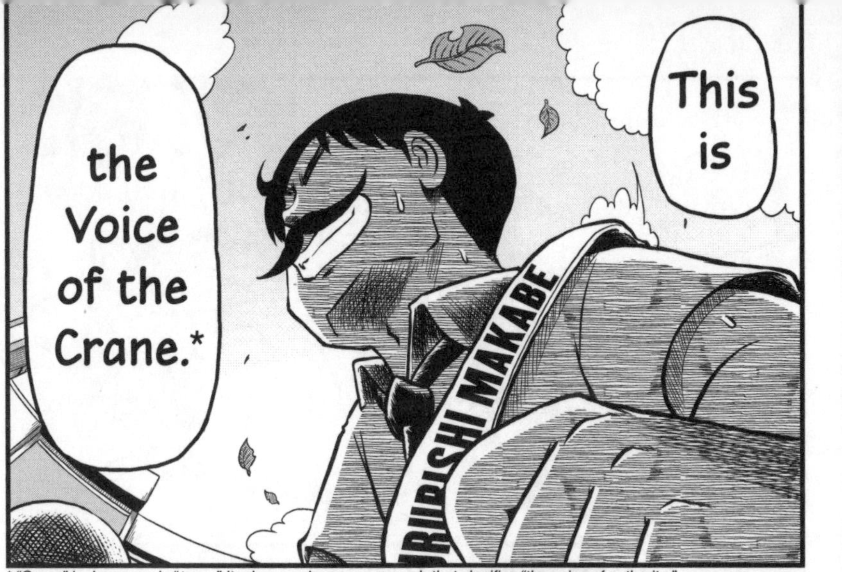
This is
the Voice of the Crane.*
TSURUBISHI MAKABE

* "Crane" in Japanese is "*tsuru.*" It mirrors a Japanese proverb that signifies "the voice of authority."

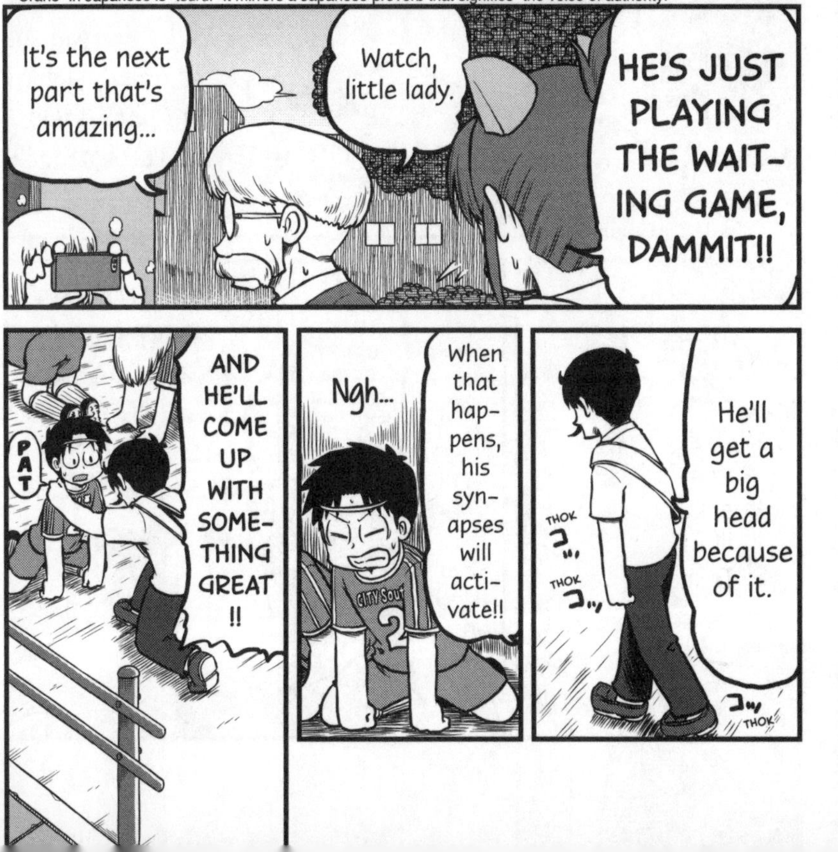
HE'S JUST PLAYING THE WAIT-ING GAME, DAMMIT!!
Watch, little lady.
It's the next part that's amazing...
He'll get a big head because of it.
THOK
THOK
THOK
When that hap-pens, his syn-apses will acti-vate!!
Ngh...
AND HE'LL COME UP WITH SOME-THING GREAT!!
PAT

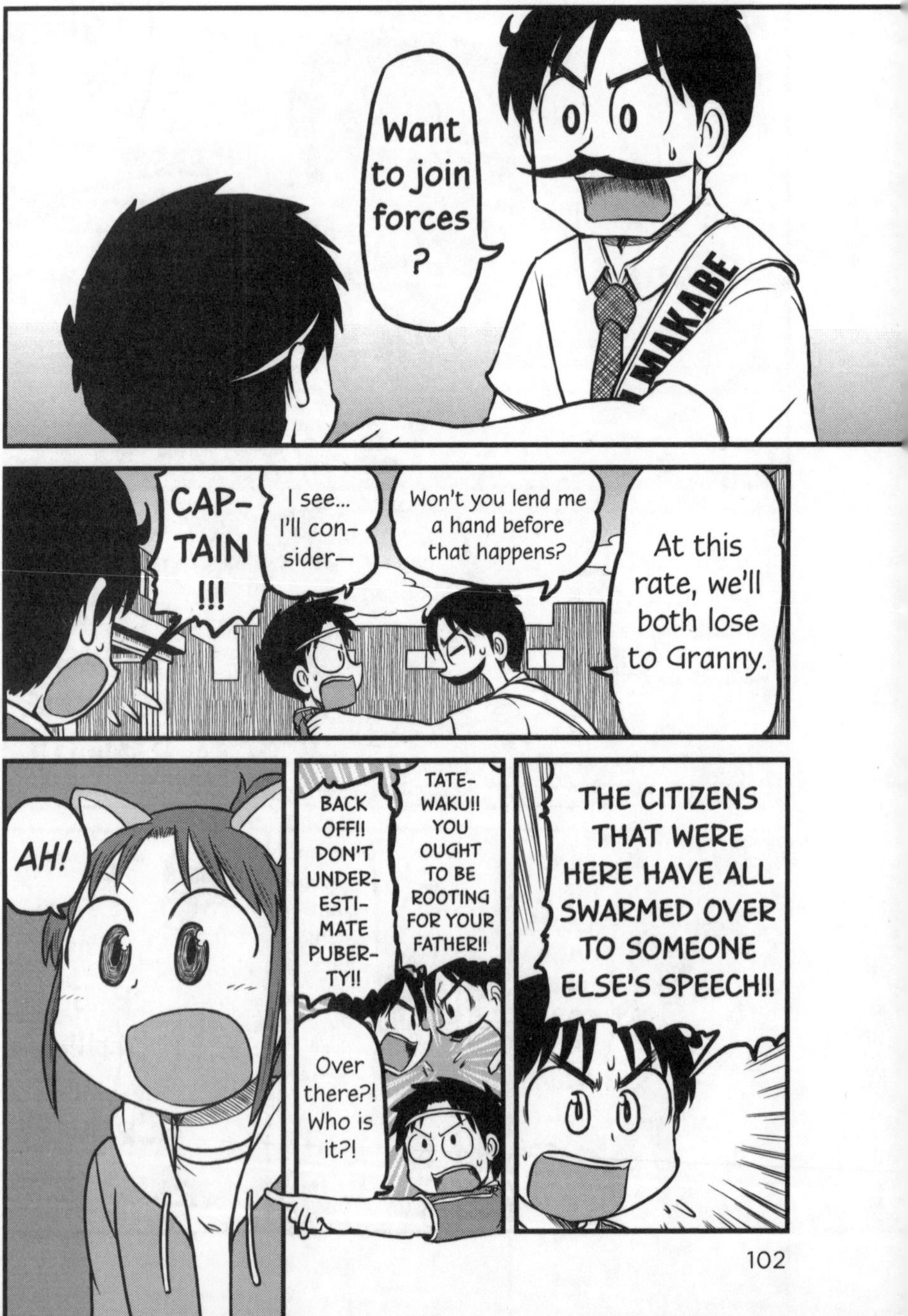
Want to join forces?
MAKABE
At this rate, we'll both lose to Granny.
Won't you lend me a hand before that happens?
I see... I'll con-sider—
CAP-TAIN!!!
THE CITIZENS THAT WERE HERE HAVE ALL SWARMED OVER TO SOMEONE ELSE'S SPEECH!!
TATE-WAKU!! YOU OUGHT TO BE ROOTING FOR YOUR FATHER!!
BACK OFF!! DON'T UNDER-ESTI-MATE PUBER-TY!!
Over there?! Who is it?!
AH!

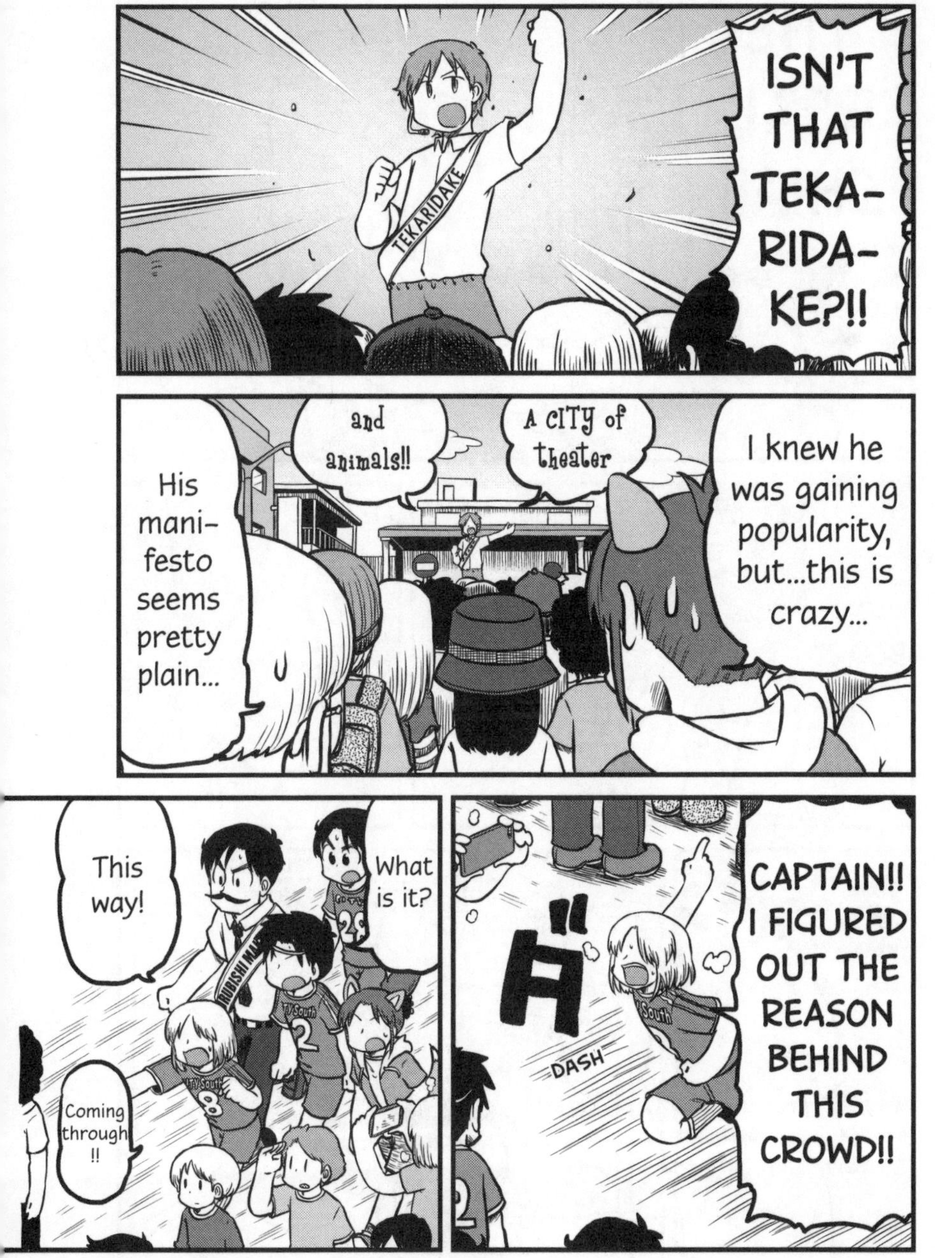
TEKARIDAKE
ISN'T THAT TEKA-RIDA-KE?!!
I knew he was gaining popularity, but...this is crazy...
A CITY of theater
and animals!!
His mani-festo seems pretty plain...
CAPTAIN!! I FIGURED OUT THE REASON BEHIND THIS CROWD!!
ダ
DASH
What is it?
This way!
Coming through !!

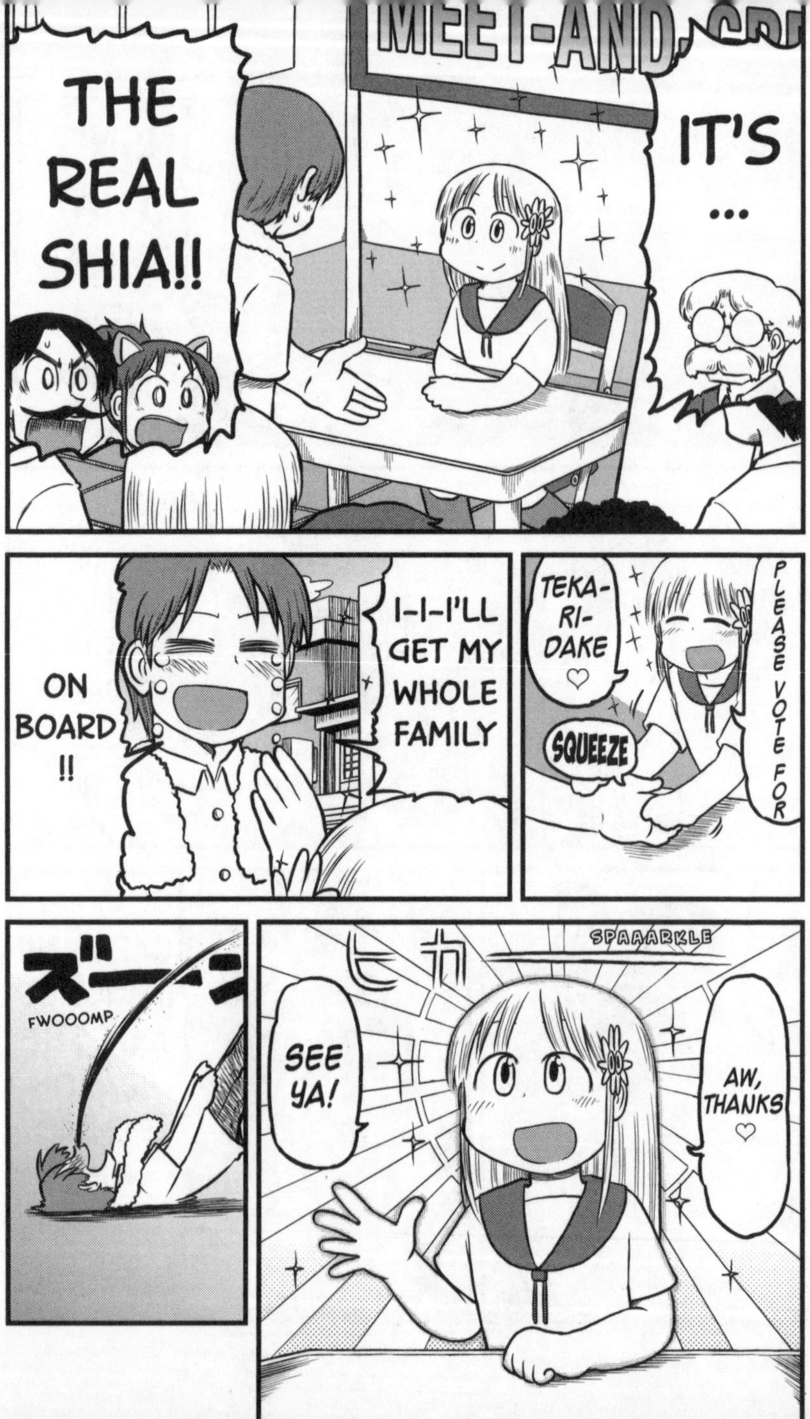
MEET-AND-
IT'S ...
THE REAL SHIA!!
PLEASE VOTE FOR
TEKA-RI-DAKE ♡
SQUEEZE
I-I-I'LL GET MY WHOLE FAMILY
ON BOARD !!
ヒカ
SPAAARKLE
AW, THANKS ♡
SEE YA!
ズーン
FWOOOMP

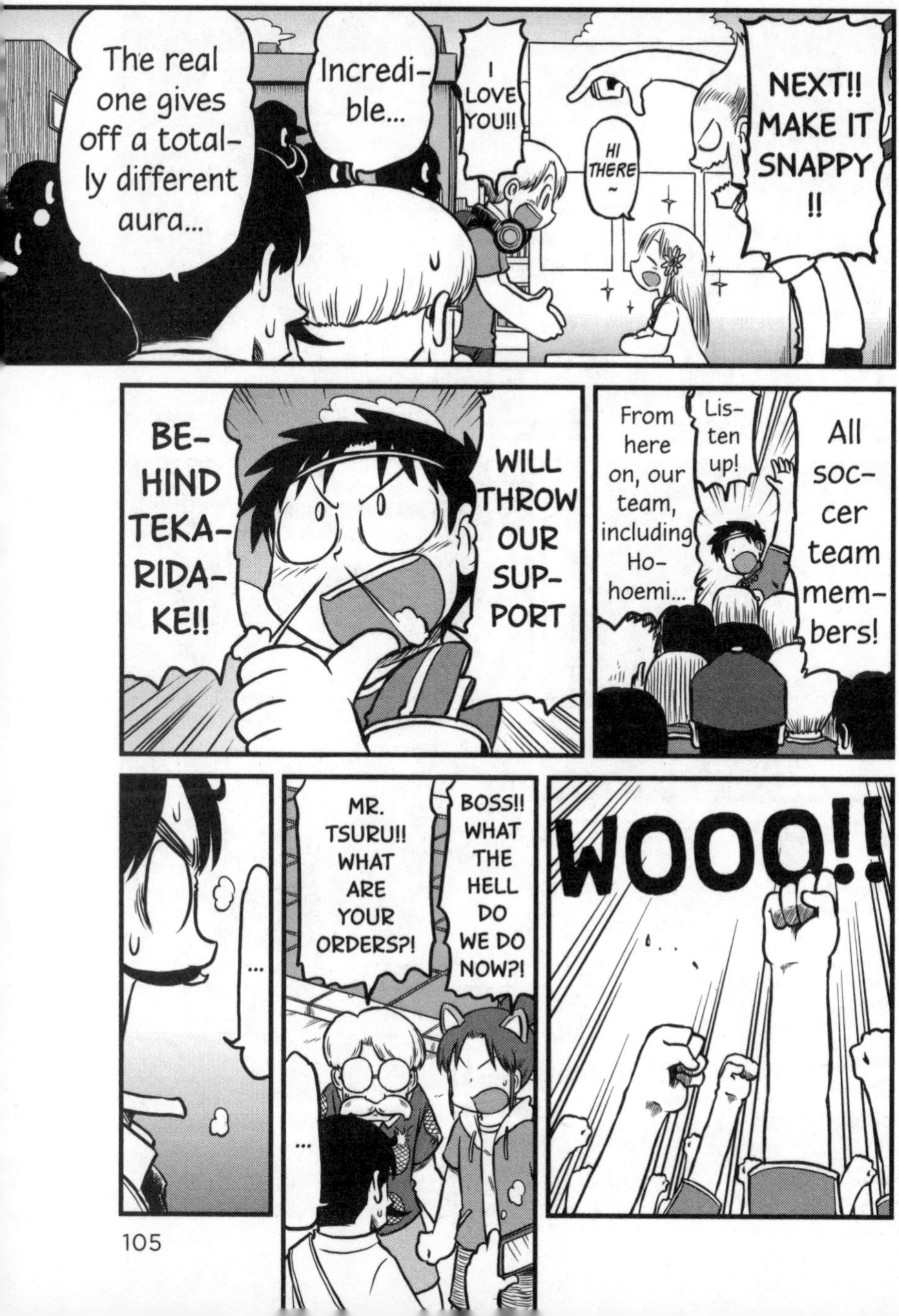
NEXT!! MAKE IT SNAPPY !!
HI THERE ~
I LOVE YOU!!
Incredible...
The real one gives off a totally different aura...
All soccer team members!
Listen up!
From here on, our team, including Hohoemi...
WILL THROW OUR SUPPORT
BEHIND TEKARIDAKE!!
WOOO!!
BOSS!! WHAT THE HELL DO WE DO NOW?!
MR. TSURU!! WHAT ARE YOUR ORDERS?!
...
...

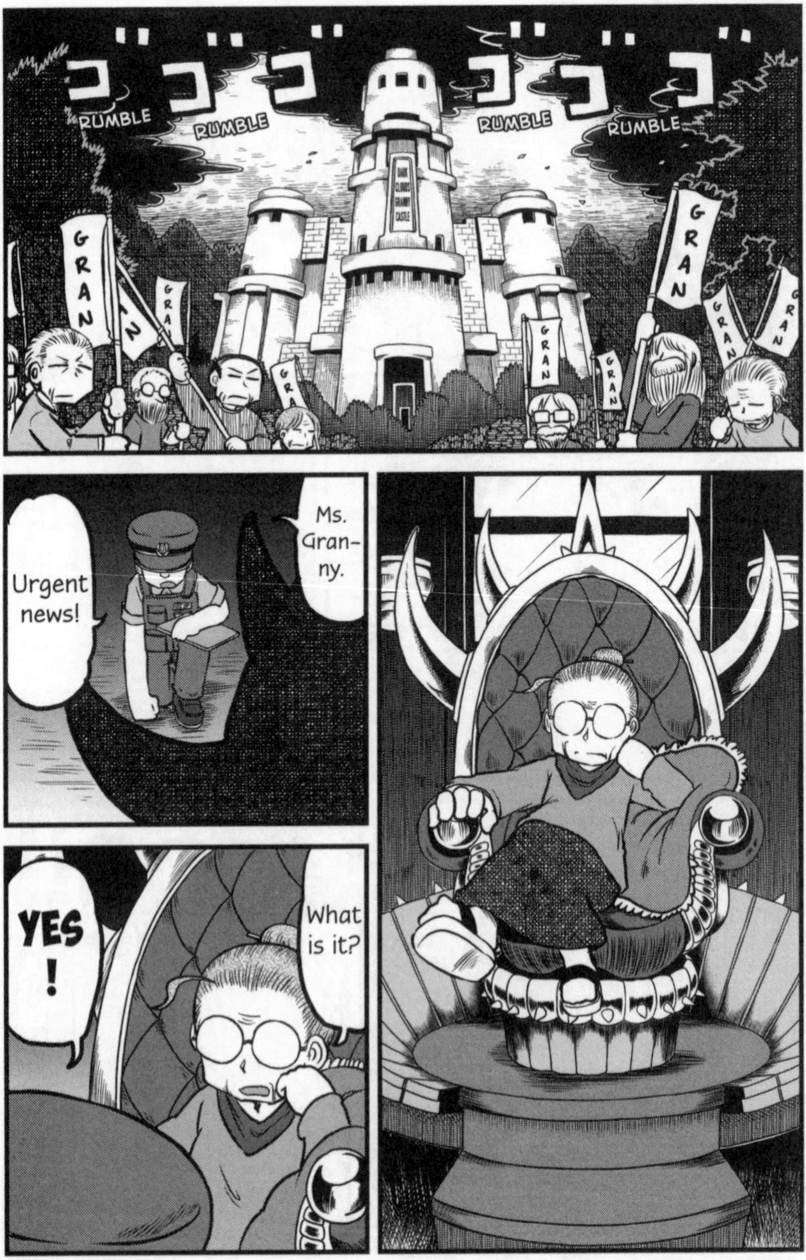

ゴゴゴゴゴゴ
RUMBLE
RUMBLE
RUMBLE
RUMBLE
DARK CLOUDS GRANNY CASTLE
GRAN
GRAN
GRAN
GRAN
GRAN
GRAN
GRAN
GRAN
GRAN
Ms. Gran-ny.
Urgent news!
What is it?
YES !

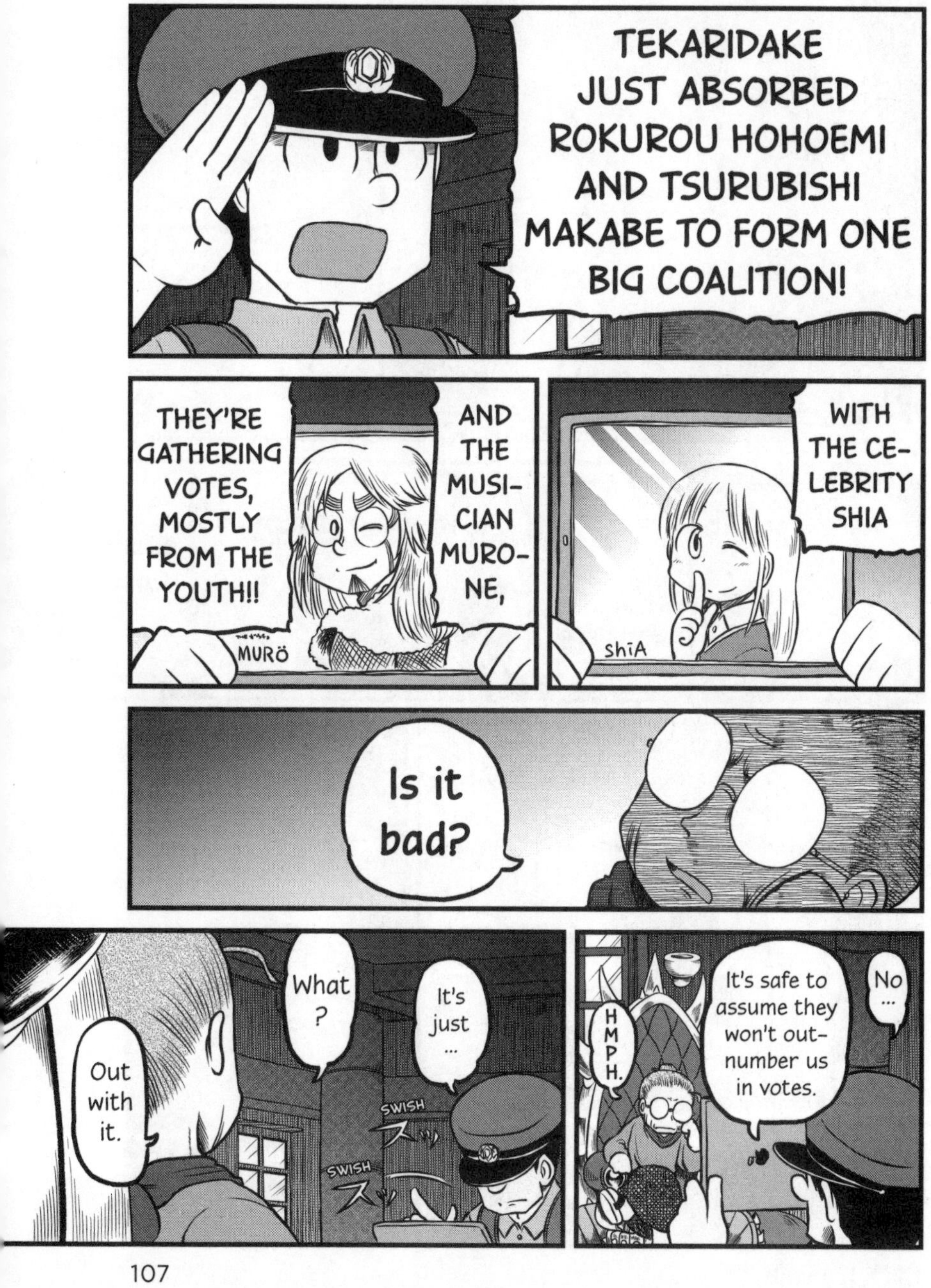
TEKARIDAKE JUST ABSORBED ROKUROU HOHOEMI AND TSURUBISHI MAKABE TO FORM ONE BIG COALITION!
WITH THE CELEBRITY SHIA
ShīA
AND THE MUSICIAN MURONE,
THEY'RE GATHERING VOTES, MOSTLY FROM THE YOUTH!!
MURÖ
Is it bad?
No ...
It's safe to assume they won't outnumber us in votes.
HMPH.
It's just ...
What?
SWISH
SWISH
Out with it.

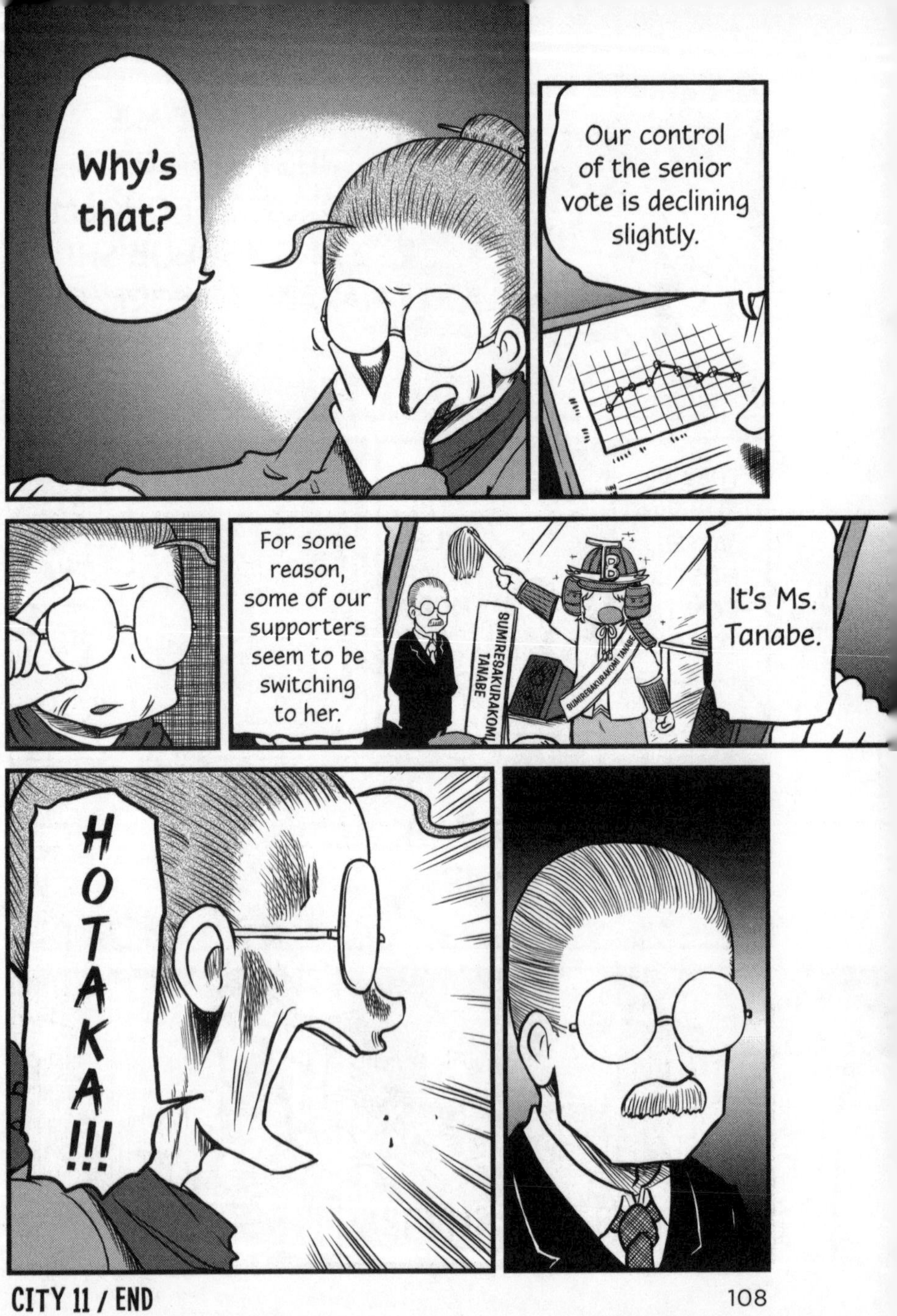
Our control of the senior vote is declining slightly.
Why's that?
It's Ms. Tanabe.
For some reason, some of our supporters seem to be switching to her.
SUMIRESAKURAKOMI TANABE
SUMIRESAKURAKOMI TANABE
HOTAKA!!!

CITY 11 / END

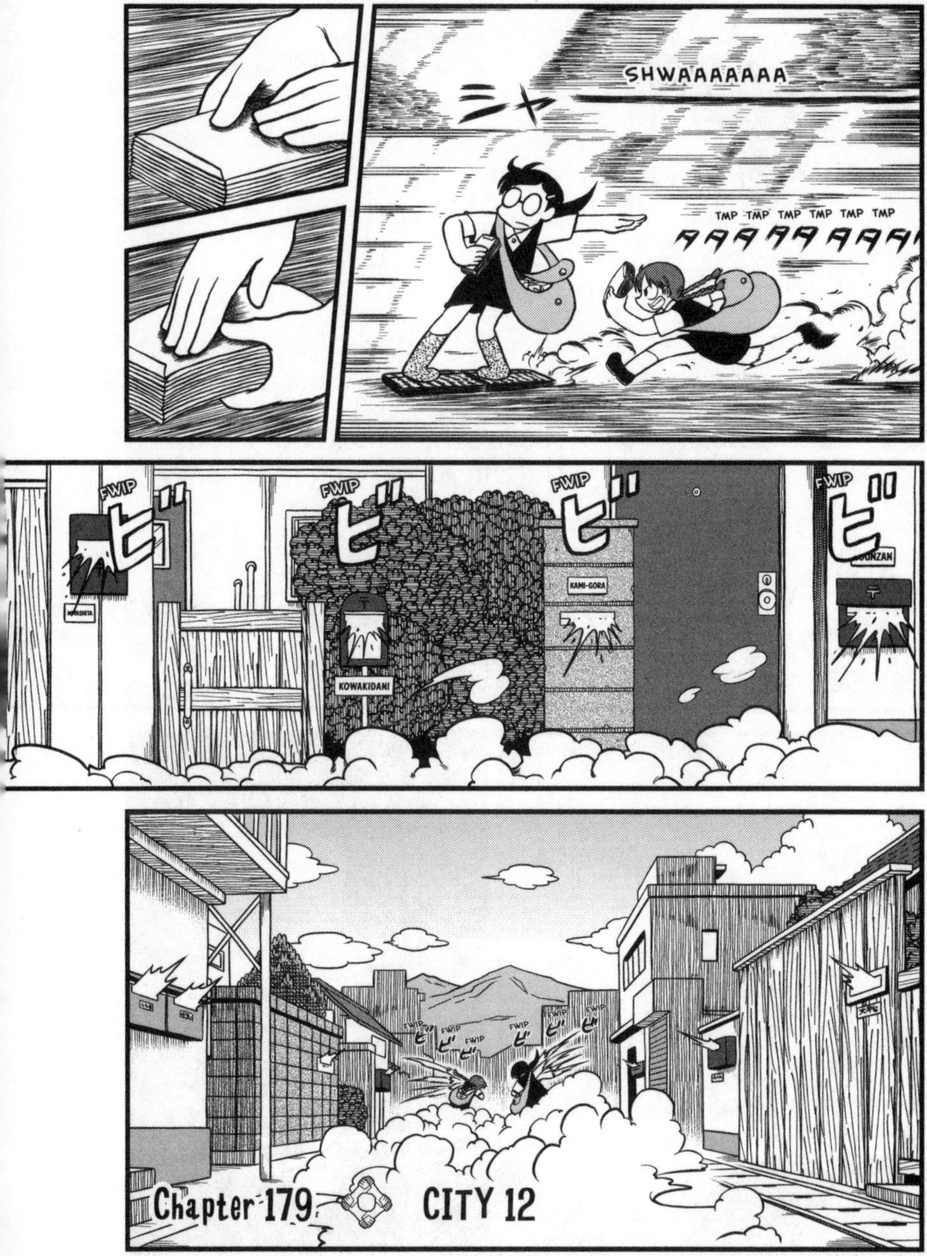
SHWAAAAAAA
TMP TMP TMP TMP TMP TMP
FWIP
KAMI-GORA
FWIP
FWIP
KOWAKIDANI
FWIP
FWIP
FWIP
FWIP
FWIP
Chapter 179 CITY 12

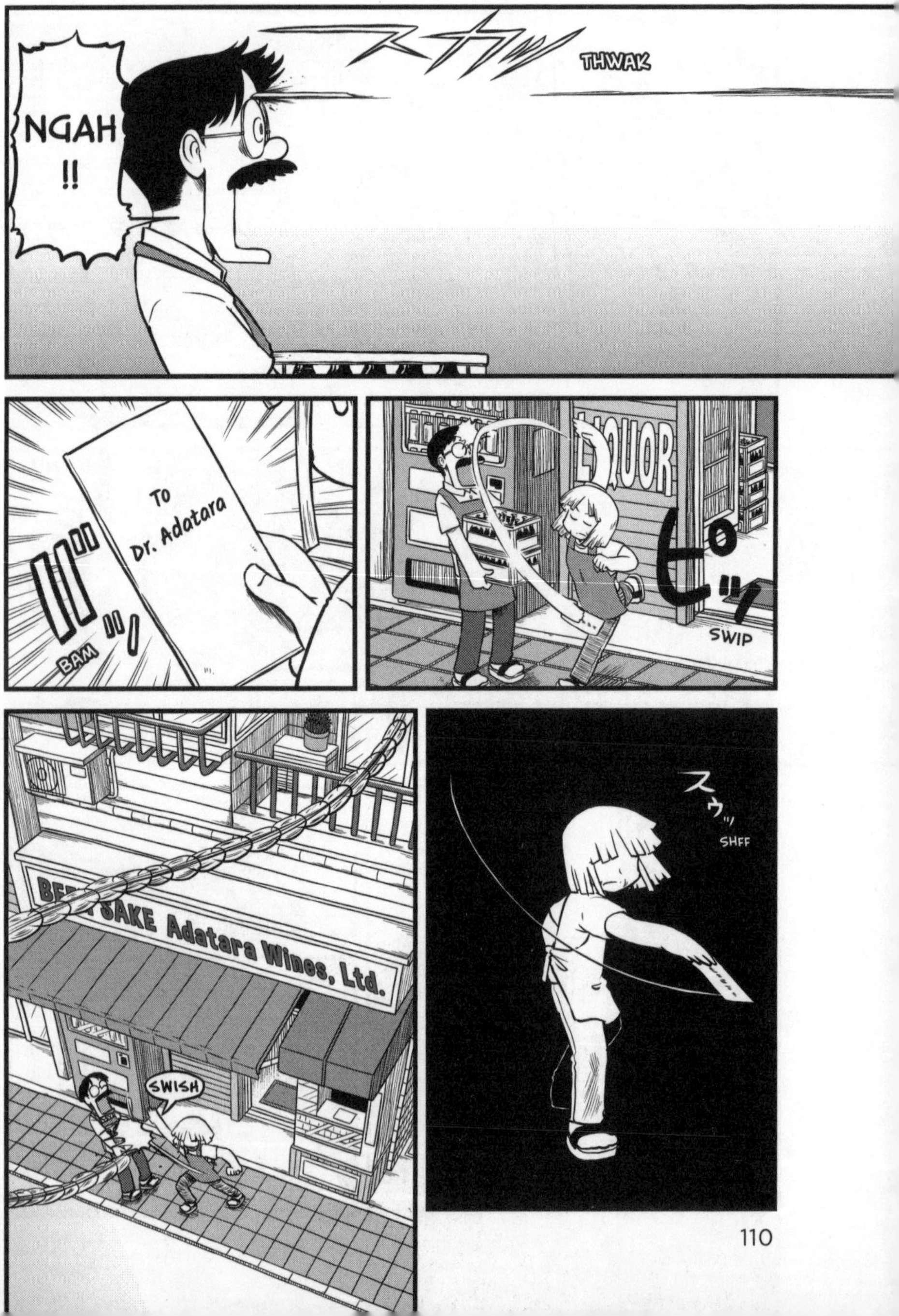
NGAH !!
スカッ
THWAK
LIQUOR
ピッ
SWIP
To Dr. Adatara
BAM
スウッ
SHFF
SAKE Adatara Wines, Ltd.
SWISH

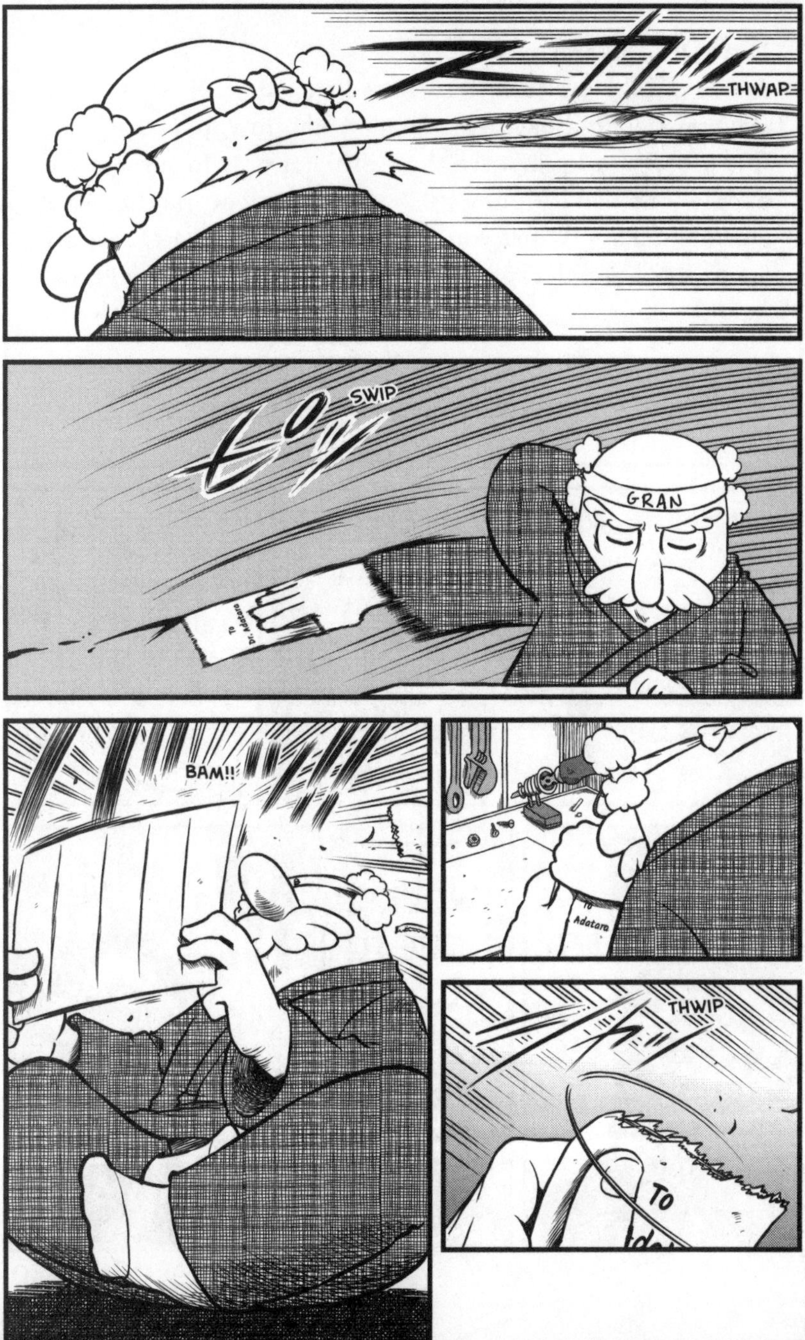
THWAP
SWIP
GRAN
To Dr. Adatara
To Adatara
THWIP
To
BAM!!

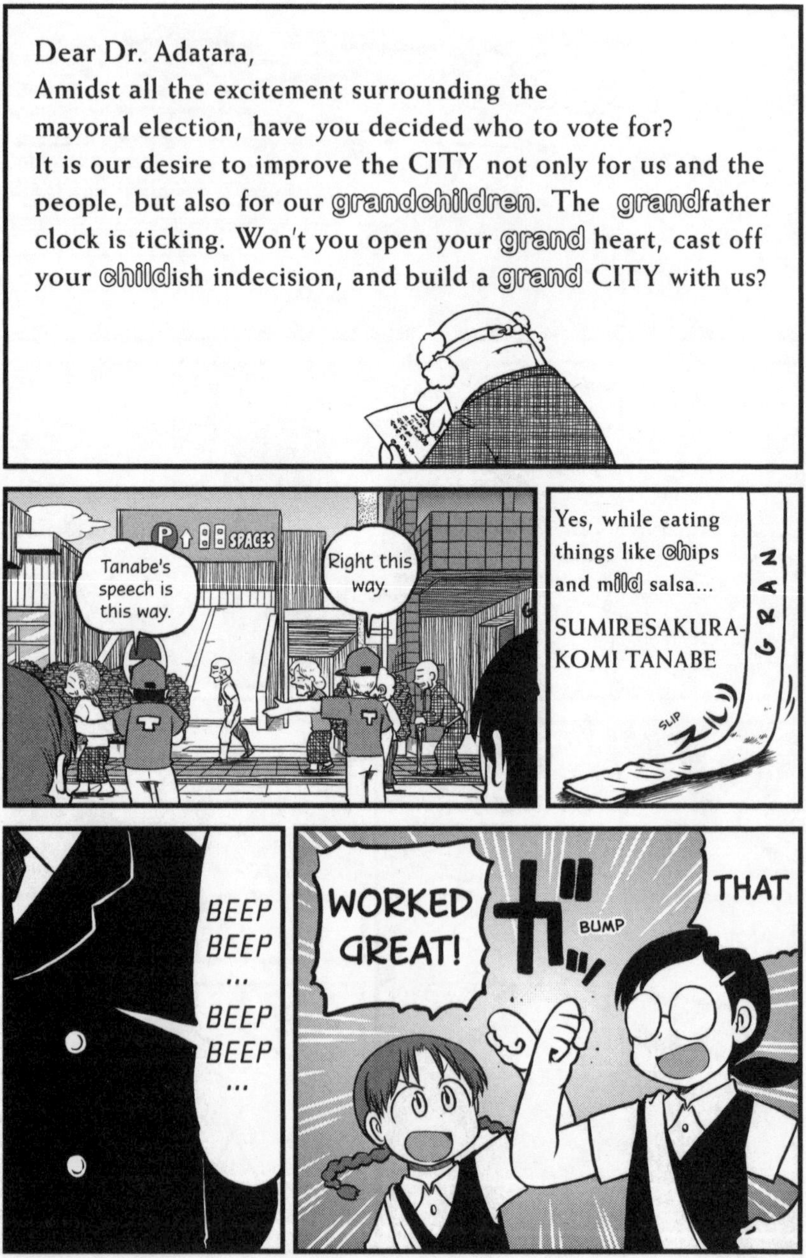
Dear Dr. Adatara,
Amidst all the excitement surrounding the mayoral election, have you decided who to vote for? It is our desire to improve the CITY not only for us and the people, but also for our grandchildren. The grandfather clock is ticking. Won't you open your grand heart, cast off your childish indecision, and build a grand CITY with us?
Yes, while eating things like chips and mild salsa...
SUMIRESAKURA-KOMI TANABE
GRAN
SLIP
SPACES
Right this way.
Tanabe's speech is this way.
THAT
WORKED GREAT!
BUMP
BEEP BEEP ... BEEP BEEP ...

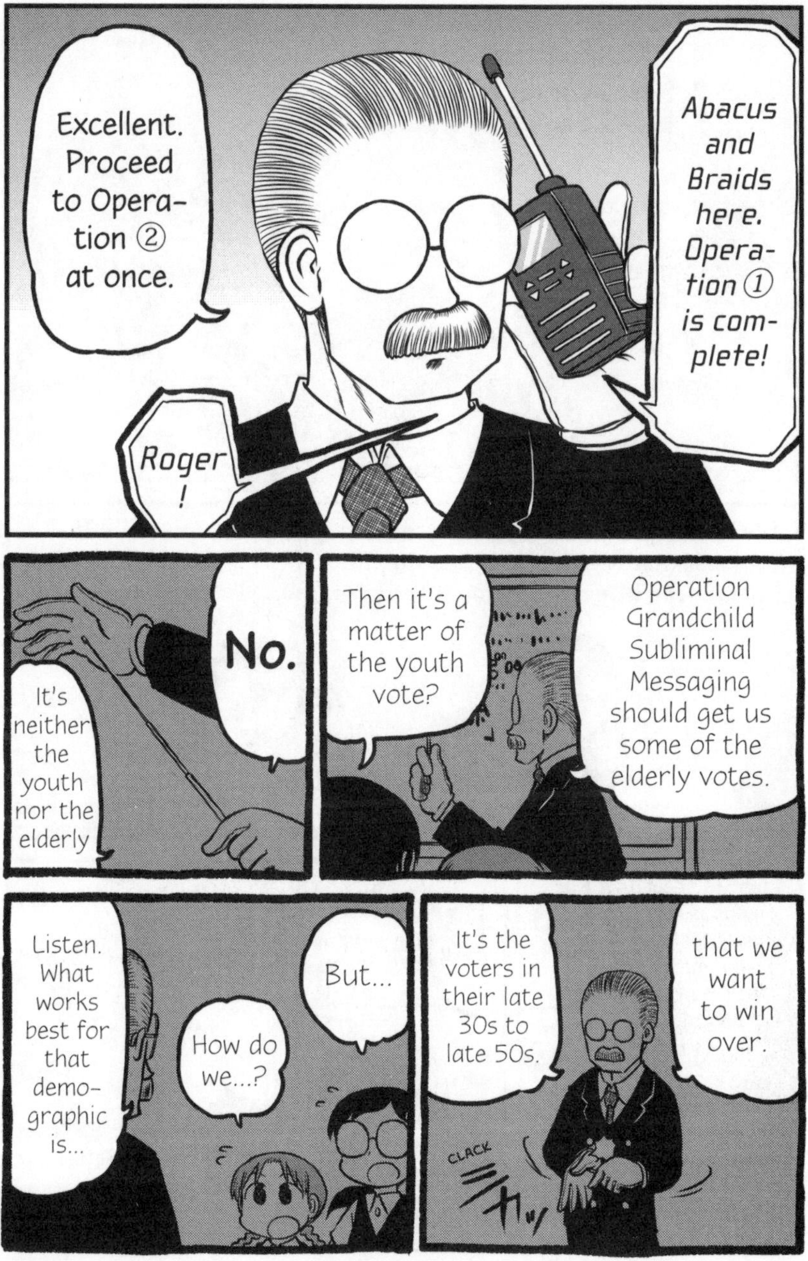
Abacus and Braids here. Operation ① is complete!
Excellent. Proceed to Operation ② at once.
Roger!
Operation Grandchild Subliminal Messaging should get us some of the elderly votes.
Then it's a matter of the youth vote?
No.
It's neither the youth nor the elderly
that we want to win over.
It's the voters in their late 30s to late 50s.
CLACK
But...
How do we...?
Listen. What works best for that demographic is...

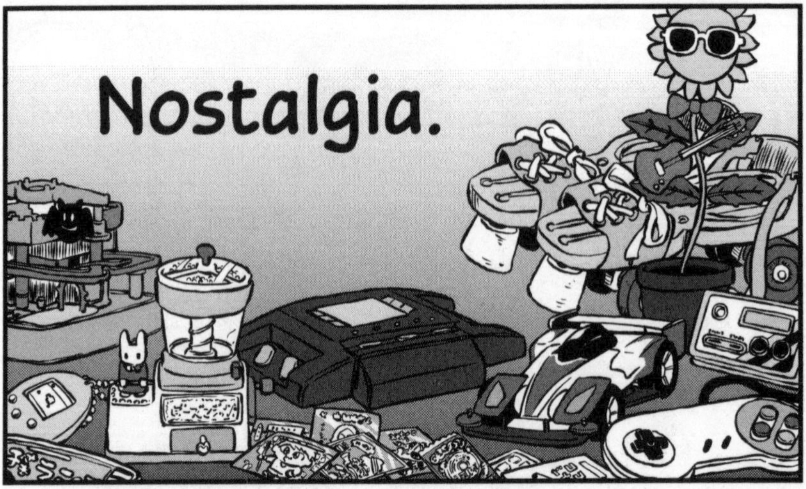
Nostalgia.

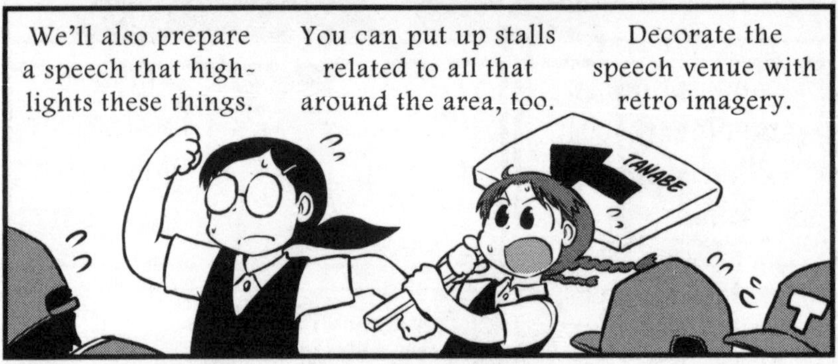
Decorate the speech venue with retro imagery.
You can put up stalls related to all that around the area, too.
We'll also prepare a speech that high-lights these things.
TANABE

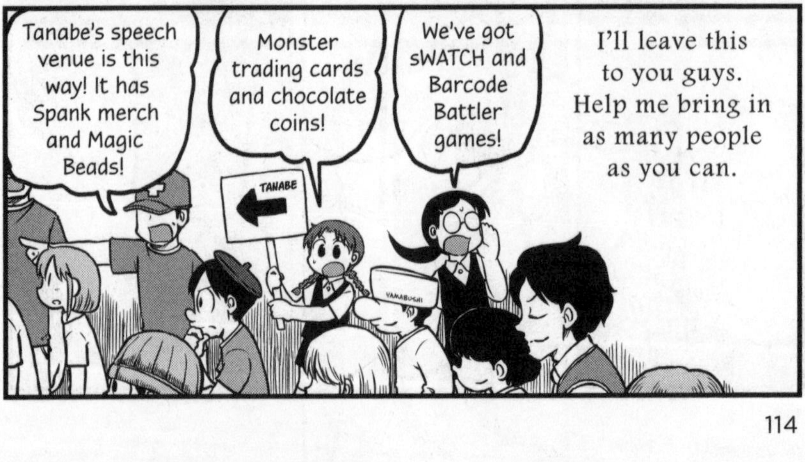
I'll leave this to you guys. Help me bring in as many people as you can.
We've got sWATCH and Barcode Battler games!
Monster trading cards and chocolate coins!
TANABE
Tanabe's speech venue is this way! It has Spank merch and Magic Beads!

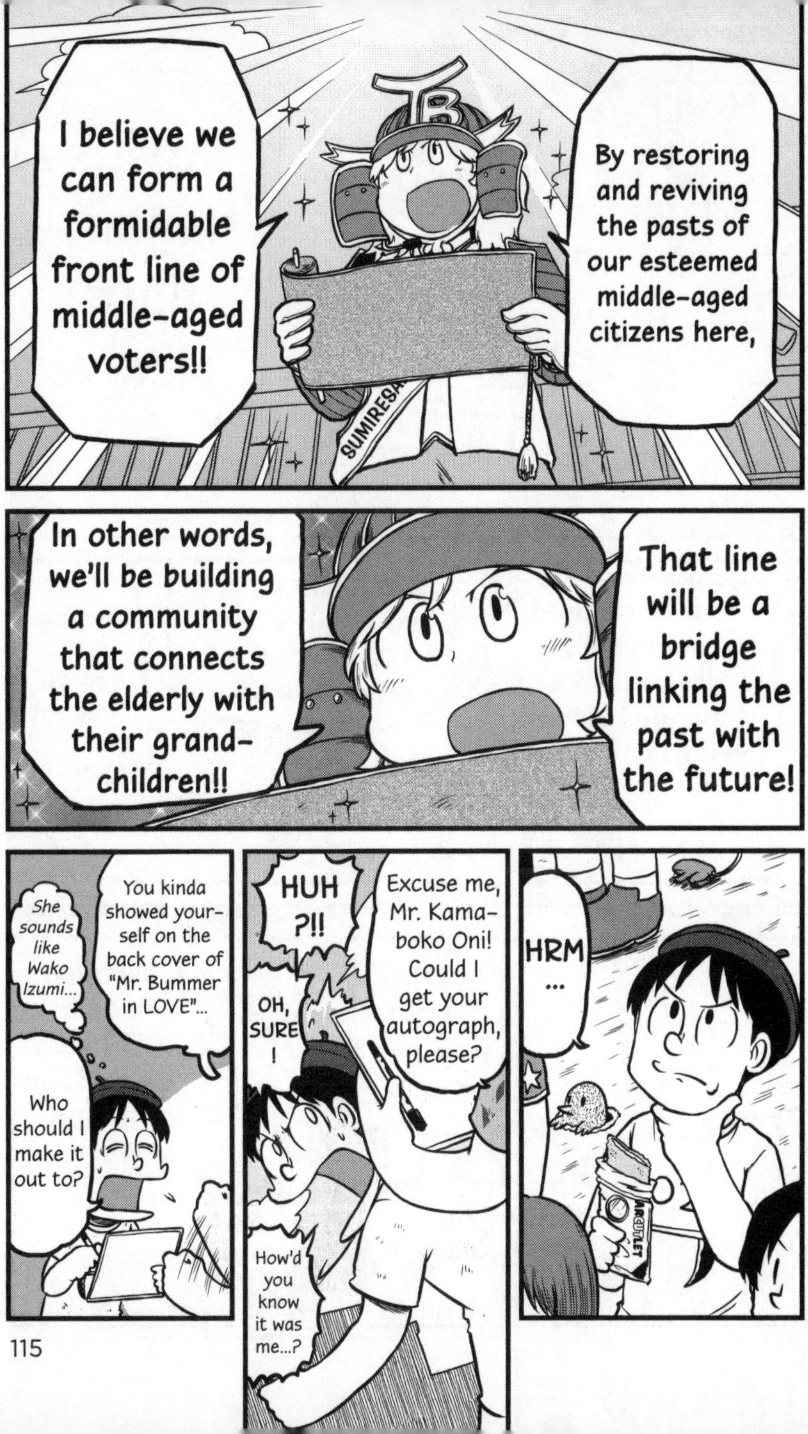
By restoring and reviving the pasts of our esteemed middle-aged citizens here,
I believe we can form a formidable front line of middle-aged voters!!
SUMIRESA
That line will be a bridge linking the past with the future!
In other words, we'll be building a community that connects the elderly with their grand-children!!
HRM ...
Excuse me, Mr. Kama-boko Oni! Could I get your autograph, please?
HUH ?!!
OH, SURE !
How'd you know it was me...?
You kinda showed your-self on the back cover of "Mr. Bummer in LOVE"...
She sounds like Wako Izumi...
Who should I make it out to?

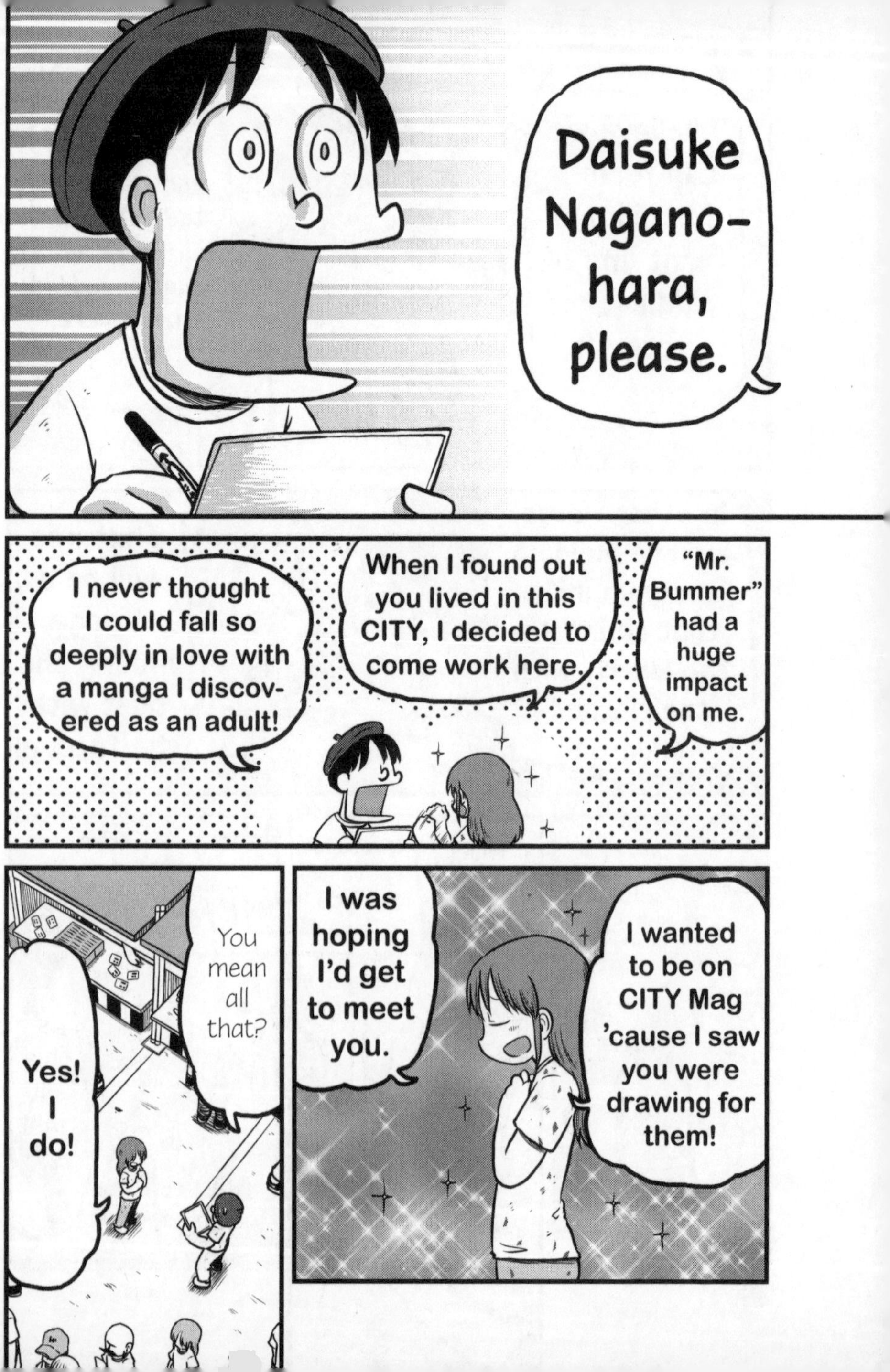
Daisuke Nagano-hara, please.
"Mr. Bummer" had a huge impact on me.
When I found out you lived in this CITY, I decided to come work here.
I never thought I could fall so deeply in love with a manga I discov-ered as an adult!
I wanted to be on CITY Mag 'cause I saw you were drawing for them!
I was hoping I'd get to meet you.
You mean all that?
Yes! I do!

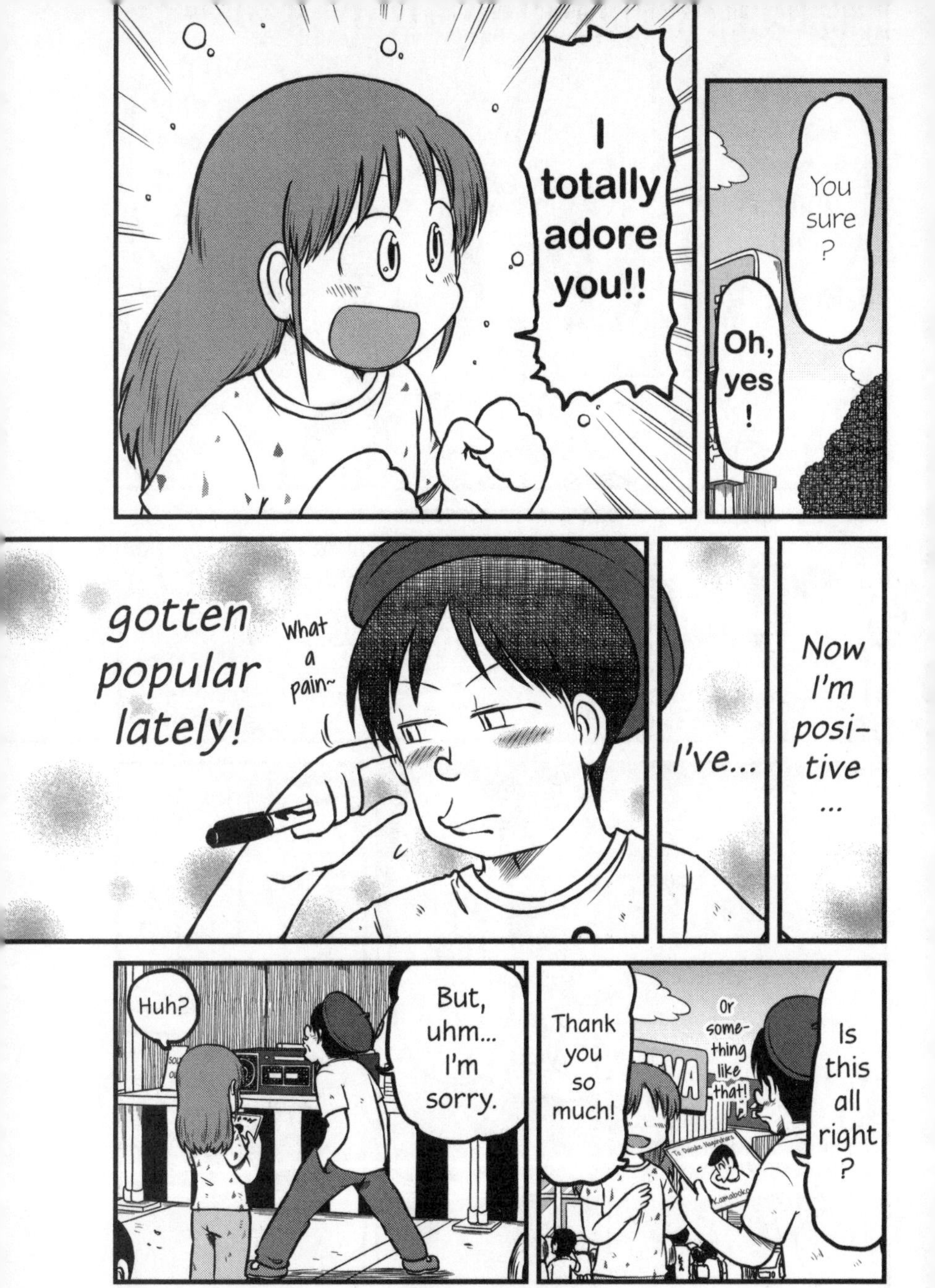
You sure?
Oh, yes!
I totally adore you!!
Now I'm positive...
I've...
gotten popular lately!
What a pain~
Is this all right?
Or something like that!
Thank you so much!
But, uhm... I'm sorry.
Huh?

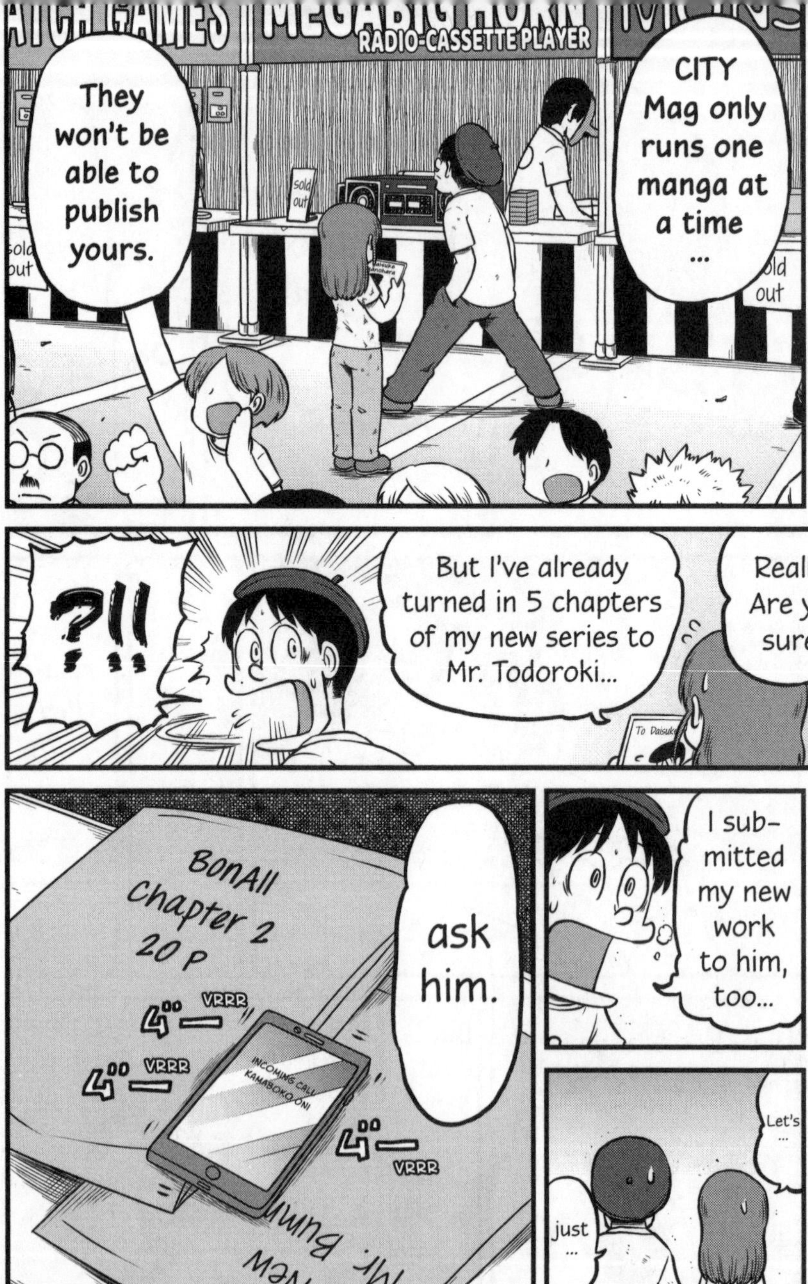
MEGABIG HORN
RADIO-CASSETTE PLAYER
CITY Mag only runs one manga at a time ...
They won't be able to publish yours.
sold out
sold out
sold out
Really? Are you sure?
But I've already turned in 5 chapters of my new series to Mr. Todoroki...
?!!
To Daisuke
I sub-mitted my new work to him, too...
Let's ...
just ...
ask him.
BonAll Chapter 2 20 P
VRRR
VRRR
INCOMING CALL KAMABOKO ONI
VRRR
New Mr. Bunn

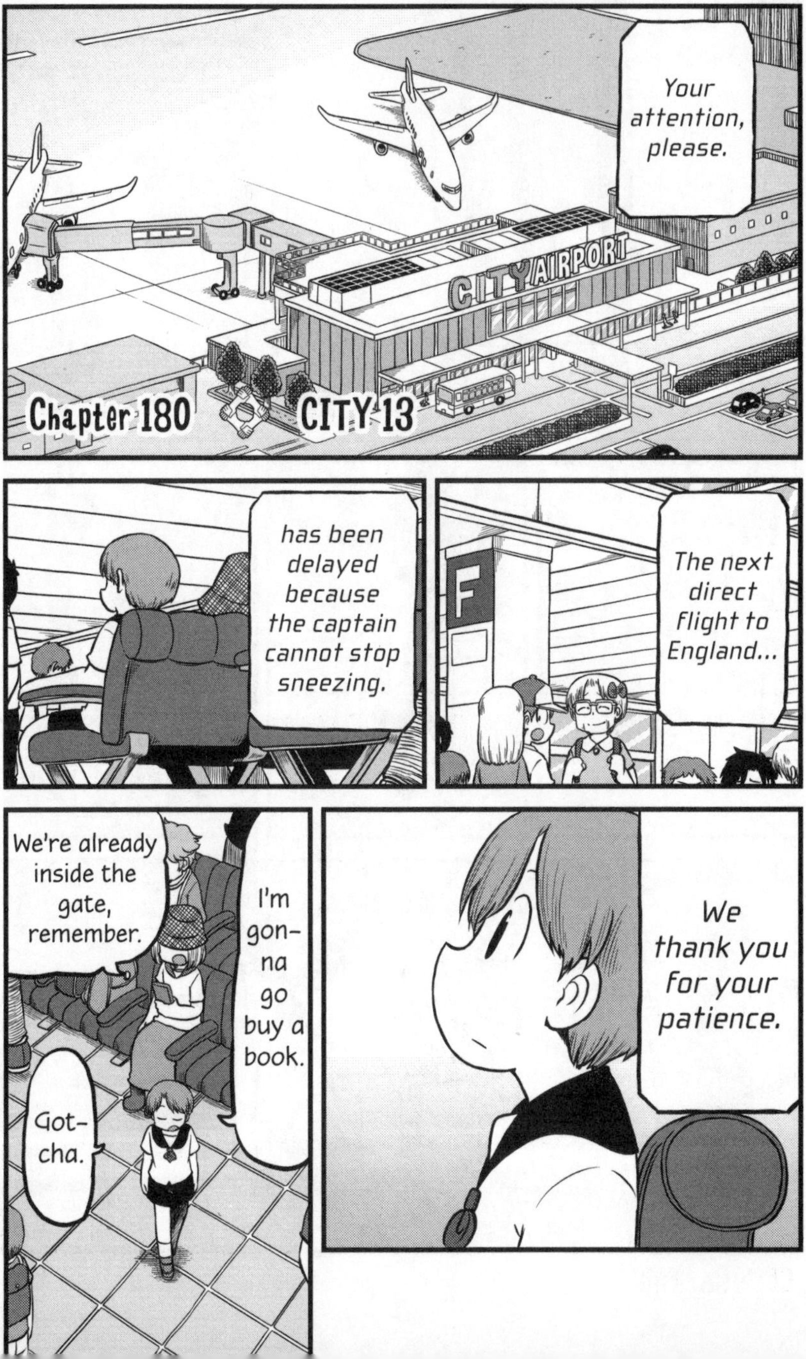
Your attention, please.
CITY AIRPORT
Chapter 180
CITY 13
The next direct flight to England...
F
has been delayed because the captain cannot stop sneezing.
We thank you for your patience.
I'm gon-na go buy a book.
We're already inside the gate, remember.
Got-cha.

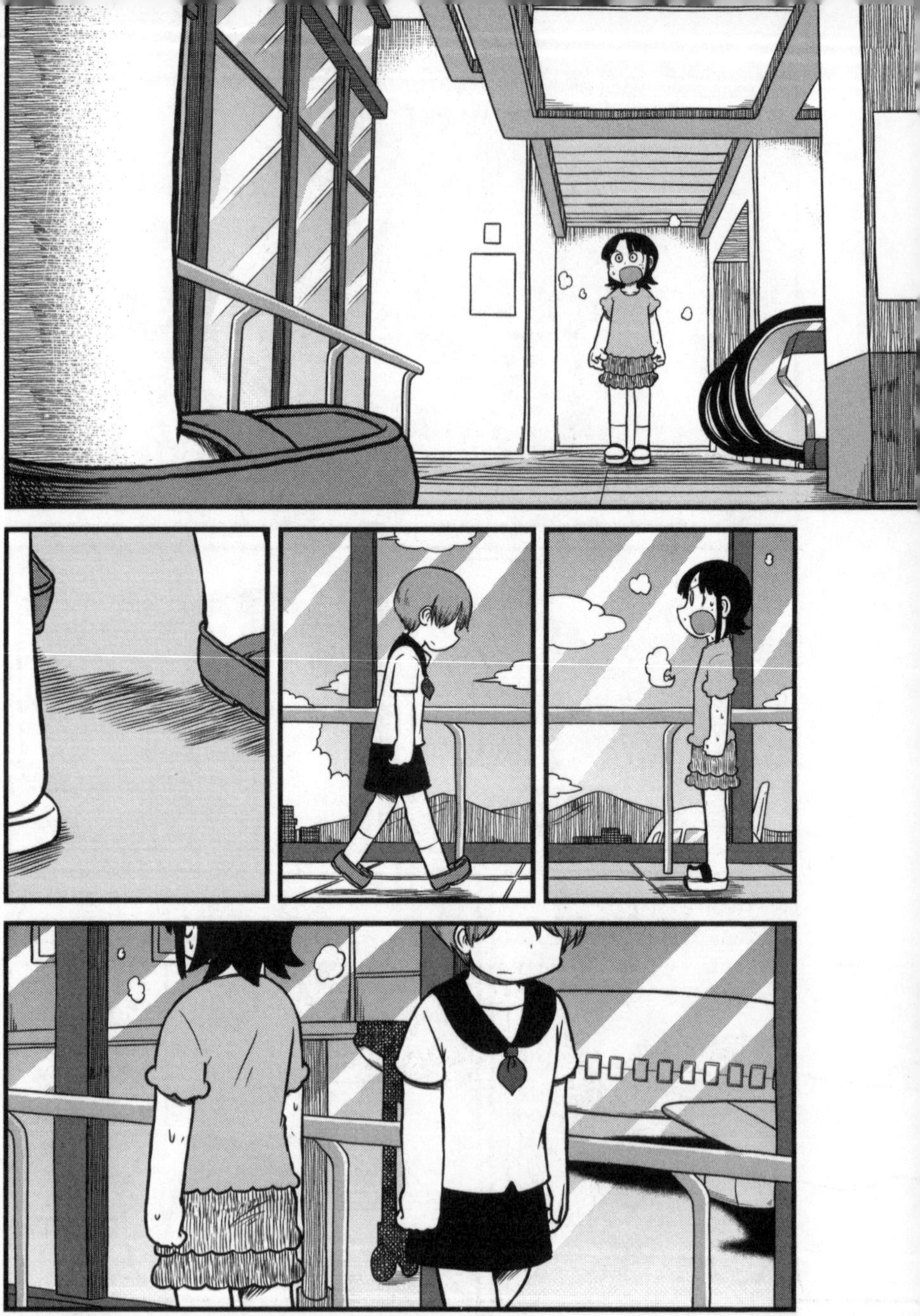

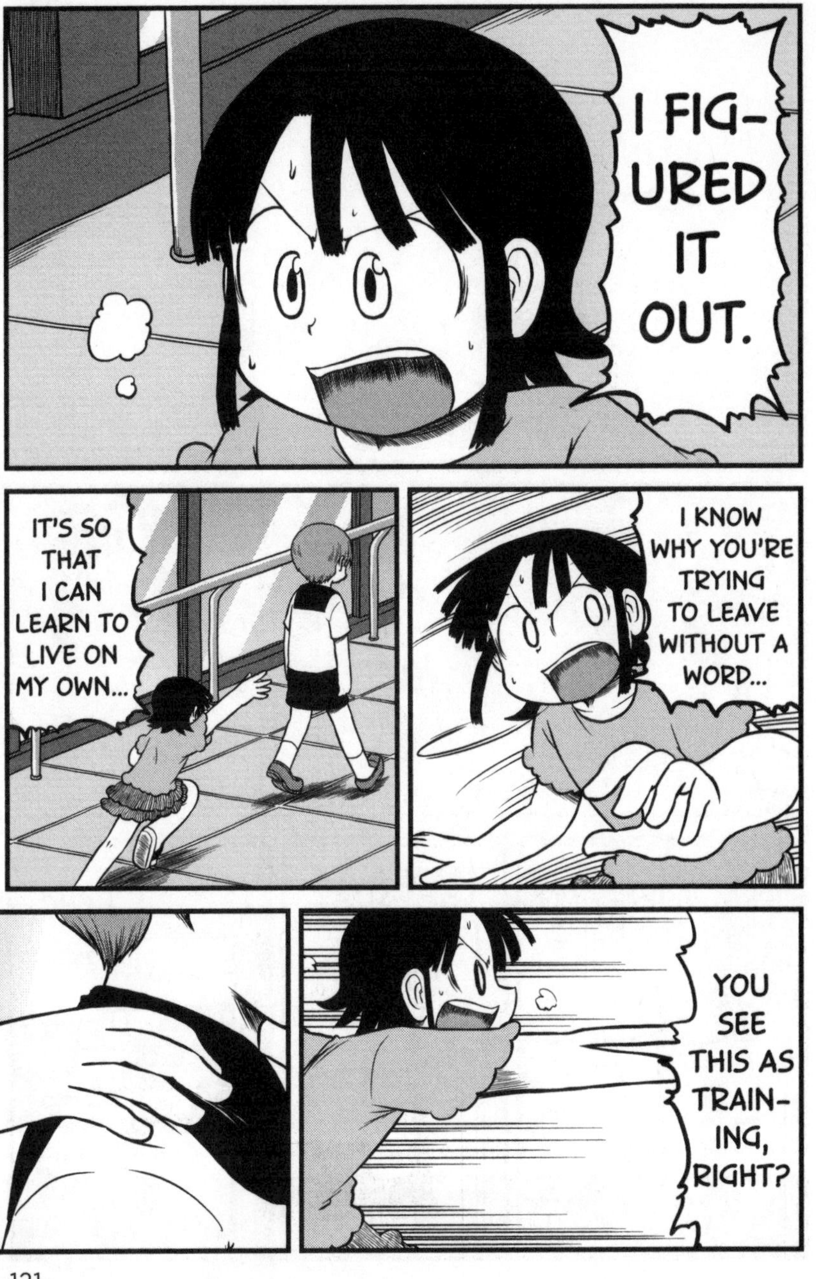
I FIG-URED IT OUT.
I KNOW WHY YOU'RE TRYING TO LEAVE WITHOUT A WORD...
IT'S SO THAT I CAN LEARN TO LIVE ON MY OWN...
YOU SEE THIS AS TRAIN-ING, RIGHT?

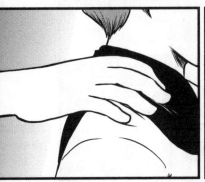

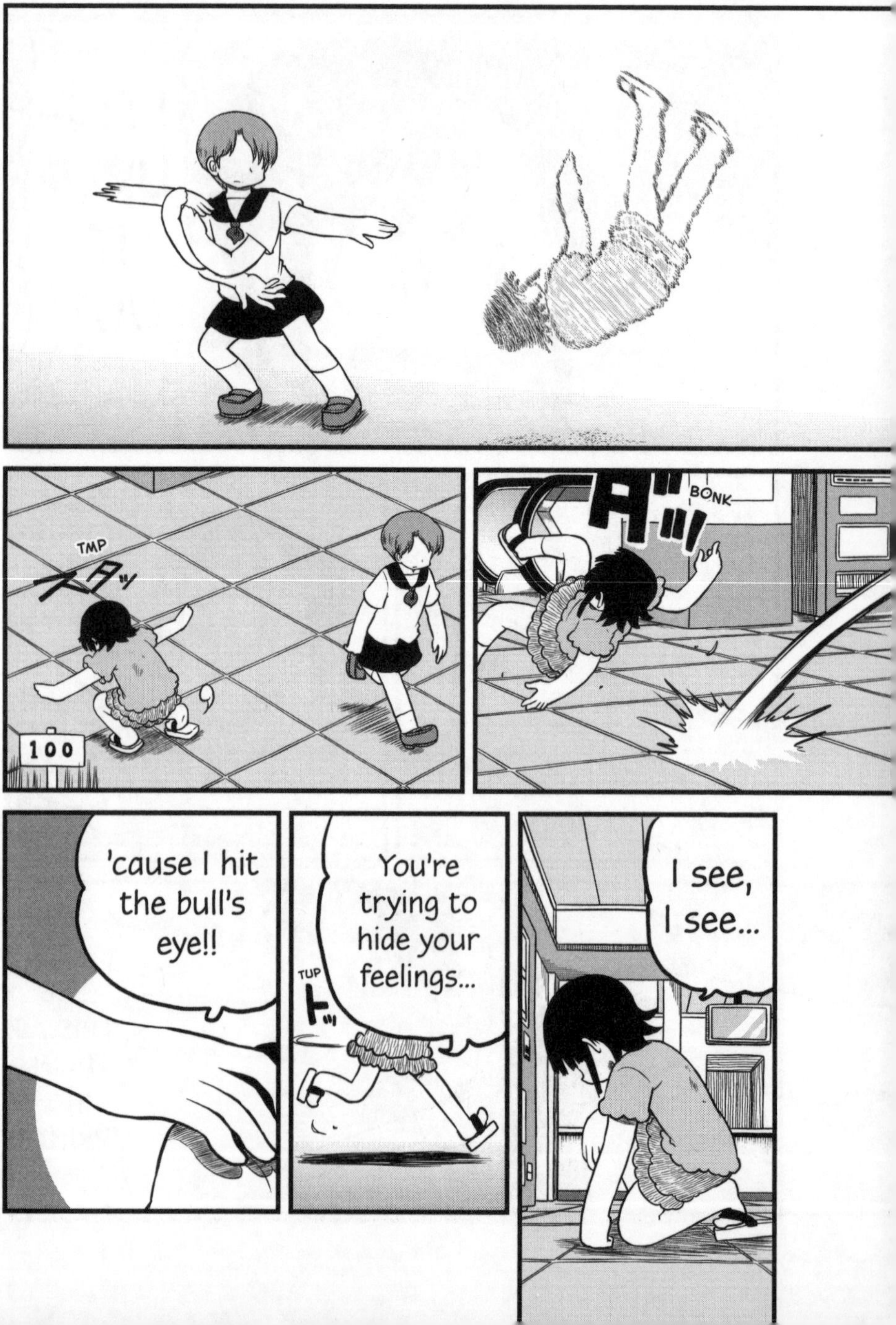
BONK
TMP
100
I see, I see...
You're trying to hide your feelings...
TUP
'cause I hit the bull's eye!!

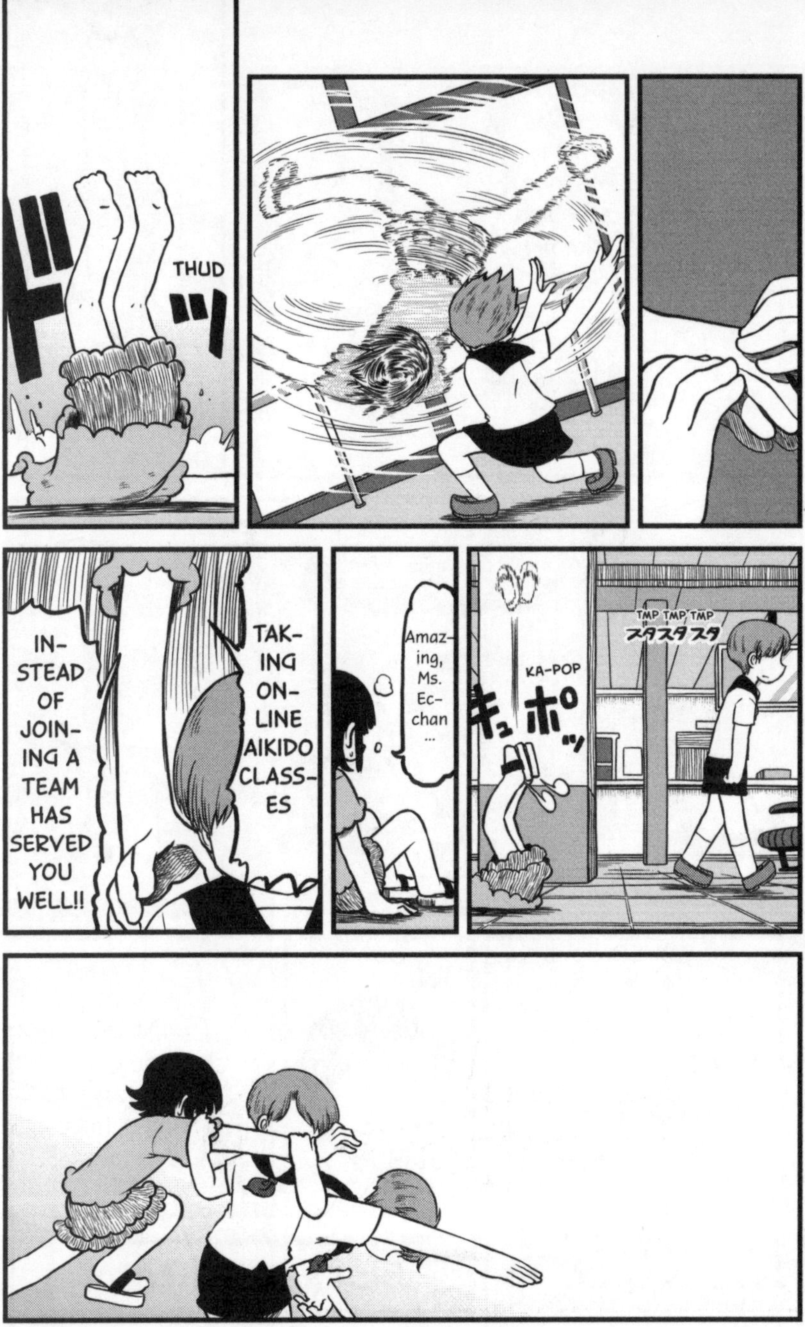
THUD
ドッ
TMP TMP TMP
スタスタスタ
KA-POP
キュポッ
Amaz-ing, Ms. Ec-chan ...
TAK-ING ON-LINE AIKIDO CLASS-ES
IN-STEAD OF JOIN-ING A TEAM HAS SERVED YOU WELL!!

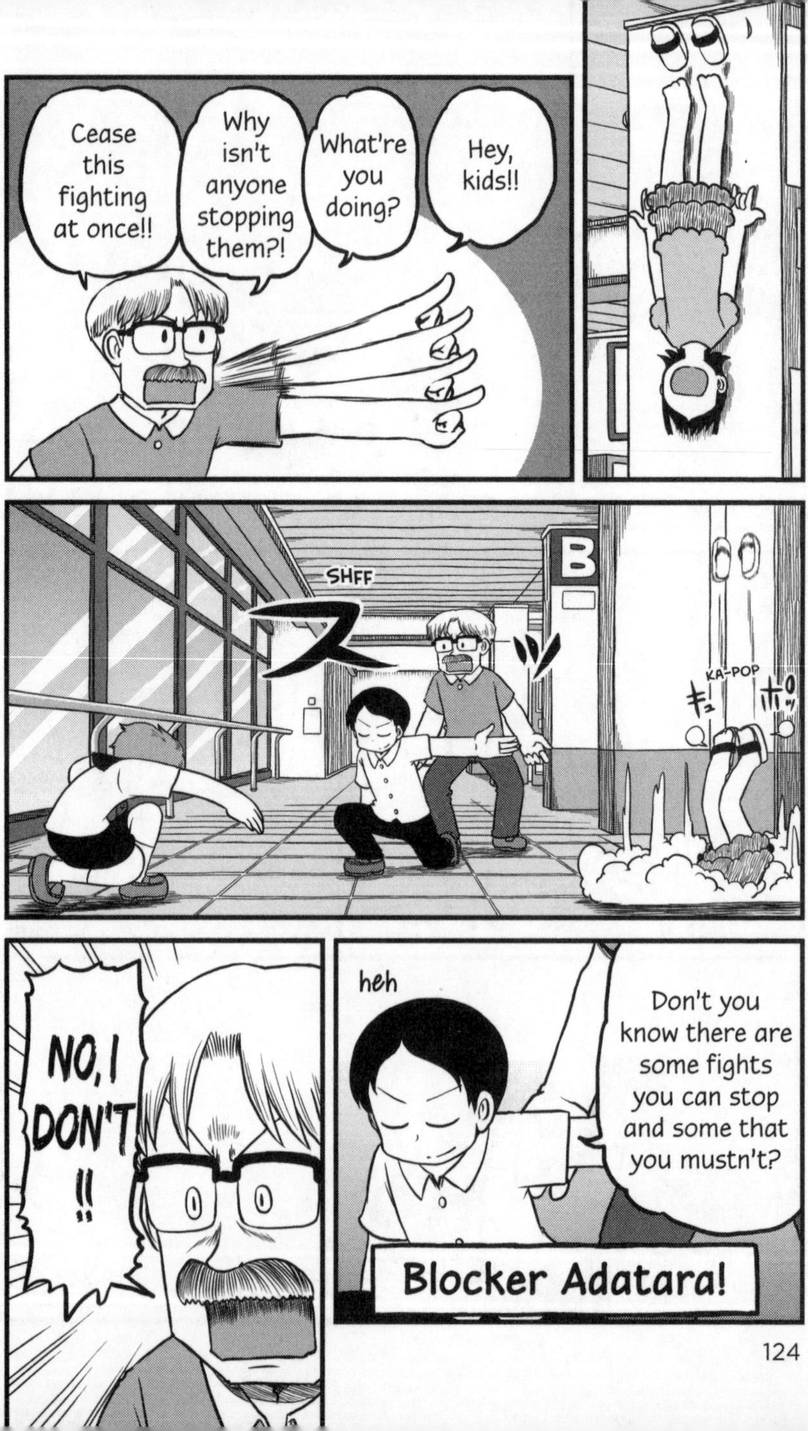
Hey, kids!!
What're you doing?
Why isn't anyone stopping them?!
Cease this fighting at once!!
KA-POP
SHFF
heh
Don't you know there are some fights you can stop and some that you mustn't?
Blocker Adatara!
NO, I DON'T!!

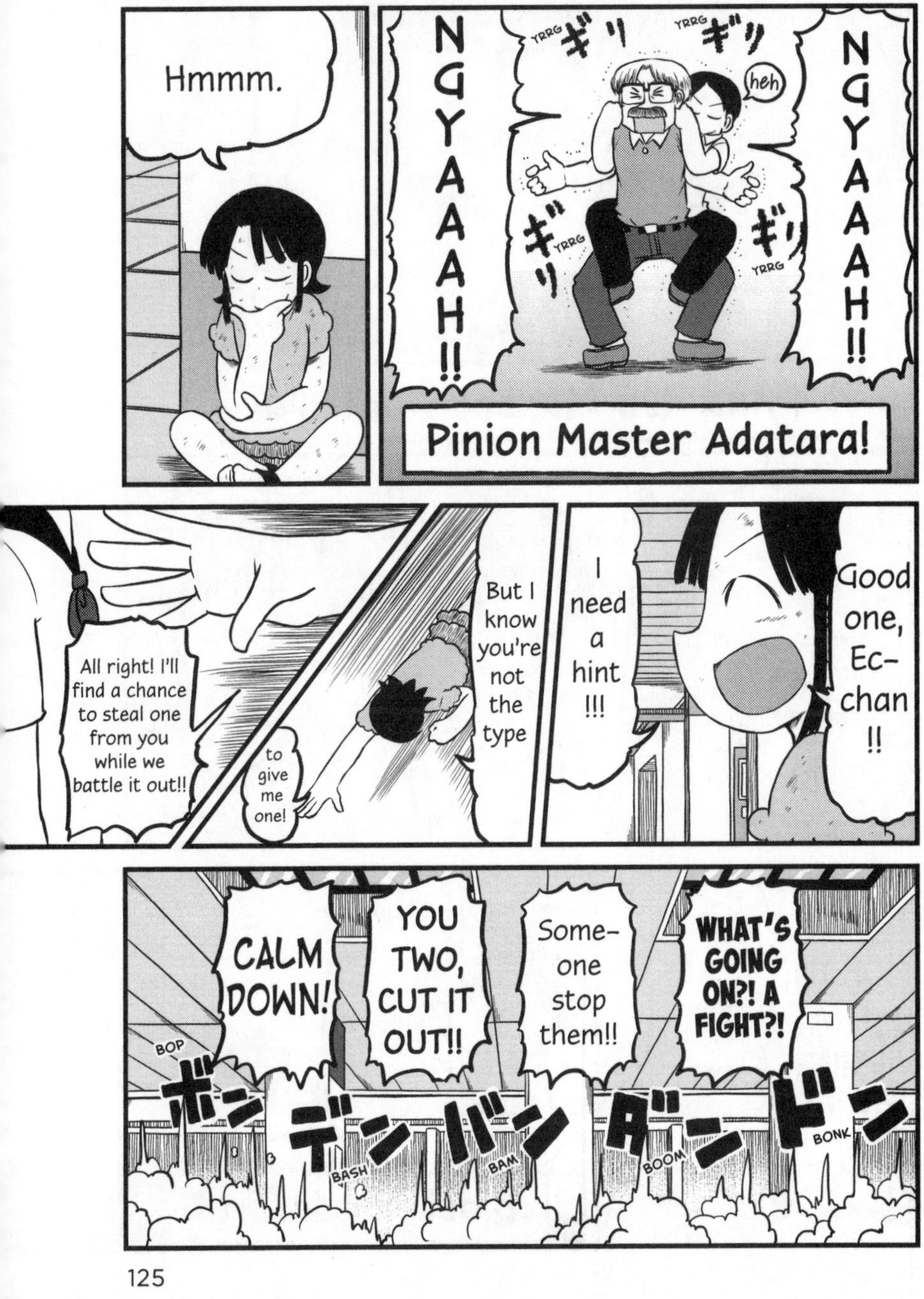
NGYAAAAH!!
YRRG ギリ
heh
YRRG ギリ
ギリ YRRG
ギリ YRRG
NGYAAAAH!!
Pinion Master Adatara!
Hmmm.
Good one, Ec-chan!!
I need a hint!!!
But I know you're not the type
to give me one!
All right! I'll find a chance to steal one from you while we battle it out!!
WHAT'S GOING ON?! A FIGHT?!
Someone stop them!!
YOU TWO, CUT IT OUT!!
CALM DOWN!
ドン BONK
ダン BOOM
バン BAM
デン BASH
ボン BOP

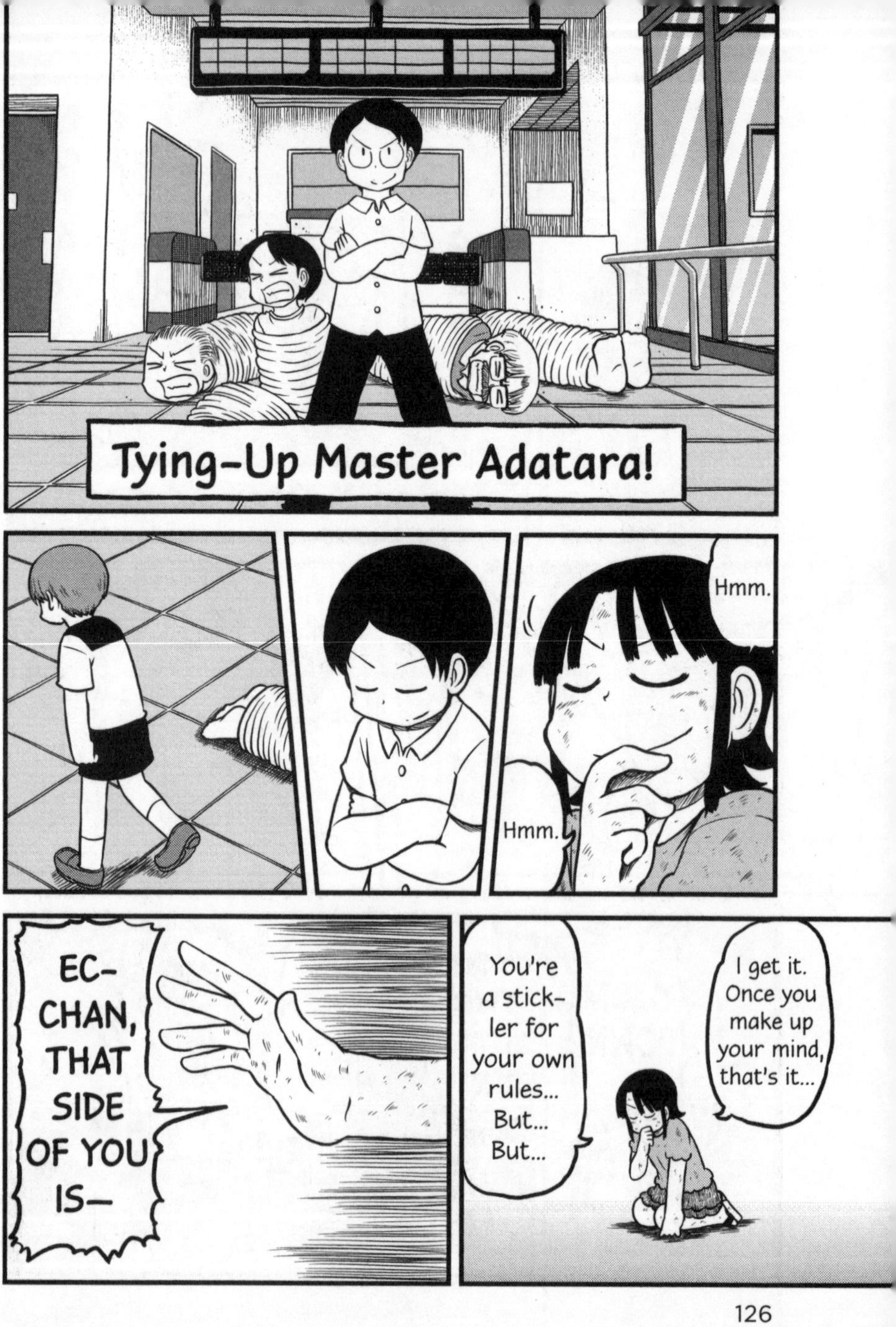
Tying-Up Master Adatara!
Hmm.
Hmm.
I get it. Once you make up your mind, that's it...
You're a stick-ler for your own rules... But... But...
EC-CHAN, THAT SIDE OF YOU IS—

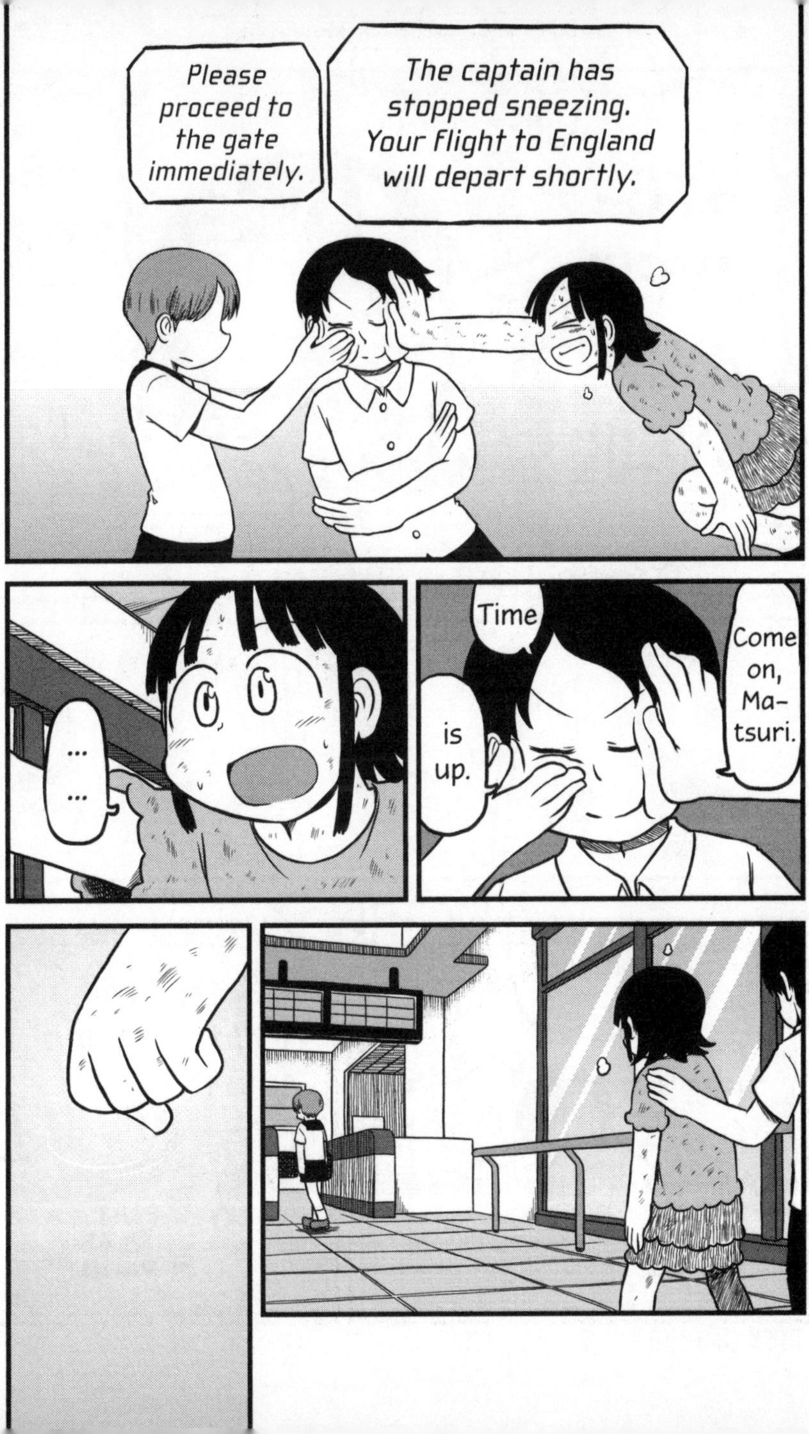
The captain has stopped sneezing. Your flight to England will depart shortly.
Please proceed to the gate immediately.
Come on, Ma-tsuri.
Time
is up.
... ...

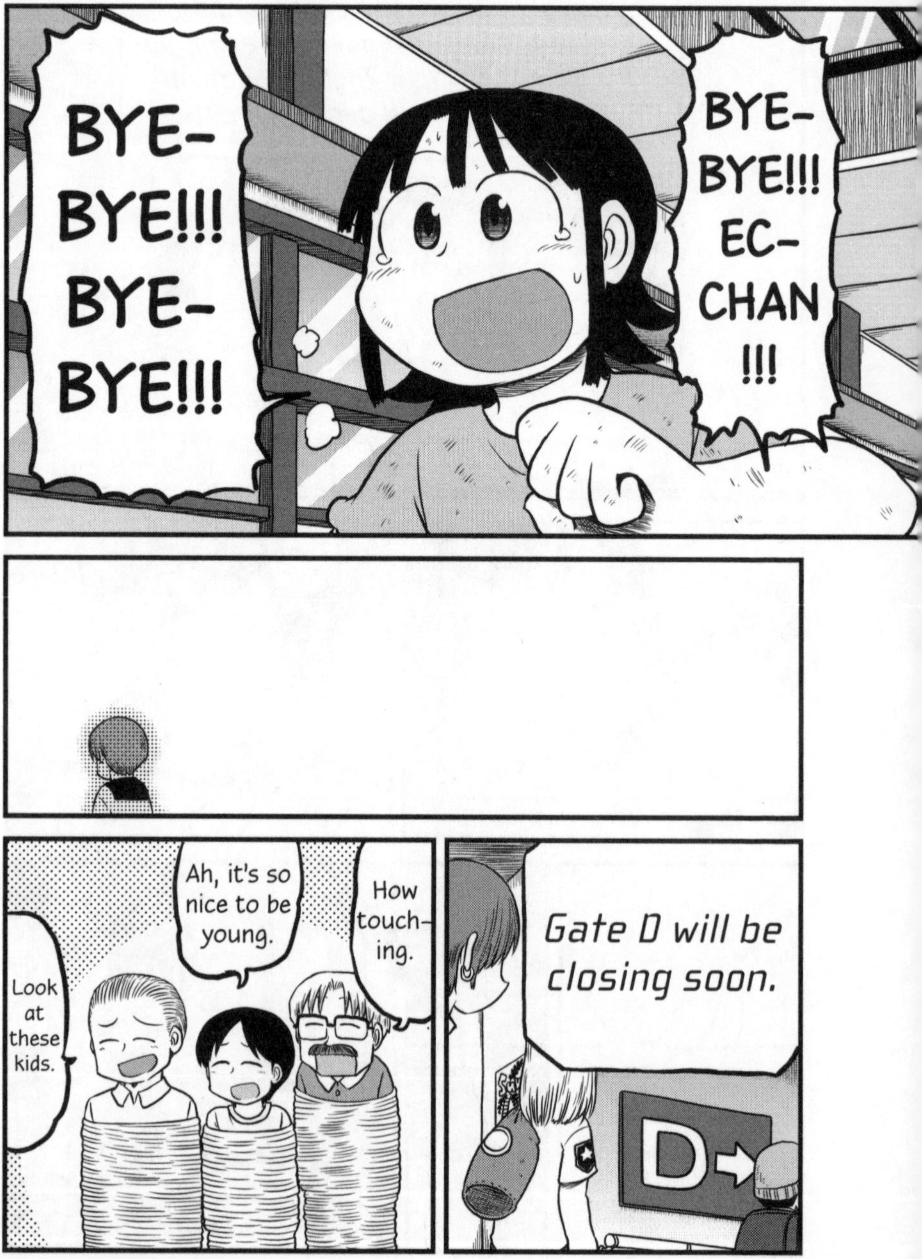
BYE-BYE!!! EC-CHAN!!!
BYE-BYE!!! BYE-BYE!!!
Gate D will be closing soon.
D
How touch-ing.
Ah, it's so nice to be young.
Look at these kids.

CITY 13 / END

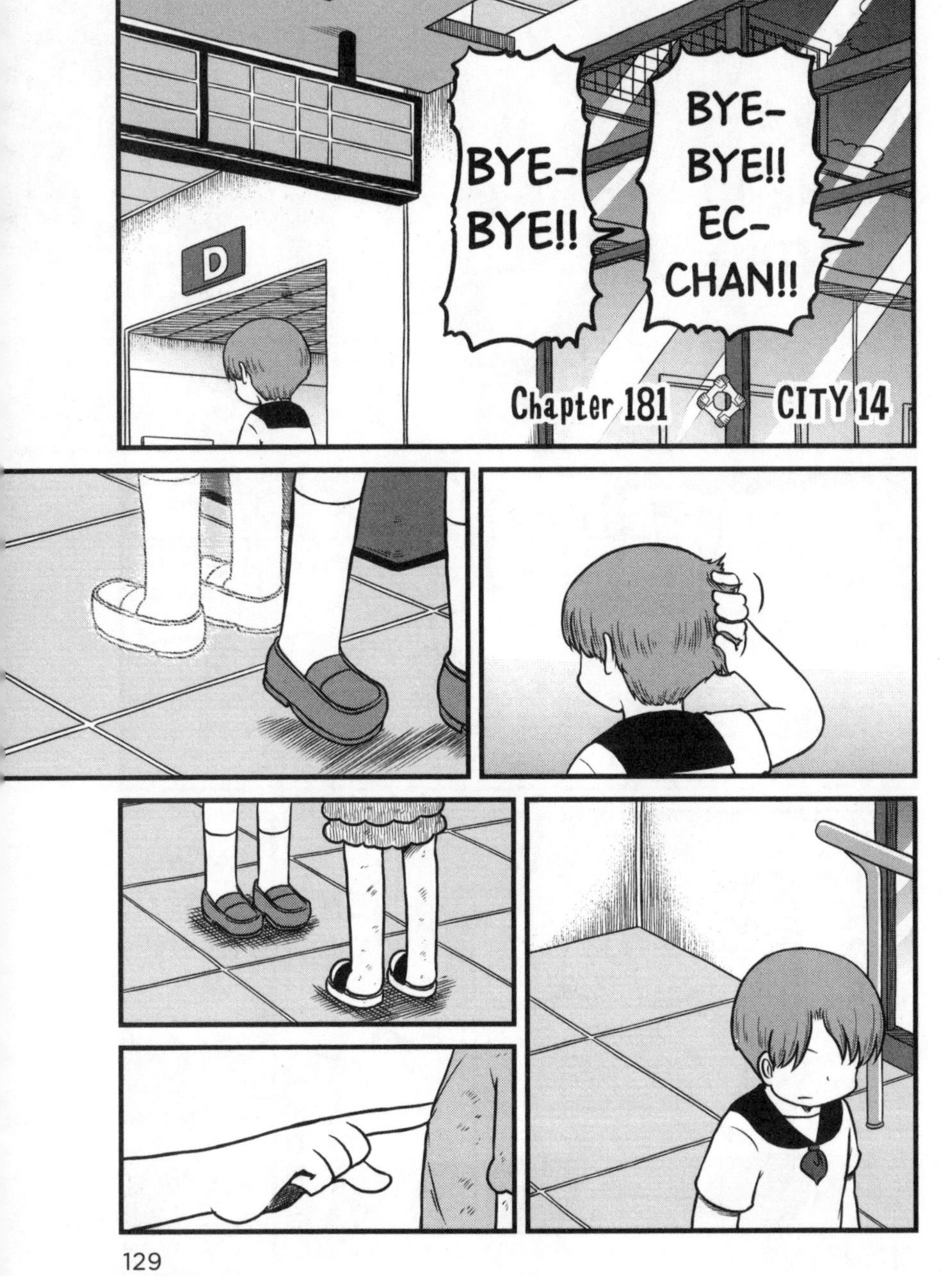
BYE-BYE!! EC-CHAN!!
BYE-BYE!!
Chapter 181 CITY 14

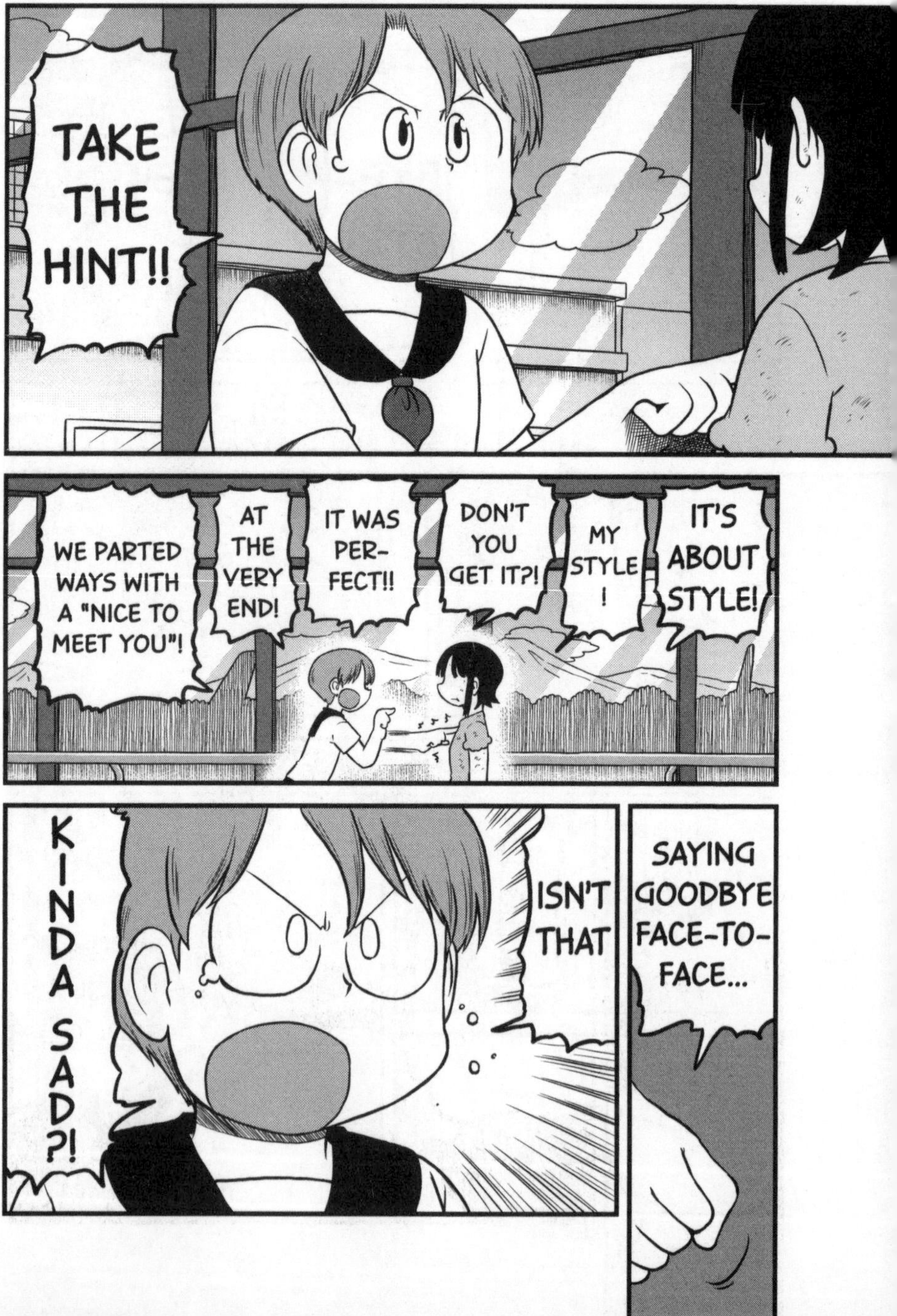
TAKE THE HINT!!
IT'S ABOUT STYLE!
MY STYLE!
DON'T YOU GET IT?!
IT WAS PERFECT!!
AT THE VERY END!
WE PARTED WAYS WITH A "NICE TO MEET YOU"!
SAYING GOODBYE FACE-TO-FACE...
ISN'T THAT
KINDA SAD?!

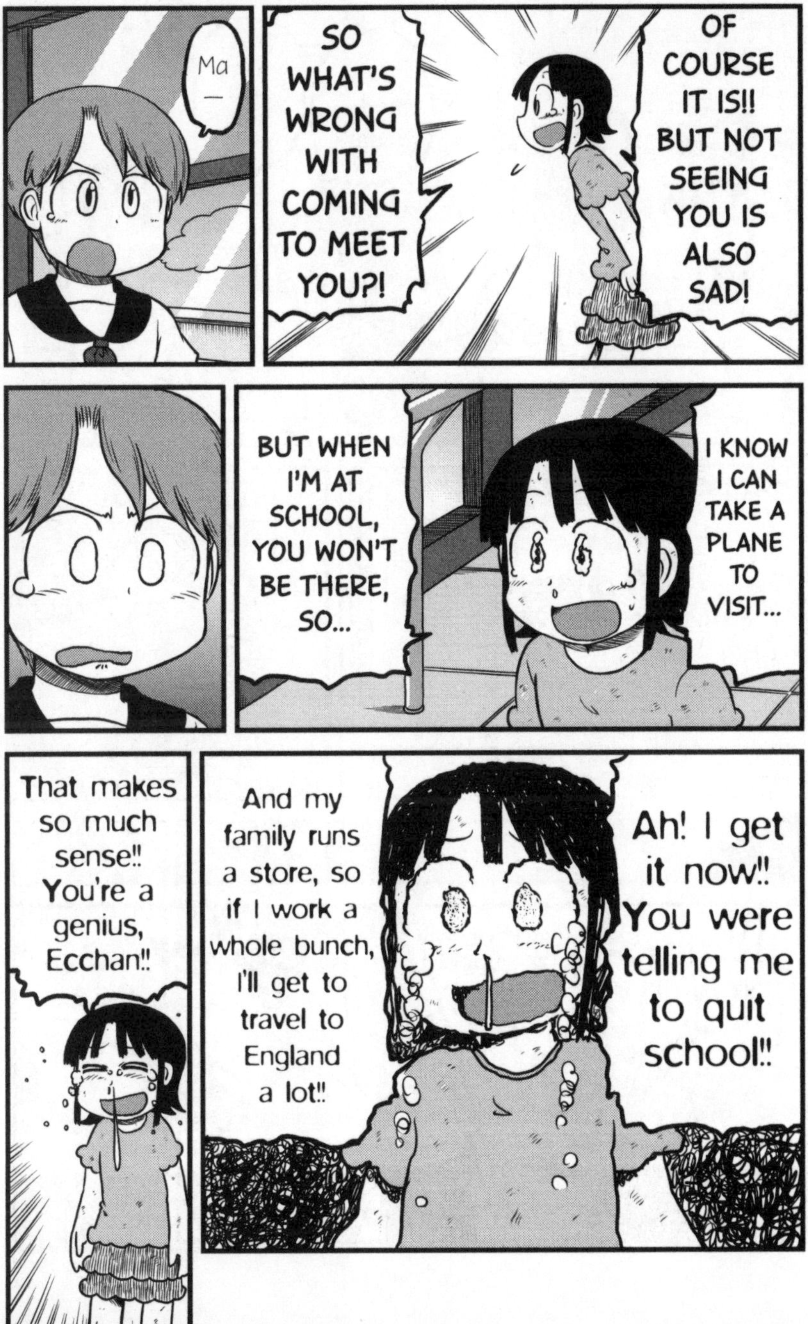
OF COURSE IT IS!! BUT NOT SEEING YOU IS ALSO SAD!
SO WHAT'S WRONG WITH COMING TO MEET YOU?!
Ma—
I KNOW I CAN TAKE A PLANE TO VISIT...
BUT WHEN I'M AT SCHOOL, YOU WON'T BE THERE, SO...
Ah! I get it now!! You were telling me to quit school!!
And my family runs a store, so if I work a whole bunch, I'll get to travel to England a lot!!
That makes so much sense!! You're a genius, Ecchan!!

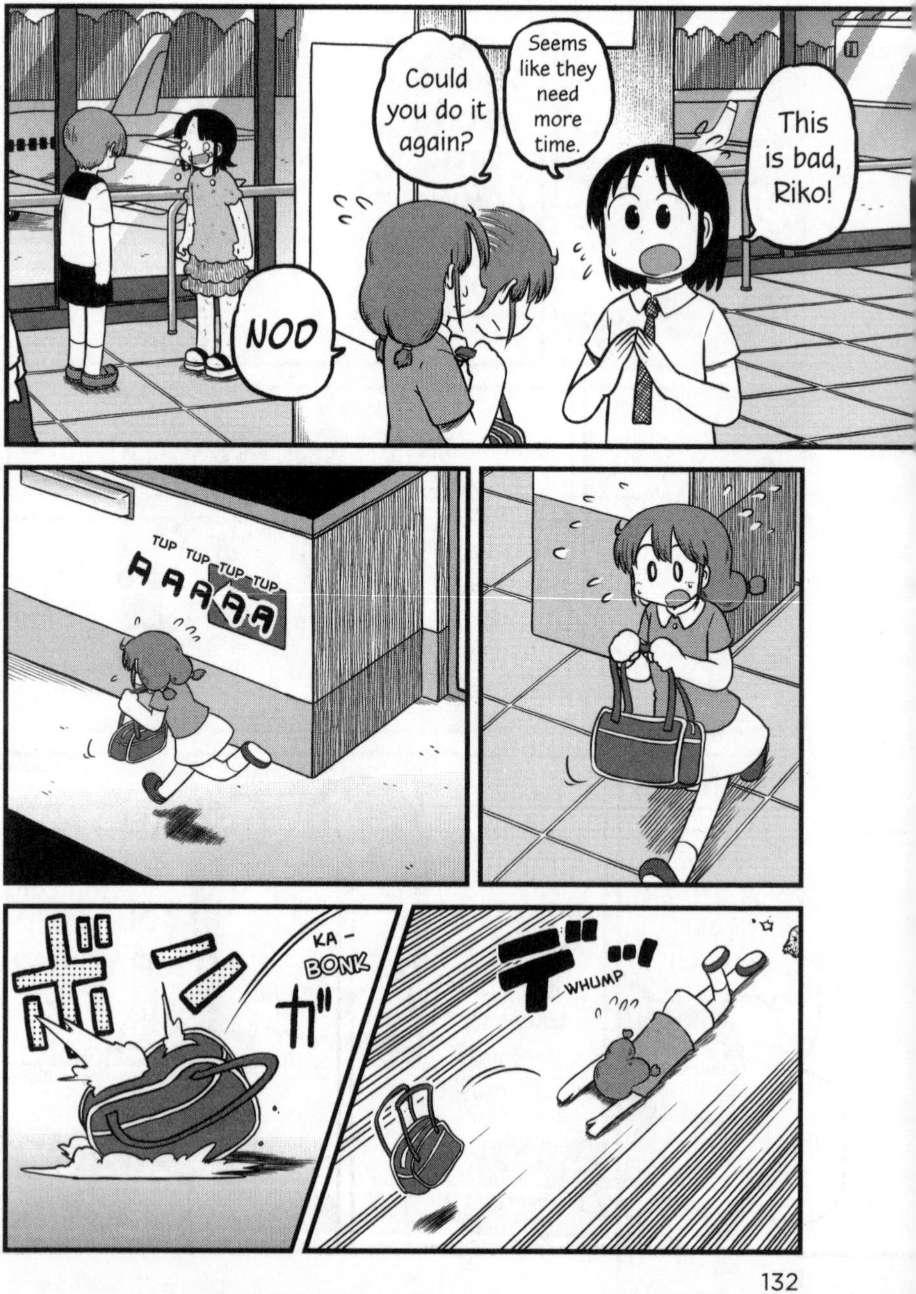
This is bad, Riko!
Seems like they need more time.
Could you do it again?
NOD
TUP TUP TUP TUP
WHUMP
KA-BONK
ボン
ガ

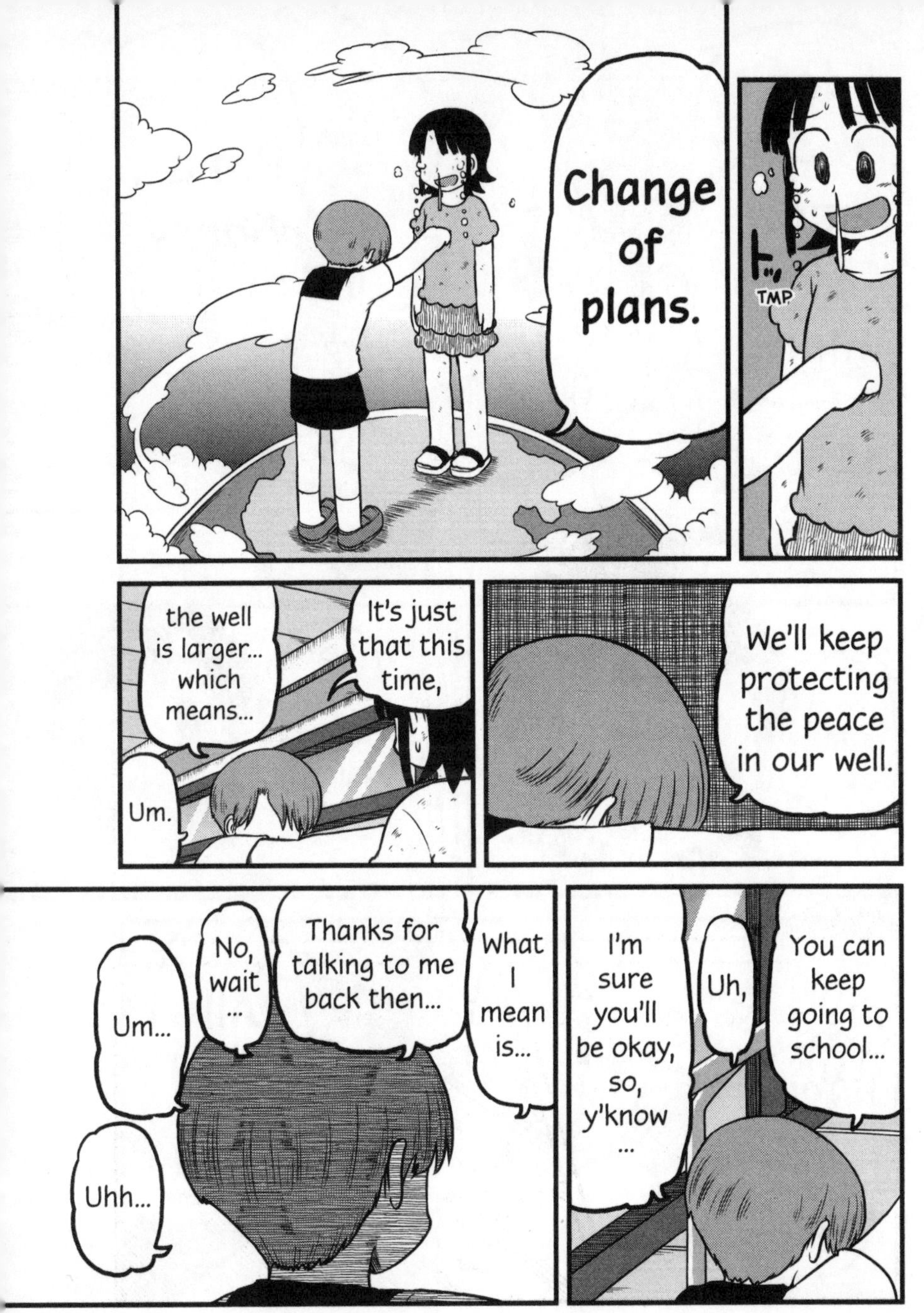
TMP
Change of plans.
We'll keep protecting the peace in our well.
It's just that this time,
the well is larger... which means...
Um.
You can keep going to school...
Uh,
I'm sure you'll be okay, so, y'know ...
What I mean is...
Thanks for talking to me back then...
No, wait ...
Um...
Uhh...

I don't really know anymore.

Haha... Sorry.

Yeah!

See ya, Matsuri.

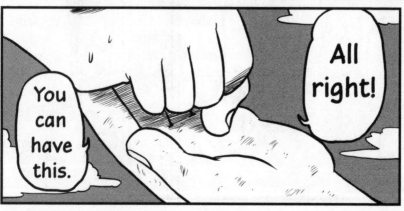

You can have this.

All right!

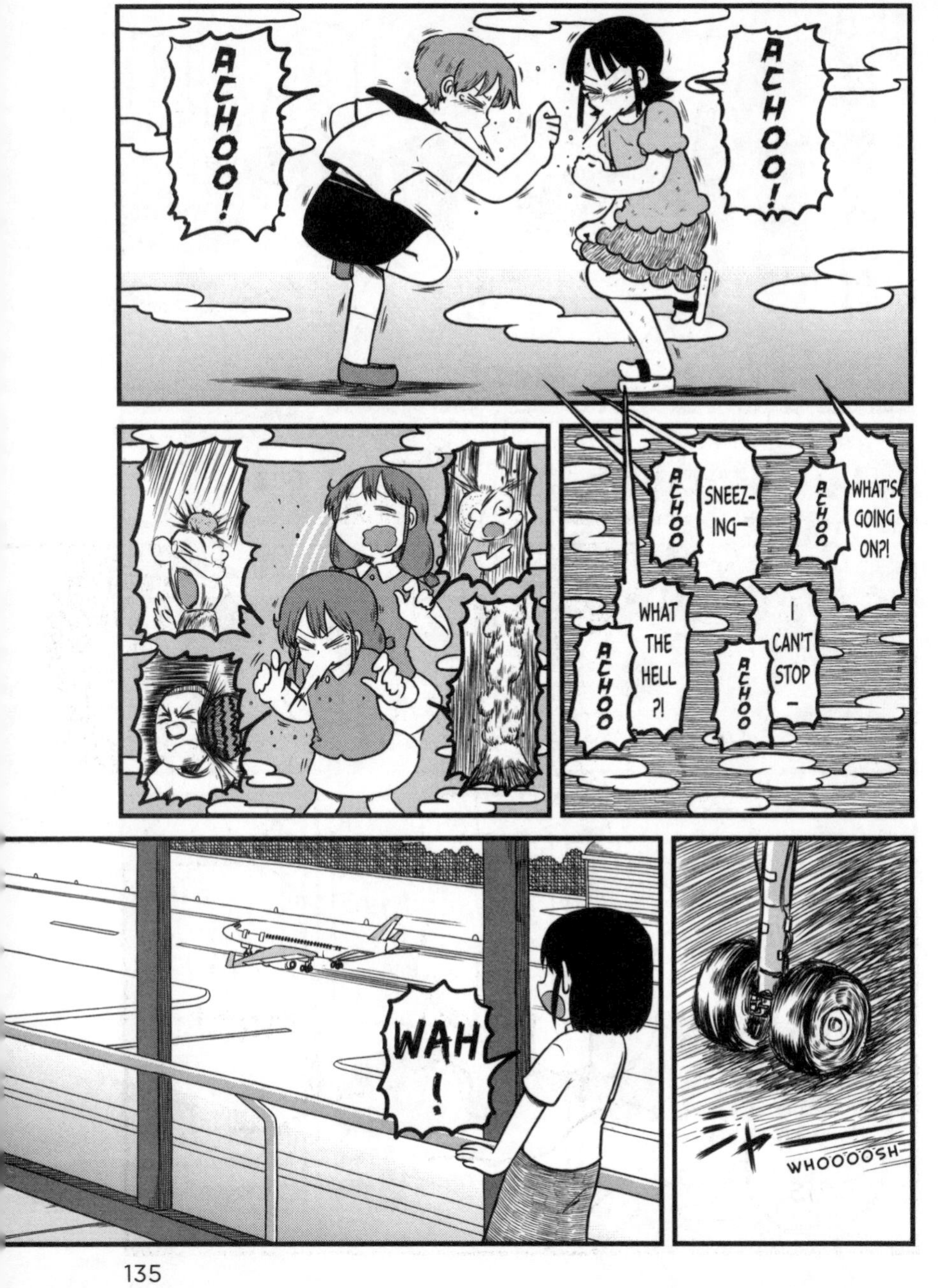
ACHOO!
ACHOO!
WHAT'S GOING ON?!
ACHOO
SNEEZ-ING—
ACHOO
I CAN'T STOP—
ACHOO
WHAT THE HELL?!
ACHOO
WHOOOOSH
WAH!

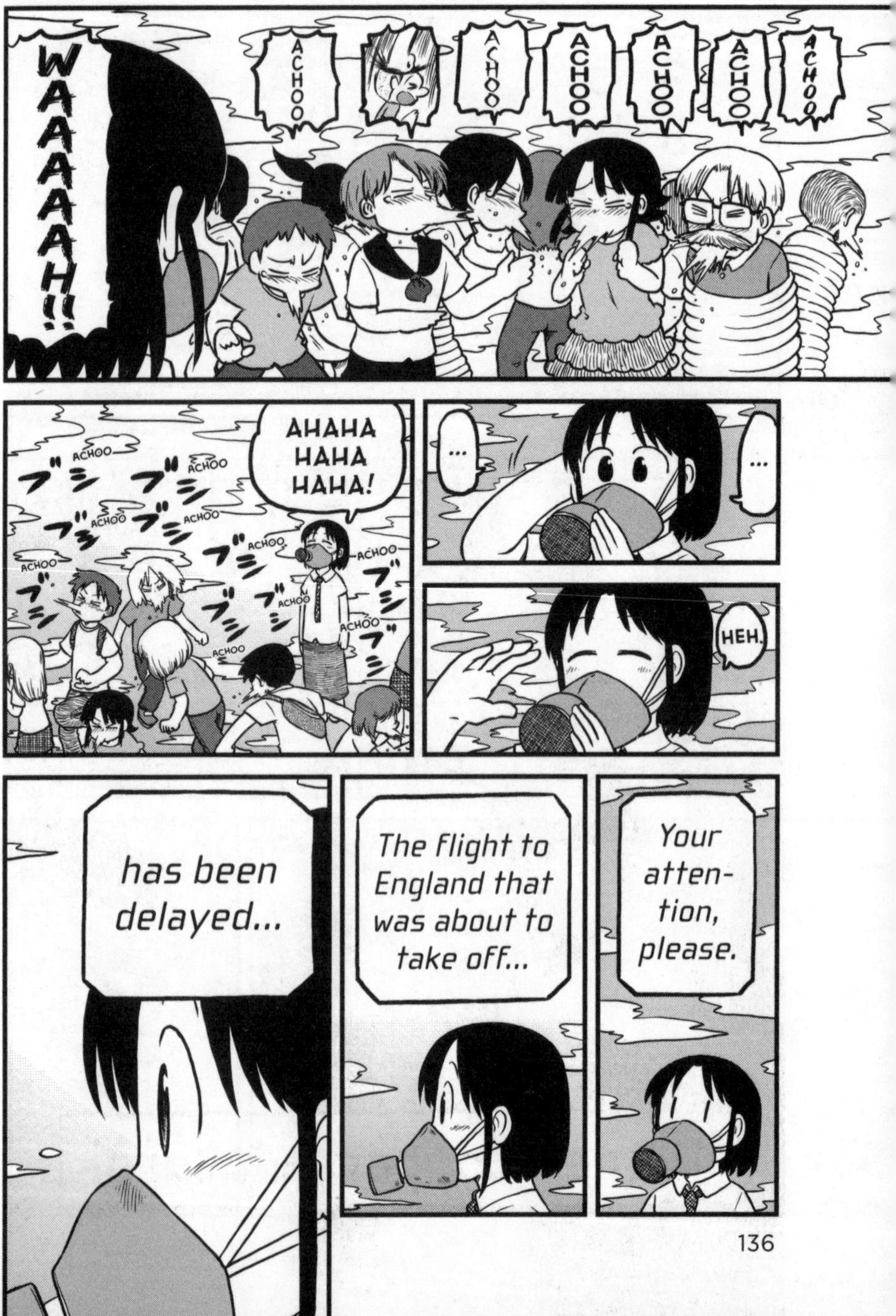
ACHOO
ACHOO
ACHOO
ACHOO
ACHOO
ACHOO
WAAAAAAH!!
...
...
HEH.
AHAHA HAHA HAHA!
ACHOO
ACHOO
ACHOO
ACHOO
ACHOO
ACHOO
ACHOO
ACHOO
ACHOO
ACHOO
Your attention, please.
The flight to England that was about to take off...
has been delayed...

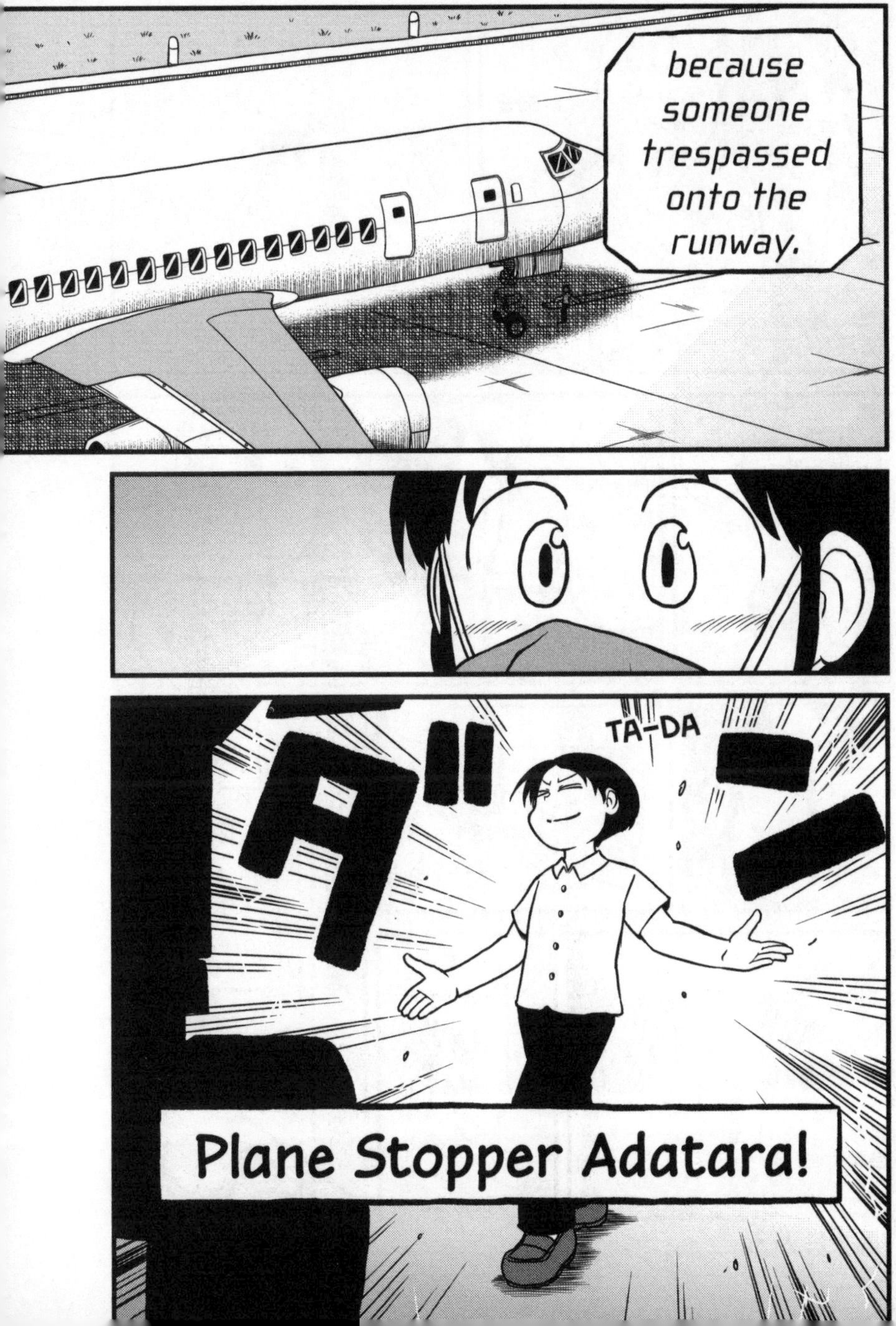
because someone trespassed onto the runway.
TA-DA
Plane Stopper Adatara!

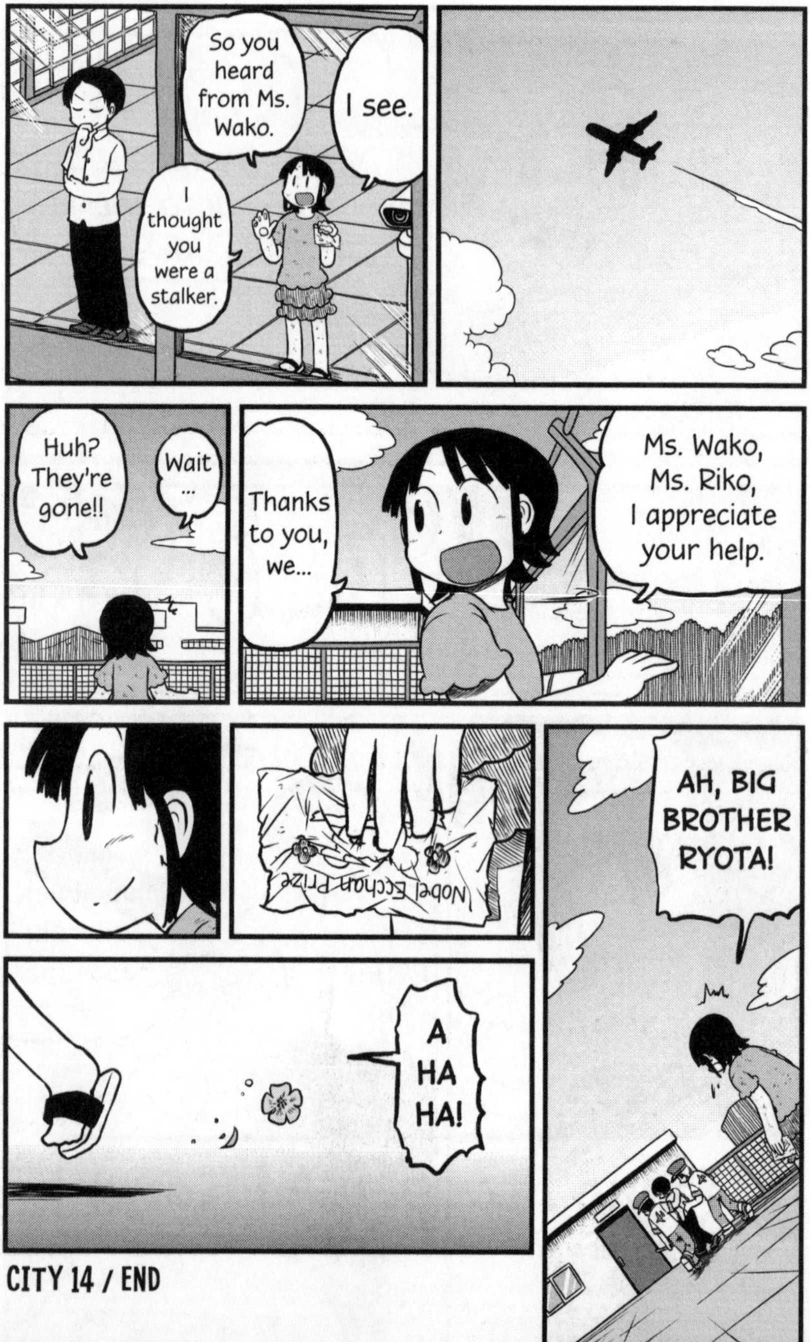
I see.
So you heard from Ms. Wako.
I thought you were a stalker.
Ms. Wako, Ms. Riko, I appreciate your help.
Thanks to you, we...
Wait ...
Huh? They're gone!!
AH, BIG BROTHER RYOTA!
Nobel Ecchan Prize
A HA HA!

CITY 14 / END

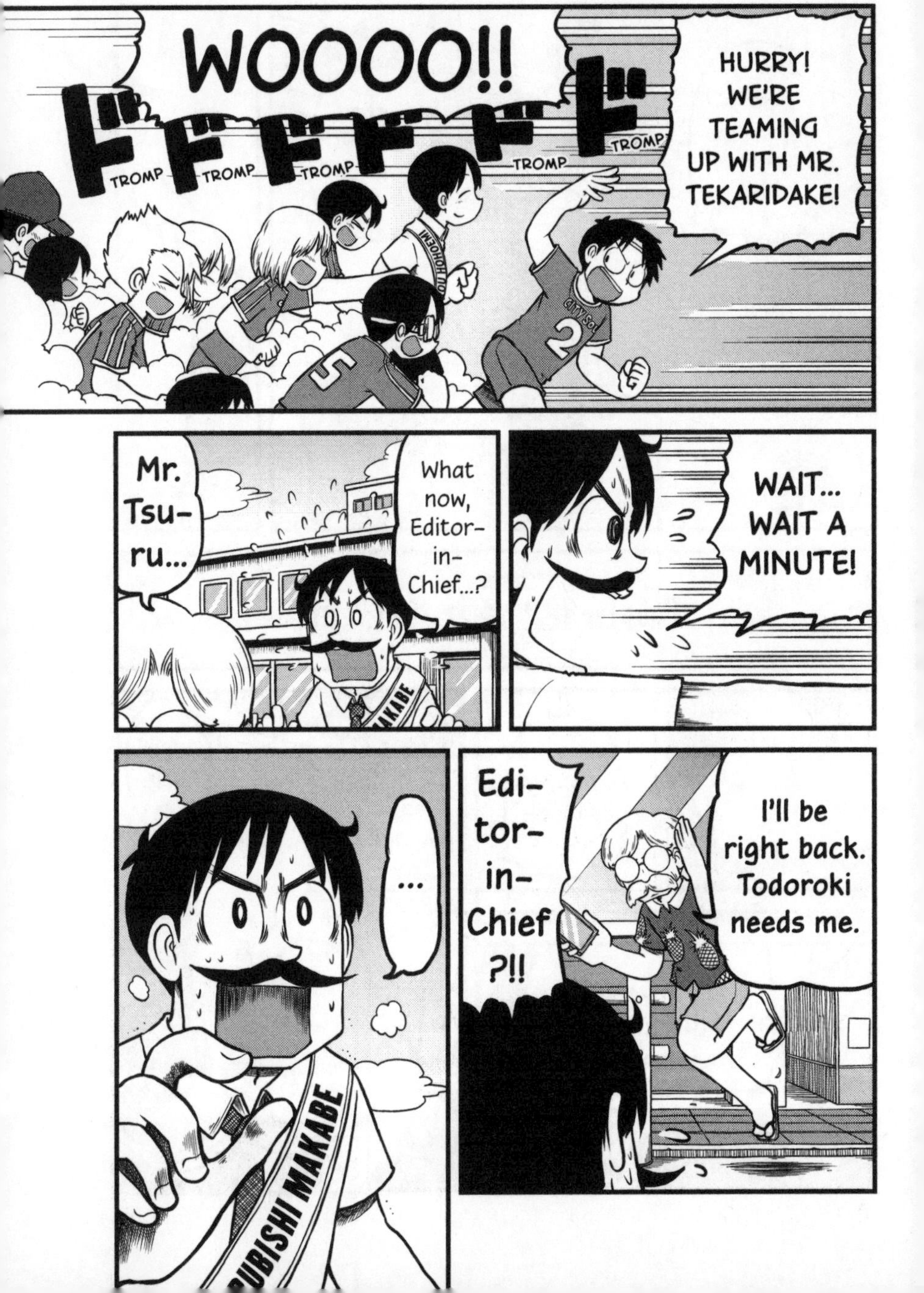
HURRY! WE'RE TEAMING UP WITH MR. TEKARIDAKE!
WOOOO!!
ドドドドドド
TROMP TROMP TROMP TROMP TROMP
WAIT... WAIT A MINUTE!
What now, Editor-in-Chief...?
Mr. Tsuru...
I'll be right back. Todoroki needs me.
Editor-in-Chief?!!
...

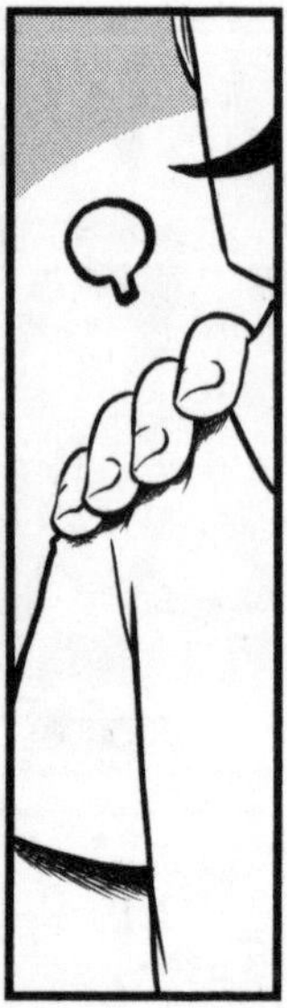

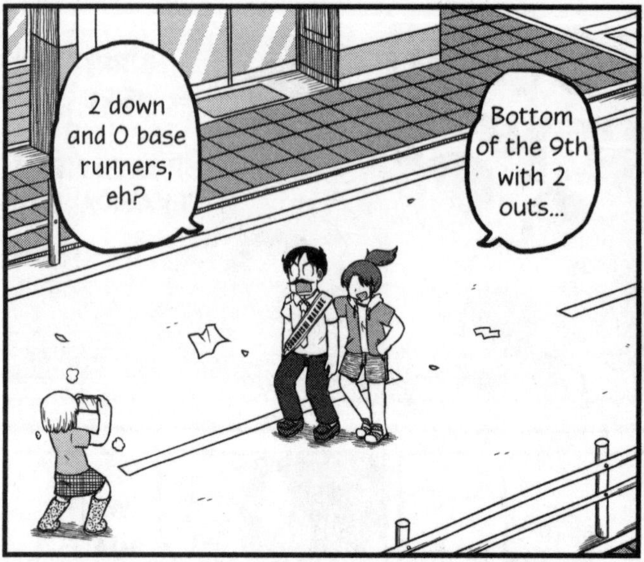
Bottom of the 9th with 2 outs...
2 down and 0 base runners, eh?

Chapter 182 CITY 15

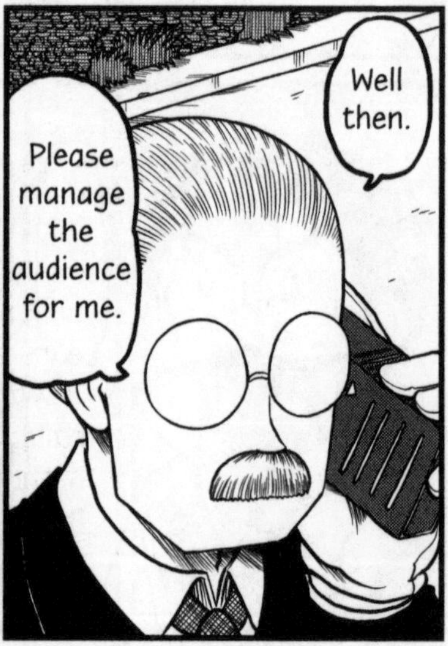
Well then.
Please manage the audience for me.

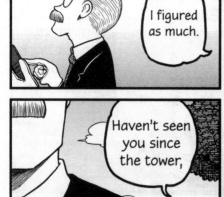

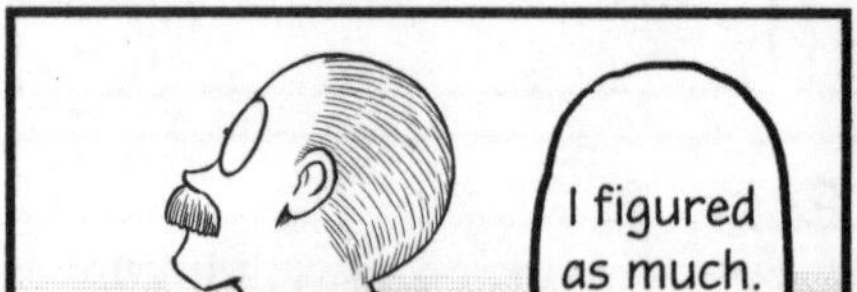
I figured as much.

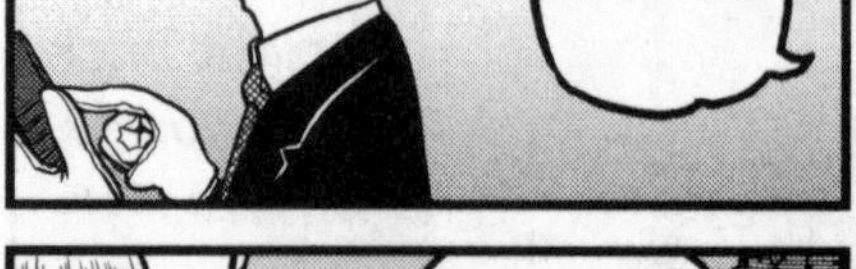
Haven't seen you since the tower,

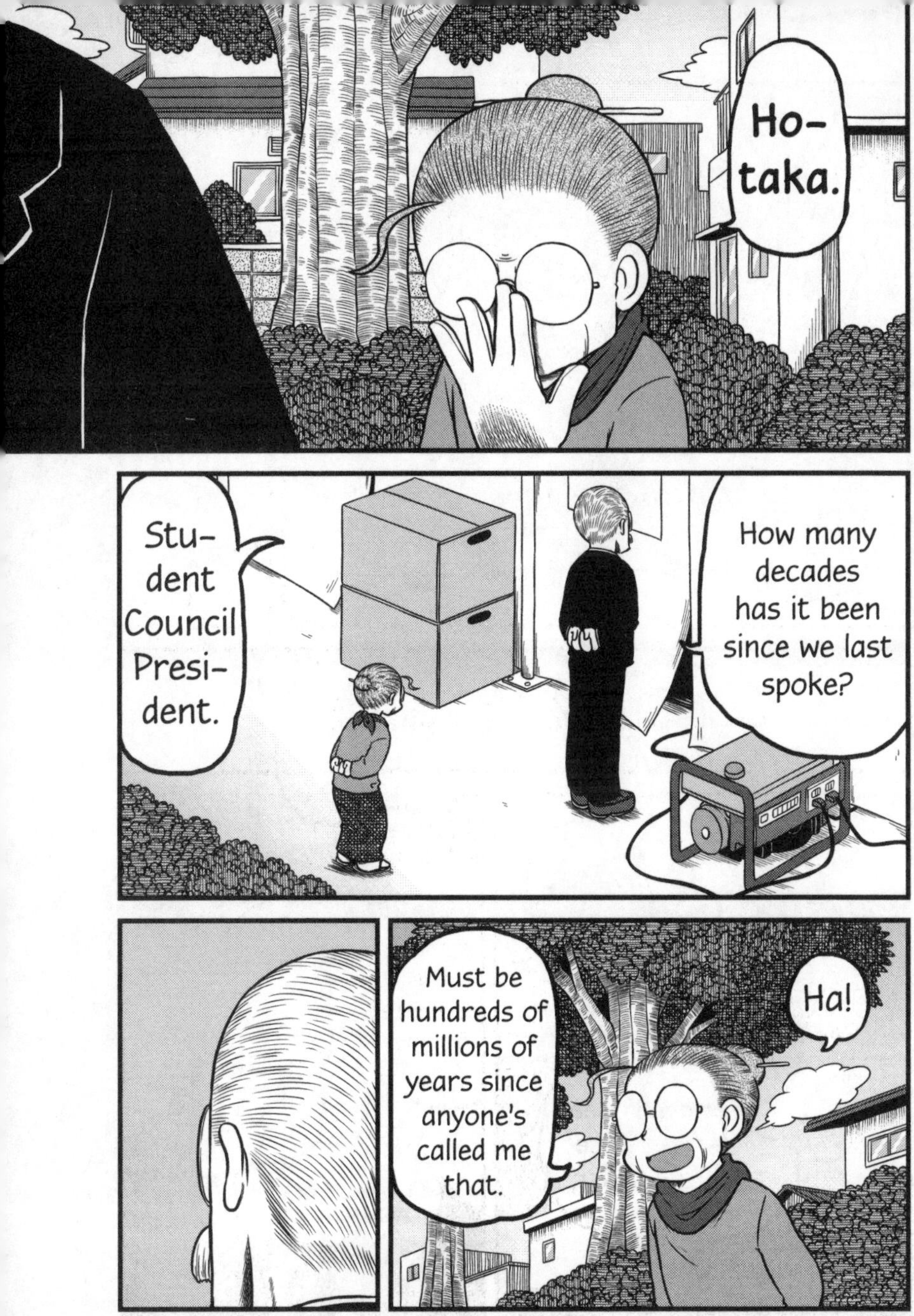
Ho-taka.
How many decades has it been since we last spoke?
Stu-dent Council Presi-dent.
Ha!
Must be hundreds of millions of years since anyone's called me that.

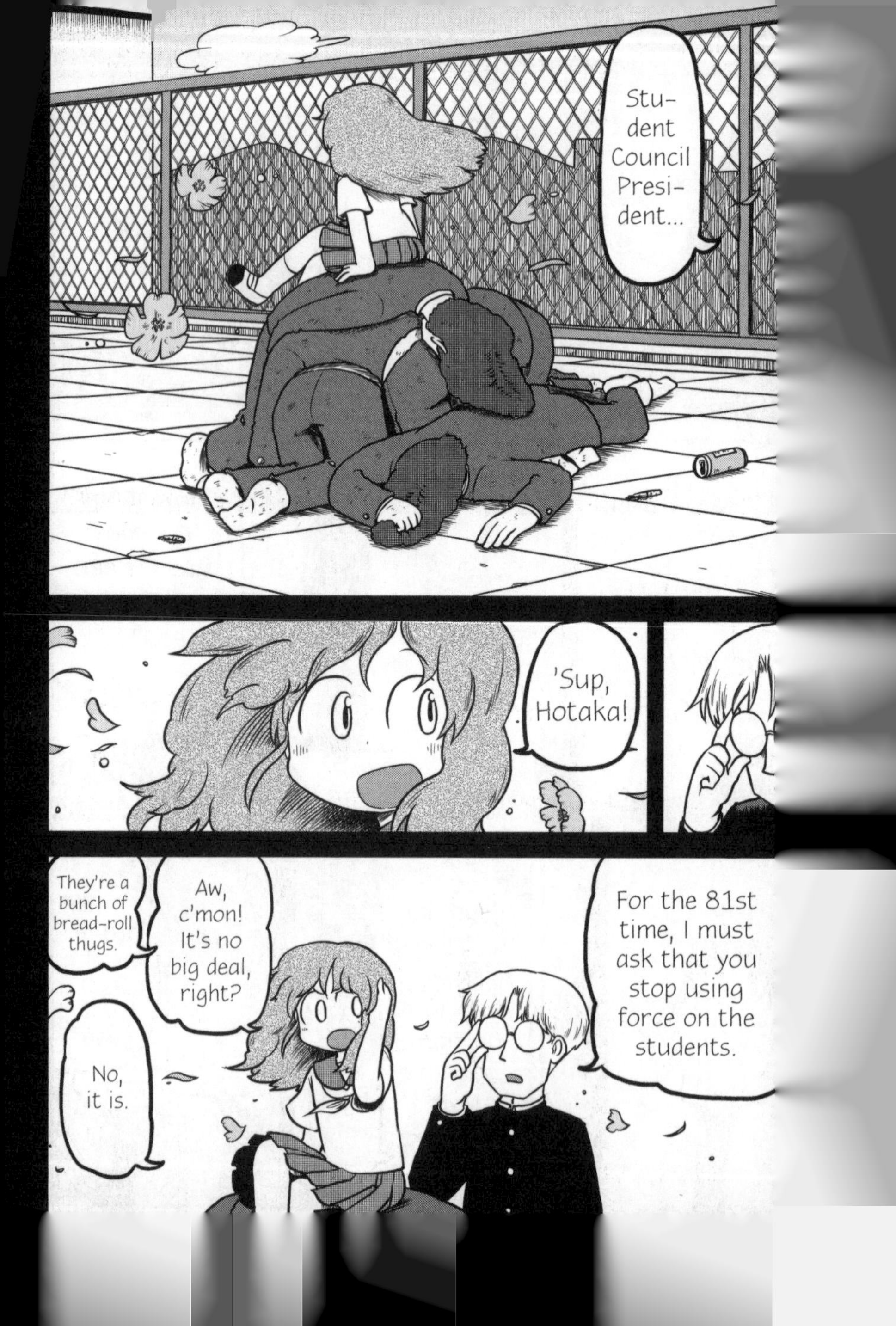
Student Council President...
'Sup, Hotaka!
For the 81st time, I must ask that you stop using force on the students.
Aw, c'mon! It's no big deal, right?
They're a bunch of bread-roll thugs.
No, it is.

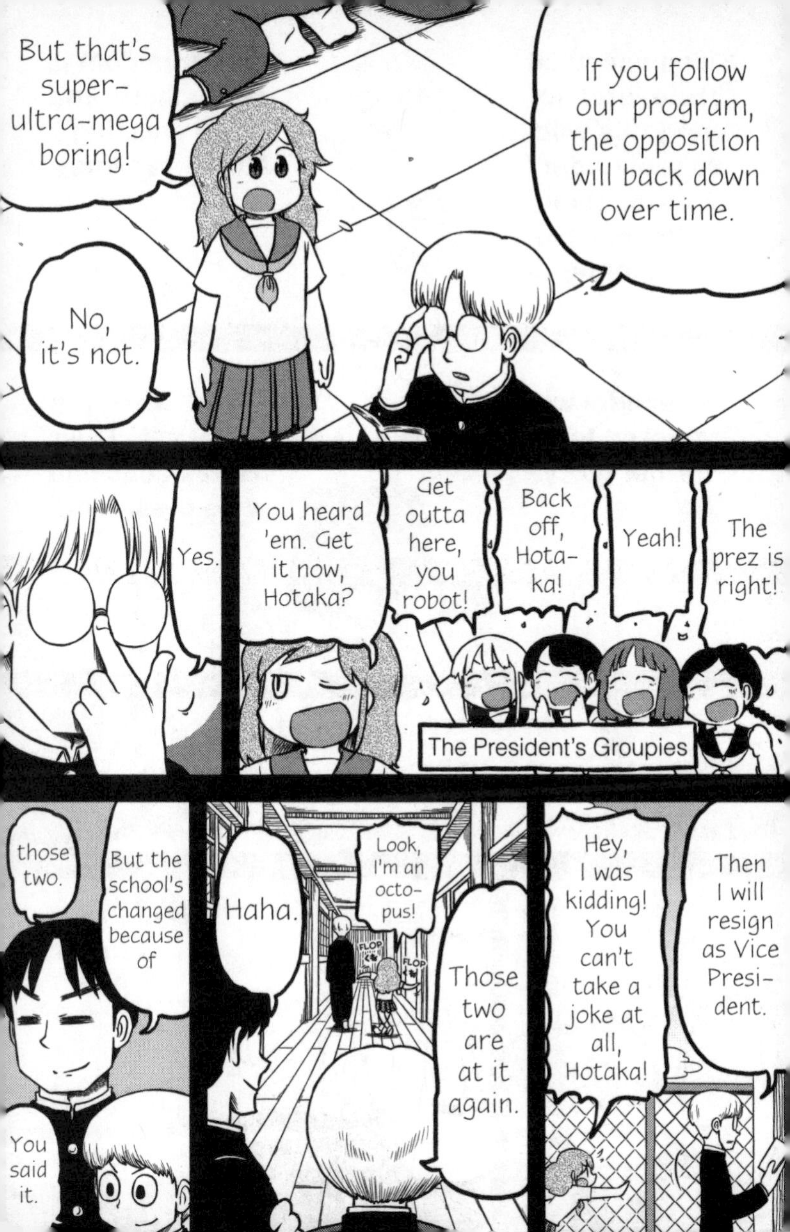
If you follow our program, the opposition will back down over time.
But that's super-ultra-mega boring!
No, it's not.
The prez is right!
Yeah!
Back off, Hotaka!
Get outta here, you robot!
You heard 'em. Get it now, Hotaka?
The President's Groupies
Yes.
Then I will resign as Vice President.
Hey, I was kidding! You can't take a joke at all, Hotaka!
Those two are at it again.
Look, I'm an octopus!
FLOP
FLOP
Haha.
But the school's changed because of
those two.
You said it.

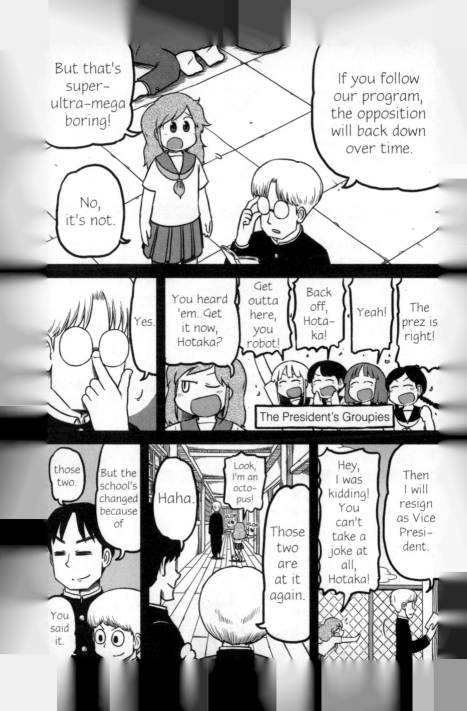

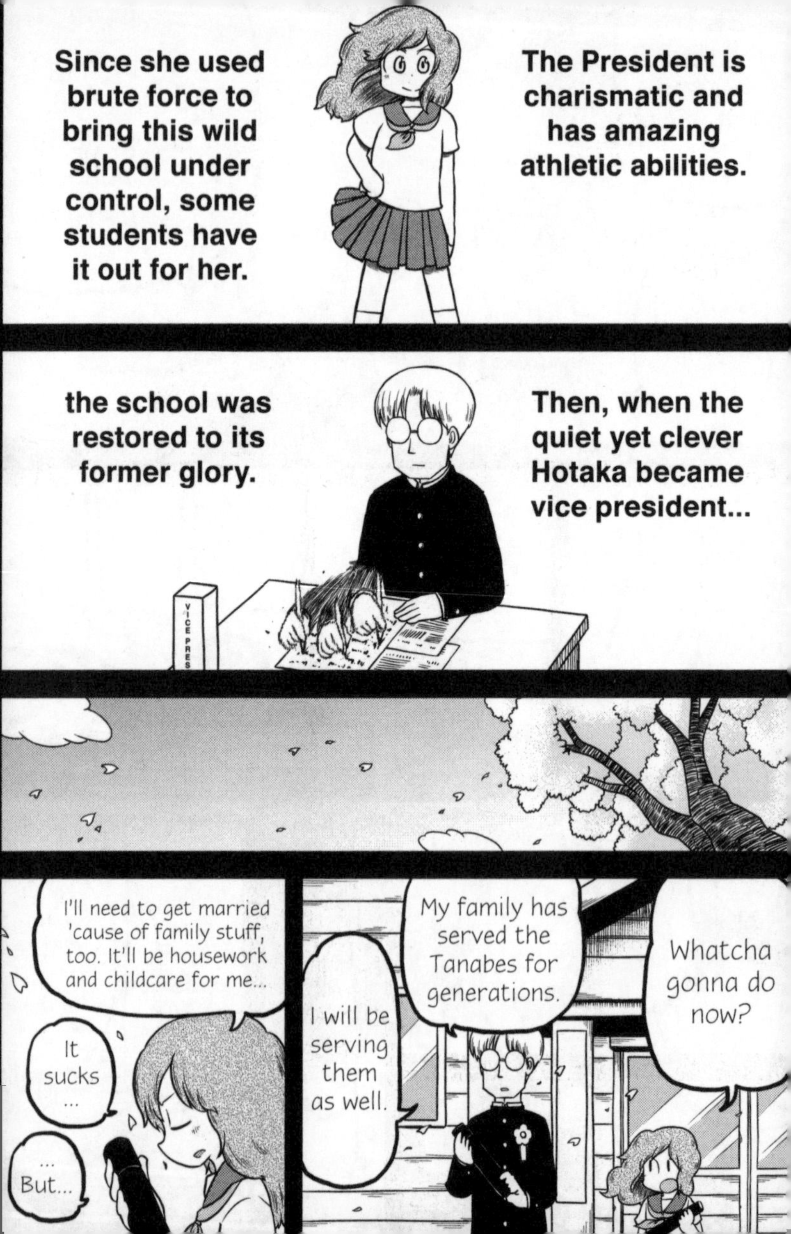
The President is charismatic and has amazing athletic abilities.
Since she used brute force to bring this wild school under control, some students have it out for her.
Then, when the quiet yet clever Hotaka became vice president...
the school was restored to its former glory.
VICE PRES
Whatcha gonna do now?
My family has served the Tanabes for generations.
I will be serving them as well.
I'll need to get married 'cause of family stuff, too. It'll be housework and childcare for me...
It sucks ...
... But...

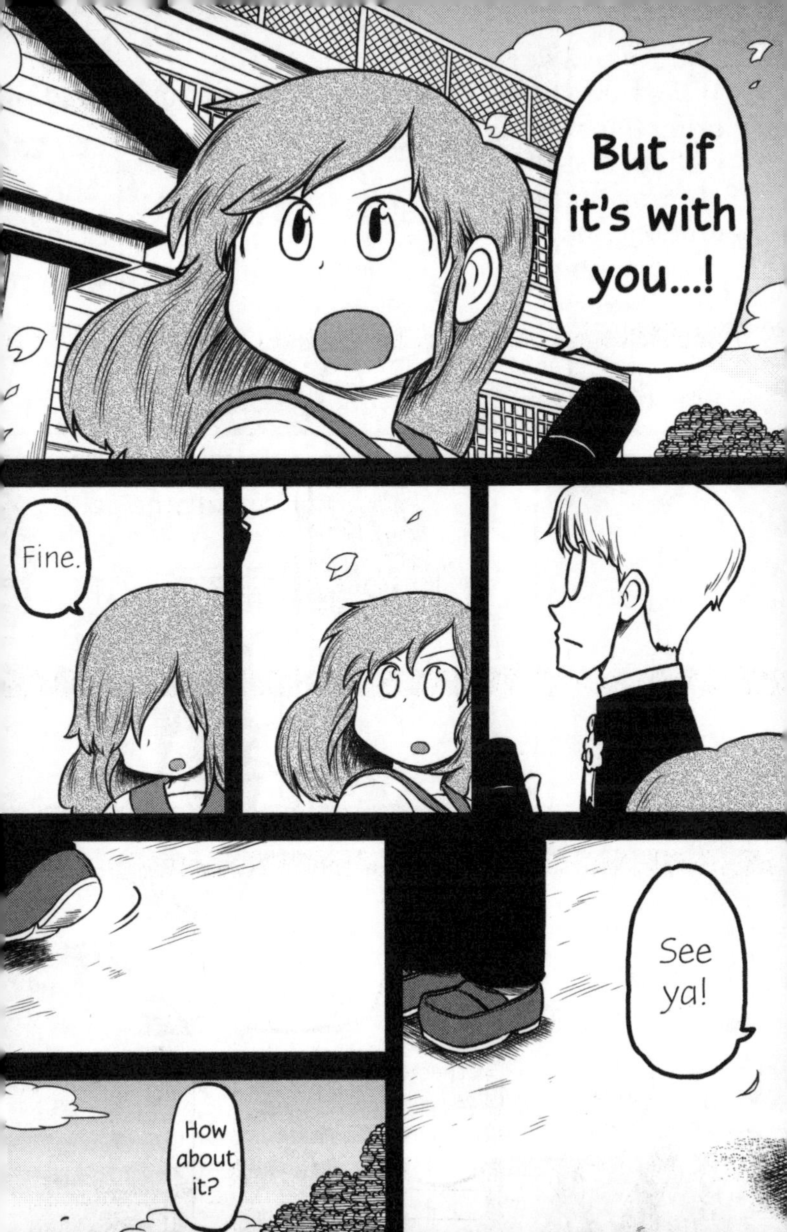
But if it's with you...!
Fine.
See ya!
How about it?

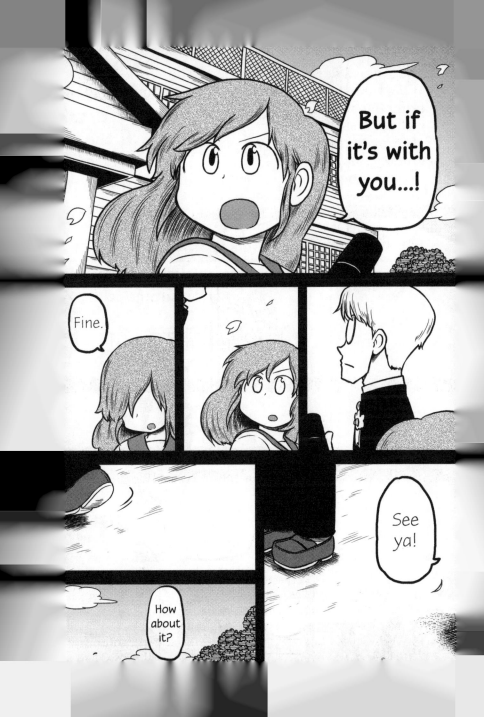

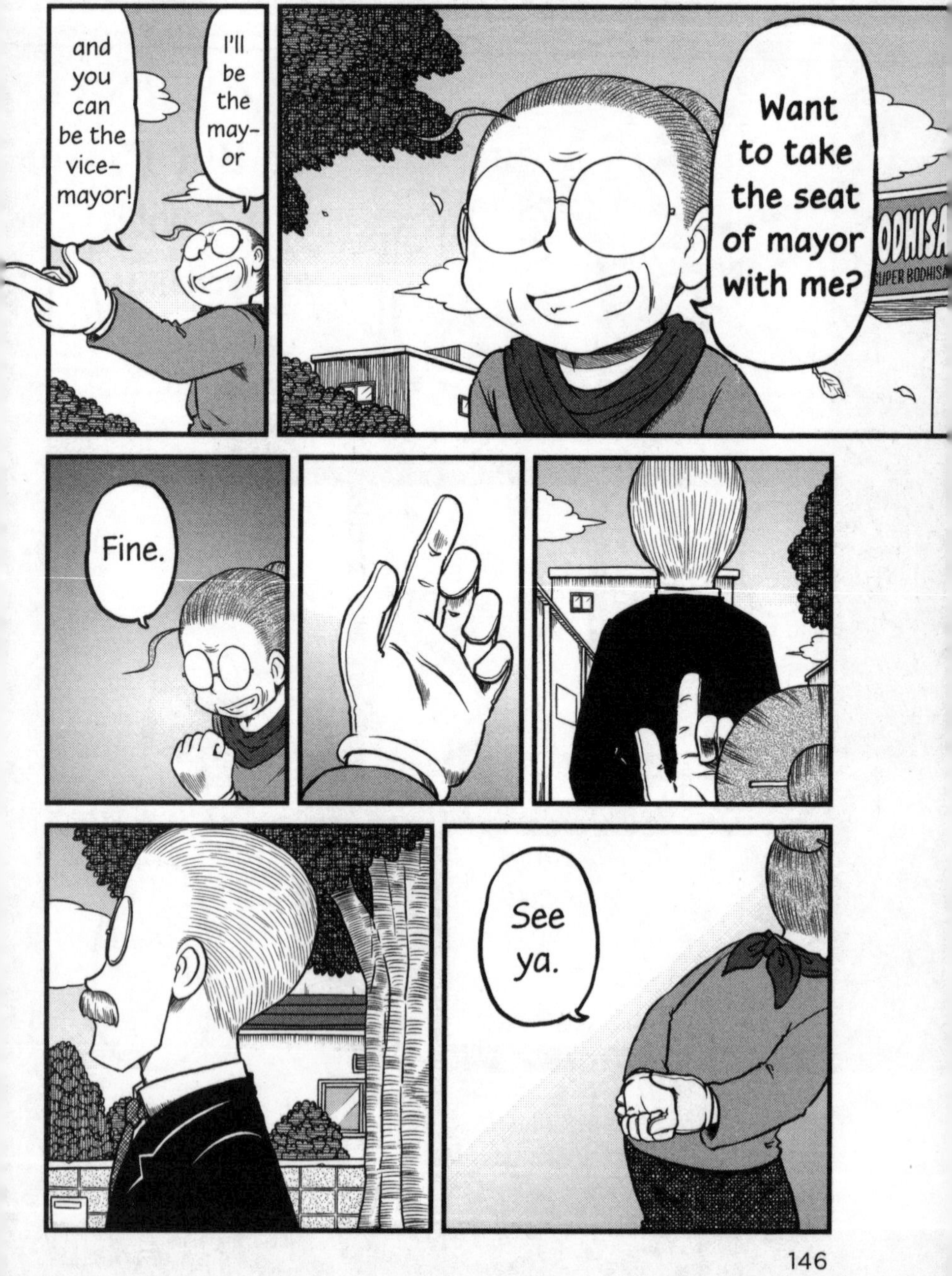
Want to take the seat of mayor with me?
I'll be the may-or
and you can be the vice-mayor!
Fine.
See ya.

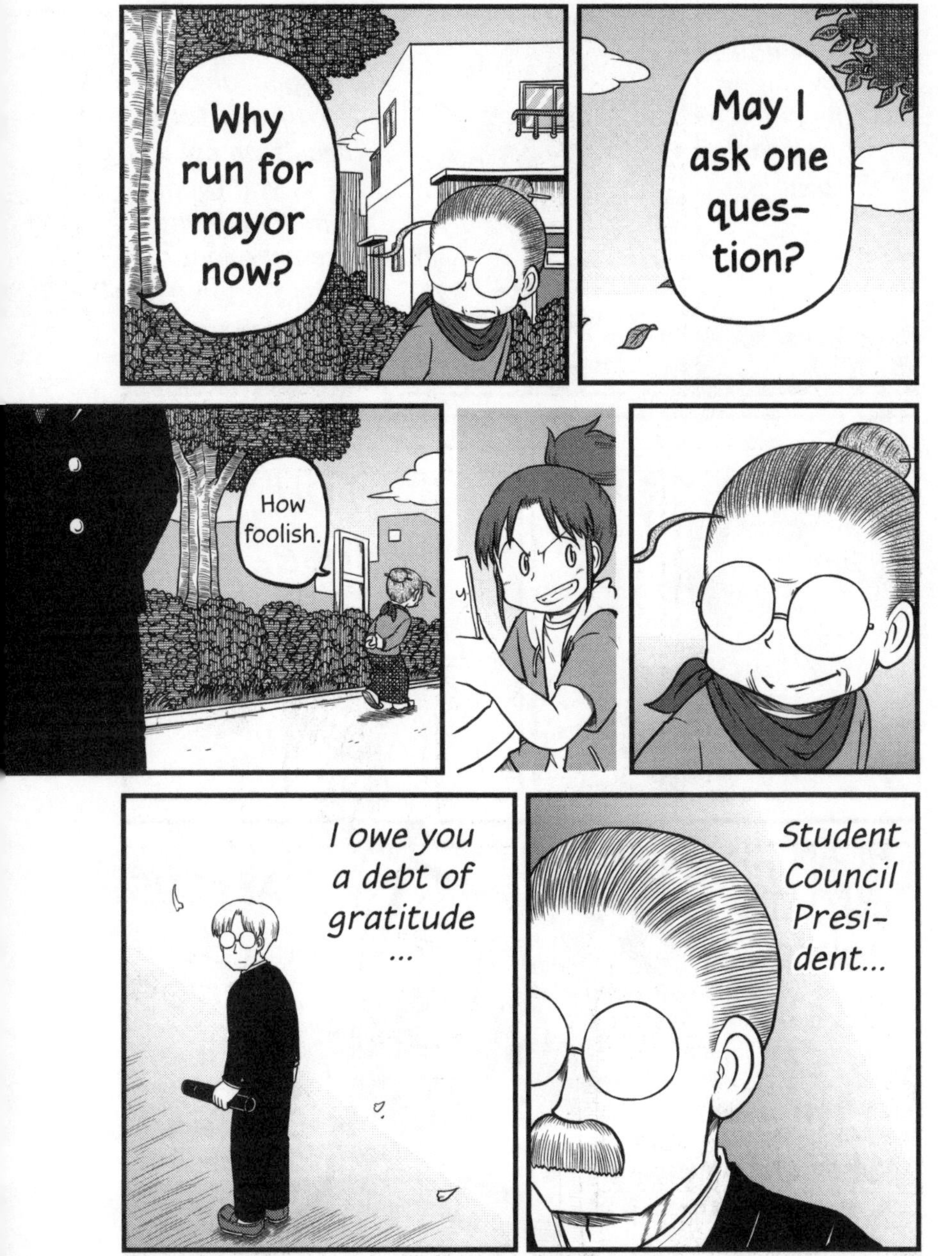
May I ask one ques-tion?
Why run for mayor now?
How foolish.
Student Council Presi-dent...
I owe you a debt of gratitude ...

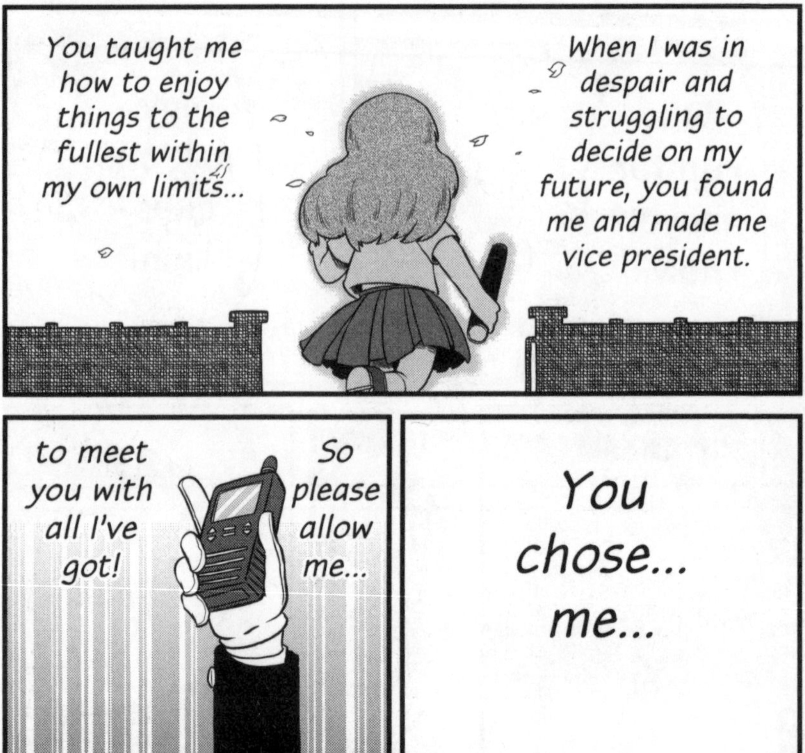

When I was in despair and struggling to decide on my future, you found me and made me vice president.
You taught me how to enjoy things to the fullest within my own limits...
You chose... me...
So please allow me...
to meet you with all I've got!
ABACUS ! BRAIDS !!
BZZZT
PLAN 2! INITIATE "OPER-ATION STEAL THE SENIOR VOTE"!!

CITY 15 / END

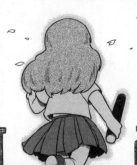

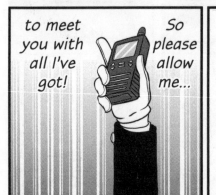

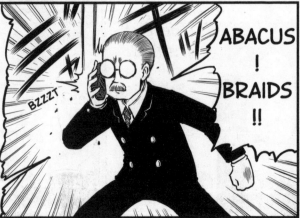

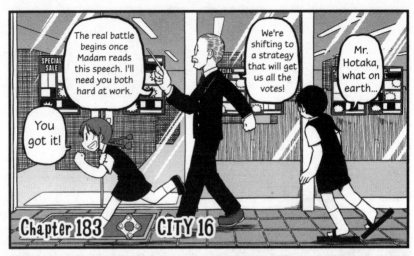

Mr. Hotaka, what on earth...
We're shifting to a strategy that will get us all the votes!
SPECIAL SALE
The real battle begins once Madam reads this speech. I'll need you both hard at work.
You got it!
Chapter 183 CITY 16
Mad-am.
AH.
HO-TAKA.
Per-fect tim-ing.
Yes?
TANABE
SUMIRESAKURAKO
I...
Yes?

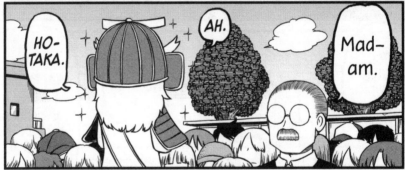

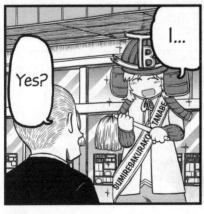

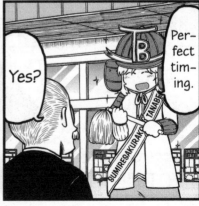

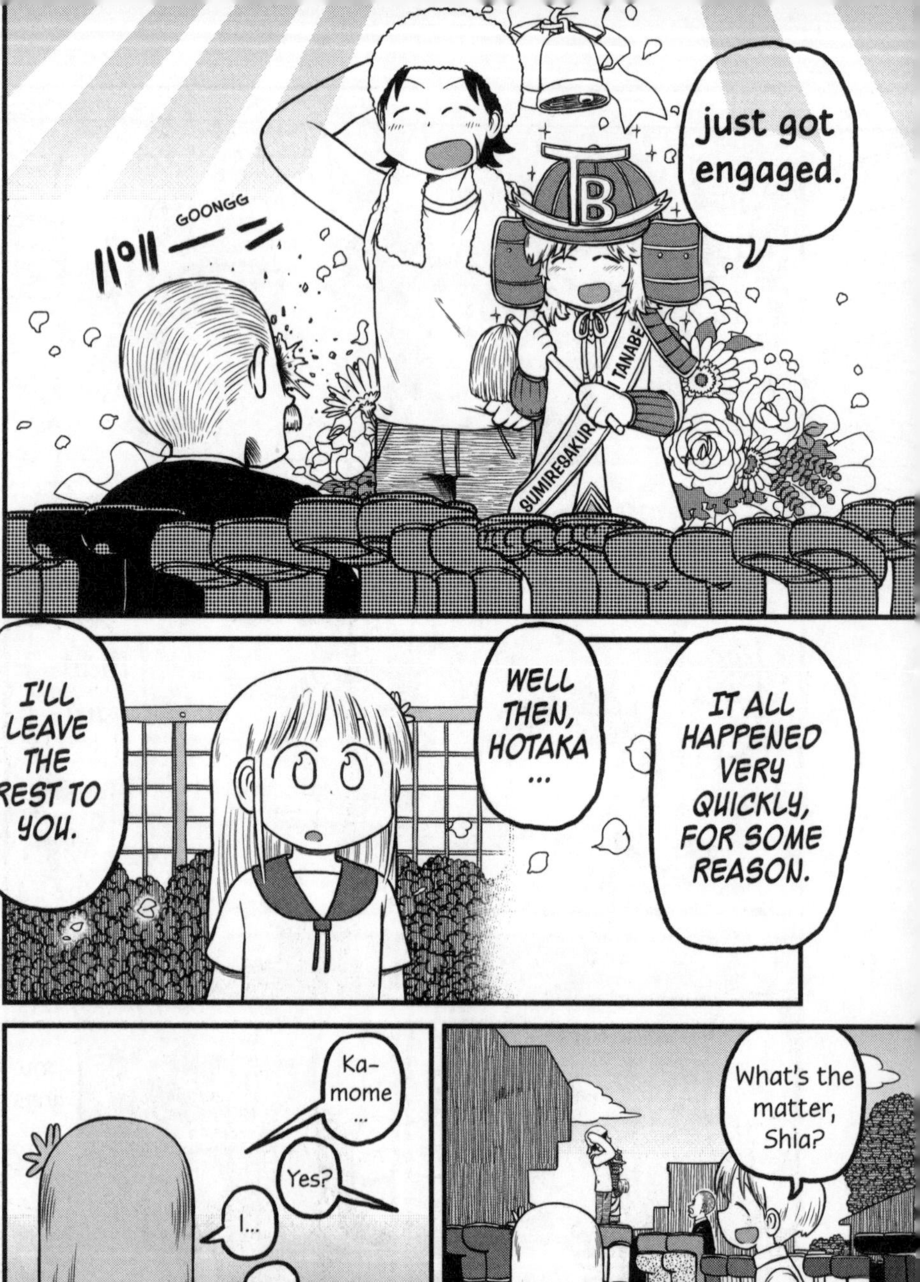

just got engaged.
GOONGG
IT ALL HAPPENED VERY QUICKLY, FOR SOME REASON.
WELL THEN, HOTAKA ...
I'LL LEAVE THE REST TO YOU.
What's the matter, Shia?
Ka-mome ...
Yes?
I...
Yes?

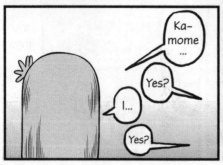

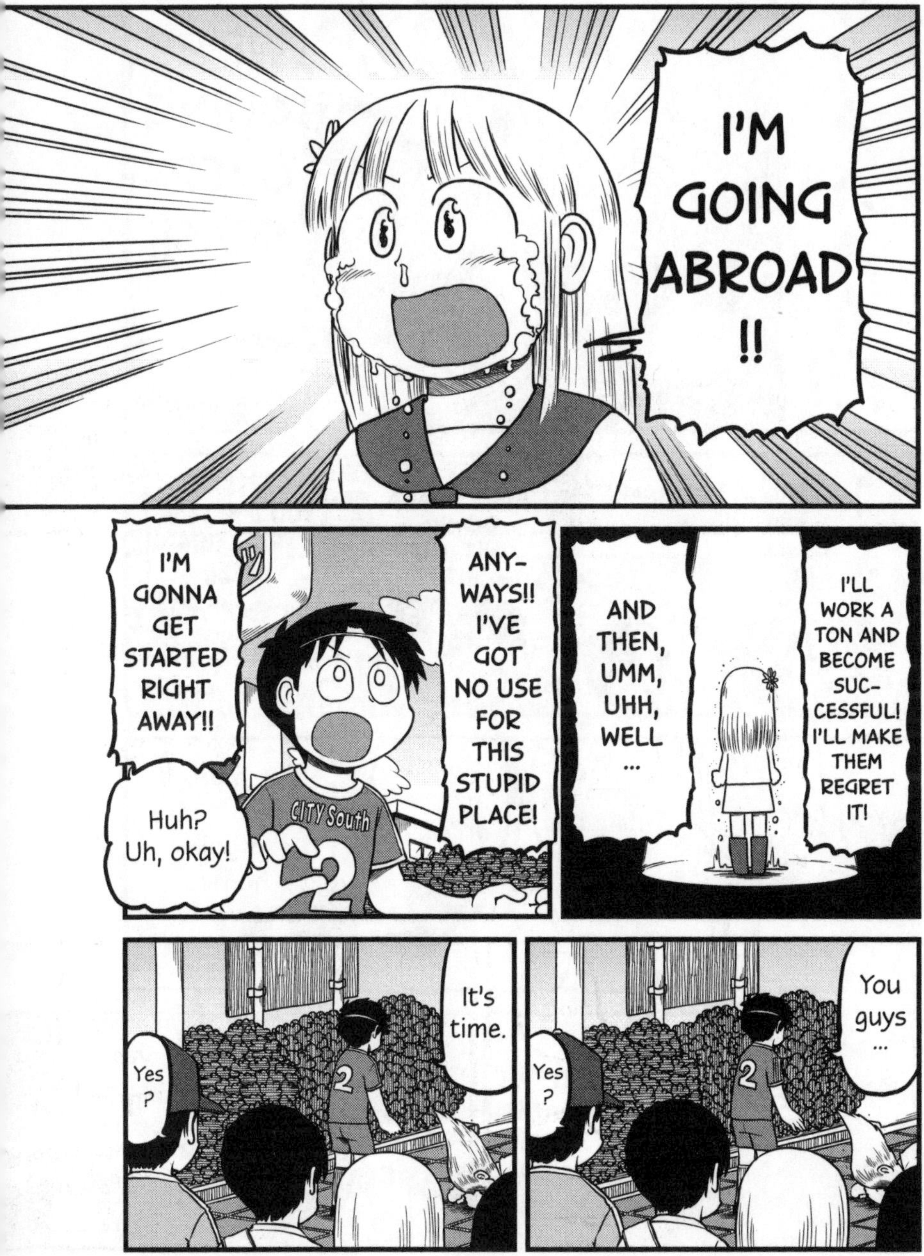
I'M GOING ABROAD !!
I'LL WORK A TON AND BECOME SUC-CESSFUL! I'LL MAKE THEM REGRET IT!
AND THEN, UMM, UHH, WELL ...
ANY-WAYS!! I'VE GOT NO USE FOR THIS STUPID PLACE!
I'M GONNA GET STARTED RIGHT AWAY!!
Huh? Uh, okay!
CITY South
2
You guys ...
Yes ?
It's time.
Yes ?

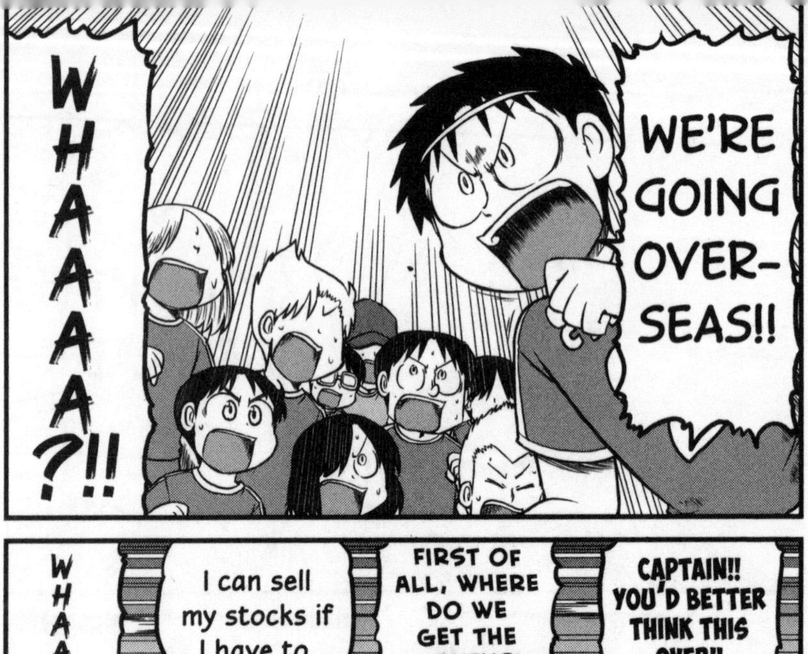
WE'RE GOING OVER-SEAS!!
WHAAAA?!!
CAPTAIN!! YOU'D BETTER THINK THIS OVER!!
FIRST OF ALL, WHERE DO WE GET THE MONEY?!
I can sell my stocks if I have to.
WHAAAAA?!!
Aw, man. If Shia's gone, I'm going home.
Wanna hit the arcade?
Let's grab a bite to eat.
Wanna play Momo-Tetsu?*
I'm down!

* Short for Momotaro Dentetsu, a Japanese role-playing video game.

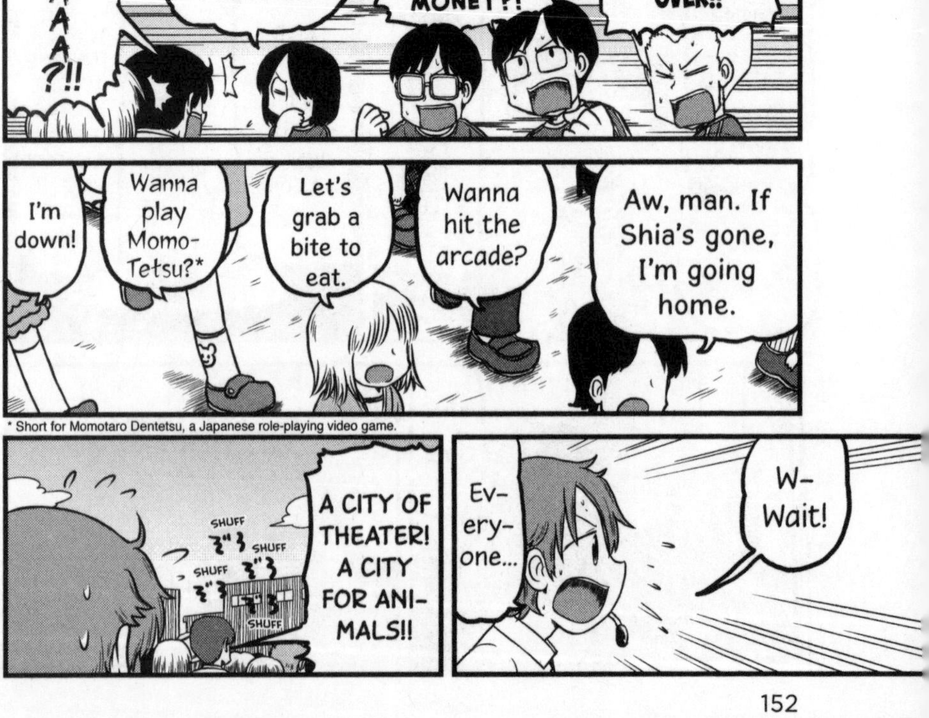
W-Wait!
Ev-ery-one...
A CITY OF THEATER! A CITY FOR ANI-MALS!!
SHUFF
SHUFF
SHUFF
SHUFF

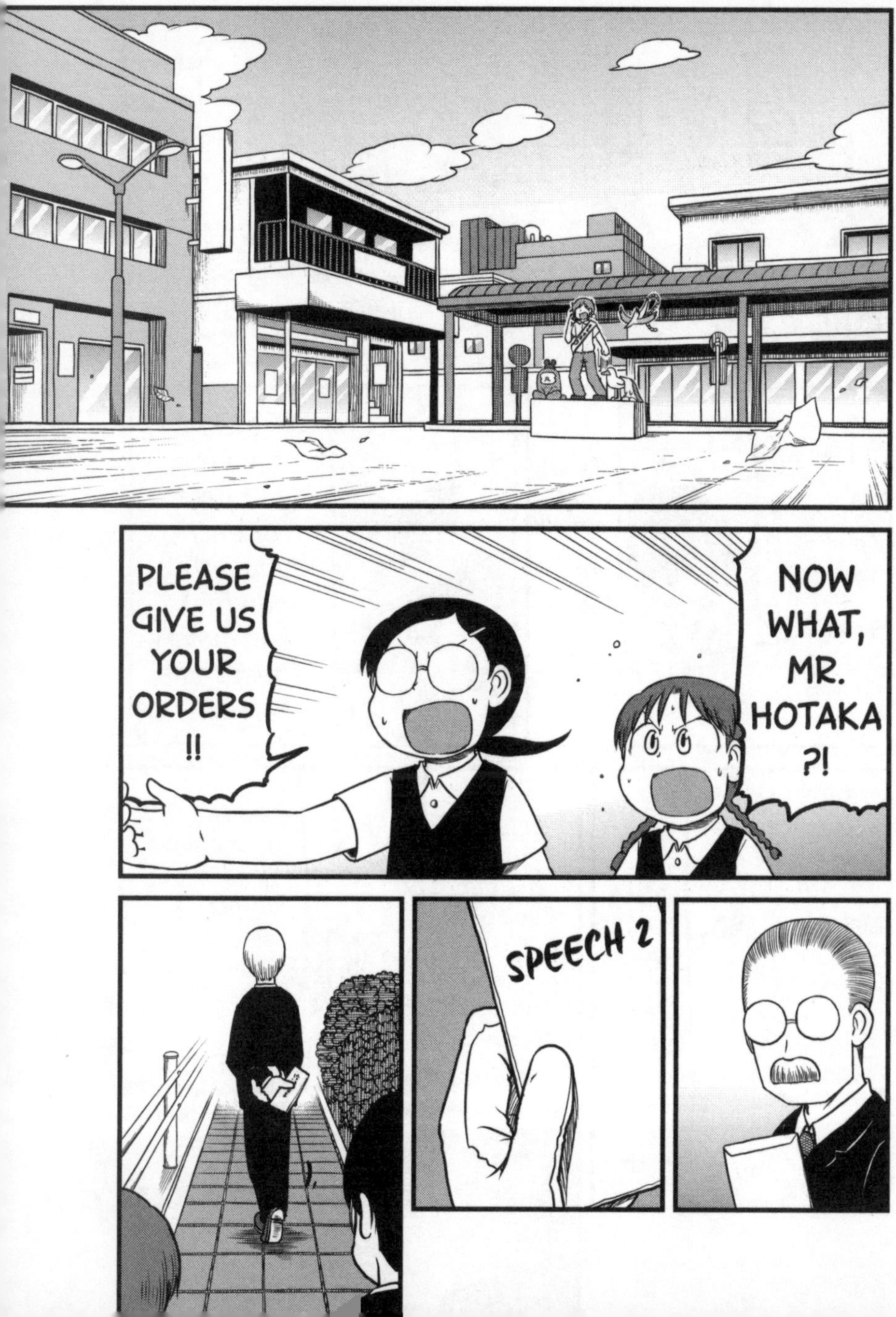
NOW WHAT, MR. HOTAKA ?!
PLEASE GIVE US YOUR ORDERS !!
SPEECH 2

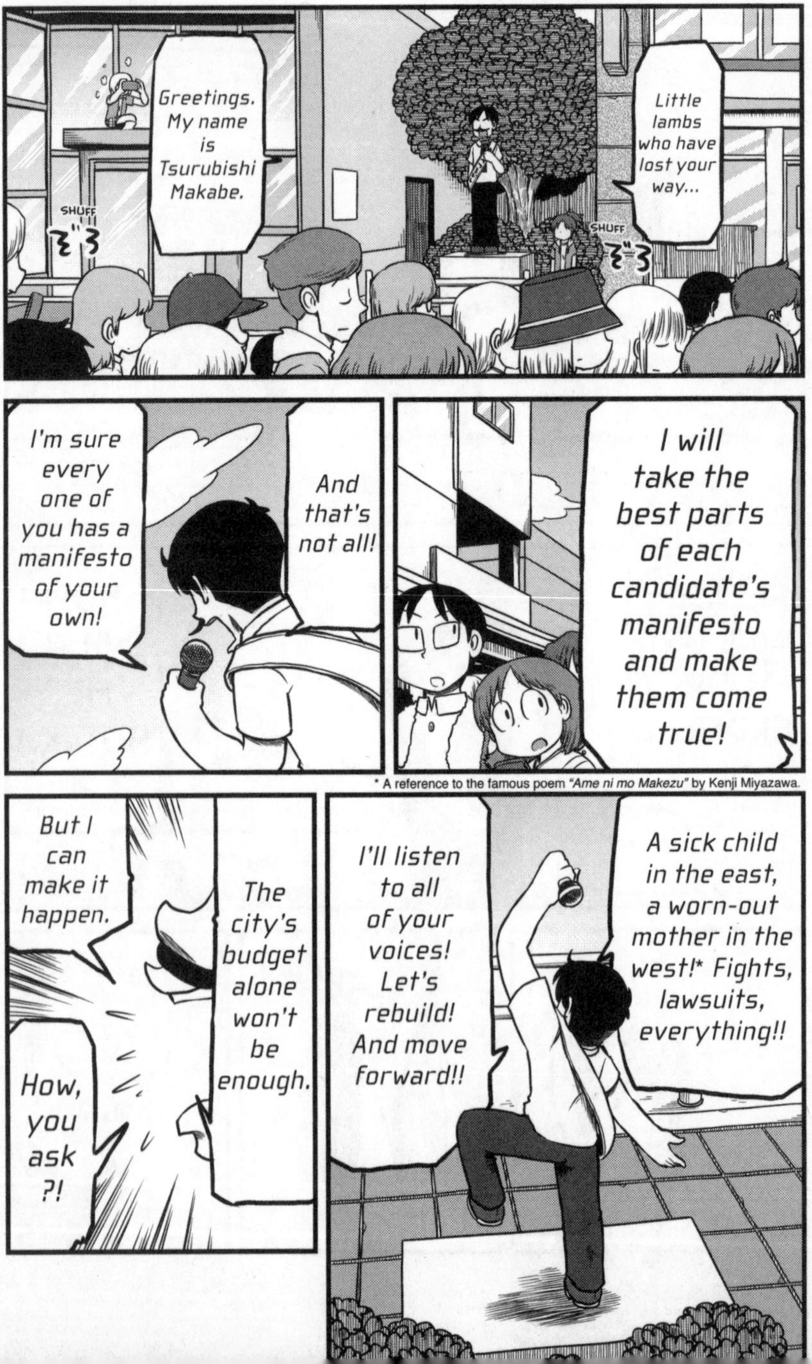
Little lambs who have lost your way...
SHUFF
Greetings. My name is Tsurubishi Makabe.
SHUFF
I will take the best parts of each candidate's manifesto and make them come true!
And that's not all!
I'm sure every one of you has a manifesto of your own!
A sick child in the east, a worn-out mother in the west!* Fights, lawsuits, everything!!
I'll listen to all of your voices! Let's rebuild! And move forward!!
The city's budget alone won't be enough.
But I can make it happen.
How, you ask?!

* A reference to the famous poem *"Ame ni mo Makezu"* by Kenji Miyazawa.

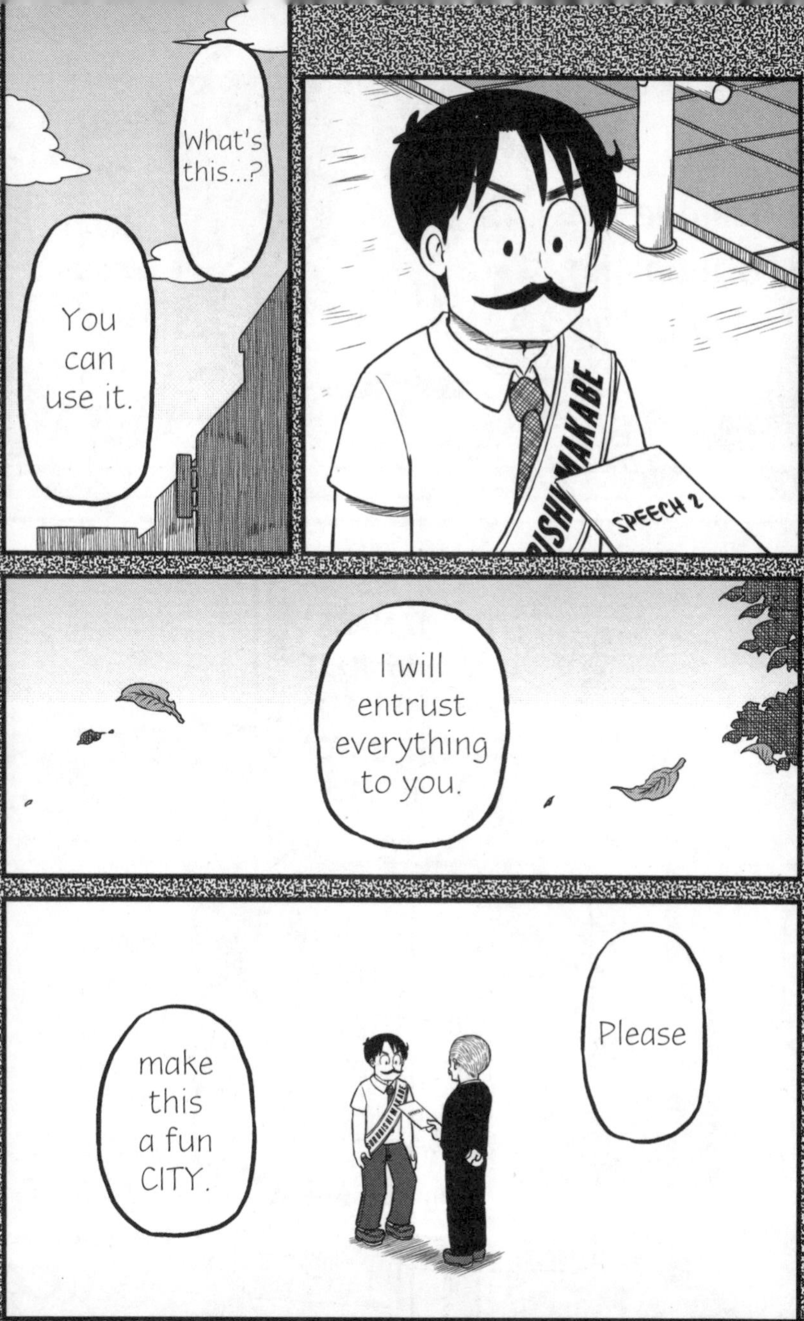
SPEECH 2
What's this...?
You can use it.
I will entrust everything to you.
Please
make this a fun CITY.

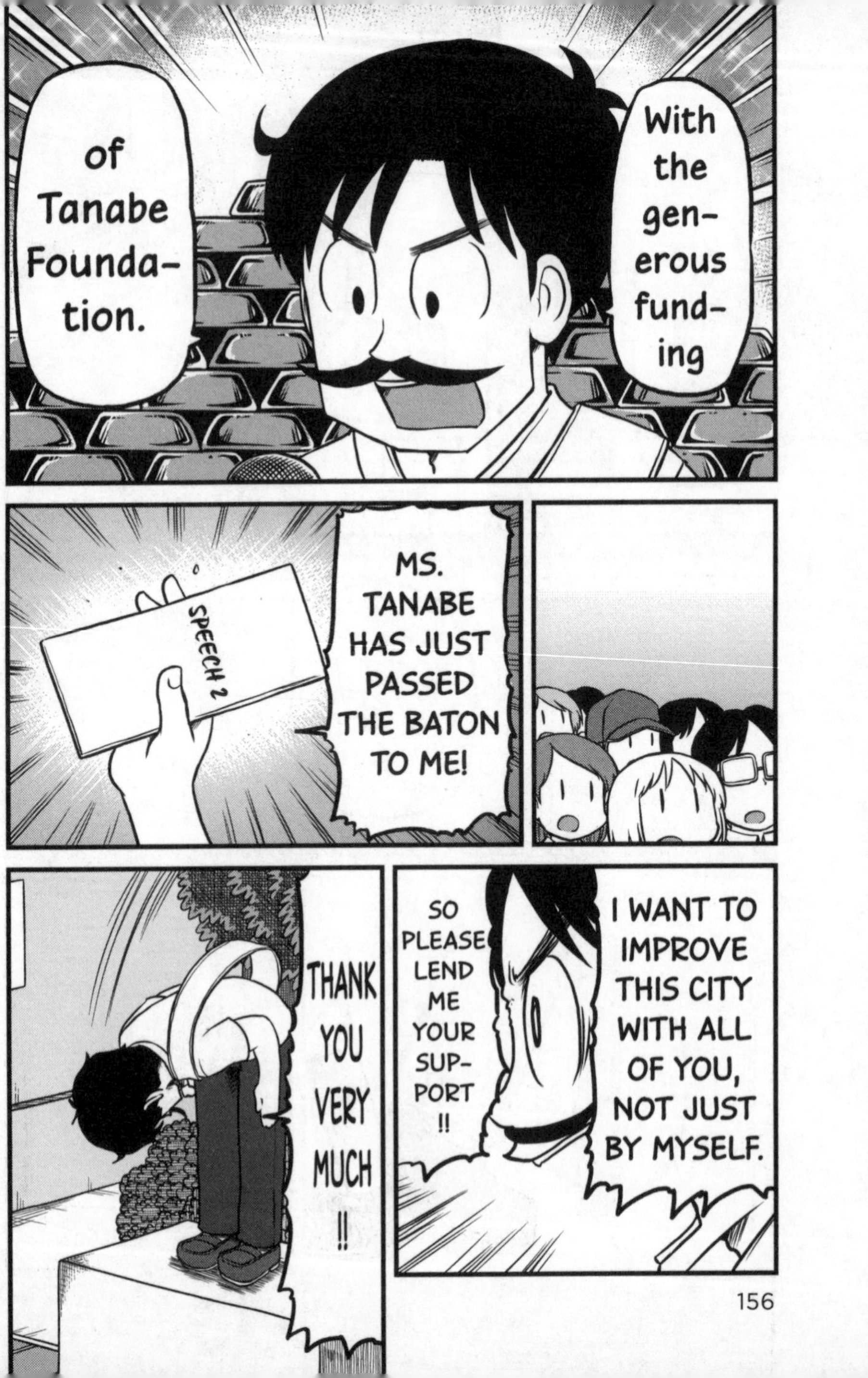
With the generous funding
of Tanabe Foundation.
MS. TANABE HAS JUST PASSED THE BATON TO ME!
SPEECH 2
I WANT TO IMPROVE THIS CITY WITH ALL OF YOU, NOT JUST BY MYSELF.
SO PLEASE LEND ME YOUR SUPPORT!!
THANK YOU VERY MUCH!!

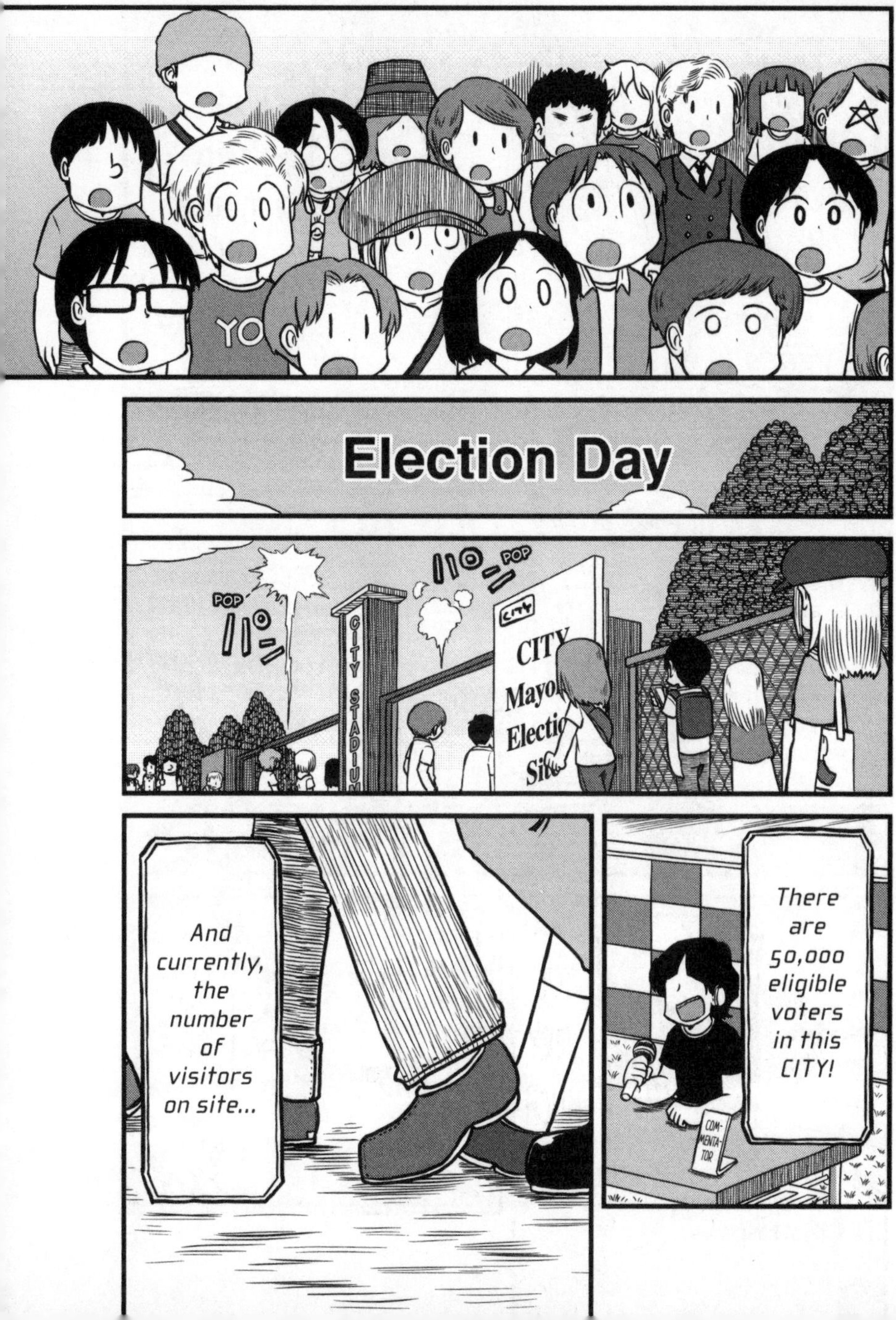
YO
Election Day
POP
POP
CITY STADIUM
CITY
Mayo
Electio
Site
There are 50,000 eligible voters in this CITY!
COM-MENTA-TOR
And currently, the number of visitors on site...

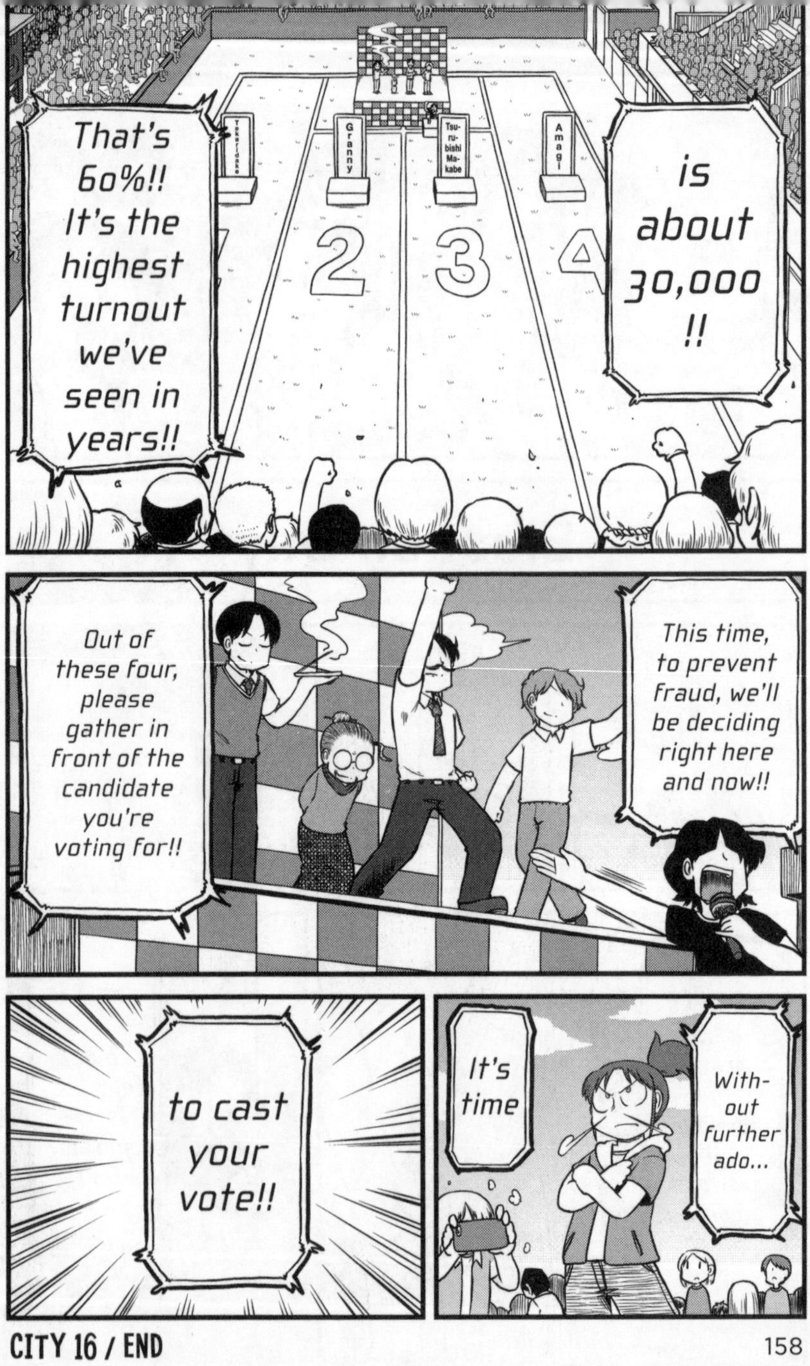
is about 30,000 !!
That's 60%!! It's the highest turnout we've seen in years!!
Amagi
Tsu-ru-bishi Ma-kabe
Granny
Tekaridake
4
3
2
This time, to prevent fraud, we'll be deciding right here and now!!
Out of these four, please gather in front of the candidate you're voting for!!
With-out further ado...
It's time
to cast your vote!!

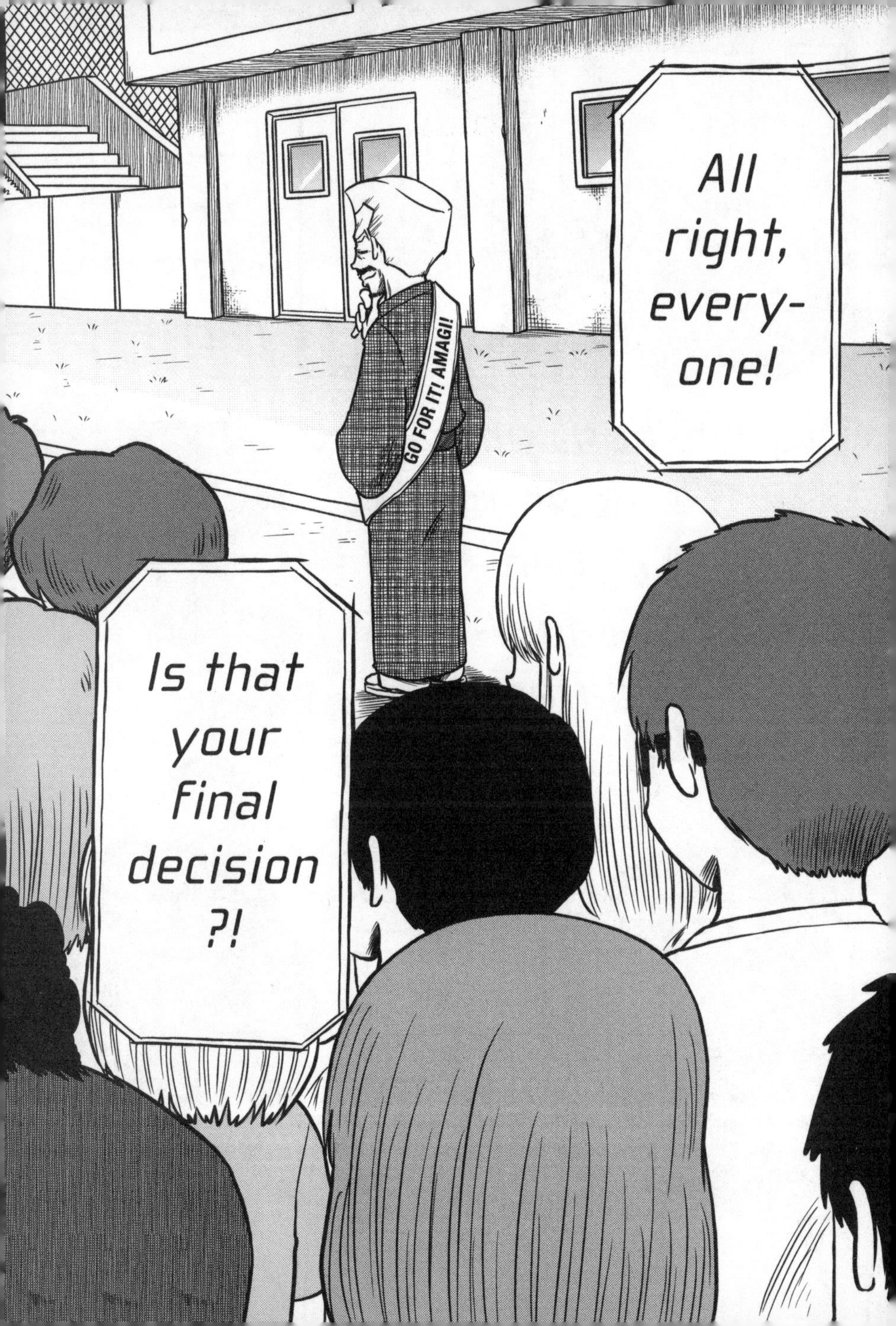
All right, every-one!
GO FOR IT! AMAGI!
Is that your final decision?!

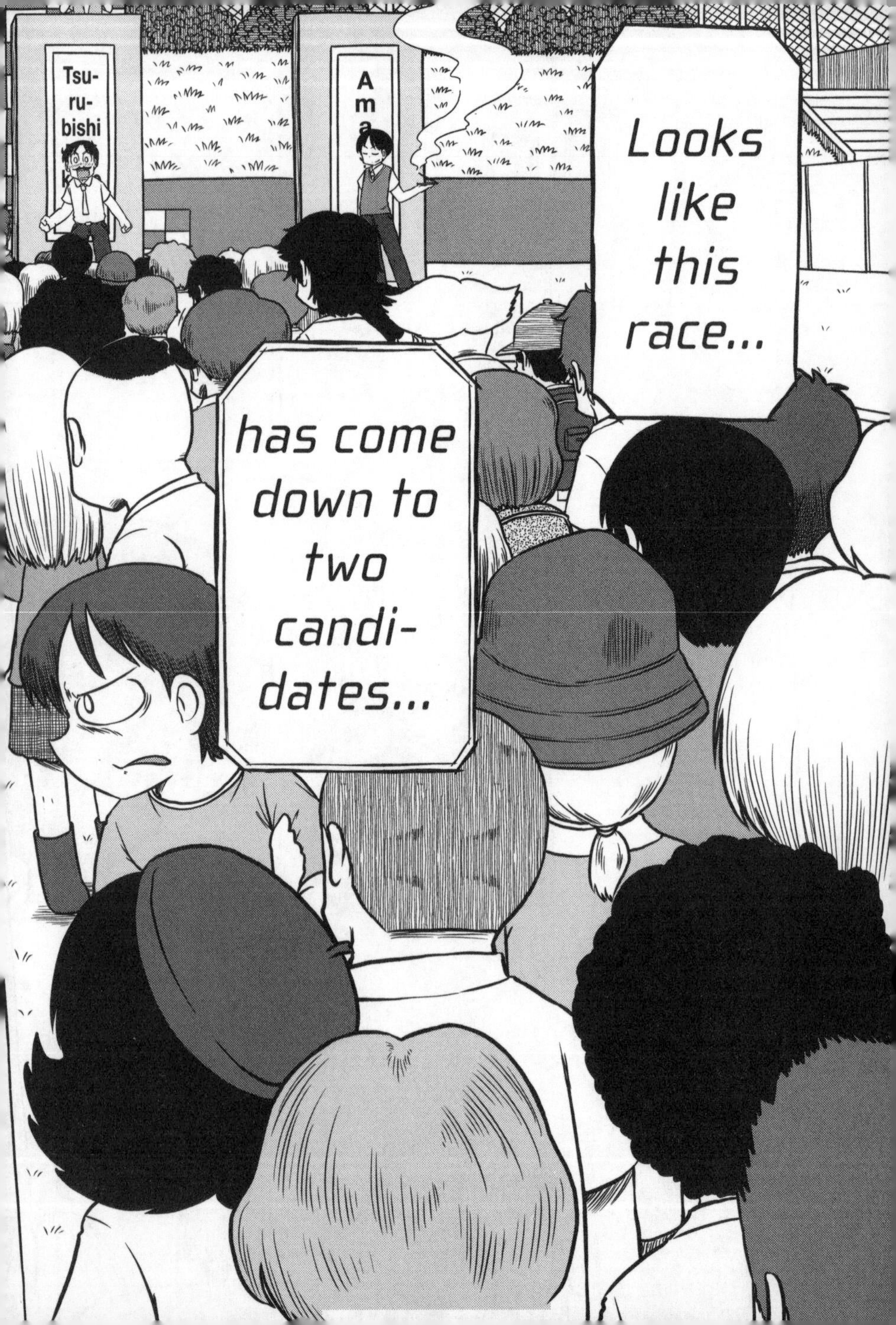
Looks like this race...
A m a
has come down to two candi- dates...
Tsu- ru- bishi

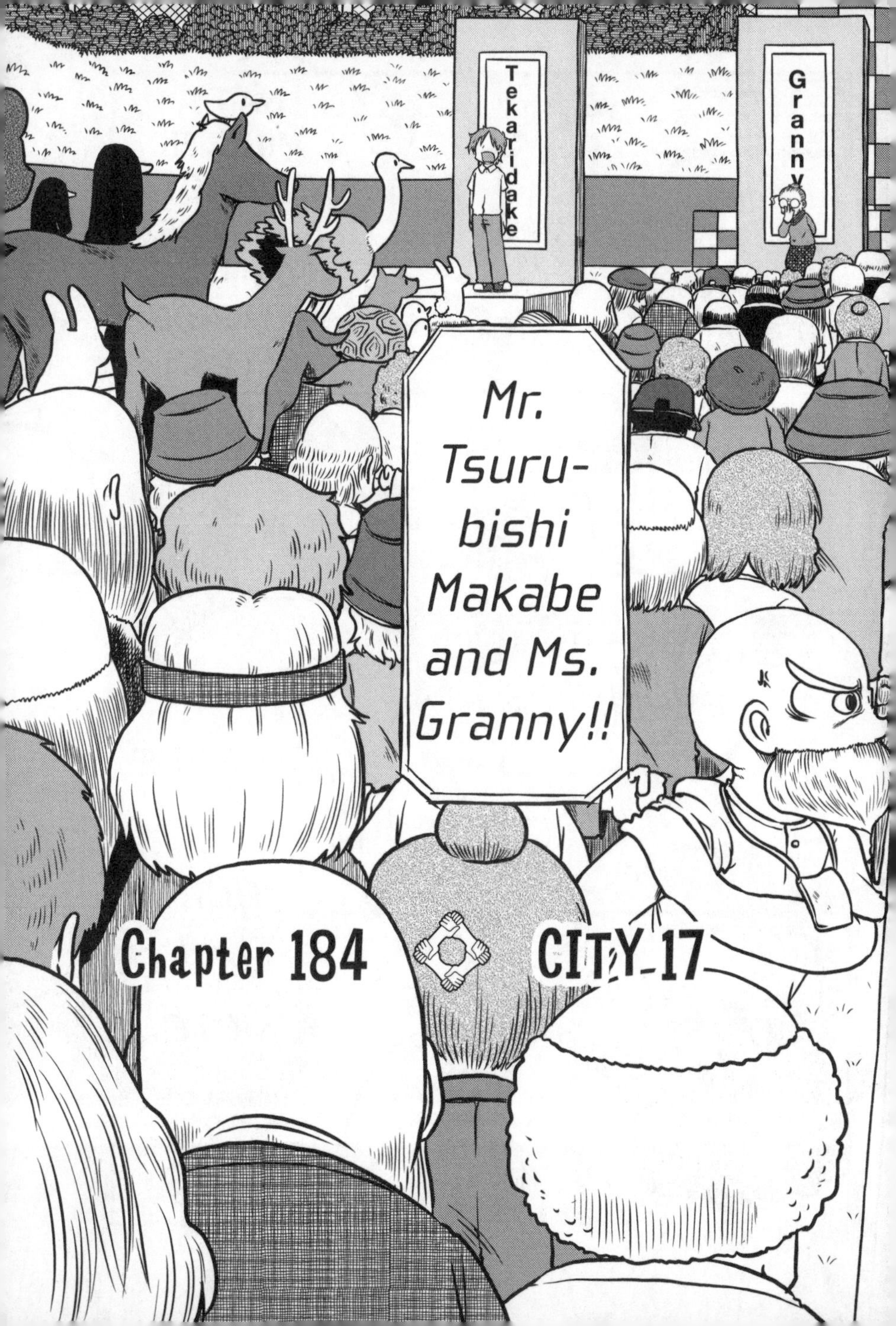
Tekaridake
Granny
Mr. Tsuru-bishi Makabe and Ms. Granny!!
Chapter 184
CITY 17

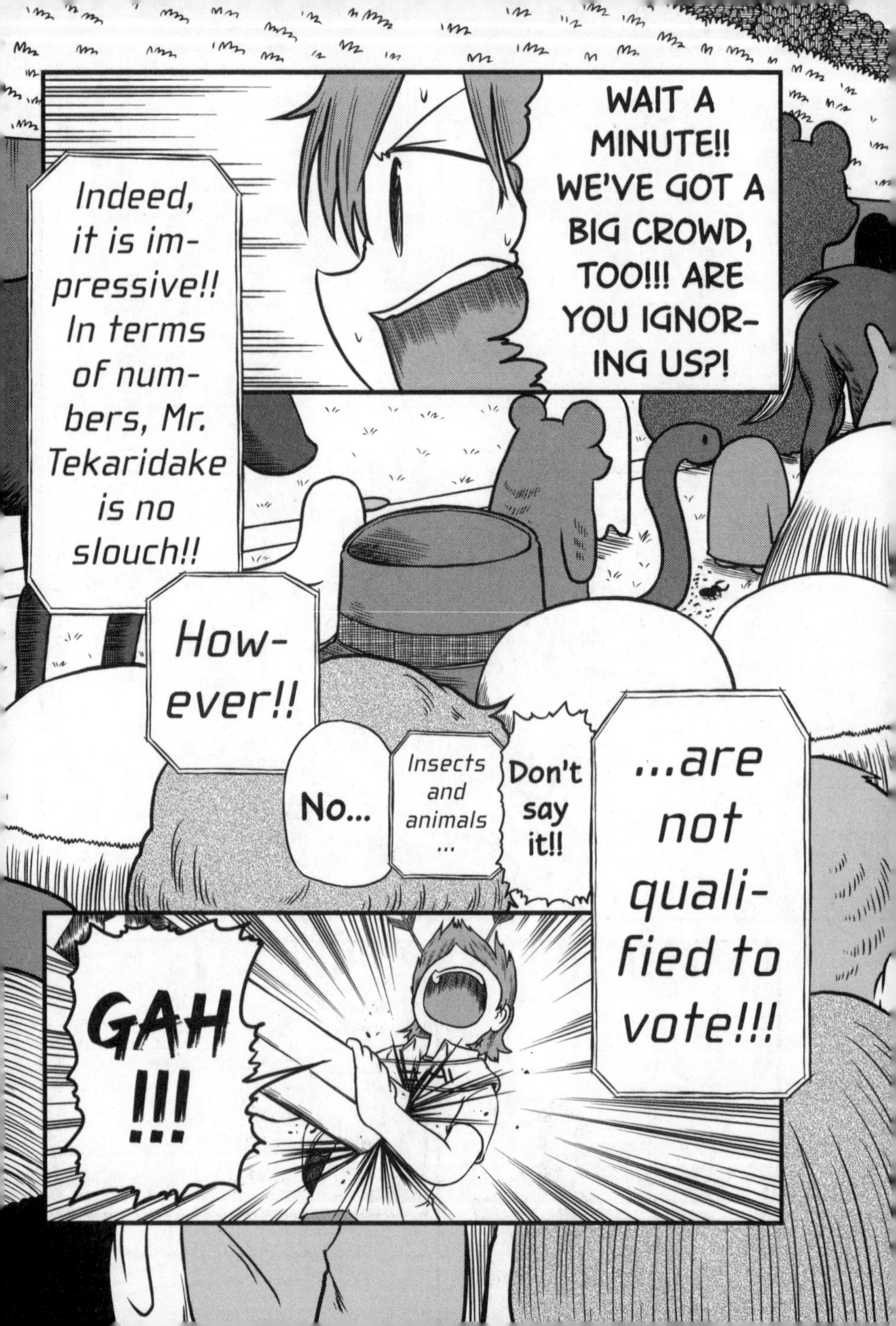
WAIT A MINUTE!! WE'VE GOT A BIG CROWD, TOO!!! ARE YOU IGNOR-ING US?!
Indeed, it is im-pressive!! In terms of num-bers, Mr. Tekaridake is no slouch!!
How-ever!!
Insects and animals ...
Don't say it!!
No...
...are not quali-fied to vote!!!
GAH !!!

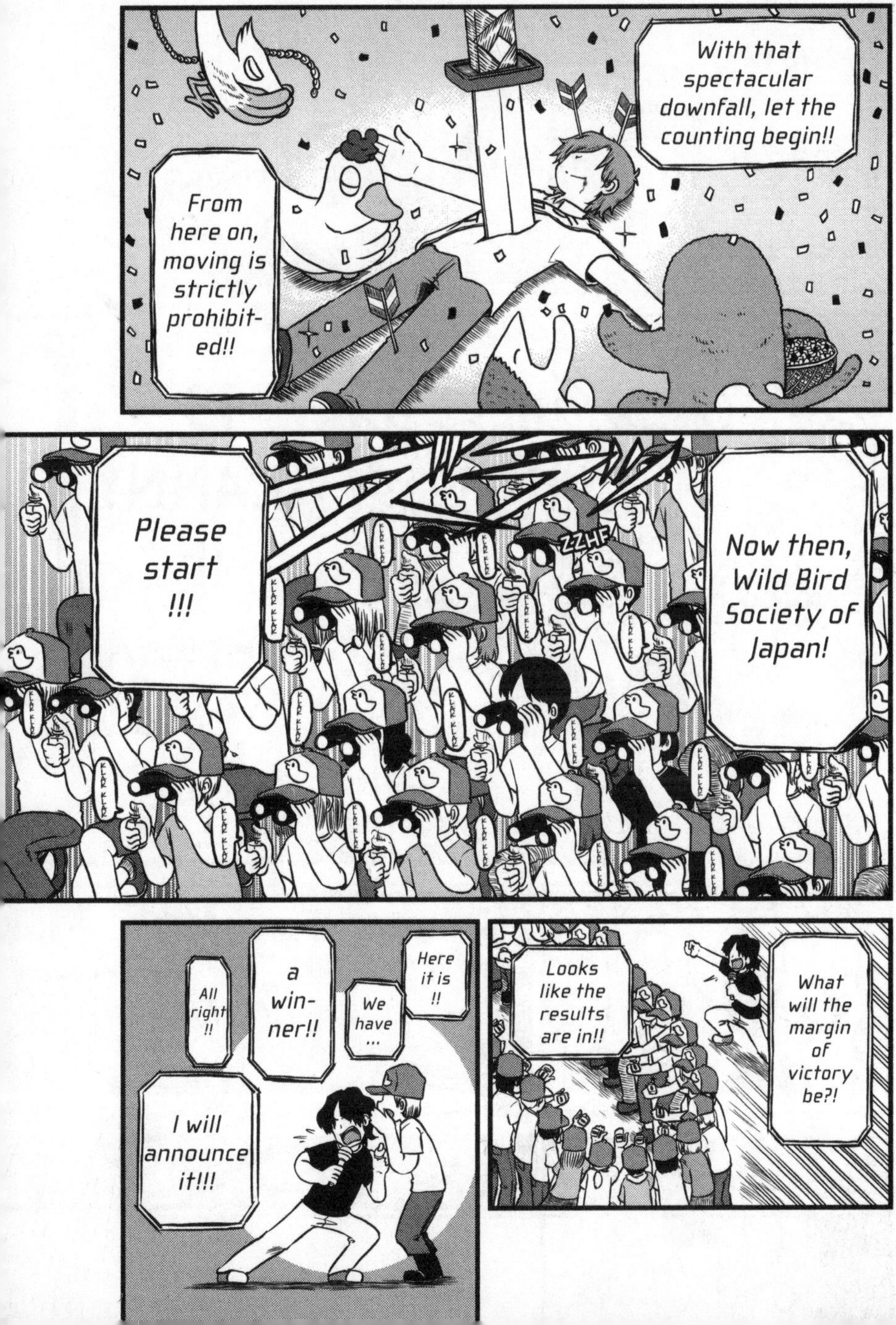
With that spectacular downfall, let the counting begin!!
From here on, moving is strictly prohibit-ed!!
Now then, Wild Bird Society of Japan!
ZZHF
Please start !!!
KLAK KLAK
What will the margin of victory be?!
Looks like the results are in!!
Here it is !!
We have ...
a win-ner!!
All right !!
I will announce it!!!

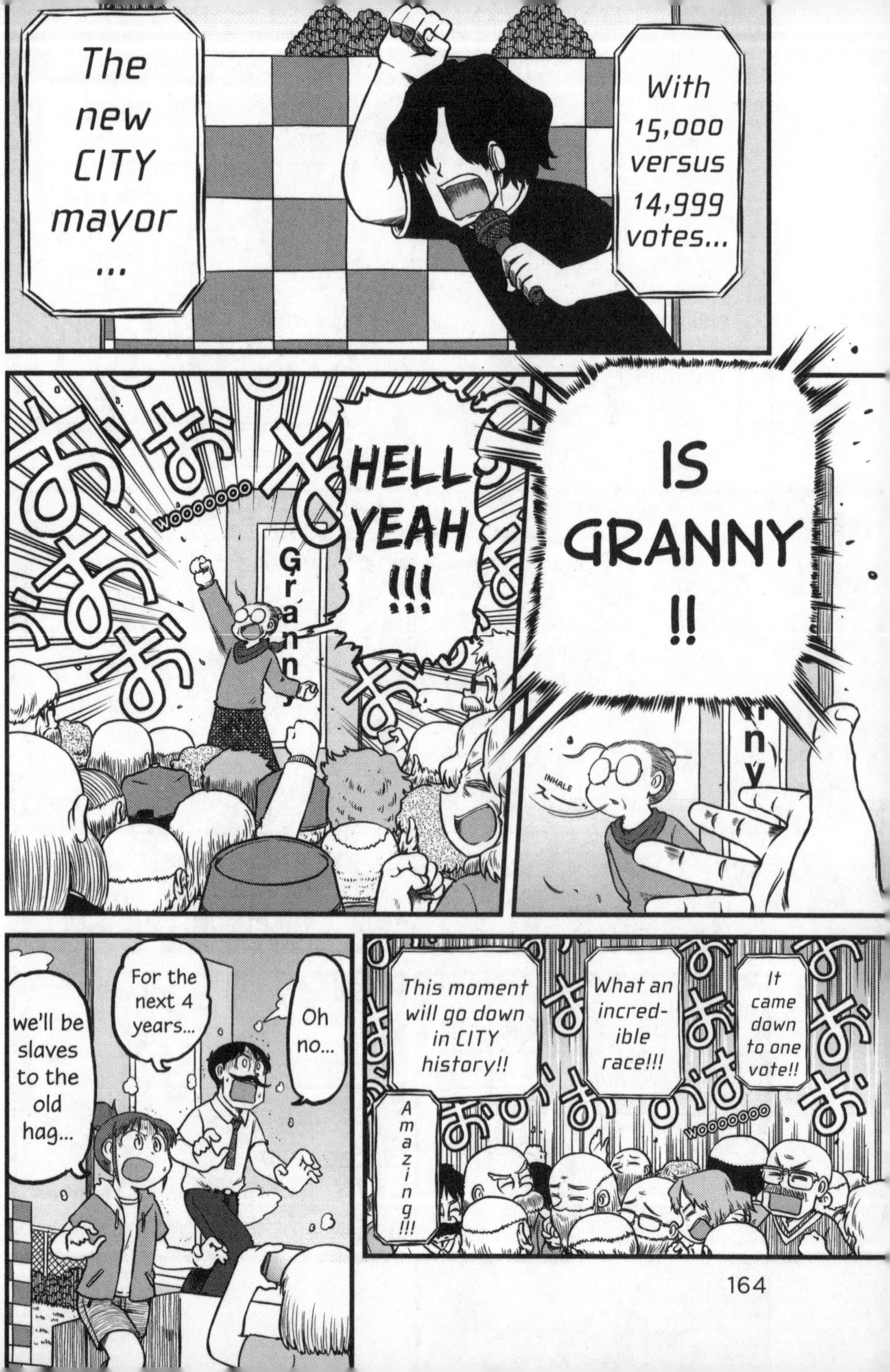
With 15,000 versus 14,999 votes...
The new CITY mayor ...
IS GRANNY !!
INHALE
HELL YEAH !!!
Granny
WOOOOOOO
It came down to one vote!!
What an incredible race!!!
This moment will go down in CITY history!!
Amazing!!!
WOOOOOOO
Oh no...
For the next 4 years...
we'll be slaves to the old hag...

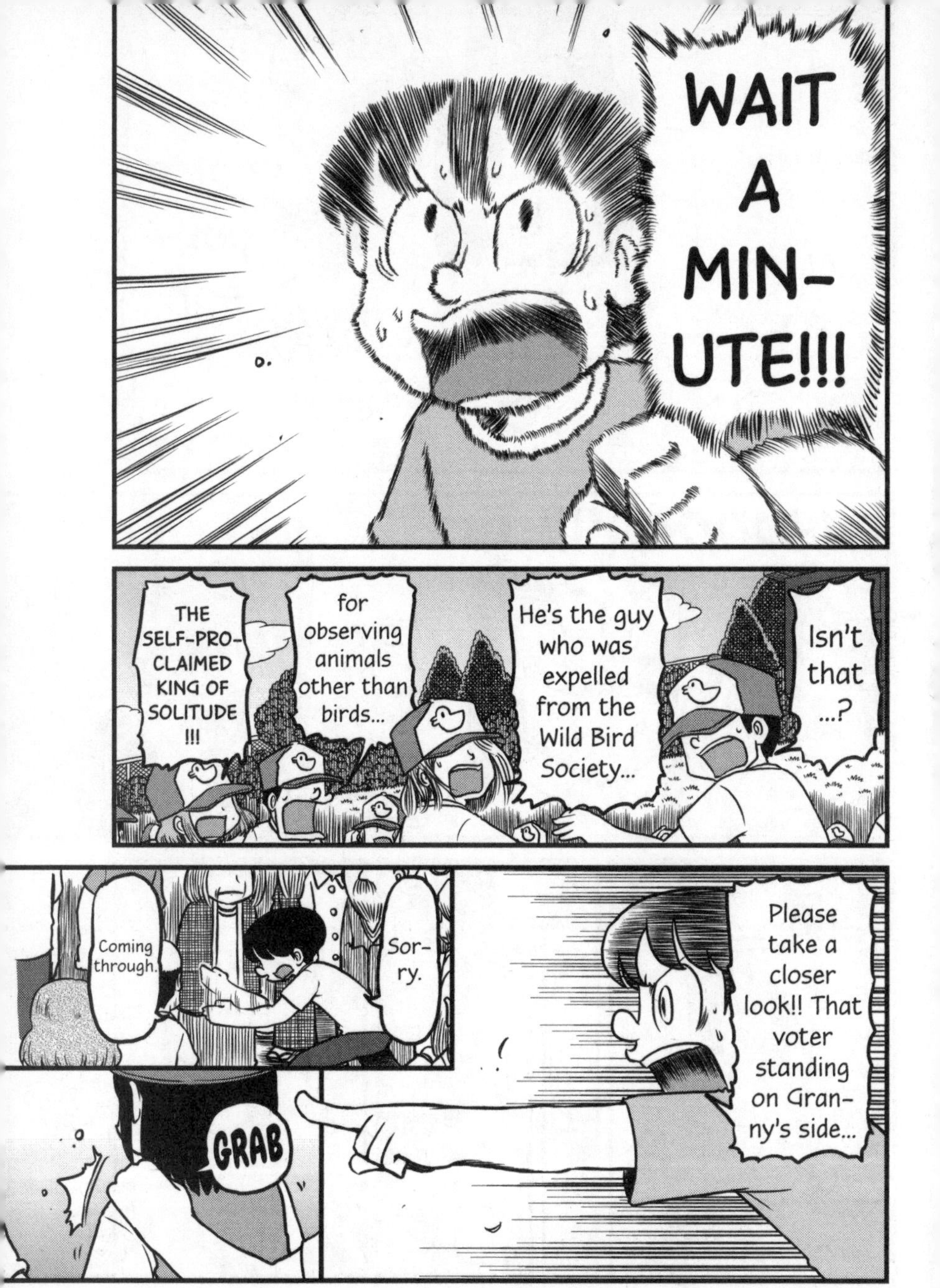
WAIT A MIN-UTE!!!
Isn't that ...?
He's the guy who was expelled from the Wild Bird Society...
for observing animals other than birds...
THE SELF-PRO-CLAIMED KING OF SOLITUDE !!!
Please take a closer look!! That voter standing on Gran-ny's side...
Sor-ry.
Coming through.
GRAB

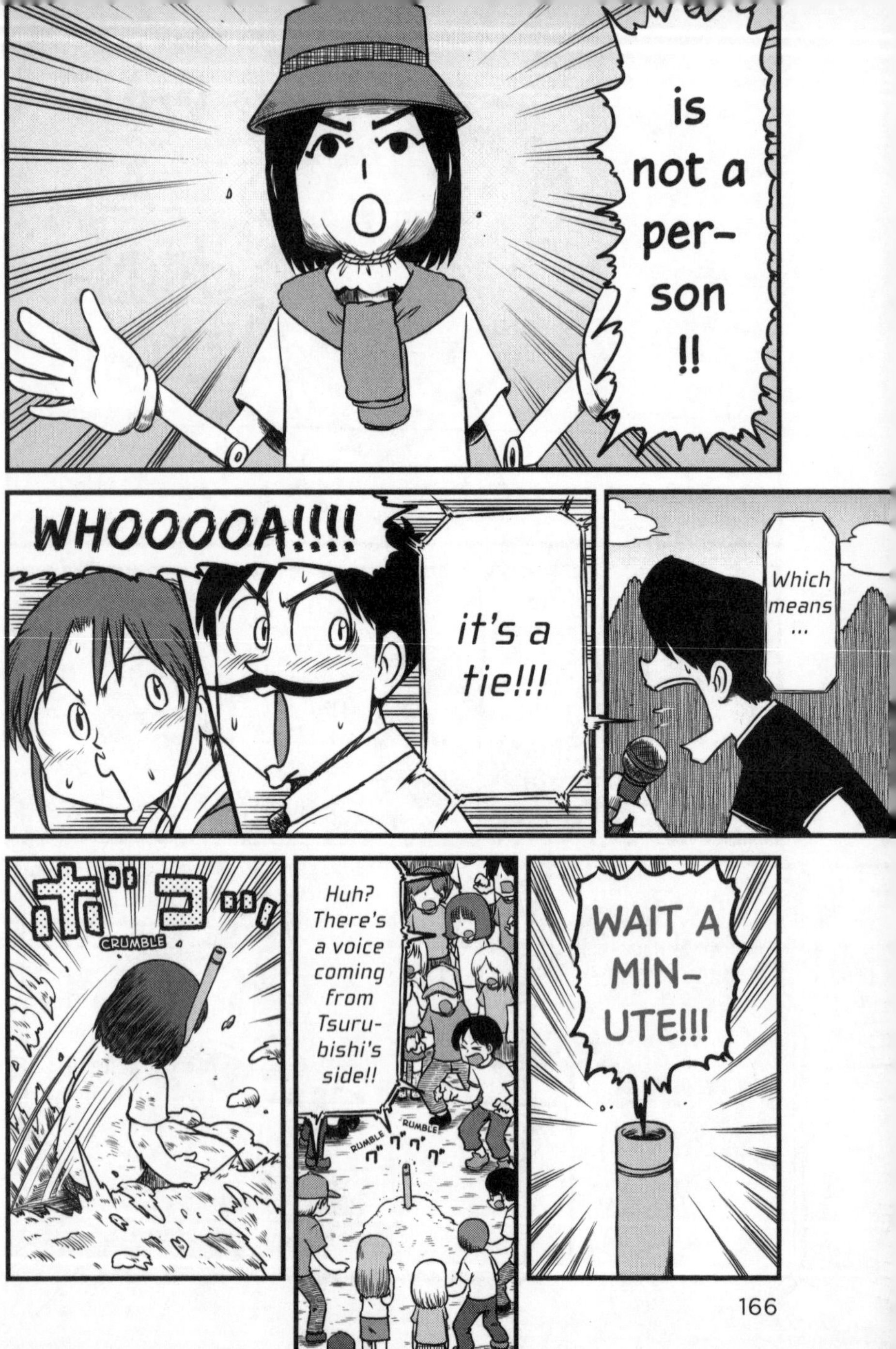
is not a per-son !!
Which means ...
it's a tie!!!
WHOOOOA!!!!
WAIT A MIN-UTE!!!
Huh? There's a voice coming from Tsuru-bishi's side!!
RUMBLE
RUMBLE
ボコッ
CRUMBLE

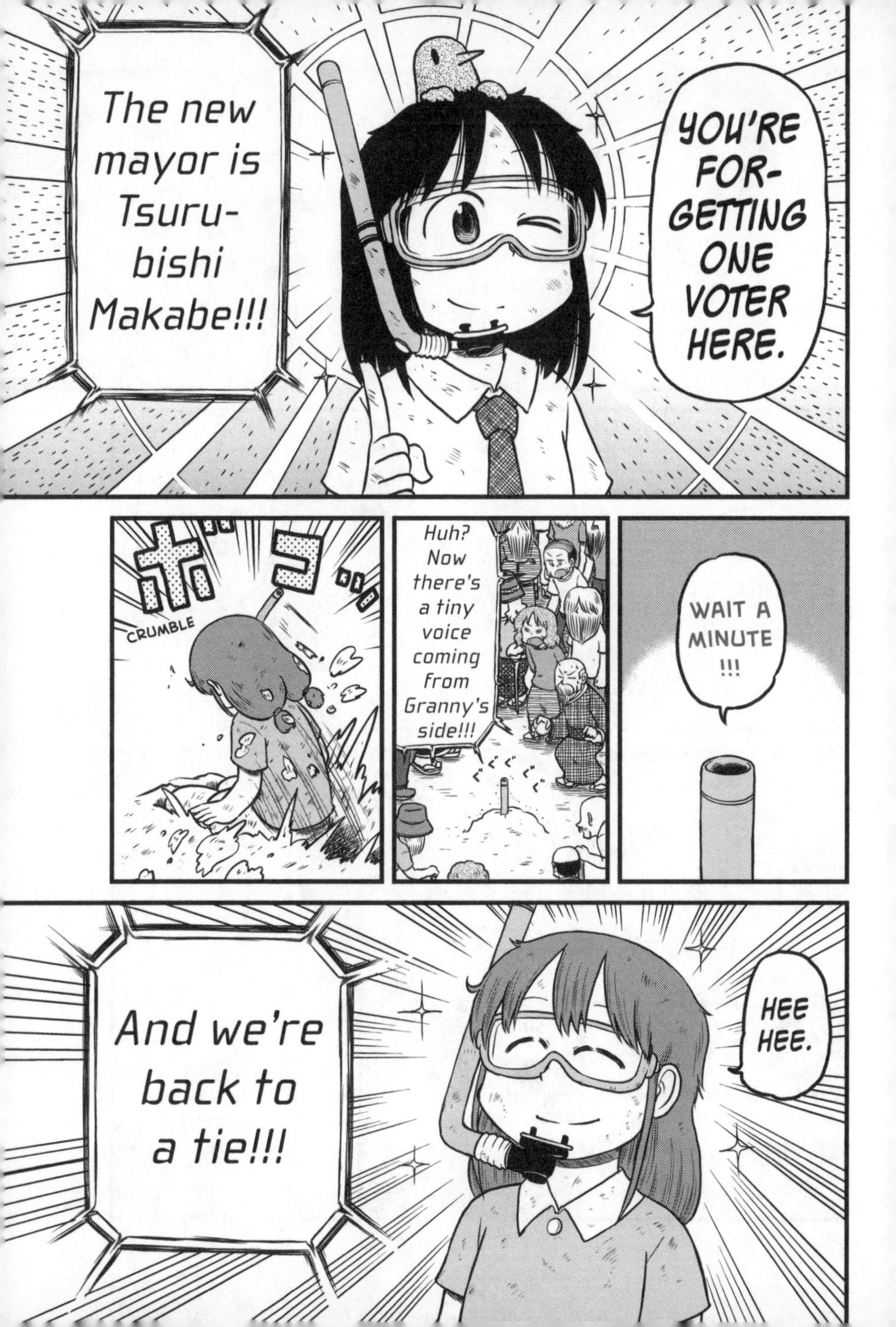
The new mayor is Tsurubishi Makabe!!!
YOU'RE FOR-GETTING ONE VOTER HERE.
WAIT A MINUTE !!!
Huh? Now there's a tiny voice coming from Granny's side!!!
CRUMBLE
HEE HEE.
And we're back to a tie!!!

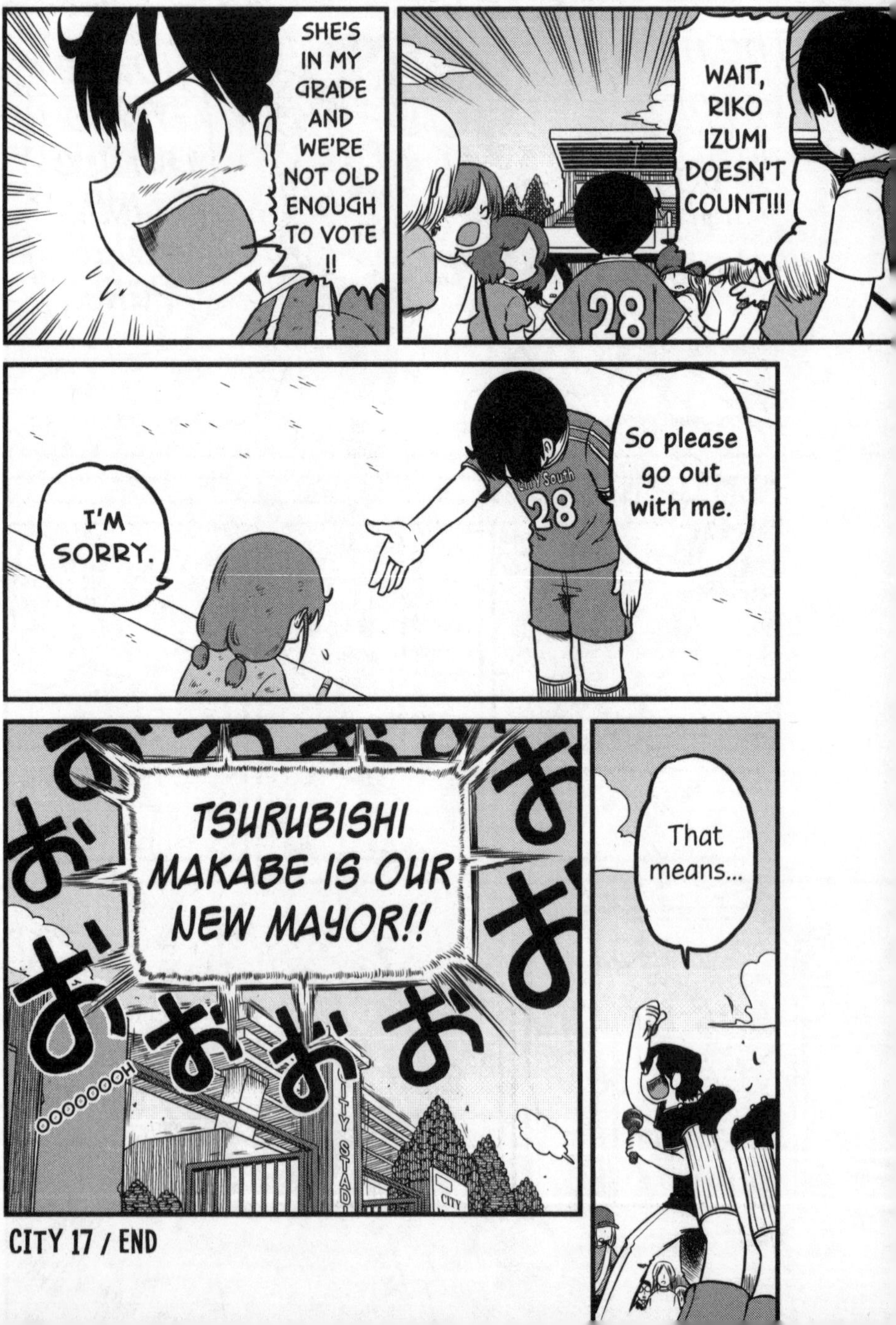
WAIT, RIKO IZUMI DOESN'T COUNT!!!
SHE'S IN MY GRADE AND WE'RE NOT OLD ENOUGH TO VOTE !!
So please go out with me.
I'M SORRY.
That means...
TSURUBISHI MAKABE IS OUR NEW MAYOR!!
おおおおおお
OOOOOOOH

CITY 17 / END

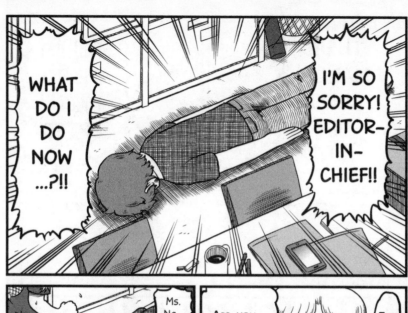

I'M SO SORRY! EDITOR-IN-CHIEF!!
WHAT DO I DO NOW ...?!!
To-do-roki ...
Are you... lying on the floor? Or are you groveling?
Ms. Na-gano-hara and Mr. Kama Oni...
I WAS TOO NICE TO BOTH OF THEM!!!
What ... do you mean ...?

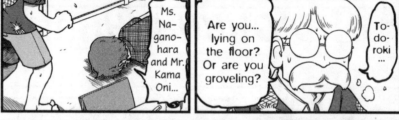

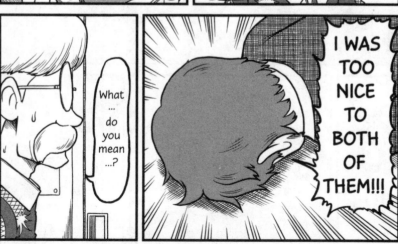

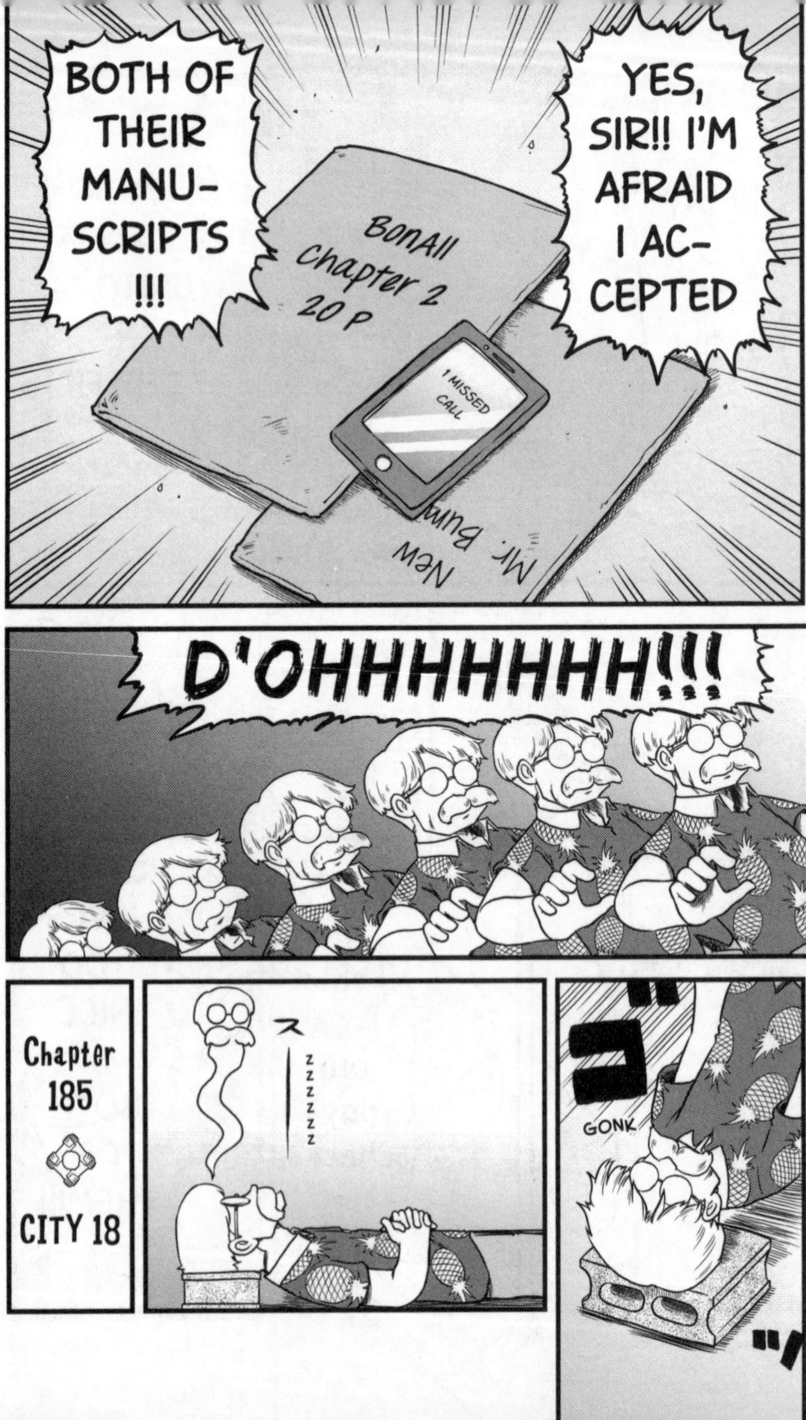
YES, SIR!! I'M AFRAID I AC-CEPTED
BOTH OF THEIR MANU-SCRIPTS !!!
BonAll Chapter 2 20 P
1 MISSED CALL
New Mr. Bum
D'OHHHHHHH!!!
ゴ
GONK
ス
ZZZZZZ
Chapter 185
CITY 18

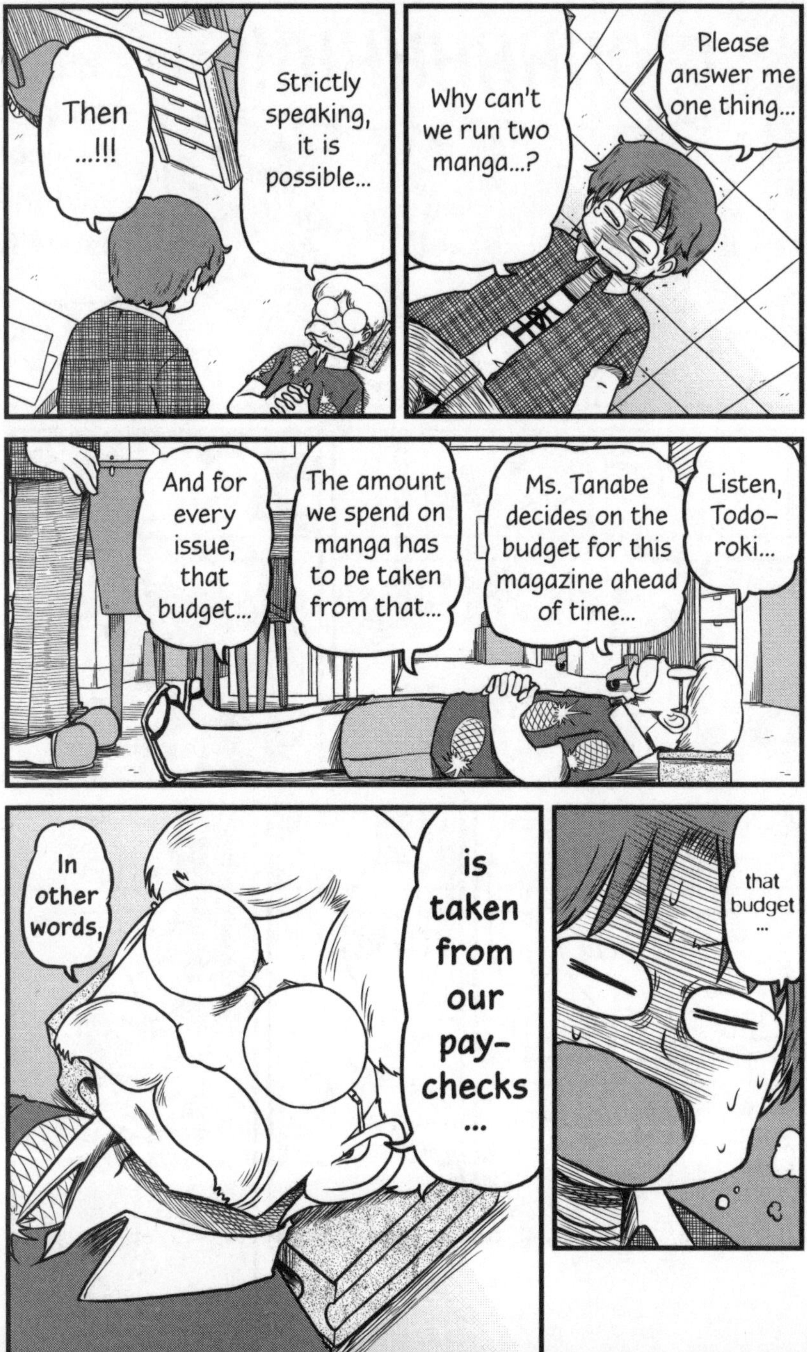
Please answer me one thing...
Why can't we run two manga...?
Strictly speaking, it is possible...
Then ...!!!
Listen, Todoroki...
Ms. Tanabe decides on the budget for this magazine ahead of time...
The amount we spend on manga has to be taken from that...
And for every issue, that budget...
that budget ...
is taken from our paychecks ...
In other words,

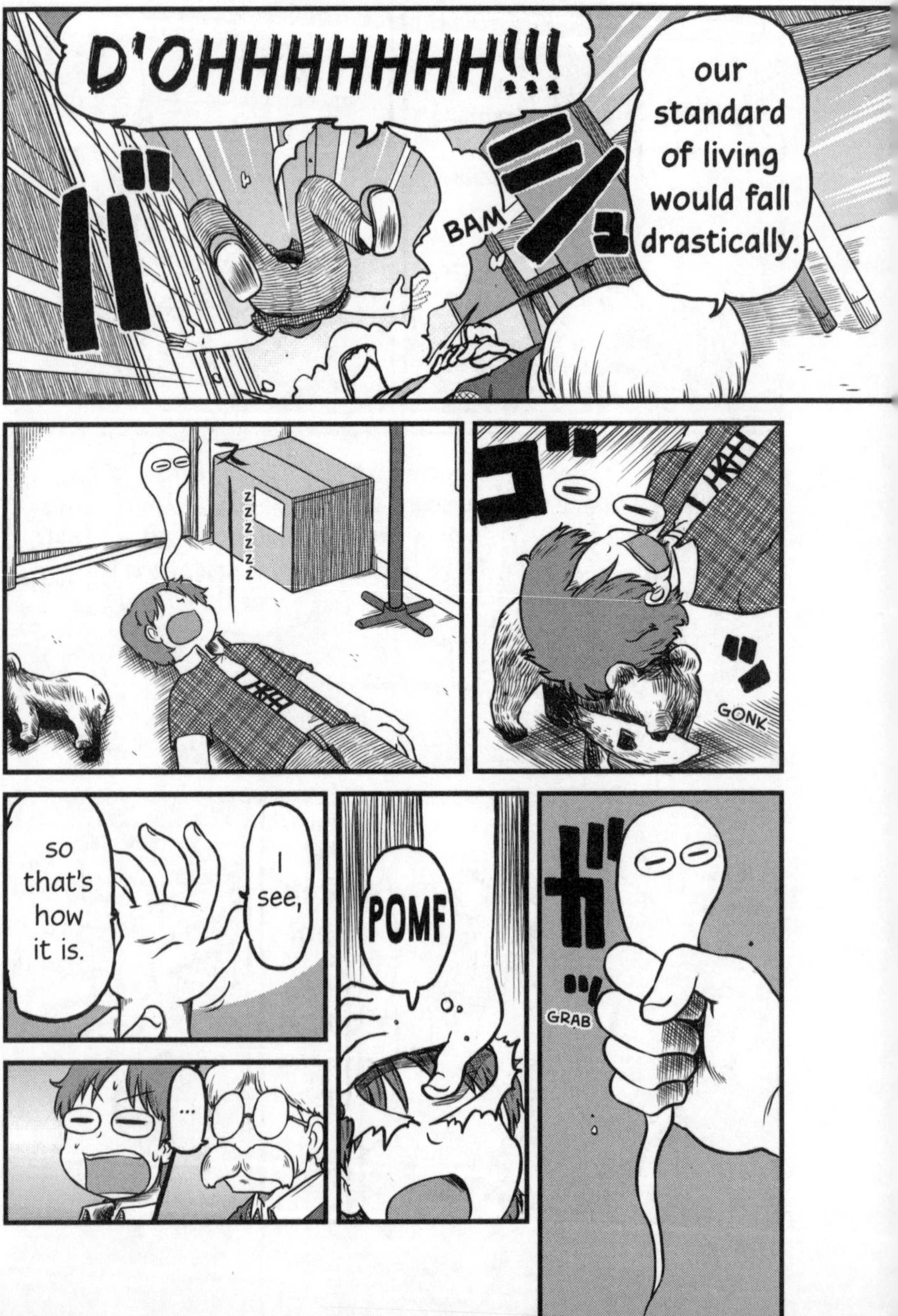
our standard of living would fall drastically.
BAM
D'OHHHHHHHH!!!
GONK
ZZZZZZ
GRAB
POMF
I see,
so that's how it is.
...

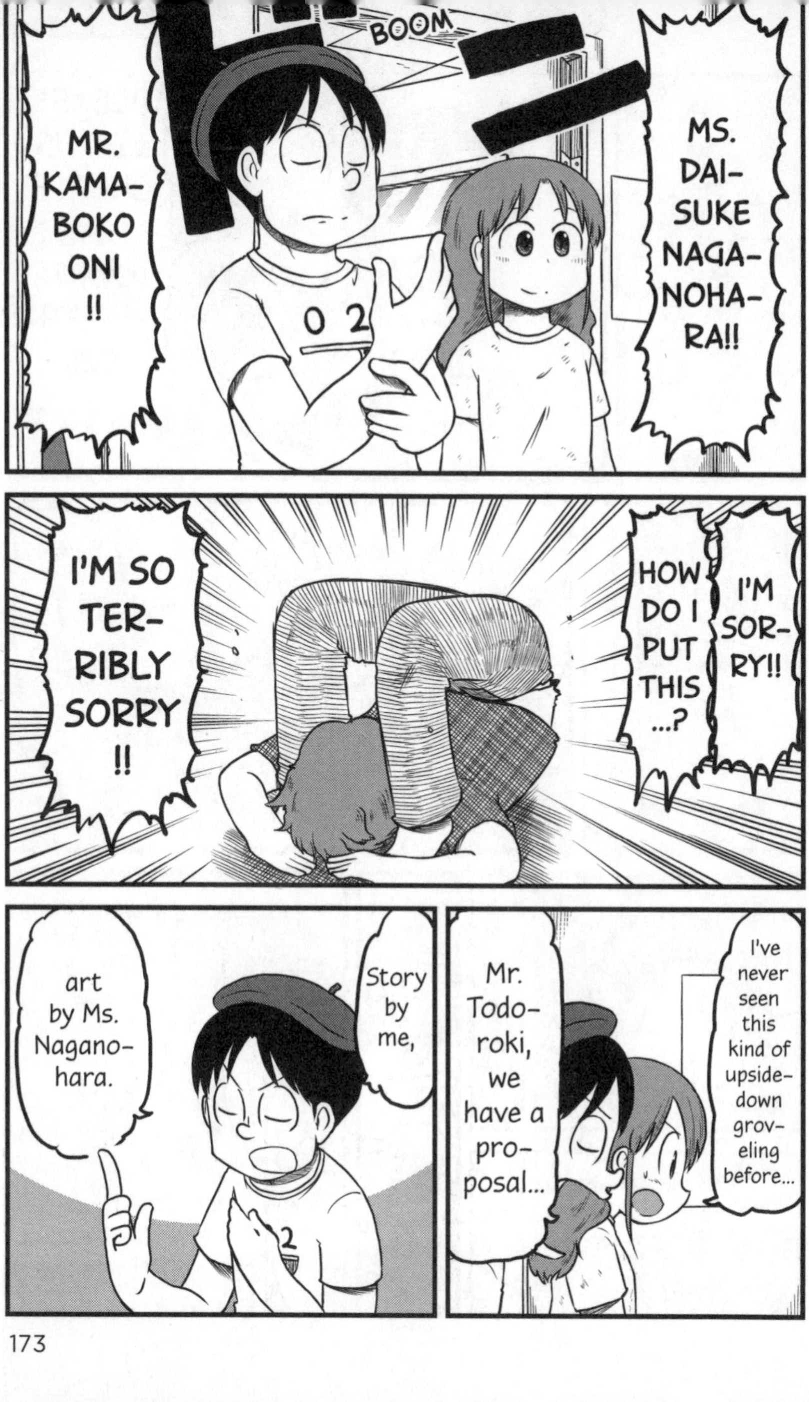
MS. DAISUKE NAGANOHARA!!
BOOM
MR. KAMABOKO ONI!!
I'M SORRY!!
HOW DO I PUT THIS...?
I'M SO TERRIBLY SORRY!!
I've never seen this kind of upside-down groveling before...
Mr. Todoroki, we have a proposal...
Story by me,
art by Ms. Naganohara.

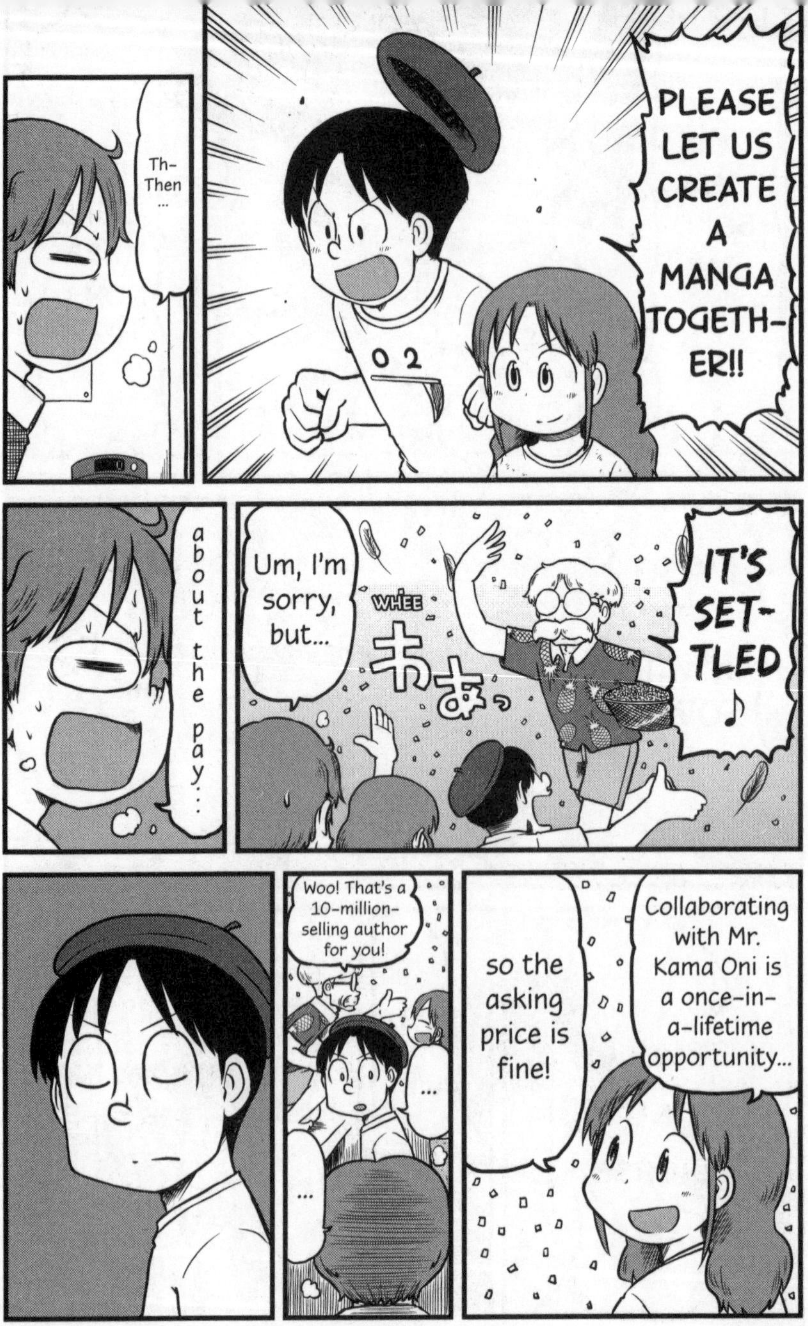
PLEASE LET US CREATE A MANGA TOGETH-ER!!
Th- Then ...
IT'S SET-TLED ♪
Um, I'm sorry, but...
WHEE
わあっ
about the pay...
Collaborating with Mr. Kama Oni is a once-in-a-lifetime opportunity...
so the asking price is fine!
Woo! That's a 10-million-selling author for you!
...
...

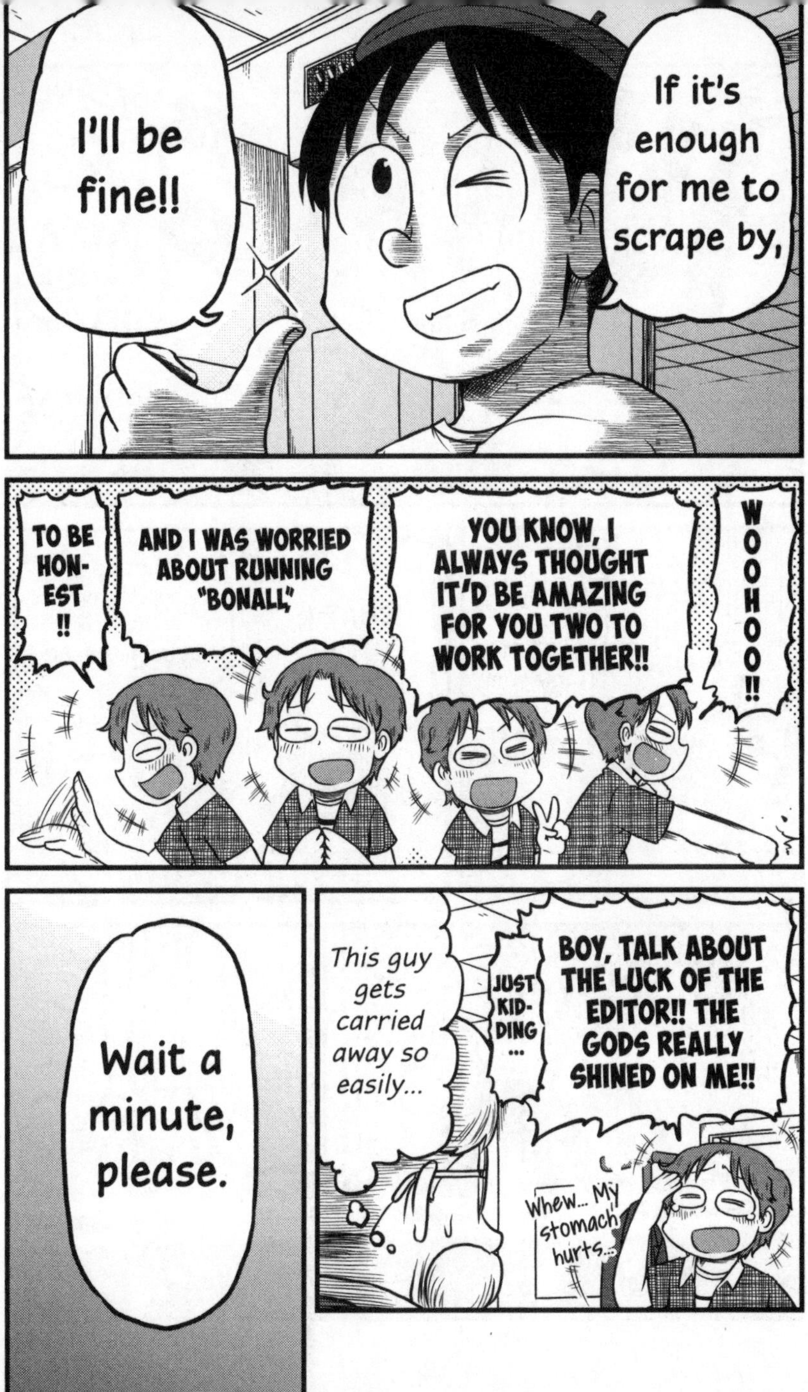
If it's enough for me to scrape by,
I'll be fine!!
WOOHOO!!
YOU KNOW, I ALWAYS THOUGHT IT'D BE AMAZING FOR YOU TWO TO WORK TOGETHER!!
AND I WAS WORRIED ABOUT RUNNING "BONALL,"
TO BE HON-EST!!
BOY, TALK ABOUT THE LUCK OF THE EDITOR!! THE GODS REALLY SHINED ON ME!!
JUST KID-DING...
This guy gets carried away so easily...
Whew... My stomach hurts...
Wait a minute, please.

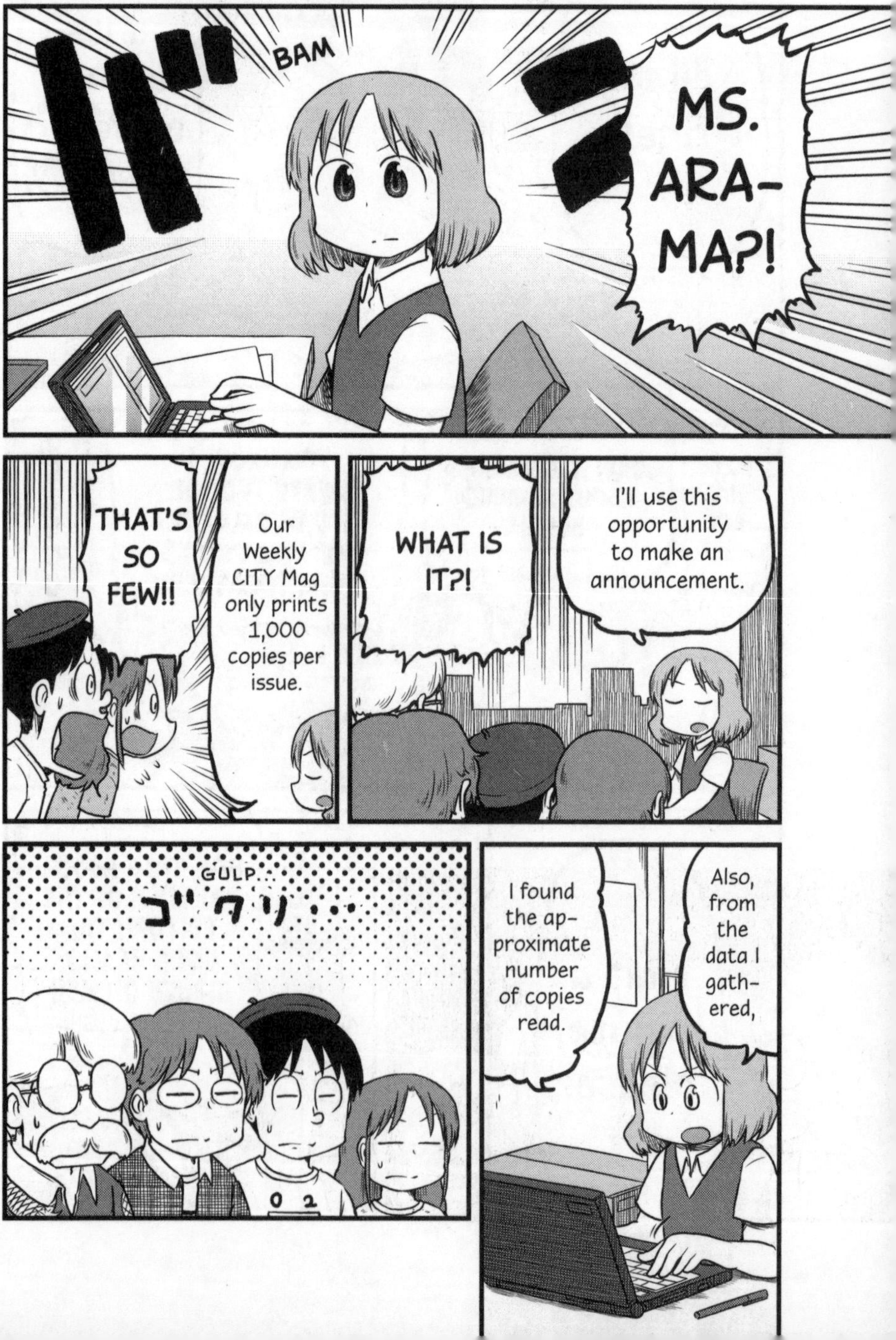
BAM
MS. ARA-MA?!
I'll use this opportunity to make an announcement.
WHAT IS IT?!
Our Weekly CITY Mag only prints 1,000 copies per issue.
THAT'S SO FEW!!
Also, from the data I gathered,
I found the ap-proximate number of copies read.
GULP...
ゴクリ…
0 2

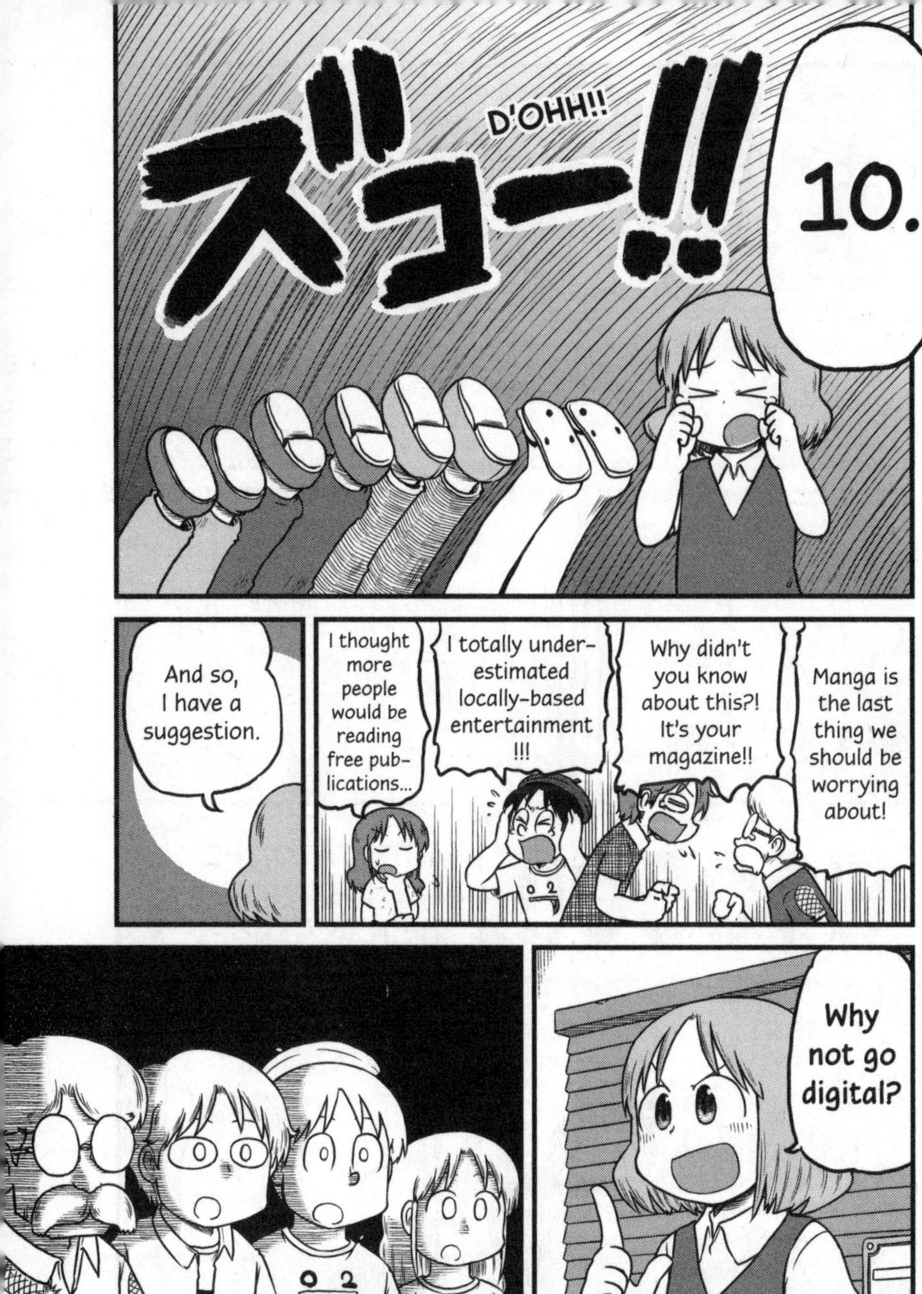
10.
ズコー!!
D'OHH!!
Manga is the last thing we should be worrying about!
Why didn't you know about this?! It's your magazine!!
I totally under-estimated locally-based entertainment !!!
I thought more people would be reading free pub-lications...
And so, I have a suggestion.
Why not go digital?

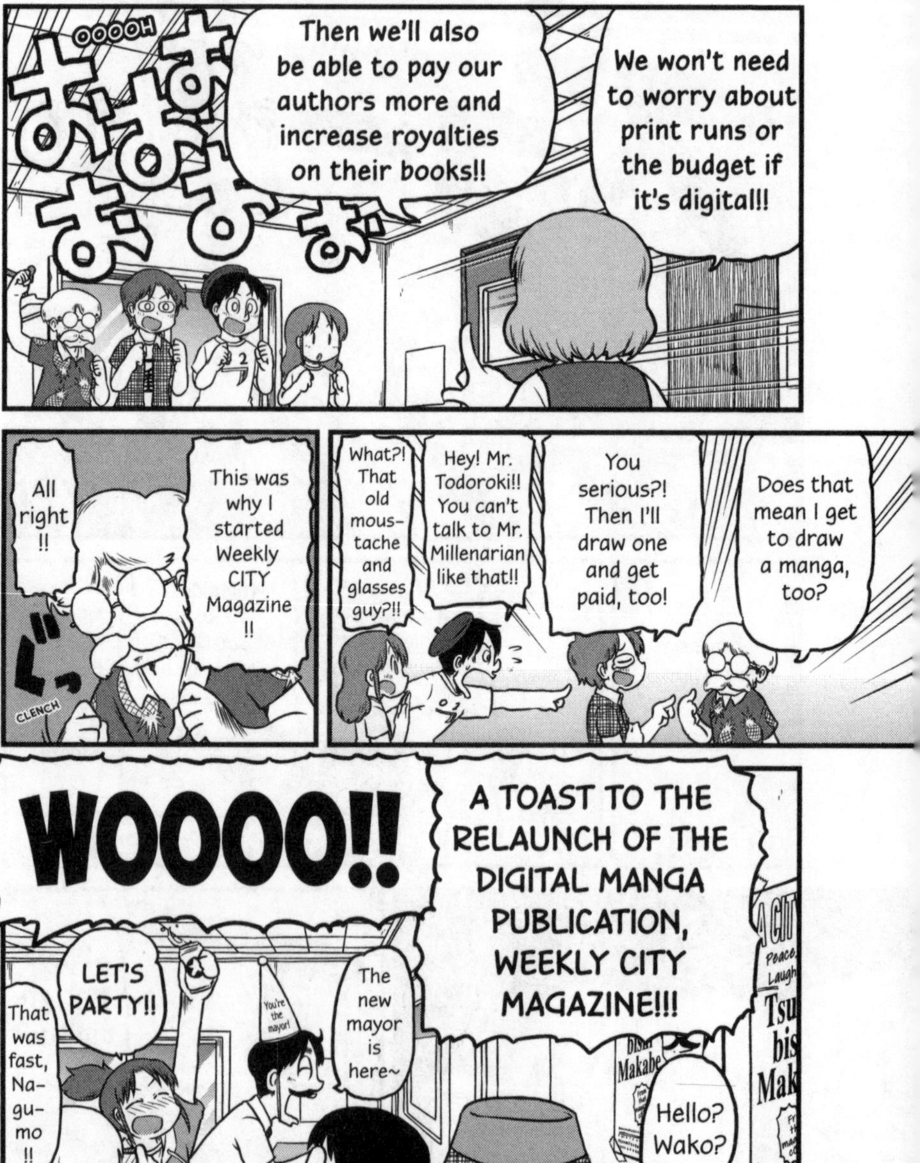
We won't need to worry about print runs or the budget if it's digital!!
Then we'll also be able to pay our authors more and increase royalties on their books!!
OOOOH
Does that mean I get to draw a manga, too?
You serious?! Then I'll draw one and get paid, too!
Hey! Mr. Todoroki!! You can't talk to Mr. Millenarian like that!!
What?! That old moustache and glasses guy?!!
This was why I started Weekly CITY Magazine !!
All right !!
CLENCH
A TOAST TO THE RELAUNCH OF THE DIGITAL MANGA PUBLICATION, WEEKLY CITY MAGAZINE!!!
WOOOO!!
Hello? Wako?
The new mayor is here~
You're the mayor!
LET'S PARTY!!
That was fast, Nagumo !!

CITY 18 / END

CONTENTS

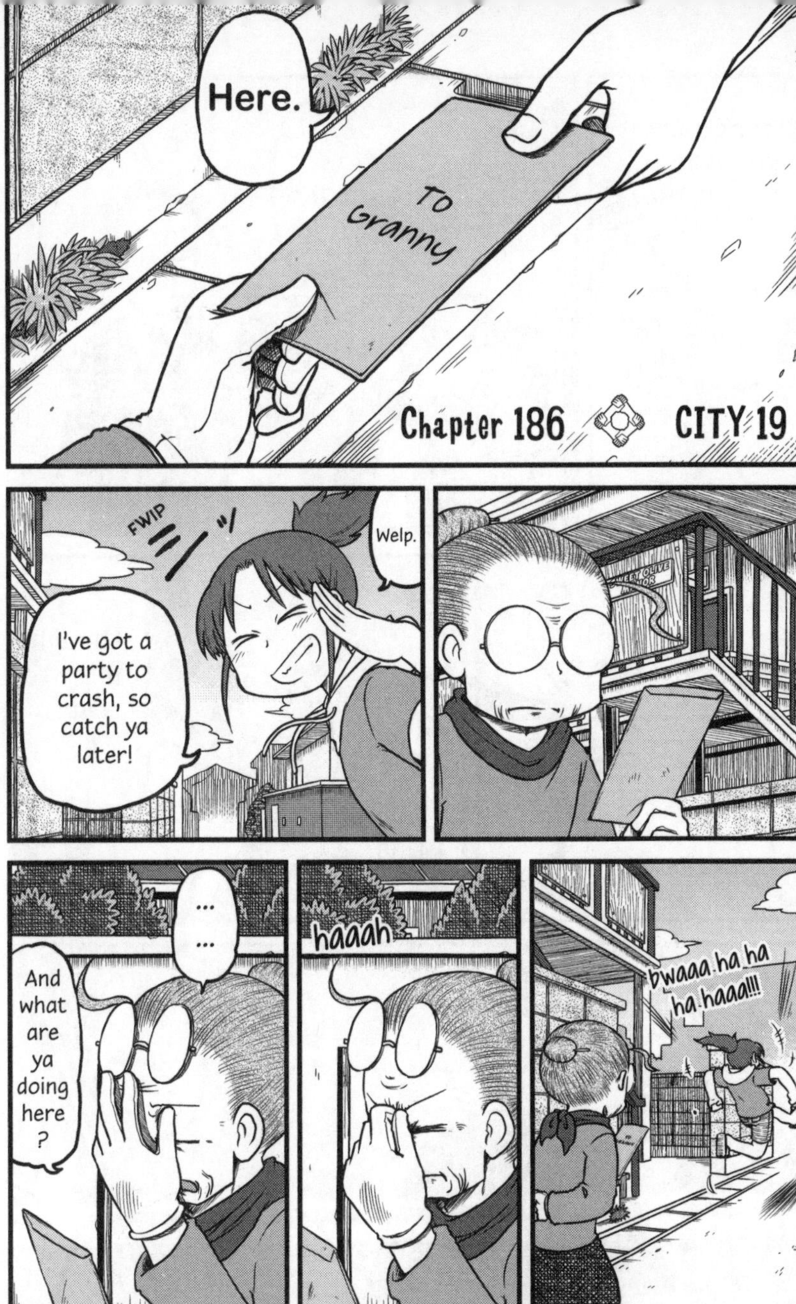
Here.
To Granny
Chapter 186
CITY 19
FWIP
Welp.
I've got a party to crash, so catch ya later!
bwaaa ha ha ha haaa!!!
haaah
... ...
And what are ya doing here?

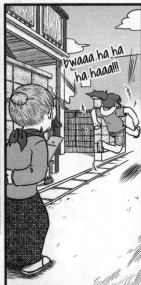

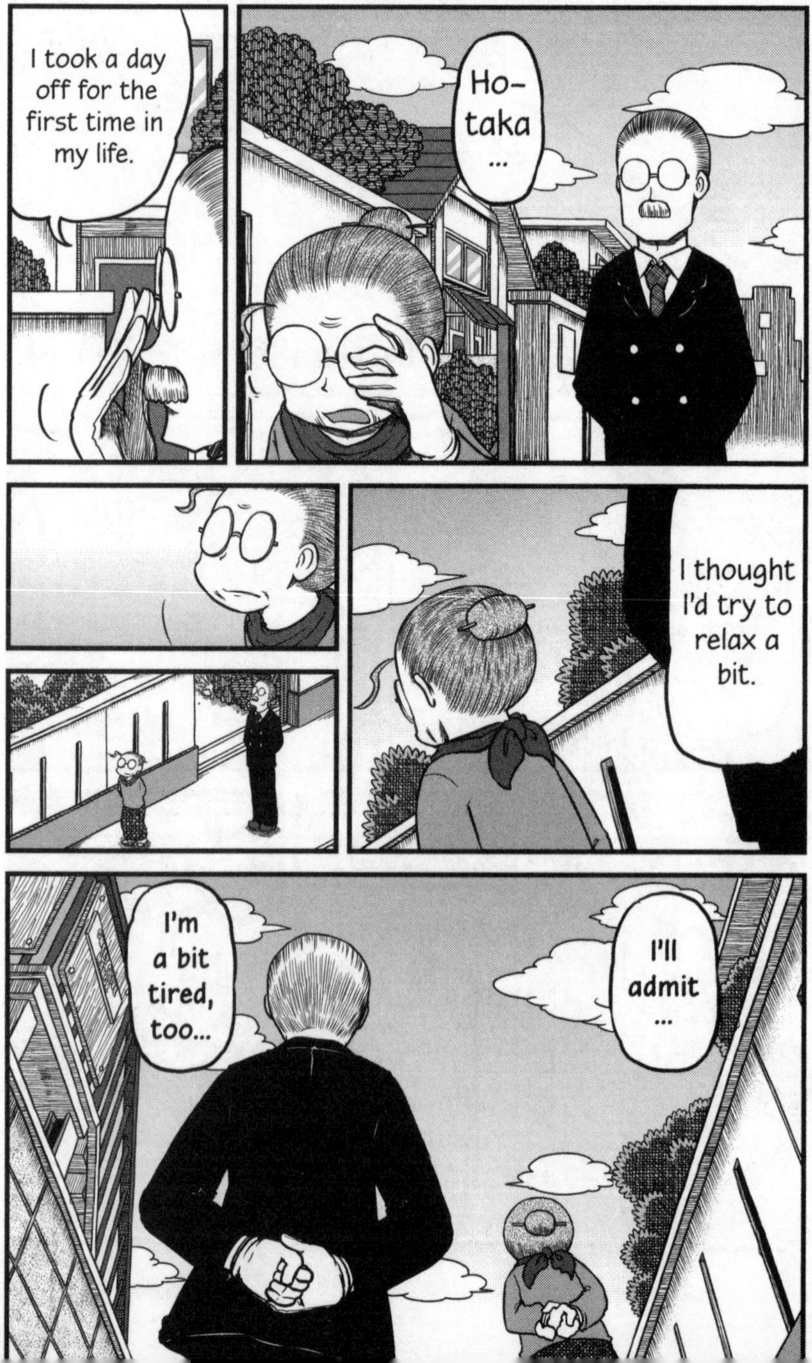
Ho-taka ...
I took a day off for the first time in my life.
I thought I'd try to relax a bit.
I'll admit ...
I'm a bit tired, too...

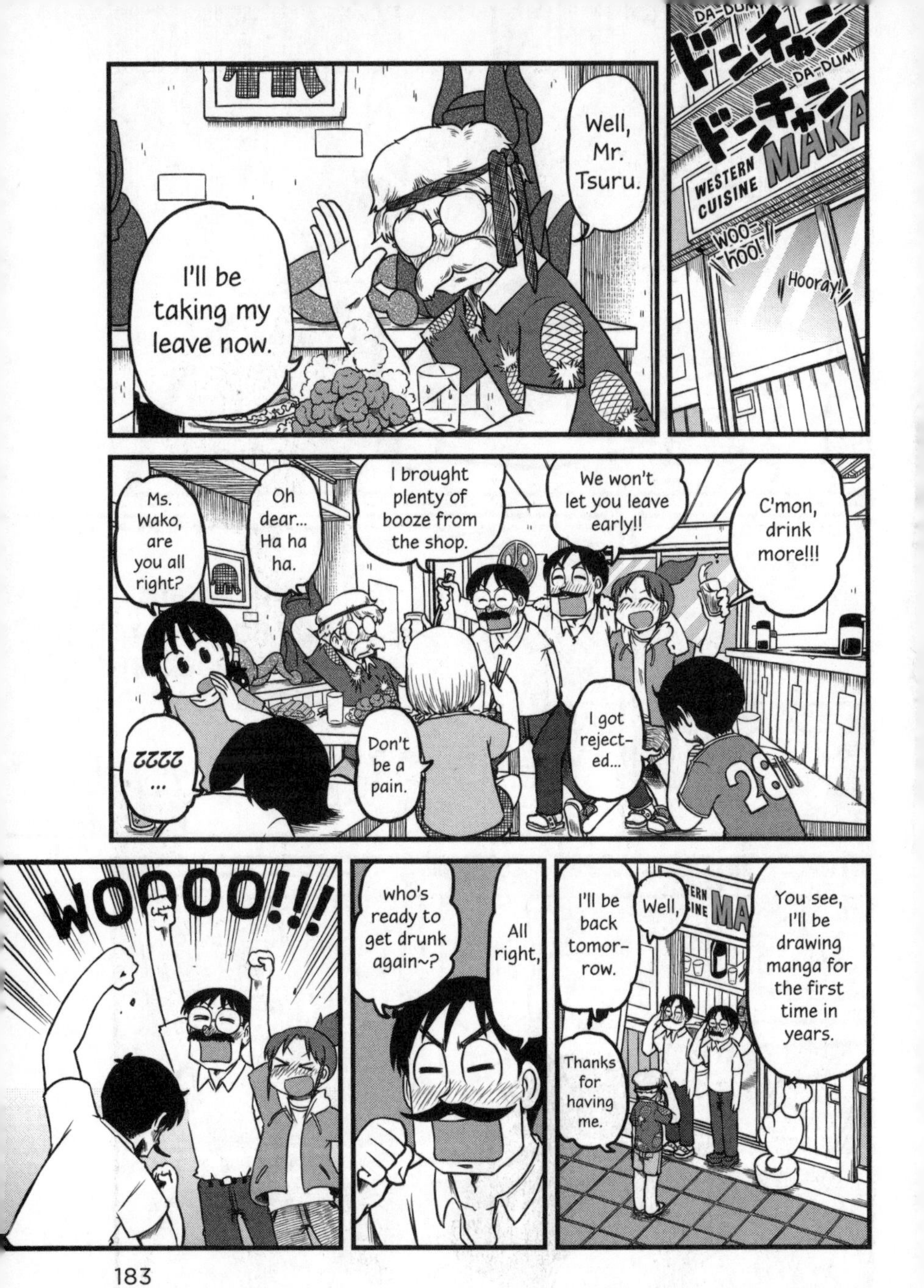
DA-DUM
ドンチャン
DA-DUM
ドンチャン
WESTERN CUISINE
MAKA
WOO-HOO!
Hooray!
Well, Mr. Tsuru.
I'll be taking my leave now.
C'mon, drink more!!!
We won't let you leave early!!
I brought plenty of booze from the shop.
Oh dear... Ha ha ha.
Ms. Wako, are you all right?
I got rejected...
Don't be a pain.
...zzzz
You see, I'll be drawing manga for the first time in years.
Well,
I'll be back tomorrow.
Thanks for having me.
All right,
who's ready to get drunk again~?
WOOOO!!!

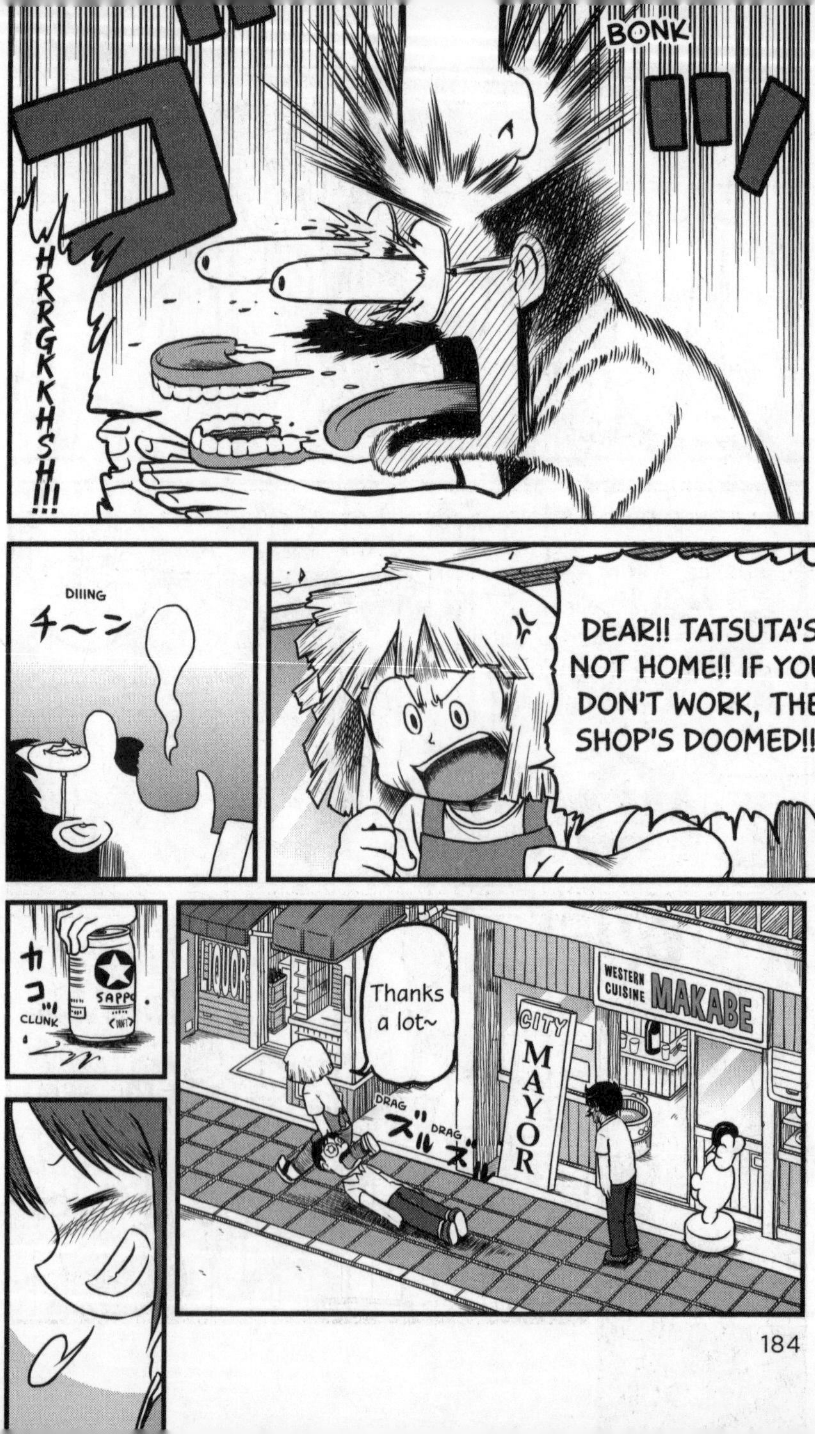
BONK
HRRGKKHSH!!!
DEAR!! TATSUTA'S NOT HOME!! IF YOU DON'T WORK, THE SHOP'S DOOMED!!!
DIIING
チ～ン
Thanks a lot~
LIQUOR
WESTERN CUISINE
MAKABE
CITY
MAYOR
DRAG
ズルズ
DRAG
カコッ
CLUNK
SAPPO

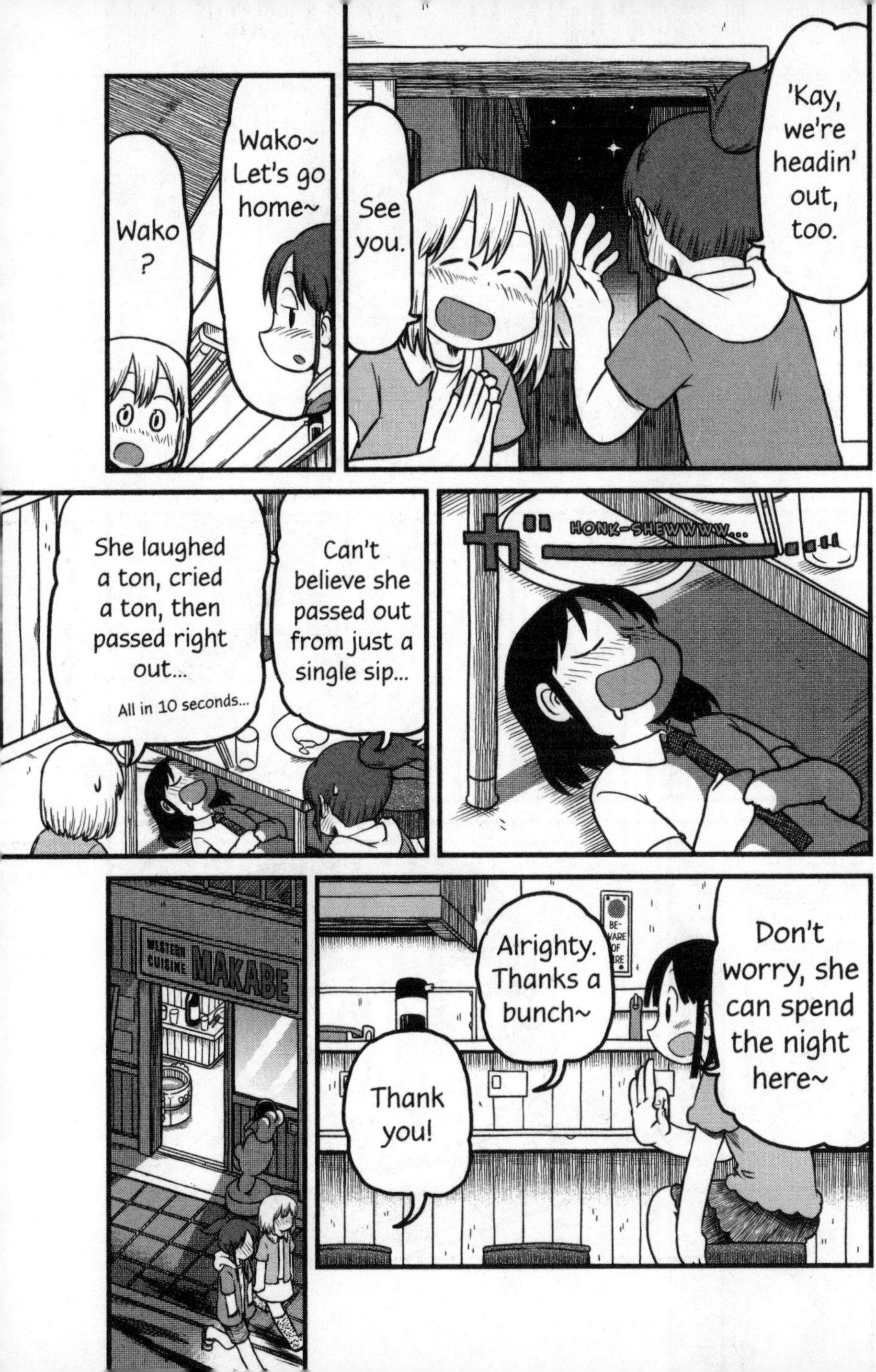
'Kay, we're headin' out, too.
See you.
Wako~ Let's go home~
Wako ?
HONK-SHEWWWWW...
Can't believe she passed out from just a single sip...
She laughed a ton, cried a ton, then passed right out...
All in 10 seconds...
Don't worry, she can spend the night here~
Alrighty. Thanks a bunch~
Thank you!
WESTERN CUISINE MAKABE

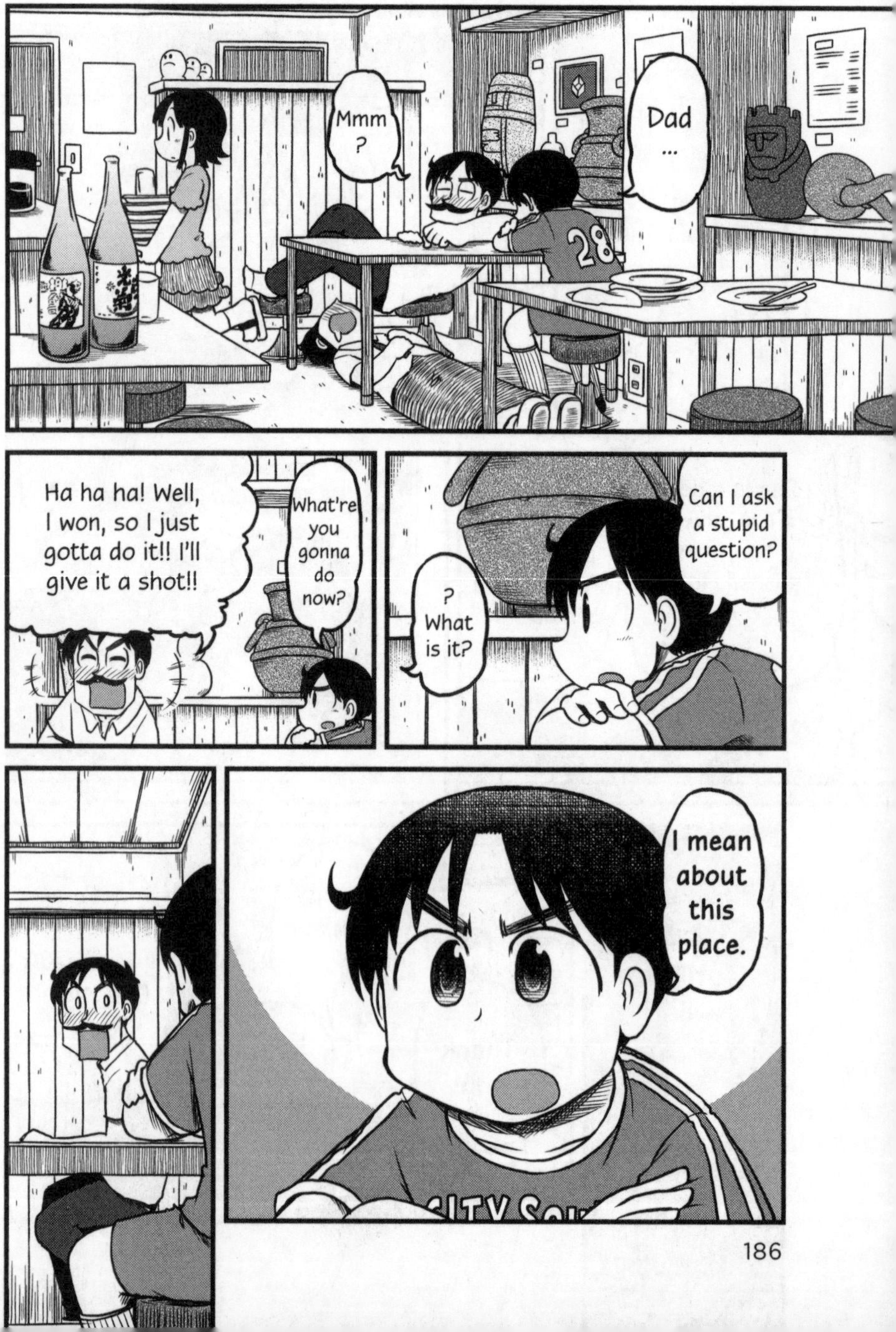
Dad ...
Mmm ?
Can I ask a stupid question?
? What is it?
What're you gonna do now?
Ha ha ha! Well, I won, so I just gotta do it!! I'll give it a shot!!
I mean about this place.

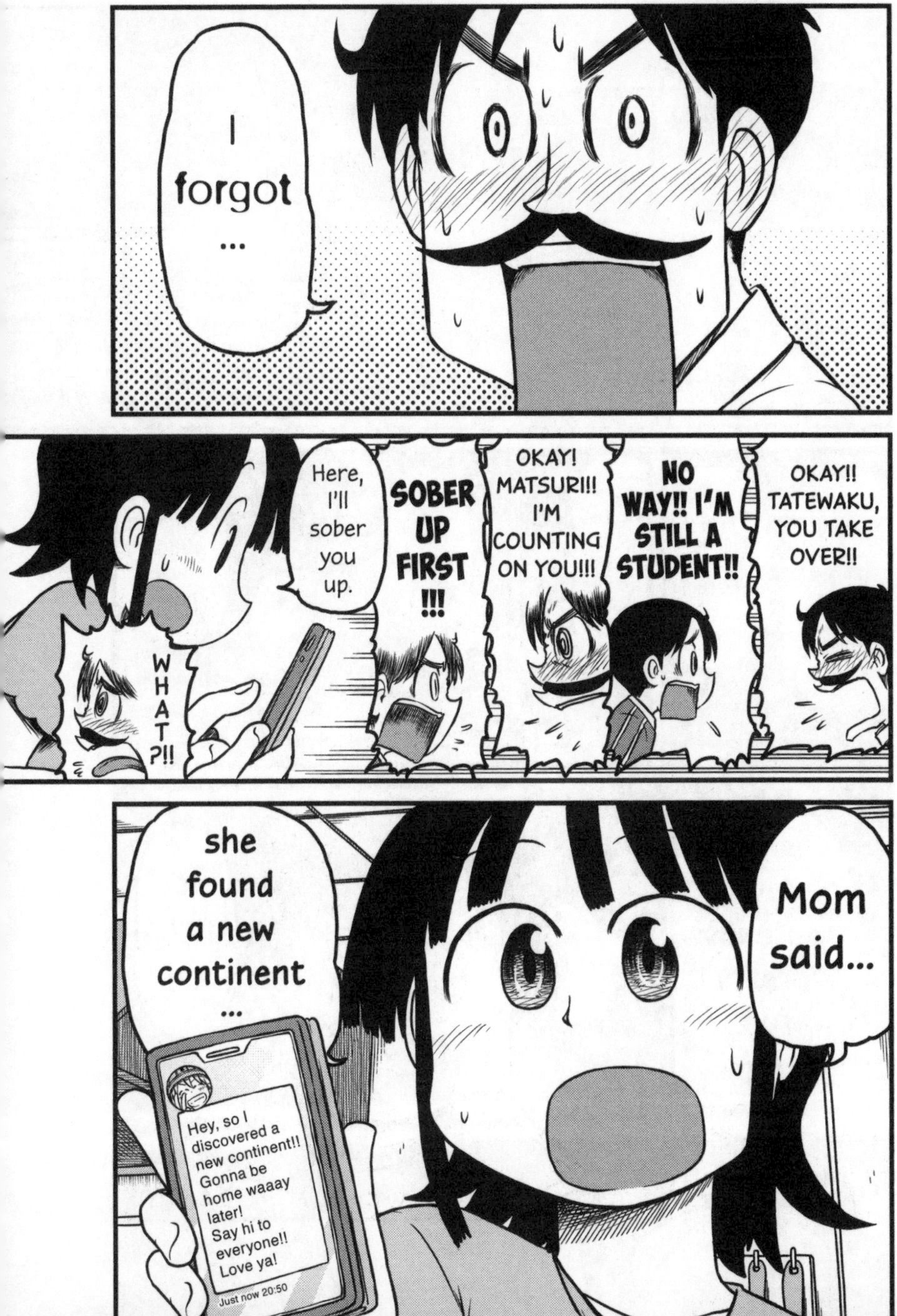
I forgot...
OKAY!! TATEWAKU, YOU TAKE OVER!!
NO WAY!! I'M STILL A STUDENT!!
OKAY! MATSURI!!! I'M COUNTING ON YOU!!!
SOBER UP FIRST!!!
Here, I'll sober you up.
WHAT?!!
Mom said...
she found a new continent...
Hey, so I discovered a new continent!! Gonna be home waaay later! Say hi to everyone!! Love ya!
Just now 20:50

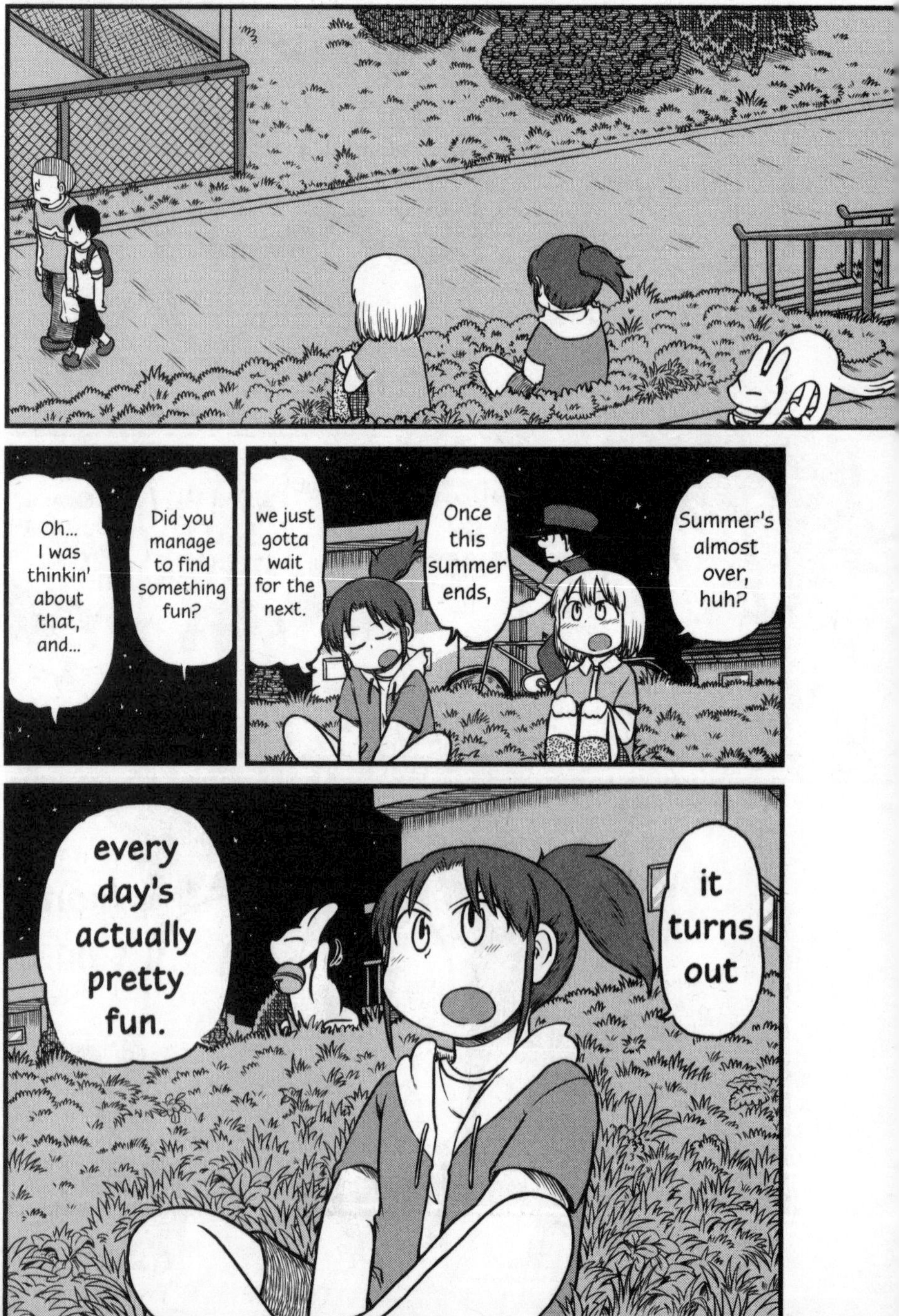
Summer's almost over, huh?
Once this summer ends,
we just gotta wait for the next.
Did you manage to find something fun?
Oh... I was thinkin' about that, and...
it turns out
every day's actually pretty fun.

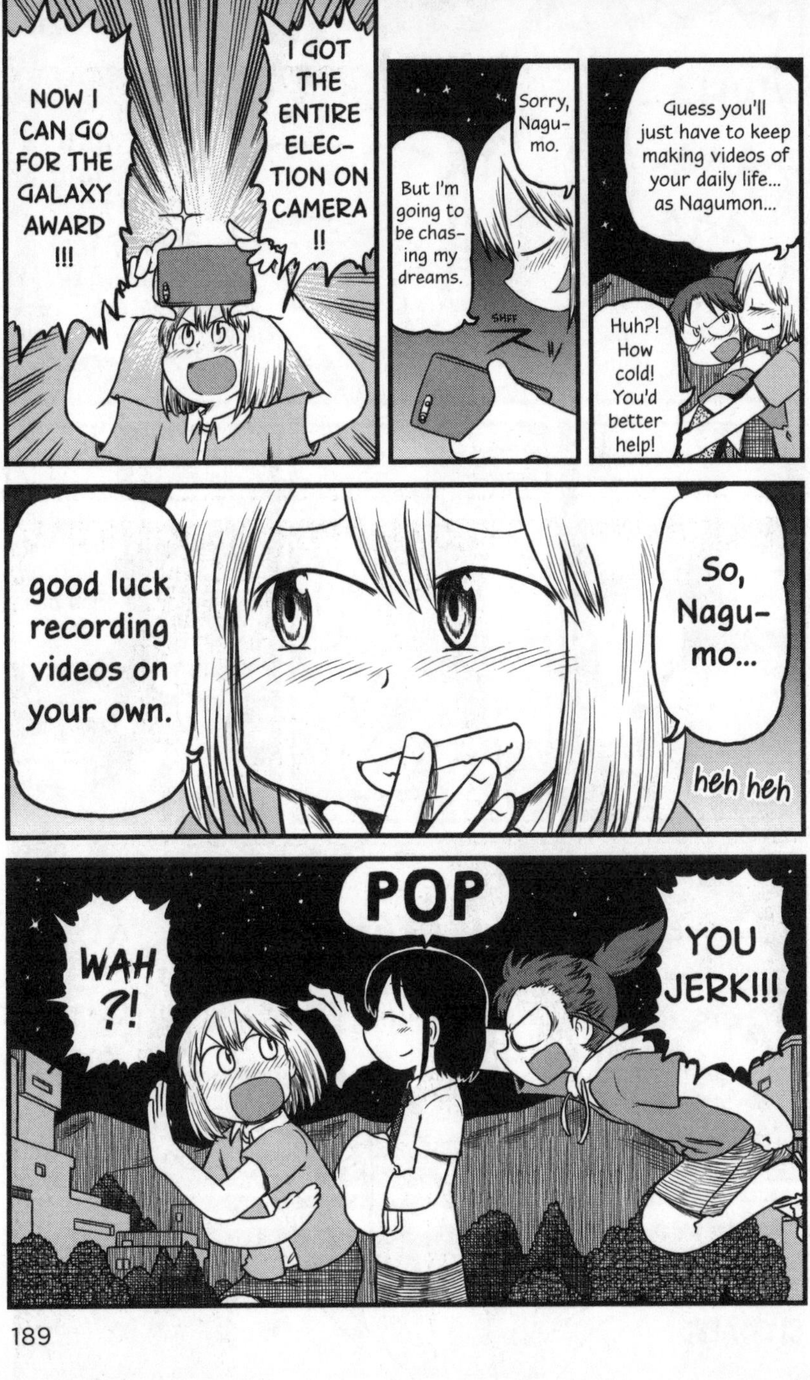

Guess you'll just have to keep making videos of your daily life... as Nagumon...
Huh?! How cold! You'd better help!
Sorry, Nagumo.
But I'm going to be chasing my dreams.
SHFF
I GOT THE ENTIRE ELECTION ON CAMERA !!
NOW I CAN GO FOR THE GALAXY AWARD !!!
So, Nagumo...
good luck recording videos on your own.
heh heh
YOU JERK!!!
POP
WAH ?!

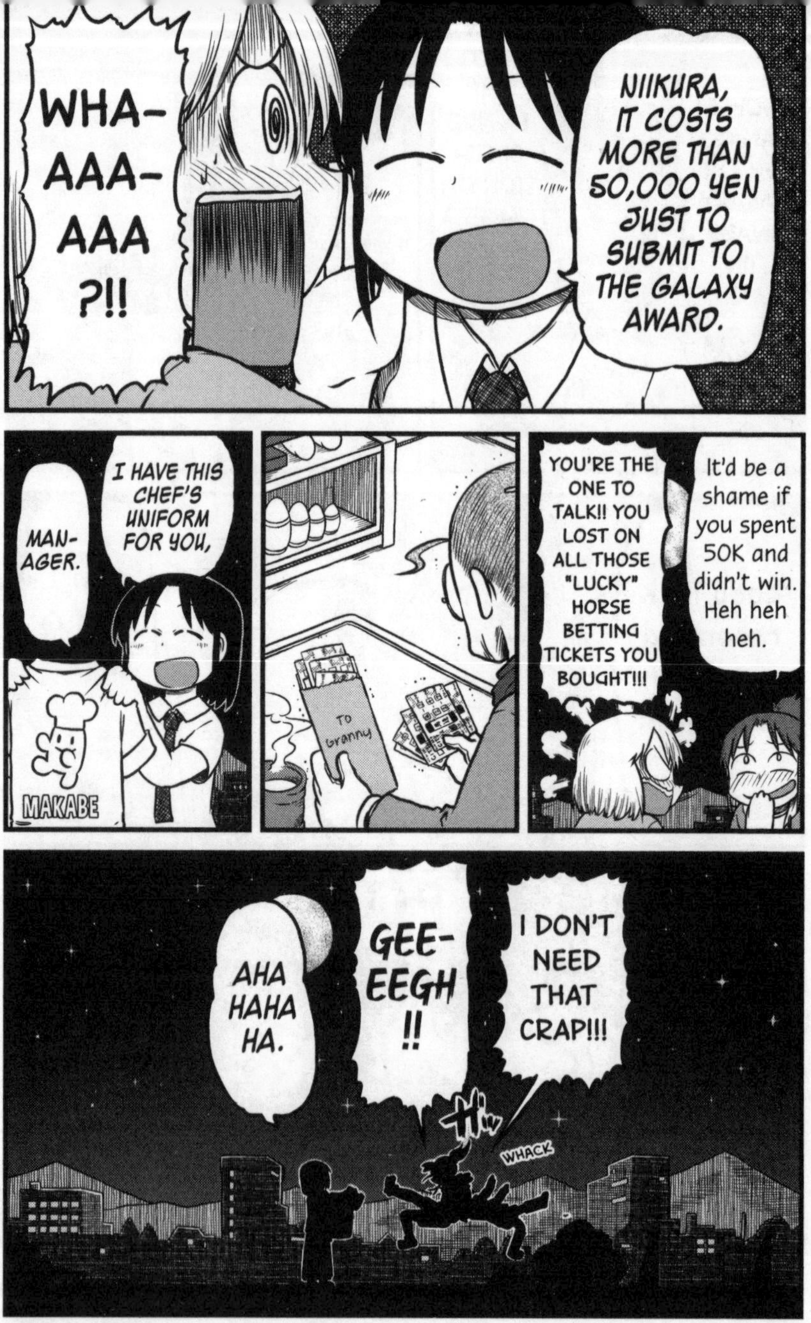
NIIKURA, IT COSTS MORE THAN 50,000 YEN JUST TO SUBMIT TO THE GALAXY AWARD.
WHA-AAA-AAA?!!
It'd be a shame if you spent 50K and didn't win. Heh heh heh.
YOU'RE THE ONE TO TALK!! YOU LOST ON ALL THOSE "LUCKY" HORSE BETTING TICKETS YOU BOUGHT!!!
To Granny
I HAVE THIS CHEF'S UNIFORM FOR YOU,
MAN-AGER.
MAKABE
I DON'T NEED THAT CRAP!!!
GEE-EEGH!!
AHA HAHA HA.
WHACK

see you in the summer somewhere.

Recent Author Photo

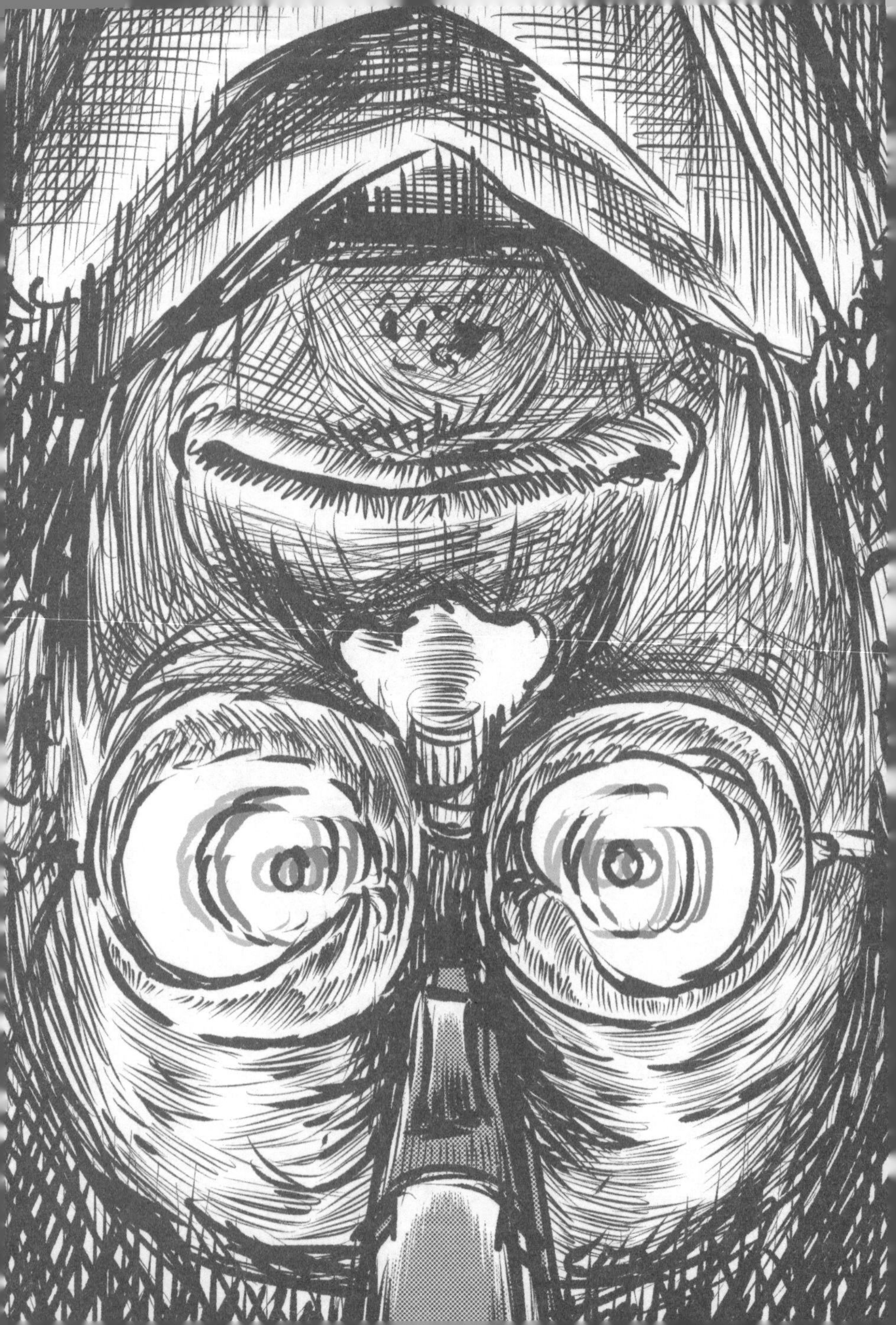

CITY
13

define "ordinary"

in this just-surreal-enough take on the "school genre" of manga, a group of friends (which includes a robot built by a child professor) grapples with all sorts of unexpected situations in their daily lives as high schoolers.

the gags, jokes, puns, and random haiku keep this series off-kilter even as the characters grow and change. check out this new take on a storied genre and meet the new ordinary.

all volumes and
a fifteenth anniversary box set
available now!

nichijou

my ordinary life

keiichi arawi

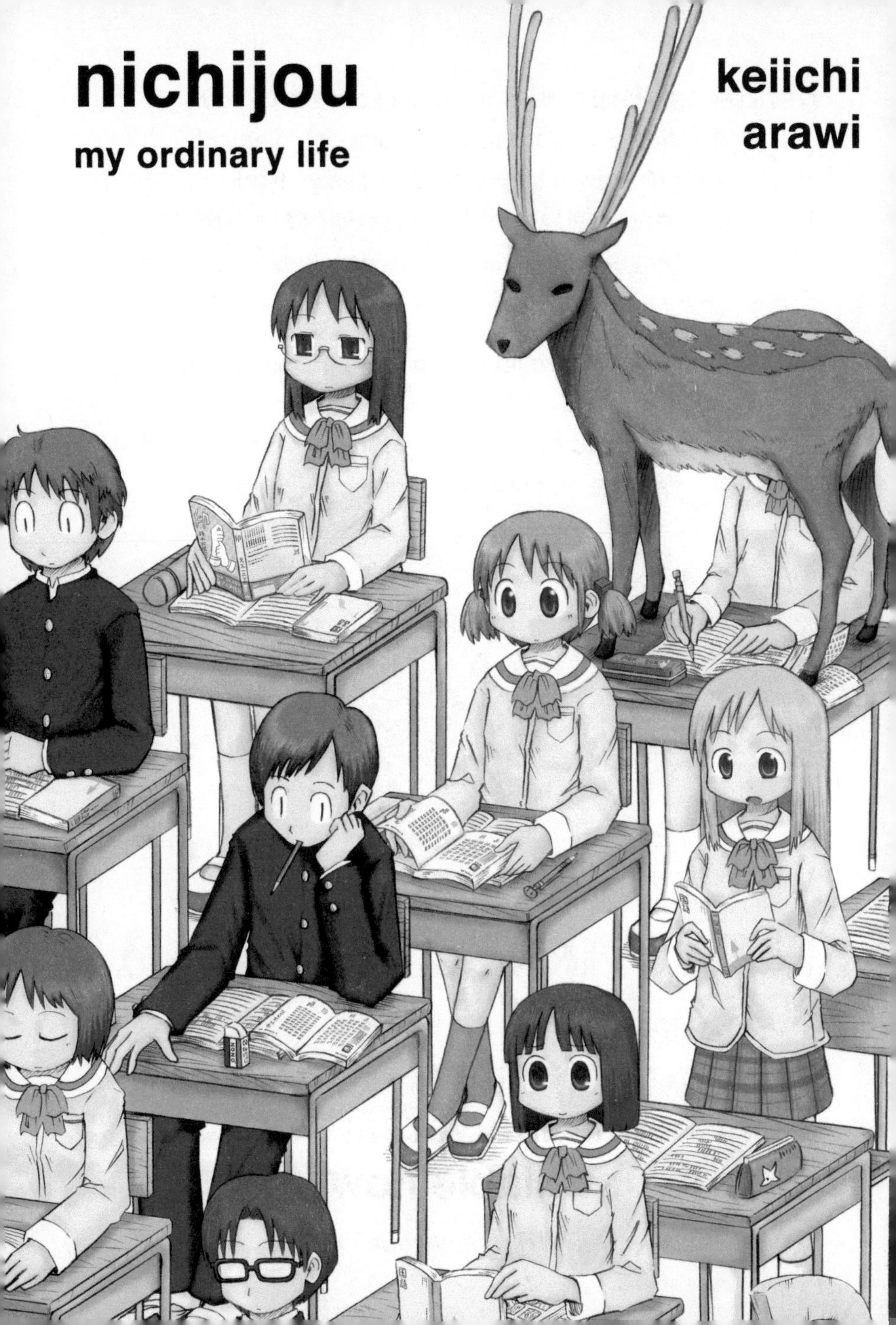

The follow-up to the hit manga series *nichijou*, ***Helvetica Standard*** is a full-color anthology of Keiichi Arawi's comic art-and-design work. Funny and heartwarming, ***Helvetica Standard*** is a humorous look at modern day Japanese design in comic form.

Helvetica Standard is a deep dive into the artistic and creative world of Keiichi Arawi. Part comic, part diary, part art and design book, ***Helvetica Standard*** is a deconstruction of the world of *nichijou*.

Helvetica Standard BOLd

Helvetica Standard ITaLic

Both Parts Available Now!

Keiichi Arawi

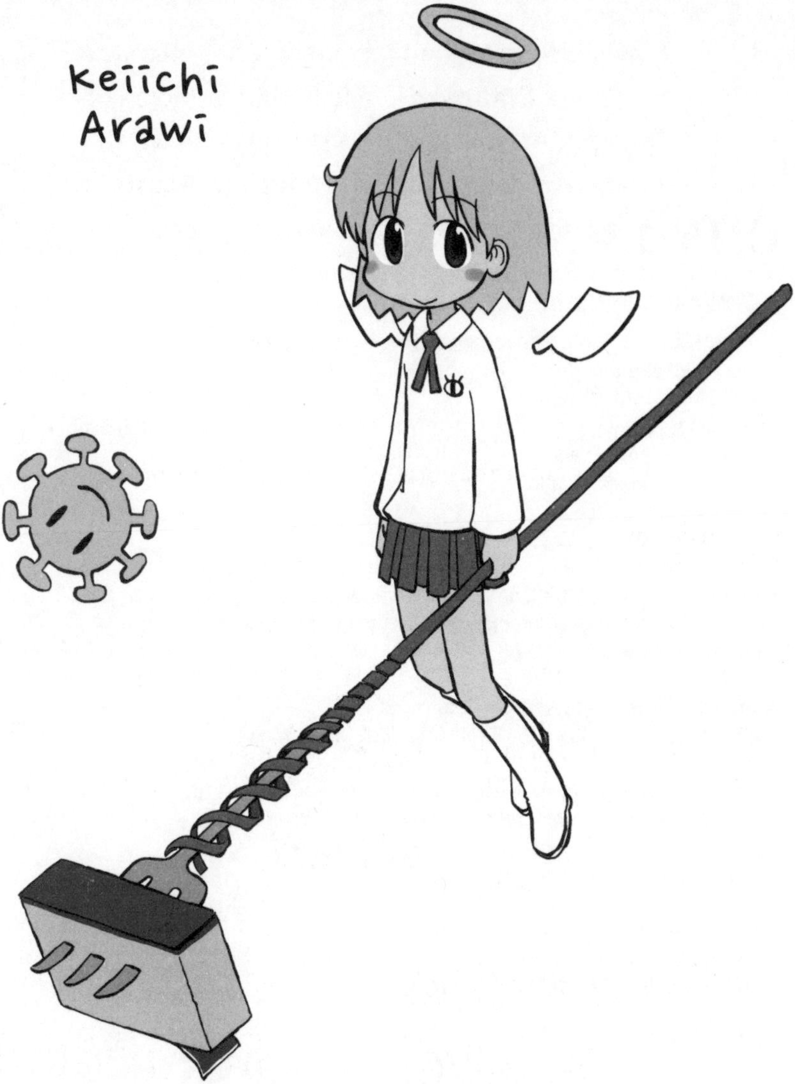

Helvetica Standard

CITY 13

A Vertical Comics Edition

Editor: Michelle Lin
Translation: Jenny McKeon
Production: Grace Lu
Shirley Fang
Hiroko Mizuno

First published in Japan in 2021 by Kodansha, Ltd., Tokyo
Publication rights for this English edition arranged through Kodansha, Ltd., Tokyo
English language version produced by Vertical Comics,
an imprint of Kodansha USA Publishing, LLC

Translation provided by Vertical Comics, 2022
Published by Kodansha USA Publishing, LLC, New York

Originally published in Japanese as *CITY 13* by Kodansha, Ltd.
CITY first serialized in *Morning,* Kodansha, Ltd., 2016-2021

This is a work of fiction.

ISBN: 978-1-64729-062-7

Manufactured in Canada

First Edition

Kodansha USA Publishing, LLC
451 Park Avenue South
7th Floor
New York, NY 10016
www.kodansha.us

Vertical books are distributed through Penguin-Random House Publisher Services.